Armies / and / Politics / in Latin America

Armies and Politics / in Latin America

Edited by

Abraham F. Lowenthal

HM

Holmes & Meier Publishers, Inc.

New York · London · 1976

Published in the United States of America 1976 by
Holmes & Meier Publishers, Inc.
101 Fifth Avenue
New York, New York 10003

Great Britain:
Holmes & Meier Publishers, Ltd.
Hillview House
1, Hallswelle Parade, Finchley Road
London NW11 0DL

LIBRARY OF CONGRESS CATALOGING IN PUBLICATION DATA

Main entry under title:

Armies and politics in Latin America.

    Includes bibliographical references and index.
    CONTENTS: Lowenthal, A. Armies and politics in Latin America.—
General interpretations: Germani, G. and Silvert K. Politics, social
structure, and military intervention in Latin America. Nun, J. The
middle-class military coup revisited. Putnam, R. D. Toward explaining
intervention in Latin American politics. Schmitter, P. Military intervention, political competitiveness, and public policy in Latin America,
1950–1967. [etc.]
    1. Latin America—Politics and government—1948-   —Ad-
dresses, essays, lectures. 2. Latin America—Armed Forces—Political
activity—Addresses, essays, lectures. I. Lowenthal, Abraham F.
F1414.2.A793   322′.5′098   76-17832
ISBN 0-8419-0281-X
ISBN 0-8419-0282-8 pbk.

PRINTED IN THE UNITED STATES OF AMERICA

For Kalman Silvert
Beloved teacher, colleague, friend

Contents

Armies
and
Politics / *in*
Latin
America

I
Introduction

Preface

La Constitución es una cosa; los militares somos otra. *

Analysts would surely agree that the armed forces are central to what happens in Latin American politics, and are likely to remain so. Yet while general books about Latin America abound, no single recent book deals with the military's political role across the region. The main regional surveys—the seminal works by Edwin Lieuwen and John Johnson published over a decade ago—are very dated; their interpretations have been superseded and indeed largely refuted by available case studies. Up to now, however, no good general work has appeared to take their place.

As my introductory essay in this anthology makes clear, there has been no scarcity of published material on armies and politics in Latin America. The numerous recent publications have been difficult to use for teaching purposes, however, because they have appeared in a wide variety of books and journals, and because individual and unrelated studies dominate the literature; few synthetic works, and even fewer comparative studies, have appeared.

The main purpose of this collection is to facilitate teaching and further systematic review by bringing together some of the best writing available on the political role of the military in Latin America. The selections have been chosen for their individual quality; for their usefulness in illustrating

---

* Attributed to a Dominican army officer, commenting on the temporary detention of the Dominican Republic's chief opposition candidate for president in the 1974 election, as quoted by *El Nacional* of Santo Domingo, March 7, 1974.

different conceptual and methodological approaches and emphases; for their coverage of the major countries; and for their treatment of armies at different levels of institutionalization and professionalization. Some of them emphasize the macrosocial context as the prime determinant of the military's political role (Germani and Silvert, and Nun), others stress the institutional history of specific armies as key (North), and still others focus on the interplay between macrosocial and institutional variables (O'Donnell, Stepan). Essays are included on highly institutionalized armies like those of Brazil and Peru; on the Dominican armed forces, which hardly qualify as a military institution at all; and on the blend of political and military roles which characterizes the civic soldier in Cuba. Among the countries considered are Peru, Brazil, and Chile, where the armed forces rule directly; Argentina, where the armed forces have spent alternate periods in the palace and out; and Mexico, where the military role in politics is more subtle and indirect, if no less real.

Most of the essays have only recently been published and have not previously been reprinted; the older and well-known essays by Germani and Silvert and by Nun are included because they are classic contributions to which many of the other articles refer, and because students should become familiar with them.

My own essay, adapted from a review article prepared for *World Politics,* provides an overview of the recently published literature, including all the selections in this volume as well as many others; it presents a theoretical framework for considering individual case materials. The extensive footnotes in my essay should also serve as a guide to further reading.

I could not have prepared this anthology in the midst of too many other activities without the efficient assistance of Victoria Garcia and Robert Bond, who turned the chore of editing this volume into something approximating a pleasure. Apart from their help in editing the selections, corresponding with authors and publishers, and preparing the manuscript for submission, they assumed the main responsibility for translating the O'Donnell essay. I also owe thanks to Anne Parks, who worked effectively on manuscript preparation, and to several of the individual authors for their willingness to have their manuscripts suffer cruel cuts in order to make them fit into the space available.

I would also like to express my thanks to Princeton's Center for International Studies and to the Council on Foreign Relations in New York for their support of my work, and to the Tinker Foundation for making it possible for me to draw on Dr. Bond's valuable assistance for this and other projects.

Abraham F. Lowenthal

Abraham F. Lowenthal  *Armies and Politics in Latin America*

I

Army officers rule in considerably more than half the countries of Latin America; in most of the rest, they participate actively in politics without currently occupying the presidential chair. In Brazil and Peru, military regimes with sharply different reputations appear entrenched. Ecuador's military government seems to waver uncertainly between the Brazilian and the Peruvian "models," as do officers in several other countries. In Chile, the armed forces deliberated long before finally taking over in September 1973, shattering the longest period any Latin American country in this century had experienced without military rule. The armed forces of Argentina relinquished office in 1973 but not without attempting to impose restrictive terms on their successors, and in 1976 the generals returned to power. In Uruguay, the army is taking an increasingly direct and expansive role, while in Paraguay it continues to serve as an instrument of prolonged per-

From Abraham F. Lowenthal, "Armies and Politics in Latin America," *World Politics* 27, no. 1 (October 1974): 107–30. Copyright © 1974 by Princeton University Press and reprinted by permission of the publisher, Princeton University Press.

Author's Note: I express here my appreciation to several colleagues who commented on this essay in draft, and particularly to Henry Bienen, Peter Cleaves, David Collier, John Fitch III, Elizabeth Hyman, Robert Kaufman, Guillermo O'Donnell, and David Ronfeldt for their valuable suggestions.

sonal rule. In Panama, nationalist reform under military auspices prevails; in Santo Domingo, there is constant reshuffling; in Bolivia, renewed "stability" exists in the context of perpetual strife. Not even Cuba's revolution has ended military participation in politics; on the contrary, the armed forces may well be Cuba's strongest and most influential political institution.[1]

Why do most Latin American armed forces participate so overtly in national political processes? Why have things changed so sharply from the time, little more than a decade ago, when only one Latin American country was ruled by a military regime and the "twilight of the tyrants" was being heralded?[2] What different political roles have been performed by Latin American military institutions? What accounts for the differences? How do Latin American armies govern? How does military rule differ from civilian rule in Latin America?

As Lyle McAlister observed in his comprehensive survey in 1966, until about a decade ago the literature on what was then called "militarism" was mostly descriptive, not explanatory.[3] It concentrated on *caudillos* (personalist military leaders) rather than on military institutional development. Authors primarily concerned with the civilian political process discussed the political activities of Latin American armed forces as a peripheral matter; their treatment tended to be normative, prescriptive, and even polemical. Scholars almost invariably grounded their analyses in a "democratic-civilist" model of civil-military relations, derived from European and North American experience, which assumed that armed forces characteristically exercise limited defense and police functions of an essentially non-political nature. When military officers played an overtly political role, that was regarded as exceptional and regrettable. It was termed "intervention," implying the temporary introduction of a coherent body into a separate system; its policy consequences were assumed to be universally regressive. Most writers dealt with all military "interventions" as if they were more or less alike, the key difference among countries being whether or not "intervention" occurred. It was assumed (or at least hoped) that military involvement in Latin America politics would decline as socioeconomic modernization and mobilization occurred, as armies became more "professional," and as the influence of announced United States support for democratic regimes made itself felt.

During the early 1960's the literature began to change, particularly in four respects. First, the political activities of Latin American armies came to be regarded as a topic sufficiently important to be studied directly. Second, authors began to highlight distinctions among the political roles played by armies in different countries, though the first attempts to classify various kinds of military participation in Latin American politics were crude and unsatisfactory.[4] Third, various writers on Latin America (John Johnson foremost among them) began to question the earlier assumption that military participation in politics was invariably regressive.[5] Fourth, it was increasingly recognized that the armed forces and civilian politics were often closely intertwined, that armies were not encapsulated institutions set apart from politics except when intervening.

In evaluating the literature published through 1965, McAlister noted that it tended to be broad and general; to begin to accept the notion that "the military is an integral component of Latin American society *interacting* with other elements rather than acting against them"; to be contributed primarily by North American scholars and mainly by historians; to lack firm data and empirical support for conclusions offered; and to be almost devoid of comparative studies.[6]

II

Writings on armies and politics in Latin America published since 1965 differ sharply from those reviewed by McAlister.[7]

1. Whereas the literature before 1966 tended to be general and regional, national case studies now predominate.[8] In fact, significant books dealing comprehensively and comparatively with the differing political roles exercised by Latin American armed forces have recently been conspicuous by their absence.

2. It has by now become the established wisdom that armed forces interact continuously with other elements in Latin American societies. Emphasis is beginning to turn, however, toward examining the educational and other institutional procedures, including recruitment and socialization, which set military forces somewhat apart from other social groups, and imbue in military officers a sense of corporate autonomy and interest.[9]

3. Some of the most insightful writing on this subject is now being done by Latin Americans.[10]

4. Historians continue to be among the most prolific writers on the political roles played by Latin American armies, but major conceptual advances have come from several political scientists.

5. Careful empirical work now characterizes this literature. For example, Robert Potash's *The Army and Politics in Argentina, 1928–1945: Yrigoyen to Perón* (Stanford 1969), draws on extensive data about the recruitment, composition, and training of Argentine officers, as well as on (almost overwhelmingly) detailed information about informal cliques within the Argentine military and their relations with civilian factions. The evidence Potash adduces—much of it from previously unavailable diplomatic records and from personal interviews—enables him to document the emergence of a highly professional, notably self-protective Argentine officer corps. The basic argument, which he spells out briefly in his conclusions (and promises to elaborate in a second book, on the Perón era), is that the Argentine army's more assertive role, reflected in Perón's rise, is attributable largely to gradual changes within the military over the preceding

fifteen years. Potash emphasizes the doubling of the Argentine officer corps between 1930 and 1945, its increasing professionalism, the establishment of the equivalent of a National War College with year-long courses for senior officers, and the creation of arsenals and factories run by the military. These changes tended to confer increasing self-confidence on the officers in their own capacity to handle national problems, and have facilitated the Argentine army's adoption of an ever more overt political role.

Alfred Stepan's *The Military in Politics: Changing Patterns in Brazil* (Princeton 1971) is also based on a wealth of data, including detailed information on the social and educational background of Brazilian officers and cadets, reports on applications to military academies, extensive interviews with Brazilian officers sympathetic to the author's research, and an imaginatively executed content analysis of several military journals and of civilian political debate. Stepan focuses mainly on explaining why the Brazilian military in 1964 turned away from what he calls a "moderator" model to its current "directive" role.

Under the "moderator" model, the military institution is repeatedly called in to preserve the political balance, but is denied the right to attempt systematically to direct lasting changes within the political system. Until 1964, acceptance of this role by Brazilian officers was contingent upon their acknowledgment of the "legitimacy and feasibility of parliamentary political forms and upon their assessment that in comparison with civilians they possess a relatively low capacity for ruling" (p. 63). In 1964, however, what Stepan terms a "boundary change" occurred. Stepan stresses the confluence of developments external to the military (Brazil's macro-social crisis and the widespread impression that the civilian political system was failing) with internal circumstances, especially the emergence of a focus on national development strategy in the Superior War College. By 1964 Brazilian officers were skeptical about the ability of civilians to solve Brazil's problems, and increasingly self-confident about their own capacity to implement a reasonably coherent development strategy (which was worked out with the aid of civilian technocrats). A full-scale, long-term takeover resulted.

Stepan concludes by examining the Brazilian regime's first four years in power; he challenges the "realist" assumption that military governments are less subject than civilian regimes to the problems of policy incoherence and instability. Stepan shows how the military's preoccupation with preserving unity has made for important discontinuities, ugly repression, and consequently eventual self-isolation, from which no escape is easily imaginable. Stepan does not directly confront the question of whether the Brazilian military might have avoided its present apparent *cul de sac,* but seems to imply that the tensions between the "military as government" and the "military as institution" will inevitably undermine the effectiveness of a long-term military regime and/or drive it to repression. It took less than five years for this process to become painfully evident in Brazil.

The impressive degree to which Peru's military regime has maintained its apparent cohesion and continuity and a reputation for tolerance for more than five years raises interesting questions, therefore. Do special circumstances in Peru account for the Velasco regime's ability to preserve its unity and self-confidence? Or is the Peruvian regime's relative success to date fragile, and eventually likely to be strained by the pressures Stepan discusses?

Important background material for analyzing the Peruvian case is provided in *100 Años del Ejército Peruano: Frustraciones y Cambios* and *El CAEM y la Revolución de la Fuerza Armada,* two recent books by Victor Villanueva, a retired Peruvian Army major.[11] In *100 Años del Ejército Peruano,* Villanueva concentrates on what he sees as a century-long "process of change in the military mind which brought it, slowly but persistently, to the need to capture political power," a need based fundamentally on a series of institutionally transmitted "traumas" and "frustrations" (p. 11). Several decades of collective experience have imbued Peruvian officers with an aversion for civilians, political parties, and "politics," a "generously positive self-estimation," a "subjective need for autonomy and power," and "confidence at being better equipped than civilians to govern the country" (p. 11).

In his most recent volume, Villanueva discusses a more specific influence on the current Peruvian regime: the mid-career education Peru's officers have been receiving since 1950 at the Centro de Altos Estudios Militares (CAEM), Peru's equivalent of the National War College. Whereas other writers on the current Peruvian regime tend generally but vaguely to attribute much of the junta's reform orientation to the CAEM program (about which little concrete information had previously emerged), Villanueva provides enough data to speculate about the specific impact of CAEM. On the basis of a reasonably well-documented (though somewhat spotty) examination of the CAEM curriculum and professional staff roster for the 1950's and 1960's, Villanueva rejects the view that CAEM was significantly influenced by Marxists and other radical civilians. Rather, Villanueva argues, the CAEM doctrine emerged from a more narrowly military concern with institutional self-protection and self-assertion in the context of national development needs; most important, it "rationalized the old rejection the military felt for the civilian" (p. 170). Villanueva's work can be criticized: some of it is more polemical than profound; insufficient evidence is provided for several key assertions (for example, that civilian professors have generally been guided by the CAEM leadership regarding their approach, rather than vice versa); and the emphasis on long-term, institutional psycho-experience is sometimes farfetched. But much can be learned from a judicious reading of Villanueva's contributions; his books are rich in detail, full of specific comments and insights, and informed by a sensitivity to personal and contextual variables that are sometimes ignored in more scholarly treatises.

6. Though excellent studies of individual countries are now available, it remains largely true that systematic comparative work is lacking on the political role of Latin American armies.

A few exceptions should be noted, however.[12] The most valuable effort so far published is Guillermo O'Donnell's *Modernization and Bureaucratic Authoritarianism: Studies in South American Politics* (Berkeley 1973), which concentrates on Argentina and Brazil. O'Donnell challenges the widely accepted notion that rising levels of modernization are conducive to democratic political arrangements. He suggests instead that there may be an "elective affinity" between situations of "high modernization" and "bureaucratic authoritarianism," which usually takes the form of a military regime that diminishes the influence of the already activated urban popular sector on national politics. O'Donnell stresses the bureaucratic and exclusionary nature of these authoritarian regimes more than their military character, implying that the latter trait may be of secondary importance or even coincidental. The key point is that technocratic elites in charge of various kinds of bureaucratic organizations try to reshape society and politics to permit more extensive application of their own expertise; in order to have their way, they cut off popular participation and even employ force.

Not all cases of "bureaucratic authoritarianism" are alike. O'Donnell distinguishes between Argentina and Brazil chiefly with regard to the degree of autonomy and organization within the "popular" (mainly labor) sector of each before the eventual turn to authoritarianism. Argentina's more highly organized and complex popular sector, O'Donnell argues, precludes thorough, long-term demobilization—short of extremely harsh repression. Brazil's lower degree of prior popular mobilization, however, has permitted the military regime to consolidate its hold. O'Donnell enriches his discussion with a brief aside on Peru, whose current regime he characterizes as "populist authoritarian," because it does not aim to exclude the present participants, but to incorporate new participants within an expansive, nationalist, and anti-oligarchical coalition like that experienced by Brazil and Argentina during the eras of Vargas and Perón.

A more extensive treatment of Peru and Brazil is provided by Luigi Einaudi and Alfred Stepan in *Latin American Institutional Development: Changing Military Perspectives in Peru and Brazil* (Santa Monica 1971).[13] They intelligently discuss why armies with essentially similar organizations, structures, and procedures, in countries with roughly comparable social and economic problems, and subject to the same kind of foreign (principally North American) doctrinal influences, forged national security doctrines that eventually led them to substitute direct, long-term rule for a previously more restricted political role. But, though well worth consulting for its concise, well-informed, and clearly written analyses of the two cases, the Einaudi-Stepan volume is essentially a juxtaposition of separately conducted studies rather than the application of a comparative framework to different cases. Disciplined comparative statements are scarce, and the study's conclusions amount to little more than a restatement of the general propositions appropriately presented in the introduction. What is particularly regrettable is that Einaudi and Stepan say so little to explain why the Brazilian and Peruvian armies, similar in so many aspects detailed by the authors, now play such apparently different roles.

Stepan begins to deal with these differences, albeit still somewhat sketchily and almost exclusively in terms of factors internal to the respective armies, in his essay "The New Professionalism of Internal Warfare and Military Role Expansion," included in this volume. Contrasting the "new professionalism" exemplified in Brazil and Peru with the "old professionalism" discussed in most of the literature on armies and politics, Stepan shows how and why the more advanced Latin American armies are playing such active political roles. Contrary to what was expected, we may be in for more, and longer-lasting, military regimes.

III

The faith of a decade ago—that military involvement in Latin American politics would decline as a result of economic development, social modernization, military professionalization, and American influence—can no longer be sustained. As it appears that the military's significant role in Latin American politics is here to stay, attention has turned increasingly not only to analyzing why this is so, but also to examining the consequences of military rule for policy outputs and outcomes.

Perhaps the most interesting aspect of the recent literature on why Latin American armed forces "intervene" is that so many writers still pose the question that way. Even a cursory familiarity with Latin America might well lead one to ask instead why armies have refrained (or appear to refrain) from taking an extensive and direct political role in a handful of Latin American countries: Costa Rica, Mexico since the 1930's, Venezuela since 1958, and Chile and Uruguay until very recently. Studies of these cases are scarce, however, and generally unilluminating.

Probably the major book on the military in Chile, *Las Fuerzas Armadas en el Sistema Político Chileno,* by Alain Joxe, disputes the conventional view that the Chilean army had not recently (before 1973) involved itself much in politics.[14] Joxe asserts—plausibly, even persuasively, but by no means in a detailed or elaborated fashion—that the Chilean army has had a "latent and permanent participation" in the political process as the middle class's principal agent in shaping and protecting the social, political, and economic systems for its benefit (pp. 40–41). Although the Chilean military has not taken office directly very often—in 1891, 1924, 1931–32 (and in 1973)—Joxe argues that each military takeover in Chile counts for ten somewhere else, because the army does such a thorough and effective job each time in rearranging the system to protect vital middle-class interests. But Joxe offers scant explanation of why the Chilean middle class, in contrast to others in Latin America, needs to rely on overt military "intervention" so infrequently.

Liisa North's essay in this volume, "The Military in Chilean Politics," goes a long way toward answering this question, and toward accounting for the brutally repressive role of today's military rulers of Chile. Emphasizing the political and institutional history of Chile's armed forces, North stresses the interplay of long-term trends and immediate situational variables in helping to account for the Chilean tragedy.

For the reader interested in analyzing why some Latin American armies participate overtly in politics less often than others, Winfield Burggraaff's *The Venezuelan Armed Forces in Politics, 1935–1959* (Columbia, Mo., 1972) is disappointing, for Burggraaff deliberately cuts off his account just when the Venezuelan army stopped "intervening." Within its purview, Burggraaff's volume provides some interesting information on how the Venezuelan army evolved from a *caudillo*'s personal instrument to an increasingly autonomous and coherent professional institution. But although Burggraaff asks "what motivated Venezuelan officers to intervene directly in politics between 1928 and 1958," he answers only by citing a catalogue of possible explanations among which it is "risky to assign weights" (p. 195).

Edwin Lieuwen's *Mexican Militarism: The Political Rise and Fall of the Revolutionary Army, 1910–1940* (Albuquerque 1968) deals with a fascinating series of questions: how a traditional army was destroyed and replaced by a revolutionary one, how the revolutionary army was professionalized, and then, how the professional army was practically withdrawn from politics and civilian authority was established.[15] Of particular interest in Mexico's experience was the Calles era in the mid-1920's, when the decision was made to professionalize the Mexican army from the bottom up by developing a corps of young professionals. The task of removing the generals from politics (some by purge, many others by payoff) was in most cases left to later—the presidents were generals until 1946—by which time the autonomy and continuity of the military institution were assured. The questions Lieuwen poses are considerably better than the answers he provides, however; this may be because the main answers involve post-revolutionary social, economic, and political circumstances beyond the scope of the data Lieuwen considers in focusing on the military itself.

Few writers, then, discuss why some Latin American armies usually avoid direct and active political roles; none do so satisfactorily. What about the question almost all of them face: why do most Latin American armed forces participate overtly in politics?

A wide variety of explanatory propositions has been advanced. Some writers emphasize institutional, "internal," or "push" factors: the size and firepower of armies; the size, class origins, socialization, training, cohort experience, and degree of professionalization of officers; and the effects of foreign military assistance. Others highlight social, "external," "environmental," or "pull" circumstances: levels of economic and political development, political culture, and social stratification systems. Not only have many variables been cited; there has been little consensus on the effects of any of them. It has been argued that smaller, or larger, armies are more likely to "intervene"; that "professionalization" expands, or restricts, an army's political activity; that the emerging predominance of middle-class officers will promote, or restrain, their political participation and will make the army's policy impact progressively redistributive, or regressive; that foreign influence leads to "interventionism," or the contrary; that rising levels of development and modernization will promote democratic, or authoritarian, politics; that the political traditions and culture of Latin America require an apolitical stance by military officers, or that they reinforce their proclivity for politics.

Robert Putnam has attempted to test a number of these contradictory propositions for the decade preceding 1966.[16] Analyzing aggregate data, Putnam relates measures of a series of independent variables, such as socioeconomic development, political development, characteristics of particular military institutions, and foreign assistance and training, to the dependent variable, "military intervention," defined as the armed forces' veering away from the management and use of controlled violence in the service of the state, to participate in or influence other, non-military agencies and functions of the state.[17] Putnam's article is useful mainly for the doubts it casts on some of the hypotheses which have been widely discussed, particularly regarding the supposed influence of foreign military missions and of "coup contagion" (i.e., the effect of coups in neighboring countries) on the incidence of military intervention. Putnam's other major findings—that "social mobilization" is strongly and negatively related to "military intervention," but that "economic development" is positively correlated—are questionable. Putnam's work may be challenged regarding the reliability of its index and the validity of its scoring criteria, regarding its technique of longitudinal inference from cross-sectional aggregate data, and particularly because the causal models suffer from multicollinearity since there are fixed relationships among the independent variables.[18] In addition to these more specific methodological difficulties, Putnam's work suffers from its undifferentiated consideration of a wide variety of armies and political roles within the phenomenon being studied—"military intervention."

The same comment applies to Martin Needler's "Political Development and Military Intervention in Latin America."[19] Needler seeks to explain the frequency and timing of *coups d'état* and to ascertain whether there is any overall trend with regard to their effects on social and economic policy. He concludes that coups occur more often than not when economic conditions are deteriorating; that they increasingly tend to occur against constitutional regimes, often just before or just after elections; that their redistributive effects on economic and social policy, if any, are regressive; and that, though their incidence is cyclical, the secular trend is descending, i.e., coups seem to occur less frequently now than before 1960. Needler's empirical observations do not appear to hold up well, however, for the years since 1966 have been punctuated by coups, at least some of them clearly reformist.

Even for the period he discusses, Needler's argument lacks explanatory power. Although he offers some hypotheses, particularly the "swing man" proposition (which focuses on the dynamics of coups themselves and how these affect timing and policy orientation), Needler cannot say much that will meaningfully explain such an undifferentiated class of phenomena as Latin American coups. Essentially, his statements about trends are grounded in the view that expanded participation is inevitable and will lead to fewer coups, but this conclusion is by no means self-evident. Needler also believes that military "intervention," being self-protective of military corporate interests, is bound to restrict participation and to protect the socioeconomic status quo. However plausible these assertions, they do not necessarily hold true either; the current rash of military regimes in Latin America undermines Needler's first assertion; Peru's current experience, at least, would appear to contradict the second.

IV

Whereas Putnam and Needler lump together all types of military coups, a growing literature on specific countries underlines the great variance among examples of military participation in politics. Each case study highlights particular circumstances, but taken together they suggest four main distinctions.[20]

First, Latin American military institutions exercise their political influence either directly and overtly, as rulers, or indirectly, as a kind of specially endowed pressure group.[21] Nowhere in Latin America (with the possible exception of Costa Rica, where the officer corps is largely disbanded by each new administration) do armed forces play an insignificant political role or even one mainly limited to national defense and police functions.

Second, among those countries where direct military rule occurs, it may be personalist, factional, or institutional. A regime is personalist when a politician in uniform uses the armed forces (or part of them) to expand and protect his power, whether exercised on his own behalf or on behalf of a civilian group or groups. Personalist regimes are most common in countries with poorly institutionalized, unprofessional armed forces.[22] Factional regimes occur when a group of officers, aspiring to accomplish an institutional coup, assumes control, usually against the will of the established military hierarchy; this formulation is bound to be transitory, for the faction will soon find itself either displaced or able to transform the military institution to its liking. Institutional regimes occur, in turn, when the leadership of the armed forces rules on the basis of established procedures likely to survive the particular chief; this may happen when the armed forces' top officers take power (purging dissenters), or when a faction successfully gains dominance within established channels.[23] Although its incidence has so far been infrequent, institutional rule is relatively stable once it has been accomplished, for no other social or political group is likely to remove from office a military establishment united in its will to govern.

Third, military regimes may be distinguished on the basis of their frequency and length. Brief, intermittent coups may be personalist (when no one *caudillo* can consolidate national control), or institutional (as was the case in Peru in 1962, and in Brazil and Argentina several times before 1964). Long-term military rule may reflect the establishment of a strongman regime in the absence of mass participation or complex social and political organizations, as in Nicaragua or Paraguay; but it may also be institutional, as it is today in Brazil and Peru.

Finally, and perhaps most important, military regimes differ sharply in their programmatic aims and consequences. In some countries, particularly in Central America and the Caribbean, armies have served mainly to enrich *caudillo* leaders, their military henchmen, and their civilian accomplices. In other cases—in Peru through 1960 and in Colombia until Rojas Pinilla, for example—armed forces have protected land-owning "oligarchies" against challenges to their wealth and power, even those posed by urban middle-class elements. In a few situations— in Chile in 1924–25, in Brazil during the Vargas period, in Argentina under Perón, and in contemporary Panama and Peru—military regimes have helped middle-class groups, including organized labor, to reduce the influence of entrenched ruling classes. In such cases, armies have aided in extending the franchise and/or other rights to new participants in politics, and have spurred redistributive economic and social reforms. But in still other cases—in contemporary Argentina and Brazil, and especially in Chile—the policy of the military has been to restrict political participation, to demobilize and depoliticize, and even to repress.

V

What accounts for the dramatically different policies adopted by military regimes in different countries, or even at successive points in one nation's history? What can explain not only the frequency and level of military participation in Latin American politics, but also its several forms: direct and indirect; personal, factional, and institutional; intermittent and longterm; reformist and regressive?[24]

Case studies, like those by Potash, Burggraaff, Einaudi, and Villanueva, tend to stress internal institutional factors. Discussions of the Peruvian case, for instance, underline the army's recruitment and promotion of officers from the provincial middle class; its training program, particularly the CAEM course and the experience of many officers in U.S. installations; its historic difficulties with and consequent distrust of civilians; and the experience of top-ranking officers who had to put down guerrilla uprisings in the mid-1960's. These factors are hardly irrelevant, but comparative data suggest that none, by itself, is a sufficient explanation for the Peruvian military's evolution. Most officer corps in Latin America come predominantly from the provincial middle class, but few (if any) parallel the Peruvian Army's current stance.[25] Peru's CAEM course is unusual among Latin American countries, but it is by no means unique, and most officers who have graduated from nearly equivalent institutions in Argentina and Brazil have emerged with attitudes and policy preferences very different from those declared by their Peruvian counterparts. Besides, not even the most extravagant proponents of the impact of education would argue that a nine-month course for mature professionals, or even shorter exposure to foreign training, could fundamentally affect their values and behavior. And other armies, in Latin America and elsewhere, have emerged from battles with guerrillas determined to repress them, rather than eager to foster structural change.[26]

If internal variables are insufficient to explain the variety of political roles played by Latin American armies, what about arguments that attribute the military's political behavior "not to the social and organizational characteristics of the military establishment but to the political and institutional structure of the society"?[27] José Nun argues that armies in Latin America have usually acted as representatives of changing middle-class interests, compensating for that class's "inability to establish itself as a well-integrated hegemonic group."[28] Samuel Huntington elaborates this insight, portraying armed forces across the world as "doorkeepers to the expansion of political participation in a praetorian society; their historic role is to open the door to the middle class and to close it to the lower class."[29]

The Nun-Huntington hypothesis, though it obviously tends to obscure somewhat the heterogeneous character and interests of the "middle class" in most Latin American countries and to play down the effects of international influences on their behavior, represents a major analytical advance. It clarifies how the military can be reformist in one context and reactionary in another while pursuing more or less consistent lines of action. Virgilio Rafael Beltrán's analysis of several different types of military participation in Argentina, for instance, shows that the army was never aligned with "popular" sectors against the "middle class," but several times joined middle-class groupings, first against the oligarchic minority and then against the majority.[30]

But the hypothesis relating the military's political role to levels and types of middle-class participation explains less than it seems to. That military officers of middle-class origin act—in any particular circumstance or even in many—compatibly with general middle-class interests does not prove that the officers are protecting the middle class. As Fitch argues (in the context of Ecuador), the officers' "strong corporate self-identification with the military institution, rather than their peripheral identification as members of the middle class," may account best for their political position.[31] If narrow institutional requirements and general class interests coincide, the explanation may relate to common responses to similar problems rather than to any similarity of origin or perceived interest. This point is important because there are cases—Argentina in the early 1930's, Peru in 1968—when a military group deposed an eminently middle-class regime. The Peruvian case, in which the military's "revolutionary" program appears to have gone beyond what all but a small fraction of Peru's middle class will support, raises this question most sharply. But the Nun-Huntington approach, by itself, also fails to account for other cases—for instance, the substantially changed character of military participation in Argentine politics between 1955 and 1966, from "legalists" to long-term rulers. How can such "exceptions" be explained?

The most persuasive writers stress the confluence and interaction of macrosocial factors with those internal to the military institution.[32] Stepan, for instance, maintains that although an army's political role cannot be deduced from its organizational characteristics, the latter importantly affect the military's exercise of a role structured in large part by wider social forces. O'Donnell emphasizes the interrelation of social and institutional forces in Argentina, arguing that the level of military "professionalization" is a key variable, but that its impact is conditioned by the wider sociopolitical setting. "The professionalization of the armed forces in the praetorian context raises the critical point from which military intervention becomes probable," O'Donnell argues, implying that the more "professional" the army, the less likely overt "intervention" becomes. But "once that point is reached, the military intervention takes place with more cohesion, with a comprehensive justificatory ideology, and with the purpose of achieving goals much more ambitious than those in coups undertaken by less professional armed forces."[33]

VI

Perhaps the most interesting series of questions regarding military participation in politics—little discussed until recently—relates to the effects of military rule.[34] How do military regimes differ from their civilian counterparts, predecessors, and successors? What difference does it make whether or not politicians, technicians, and bureaucrats wear uniforms?

By far the most systematic and comprehensive effort to deal with the consequences of military rule in Latin America is Philippe Schmitter's "Military Intervention, Political Competitiveness, and Public Policy in Latin

America: 1950–1967."[35] Noting that the supposed impact of different types of regimes on public policy is rarely accompanied by evidence, Schmitter draws on the literature to formulate a series of "speculative contradictory hypotheses" susceptible to testing against available socioeconomic data and indicators of public policy variables. (Schmitter limits his review to analyzing expenditures; dimensions of civil liberty, for instance, are deliberately ignored.) Some of Schmitter's arguments may scare off readers unfamiliar with quantitative analytical techniques and their argot; those not so handicapped may question his eclectic application of several methods and wonder about the quality of some of the basic data.[36] But Schmitter's exercises provide a very useful start, suggesting several effects that various types of regimes may have on patterns and results of public policy. Military regimes apparently spend more than their civilian counterparts on "defense" and less on social welfare; the highest defense expenditures occur when the military is an intermittent ruler.[37] The type of regime affects "how much Latin American polities can extract from their environments (i.e., total government expenditures and revenues), upon whom the burden of this extractive process will fall (i.e., taxation), how much of these scarce resources will be plowed back into the system to develop it (i.e., public investment), and which social groups will be benefited (i.e., sectoral expenditures)." But "indicators of overall system performance (*outcomes*) are much less predictably affected by regime-type . . . than are indicators of direct governmental allocation (*outputs*). How much Latin American countries invest, industrialize, increase their GNP, raise their cost of living, increase their school enrollment and/or engage in foreign trade seems more the product of environmental or ecological factors than the willful acts of politicians grouped according to their competitiveness or civilian-military status."

Schmitter's essay, though making imaginative use of a wide variety of available data, points up the need for improved and more comprehensive data sets on specific countries. Even more, as Schmitter himself suggests, his study indicates the need for careful analysis of causality and process in individual cases or pairs of cases, conforming to or deviating from the modal patterns. To date, however, there is only one such study. Barry Ames, in "Rhetoric and Reality in a Militarized Regime: Brazil Since 1964," looks at how the Brazilian military government and its civilian predecessors handled a series of issue areas: housing, tax, and educational policies.[38] He suggests that the policy-making process did not differ equally across the various issue areas from one type of regime to another; rather, it differed according to the priority given the particular issue by the military, the degree (if any) of prior policy commitments and clearly articulated goals, and the strength of clientele groups.

Ames's analysis, like Schmitter's, suggests that military regimes do affect public policies, but not as much as they claim or their critics assert. But lumping together all "military" regimes and distinguishing them from all "civilian" regimes may be profoundly misleading. As O'Donnell hints, certain social circumstances may produce regimes, whether civilian or military, that resemble each other much more than they do other civilian or military regimes under different socioeconomic circumstances.[39] The incipient literature on public policy making in Latin America should illuminate this point.

VII

The recent literature on the political role of Latin American armed forces is extensive, empirically based, and increasingly subtle conceptually. Obvious differences between the political activities and impacts of armies in countries like Brazil and Peru, the Dominican Republic and Argentina, Bolivia and Chile—indeed, the vast differences among the military institutions themselves and between the political roles played by the same army at different times in a given country's history—have dissolved easy assumptions about the nature of military involvement in Latin American politics. It becomes increasingly clear that armies participate in Latin American politics in several different ways, and that no simple explanation accounts for all. More important, it becomes evident that approaches relating characteristics of the military institutions themselves to the social context in which they operate provide the most promising avenues for explaining the various political roles played by Latin American officers.

What remains to be done?

1. Additional case studies are needed to help us analyze how the political roles of armies have evolved within different national contexts, why coups sometimes occur and sometimes do not, why military regimes are sometimes brief and sometimes long, sometimes reformist and sometimes reactionary, how armies have been affected by macrosocial and institutional changes, and what effects various forms of military participation have had on national politics and policy. Research on cases where military participation has become less overt (e.g., Venezuela), or where military rule has now entrenched itself (e.g., Peru), would be of greatest interest.

2. Contextually sensitive analysis is particularly needed on how armies govern in Latin America, what coalitions they form, what clienteles they respond to, how they make and execute decisions, and generally whether, how, and why the substance and style of military regimes differ in Latin America from those of civil governments.

3. Research is required on pairs of cases chosen to highlight theoretically significant differences: Peru and Brazil, Argentina and Chile, Panama and Nicaragua, for example. Emphasis should be given particularly to specific institutional aspects that may vary from country to country: recruitment, socialization, and training patterns, for instance. Because it may be unreal-

istic to expect individual researchers to attain the necessary degree of access to military institutions in more than one country, carefully designed collaborative projects seem indicated.

4. How soldiers affect Latin American politics should be compared with what we know of their role elsewhere, particularly in other Third-World regions. "Neo-realist" writings on the Middle East and Asia distorted North American perceptions of the Latin American military in the 1960's.[40] Writings on Latin America, in turn, are said to have misled scholars when they turned to analyzing sub-Saharan armies.[41] Recent "revisionist" writings on the military role in African and Arab polities, together with those here reviewed on Latin America, should provide for a mutual correction of focus.[42]

5. The most exciting task is to synthesize and integrate within an inclusive theoretical formulation the by now abundant literature on the political roles armies play in Latin America and in other regions.

It is not possible in this brief essay to take up that final challenge. It may be appropriate, however, to advance one central proposition suggested by the literature reviewed here: that the relation between the level of military institutionalization and the institutionalization of civilian political procedures may be a key determinant of the varying political roles army officers play.[43]

As Huntington argues, the single most important variable affecting military participation in politics is the ratio between the scope of political participation and the strength (autonomy, coherence, complexity, and adaptability) of civilian political institutions. Whenever popular participation exceeds the capacity of political institutions to channel it in a routinized, stable manner, "praetorianism" of one kind or another results, no matter what the absolute level of popular participation. Extensive and unmediated political activity takes place, not only by soldiers but also by priests, students, and labor leaders.

Important variations mark the spectrum of "praetorian" cases, however. Some armies "moderate" or "arbitrate"; others "direct" or "rule." Some act overtly for brief periods only; others take power for an extended time. Some push progressive, redistributive policies; others are conservative, if not reactionary.

Huntington postulates that the policy impact of military rule varies with the level of civilian political participation. In the "oligarchic" phase of limited participation, military *caudillos* (like civilian leaders) do not challenge the structure of power and rewards; they merely seek to assure themselves that they will benefit from it. Armies entering politics during a period of expanding middle-class participation in a previously aristocratic society are likely to play a "radical" role, opening the system and distributing resources and rewards more equitably than was previously done. But the impact of military involvement in an already highly participant polity (i.e., at the "mass praetorian" phase) is bound to be restrictive and repressive, Huntington argues, for the popular majority now threatens the prerogatives of the middle class, including the armed forces.

Huntington's persuasive argument does not fully explain, however, why military participation in different "praetorian" societies varies so much in duration, intensity, and style. Why do officers in Peru and Panama seem to go way beyond middle-class civilian politicians in their reformist zeal, for instance? Or, why is military involvement in the politics of Santo Domingo, Haiti, or Nicaragua so much closer to gang plunder than to institutional exercise of national responsibility?[44]

A study of the differing levels of institutional strength among Latin American armies and the comparative strengths of civilian and military organizations in specific countries might be most illuminating in this connection.

An army's institutional strength may be measured, at least roughly, with reference to: (1) its resources (e.g., percentage of GNP and of national budget spent on defense, percentage of eligible men under arms, expenditure per soldier); (2) its professional level (e.g., years of schooling required of senior officers, number of military journals published, extent to which academic achievement and other "objective" measures affect promotions); and (3) its institutional cohesion and coherence, reflected also by its autonomy in such spheres as recruitment, assignments, and promotion.

If we were to rank the institutional strength of past and present Latin American armies, I suspect we would discover that military involvement in politics changes in a curvilinear fashion as armies gain in organizational strength and coherence.[45] At the lowest level of military institutionalization, officers participate in politics overtly, frequently, on a personalist basis, and often for long periods. At the intermediate level of military institutionalization, after "professionalization" has been emphasized, officers tend to participate less overtly (and if overtly, for briefer periods) than at an earlier stage, perhaps because they are protecting their still fragile corporate autonomy. At this intermediate stage, tensions are common between personalist leadership and institutional considerations; it is not unusual for the most professional officers (the best educated, least dependent on political ties for their previous promotions, etc.) eventually to displace the *caudillo* and restore civilian rule. At a still higher stage of military institutionalization, in turn, armies are again more likely to play an overt role, this time long-term and directive, as officers achieve a self-confident sense of corporate autonomy and even superiority. At this stage, "intervention" may be reluctant, but when it comes it will probably be intensive and long-lasting.

Analyzing the relation between the strength of military institutions, the strength of civilian institutions, and the level of civilian political participation would also be of interest. If military institutionalization outpaces the evolution of parties and other civilian institutions, long-term, directive, and institutional rule by the armed forces is likely. The policy impact of military involvement will vary, however, with the level of mobilization and participation. At an intermediate stage, officers may self-confidently help to expand participation and even redistribute rewards, assured by their predominant strength that their own corporate interests are unendangered. At a high level of participation, rule by a well-institutionalized army may be equally overt, directive, and extended. But as military rule is occasioned precisely because mass participation was deemed threatening to the armed forces, its impact will be restrictive and regressive.

Conversely, when military institutionalization lags behind, as it does in most of Central America and the Caribbean at the intermediate level of civilian participation, or perhaps in Uruguay at a higher level, the consequences are also predictable. At the intermediate level of participation, officers are more likely to participate overtly, as personalist instruments, and for more extended periods than are the more professional units characteristic of other such politics. At a high level of participation, officers will participate less overtly and directively than would the highly institutionalized armies usually associated with high-participation situations.

The foregoing argument obviously needs elaboration and testing. No doubt it needs to be further qualified as well—particularly with regard to the impact of the specific previous experience of each country on participation of the military in politics, and of the relative timing of each country's economic growth and social mobilization.[46] It is offered in this preliminary form, however, as one contribution to the theory-building process that the extensive literature on armies and politics in Latin America now clearly invites.

Notes

1. More than half the members of the Central Committee of Cuba's Communist Party are army officers. See Jorge Domínguez, "The Civic Soldier in Cuba," reprinted in this volume. See also Eduardo Gonzalez "The New Role of the Revolutionary Armed Forces in Cuba," paper presented at the Conference on the Latin American Military, University of California, Riverside, April 1970; and Gonzalez, "Political Succession in Cuba: After Fidel . . . ?" paper presented to the 1973 Annual Meeting of the American Political Science Association, New Orleans, September 1973.
2. Late in 1961, Paraguay's was the only military government in all of South America. See Tad Szulc, *Twilight of the Tyrants* (New York 1959), and Edwin Lieuwen, *Arms and Politics in Latin America* (New York 1961), for the view that military participation in Latin American politics was declining.
3. See Lyle McAlister, "Recent Research and Writing on the Role of the Military in Latin America," *Latin American Research Review,* II (Fall 1966), 5–36.

4. Lieuwen (n. 2), for instance, distinguished among three groups of countries: those in which the military dominated politics, those in which armies were in transition from political to non-political bodies, and those in which they were non-political. At least six of the seven cases in the supposedly transitional category, however, have since then moved in the direction contrary to Lieuwen's argument, and some of his "non-political" armies have taken an active political role. In any case, Lieuwen's three descriptive categories lacked explanatory power; little was said to indicate why particular countries fell into one category or another. Essentially similar criticism may be made of Theodore Wyckoff's "The Role of the Military in Latin American Politics," *Western Political Quarterly*, XIII (September 1960), 745–63.

5. They suggested that the military's institutional characteristics—its coherence and continuity, its technical orientation, its national perspective, and particularly its recruitment of officers from the upwardly mobile lower middle class—might dispose officers to support economic development, expanded participation, democratic procedures, and progressive redistribution. See John Johnson, ed., *The Role of the Military in Underdeveloped Countries* (Princeton 1962), and *The Military and Society in Latin America* (Stanford 1964).

6. See McAlister (n. 3), 32–36.

7. See Elizabeth Hyman, "Soldiers in Politics: New Insights on Latin American Armed Forces," *Political Science Quarterly*, LXXXVII (September 1972), 401–18; and David Ronfeldt, "Patterns of Civil-Military Rule," in Luigi Einaudi, ed., *Beyond Cuba: Latin America Takes Charge of Its Future* (New York 1974), 107–28. A comprehensive bibliography is provided by Klaus Lindenberg, *Fuerzas Armadas y Política en América Latina: Bibliografía Selecta* (Santiago, Chile 1972).

8. Among the major country studies published since 1966, other than those published in this volume or mentioned elsewhere in this article, are: on Argentina, Dario Canton, *La Política de los Militares Argentinos, 1900–1971* (Buenos Aires 1971); Marvin Goldwert, *Democracy, Militarism and Nationalism in Argentina, 1930–1966: An Interpretation* (Austin 1972); Carlos Astiz, "The Argentine Armed Forces: Their Role and Political Involvement," *Western Political Quarterly*, XXII (December 1969), 862–78; Virgilio Rafael Beltrán, "The Army and Structural Changes in 20th Century Argentina," in Jacques Van Doorn, ed., *Military Profession and Military Regimes: Commitments and Conflicts* (The Hague 1969), 317–41; on Bolivia, William H. Brill, *Military Intervention in Bolivia: The Overthrow of Paz Estenssoro and the MNR* (ICOPS, Washington, D.C. 1967); on Brazil, Georges-André Fiechter, *Le Régime Modernisateur du Brésil, 1964–1972* (Geneva 1972); Ronald Schneider, *The Political System of Brazil: Emergence of a "Modernizing" Authoritarian Regime, 1964–1970* (New York 1971); Frederick M. Nunn, "Military Professionalism and Professional Militarism in Brazil, 1870–1970: Historical Perspectives and Political Implications," *Journal of Latin American Studies*, IV, No. 1 (1972), 29–54; Riordan Roett, "A Praetorian Army in Politics: The Changing Role of the Brazilian Military" in Roett, ed., *Brazil in the Sixties* (Nashville 1972), 3–50; on Chile, Frederick M. Nunn, *Chilean Politics, 1920–1931: The Honorable Mission of the Armed Forces* (Albuquerque

1970); Roy A. Hansen, "Military Culture and Organizational Decline: A Study of the Chilean Army," Ph.D. diss. in sociology (University of California, Los Angeles 1967); on Colombia, Richard Maullin, *Soldiers, Guerrillas, and Politics in Colombia* (Lexington, Mass. 1973); Francisco Leal Buitrago, "Política e intervención militar en Colombia," *Revista Mexicana de Sociologia*, XXXII, No. 3 (1970), 491–538; Anthony Maingot, "Colombia," in Lyle McAlister and others, *The Military in Latin American Socio-political Evolution: Four Case Studies* (Washington, D.C. 1970); on Ecuador, John S. Fitch III, "Toward a Model of Coups D'Etat as a Political Process in Latin America: Ecuador, 1948–1966," Ph.D. diss. in political science (Yale University 1973); on Guatemala, Richard Adams, "The Development of the Military" in Adams, ed., *Crucifixion by Power: Essays on Guatemalan National Social Structure, 1944–1966* (Austin 1970), 238–77; Jerry Weaver, "Political Style of the Guatemalan Military Elite," *Studies in Comparative International Development*, V (1969–70), 63–81; on Mexico, Jorge Alberto Lozoya, *El ejército mexicano (1911–1965)* (Mexico 1970); on Panama, Steve Ropp, "Military Reformism in Panama: New Directions or Old Inclinations," *Caribbean Studies*, XII (October 1972), 45–63; on Peru, Carlos Astiz and José Garcia, "The Peruvian Military: Achievement Orientation, Training, and Political Tendencies," *Western Political Quarterly*, XXV (December 1972), 667–85; François Bourricaud, "Los militares: por qué y para qué?" *Aportes* (April 1970), 13–55; Bourricaud, "Voluntarismo y experimentación: los militares peruanos: manos a la obra," *Mundo Nuevo* (December 1970), 4–16; Julio Cotler, "Crisis política y populismo militar," in José Matos Mar and others, *Peru: Hoy* (Mexico 1971), 87–174, and "Bases del corporativismo en el Peru," *Sociedad y Política*, No. 2 (November 1972), 3–11; Jane Jaquette, "Revolution by Fiat: The Context of Policy-making in Peru," *Western Political Quarterly*, XXV (December 1972), 648–66.

9. Cf. Robin Luckham, *The Nigerian Military: A Sociological Analysis of Authority and Revolt, 1960–67* (Cambridge 1971).

10. In addition to the works by Nun and O'Donnell reprinted in this volume and the works cited above, see Oscar Cuellar, "Notas sobre la participación de los militares en América Latina," *Aportes* (January 1971), 6–41; Liliana de Riz, "Ejército y política en Uruguay," *Revista Latinoamericana de Sociologia*, No. 3 (September–December 1970), 420–42; and Alberto Sepulveda, "El Militarismo Desarrolista en América Latina," *Foro Internacional*, XIII (July–September 1972), 45–65.

11. For further discussion of Villanueva, see James M. Malloy, "Dissecting the Peruvian Military," *Journal of Inter-American Studies and World Affairs*, XV (August 1973), 375–82.

12. Four additional comparative efforts deserve mention. McAlister and others (n. 8), contains competent but not closely related studies of Peru, Argentina, Colombia, and Mexico, with a useful final attempt by McAlister to derive comparative generalizations. Brady Tyson's "The Emerging Role of the Military as National Modernizers in Latin America: The Cases of Brazil and Peru," in David Pollock and Arch Ritter, eds., *Latin American Prospects for the 1970's: What Kind of Revolution?* (New York 1973), 107–30, presents insightful but inconclusive speculation on the possibility that

Peru's regime will eventually evolve in a direction similar to Brazil's. James Malloy's "Populismo militar en el Peru y Bolivia: Antecedentes y posibilidades futuras," *Estudios Andinos*, II (1971–72), 113–36, strains somewhat to fit limited data on the Peruvian regime's first three years into a framework Malloy had developed in his earlier work on Bolivia. Charles Corbett's *The Latin American Military as a Sociopolitical Force: Case Studies of Argentina and Bolivia* (University of Miami, Center of Advanced International Studies 1972), brings together two very unlikely objects of comparison, apparently chosen simply because the author (formerly a U.S. military attaché) had first-hand familiarity with each.

13. See also Einaudi's *The Peruvian Military: A Summary Political Analysis* (Rand, Santa Monica 1969), "U.S. Relations with the Peruvian Military," in Daniel Sharp, ed., *U.S. Foreign Policy and Peru* (Austin 1972), 15–56, and "Revolution from Within—Military Rule in Peru Since 1968," *Studies in Comparative International Development*, VIII (Spring 1973), 71–87.

14. The Joxe volume was published in 1970 in Santiago, Chile by Editorial Universitaria. There is, interestingly, no book-length study in English of the Chilean military which deals with the post–World War II period.

15. For knowledgeable skepticism regarding the degree to which the Mexican army has actually withdrawn from politics, see David Ronfeldt, "The Mexican Army and Political Order Since 1940," reprinted in this volume. See also Franklin Margiotta, "Changing Patterns of Political Influence: The Mexican Military and Politics," paper presented at the 1973 Convention of the American Political Science Association, New Orleans.

16. See Robert D. Putnam, "Toward Explaining Military Intervention in Latin American Politics," reprinted in this volume.

17. *Ibid.* The definition is paraphrased from Robert L. Gilmore, *Caudillism and Militarism in Venezuela* (Athens, Ohio 1964), 4–5.

18. See Edward Tufte, "Improving Data Analysis in Political Science," *World Politics*, XXI (July 1969), 654; and Jerry L. Weaver, "Assessing the Impact of Military Rule: Alternative Approaches," in Philippe C. Schmitter, ed., *Military Rule in Latin America: Functions, Consequences, and Perspectives* (Beverly Hills 1973), 84–86, 96–98. I am indebted to John S. Fitch III and Jeffrey Hart for help on this point.

19. *American Political Science Review*, LX (September 1966), 616–26.

20. Cf. Manfred Kossok, "The Armed Forces in Latin America: Potential for Changes in Political and Social Functions," *Journal of Inter-American Studies and World Affairs*, XIV (November 1972), 375–98.

21. On the limitations of the "pressure group" concept for analyzing the political role of Latin American armies, see Hyman (n. 7), 410–11.

22. Cf. Samuel Decalo, "Military Coups and Military Regimes in Africa," *Journal of Modern African Studies*, II, No. 1 (1973), 105–27.

23. For an interpretation of the current Peruvian regime (generally regarded as eminently institutional), as deriving primarily from the dominance of one army faction, see Abraham F. Lowenthal, "Peru's Ambiguous Revolution" in Lowenthal, ed., *The Peruvian Experiment: Continuity and Change Under Military Rule* (Princeton 1975).

24. Amos Perlmutter, in an article based primarily on Middle Eastern and Asian cases but explicitly generalized to Africa and Latin America as well,

distinguishes between two subtypes of institutional military regimes: "arbitrator-types" and "ruler-types." Arbitrator-types are only briefly direct, if at all; they are "professionally-oriented," and are little interested in political ideology or organization. "Ruler-types" are more likely to be long-term and direct, to submerge professional considerations to others, and are much concerned about ideology and organization. But Perlmutter's observation about professional orientation does not appear to apply in the Latin American context (e.g., Peru and Brazil) unless one defines "professional orientation" as excluding long-term civilian responsibility, in which case Perlmutter's point is somewhat circular. See Perlmutter, "The Praetorian State and the Praetorian Army: Toward a Taxonomy of Civil-Military Relations in Developing Polities," *Comparative Politics,* I (April 1969), 382–404.

25. Fitch shows that Ecuadorean officers come from socioeconomic origins very similar to those of their Peruvian colleagues, for instance. See Fitch (n. 8), 248–49.

26. This seems to have been the case, for instance, in the Dominican Republic and Bolivia. For another case where counterinsurgent activities have apparently stimulated military interest in structural reform, however, see Maullin (n. 8).

27. Samuel P. Huntington, *Political Order in Changing Societies* (New Haven 1968), 194. For an earlier, still useful formulation, see Gino Germani and Kalman Silvert, "Politics, Social Structure and Military Intervention in Latin America," *European Journal of Sociology,* II (1961), 62–81, reprinted in this volume.

28. See "The Middle-Class Military Coup Revisited," reprinted in this volume.

29. Huntington (n. 27), 222.

30. Beltrán (n. 8).

31. Fitch (n. 8), 331–32.

32. The best recent literature on the political roles of African armies shares this emphasis. See, for instance, Claude E. Welch, "Radical and Conservative Military Regimes: A Typology and Analysis of Post-Coup Governments in Tropical Africa," paper presented at the 1973 Convention of the American Political Science Association, New Orleans; and Henry Bienen, "Military and Society in East Africa: Thinking Again about Praetorianism" *Comparative Politics,* VI (July 1974), 489–517.

33. See O'Donnell, "Modernization and Military Coups: Theory, Comparisons and the Argentine Case," reprinted in this volume.

34. The volume Schmitter has edited (n. 18) contributes much less than its title promises on this point. Only Weaver's essay deals systematically with the effects of military rule.

35. An edited reprint of Schmitter's article appears in this volume. Cf. Eric Nordlinger, "Soldiers in Mufti: The Impact of Military Rule Upon Economic and Social Change in the Non-Western States," *American Political Science Review,* LXIV (December 1970), 1131–48.

36. For a critique of Schmitter's methodology, see Barry Ames and Edward Goff, "A Longitudinal Approach to Latin American Public Expenditures," paper presented at the 1973 Convention of the American Political Science Association, New Orleans, 9–11. See also Weaver (n. 18), 93 ff.

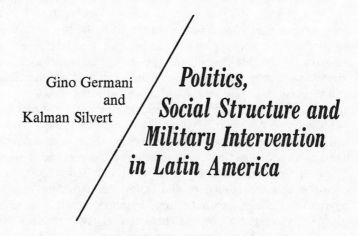

Gino Germani
and
Kalman Silvert

Politics, Social Structure and Military Intervention in Latin America

The recent politico-military events of Turkey, Pakistan, Egypt, and even France demonstrate that the application of unabashed armed might to the solution of civic problems is not peculiar to Latin America, nor indeed a phenomenon to be correlated only with economic underdevelopment. Public violence and political instability in Latin America have all too often been treated either as merely comic or else a manifestation of "spirit," "temperament," or "Latin blood." Riots in the streets of Buenos Aires are no less tragic than riots in the streets of Algiers—and no less related to the basic facts of social disorganization as they may be reflected in crises of political legitimacy and consensus.

Military intromission in the political power structure always indicates, of course, at least a relative inability of other social institutions to marshal their power effectively, and at most an advanced state of institutional decomposition. This is to say, if the armed forces are viewed as having a limited and specialized set of functions having only to do with internal

From Gino Germani and Kalman Silvert, "Politics, Social Structure and Military Intervention in Latin America," *European Journal of Sociology* 2 (1961): 62–81. Reprinted by permission of the authors and the publisher. [Table II has been omitted from this edition.—Ed.]

order and external defense, then a widening of castrensic activities into
other social domains implies a generally weakened and sick social system,
no matter the country or even the special cultural conditions concerned.
This premise suggests several ways of constructing typologies of civil-
military relations: one possibility is to order the types of social pathology
to be found, and then to relate them to the historical facts of politico-
military action; another is to order types of public violence, and once again
to relate these to the real types of military interventions; and still a third
alternative suggests itself in the direct listing of the institutional arrangements between the military establishment and the political institution
treated as a variable dependent upon other social factors. This article will
employ the latter procedure as being of the most immediate analytical
utility, even though direct correlations between military action and the
general state of social and economic development are at best vague.

Most Latin American countries have reached their first century and a
half of independent existence. However, their social development into
national states lagged behind formal independence and it is only now that
a few of them are reaching a stage of full nationhood. While in some
countries the breakdown of the traditional structure began in the last
quarter of the nineteenth century, in many others a similar process of
structural change did not start until the last two or three decades of the
present century. Furthermore, one must remember that nowhere, not even
in the most "advanced" Latin American nations, may it be said that the
transition is complete.

In this transitional process we shall distinguish a series of successive
"stages" so that the degree of development reached by any single Latin
American country can then be described and compared with others. It is
hardly necessary to emphasize the intrinsic limitations of such a procedure:
nevertheless, it seems the most convenient one to yield a short-hand description of the present situation, while at the same time retaining a clear
awareness of the total dynamics of the process. It must be added that this
"model" of the transition is the result of a schematization of the actual
historical process as it has been observed to take place in Latin America.

A tentative simple typology of the social structure of the twenty Republics has been summarized in Table I. In constructing it we have taken
into account those traits which we consider most relevant to the problem
at hand: namely, economic structure; the social stratification system (especially the existence of a self-identifying middle stratum); the degree of
economic and cultural homogeneity and of participation in a common culture and in national life; the degree of national identification; and geographical discontinuities in the socio-economic level of the various regions
within each country.[1] While we do not identify the successive "stages" of
the historical scheme with the different "types" of social structure described
in the Table, we suggest that various degrees of "delayed development"
may have resulted in situations similar to those indicated in the typology.

Table I

[. . .] *No data.* *1940.   (1950 *circa*)

COUNTRIES	% MIDDLE AND UPPER STRATA	% IN PRIMARY ACTIVITIES	% IN CITIES OF 20,000 AND MORE INHABITANTS	% MIDDLE AND UPPER URBAN STRATA	% LITERATES	UNIVERSITY STUDENTS PER 1,000 INHABITANTS

Group A: (a) *Middle strata: 20% and more;* (b) *cultural, psychological and political existence of a middle class;* (c) *ethnic and cultural homogeneity; national identification and considerable level of participation in different spheres;* (d) *urban/rural differences and geographical discontinuity exist, but to a lesser extent than in other Latin American countries.*

COUNTRIES	% MIDDLE AND UPPER STRATA	% IN PRIMARY ACTIVITIES	% IN CITIES OF 20,000 AND MORE INHABITANTS	% MIDDLE AND UPPER URBAN STRATA	% LITERATES	UNIVERSITY STUDENTS PER 1,000 INHABITANTS
Argentina } urban predominance {	36	25	48	28	87	7.7
Uruguay	...	22	50	...	95	5.2
Chile	22	35	43	21	80	3.9
Costa Rica rural predominance	22	57	18	14	80	3.9

Group B: (a) *Middle strata: between 15 and 20% (approx.) heavily concentrated in some areas of the country;* (b) *cultural, psychological and political existence of a middle class;* (c) *ethnic and cultural heterogeneity; pronounced inequalities in the degree of participation in national society and in other aspects;* (d) *strong regional inequalities with concentration of urbanization and industrialization in certain areas and rural predominance in the greater part of the country.*

COUNTRIES	% MIDDLE AND UPPER STRATA	% IN PRIMARY ACTIVITIES	% IN CITIES OF 20,000 AND MORE INHABITANTS	% MIDDLE AND UPPER URBAN STRATA	% LITERATES	UNIVERSITY STUDENTS PER 1,000 INHABITANTS
Mexico lesser survival of traditional pattern	17*	56	24	...	59	0.9
Brazil greater survival of traditional pattern	15	62	20	13	49	1.2

Group C: (a) *Middle strata between 15 and 20% (approx.);* (b) *emerging middle class (but there is no agreement as to its degree of auto-identification);* (c) *ethnic and cultural heterogeneity, pronounced inequalities in the degree of participation in national society and other aspects;* (d) *pronounced discontinuity between rural/urban areas and strong regional inequalities:*

COUNTRIES	% MIDDLE AND UPPER STRATA	% IN PRIMARY ACTIVITIES	% IN CITIES OF 20,000 AND MORE INHABITANTS	% MIDDLE AND UPPER URBAN STRATA	% LITERATES	UNIVERSITY STUDENTS PER 1,000 INHABITANTS
Cuba } urban predominance {	22	44	37	21	76	3.9
Venezuela	18	44	31	16	52	1.3
Colombia rural predominance	22	58	22	12	62	1.0

Group D: (a) *Middle strata: less than 15%; emergent middle strata in some countries, but clear persistence in all, in varying degrees, of the traditional pattern;* (b) *ethnic and cultural heterogeneity in almost all;* (c) *vast sectors of the population still marginal;* (d) *rural predominance in general; regional inequalities.*

COUNTRIES	% MIDDLE AND UPPER STRATA	% IN PRIMARY ACTIVITIES	% IN CITIES OF 20,000 AND MORE INHABITANTS	% MIDDLE AND UPPER URBAN STRATA	% LITERATES	UNIVERSITY STUDENTS PER 1,000 INHABITANTS
Panama	15	55	2?	15	70	2.6
Paraguay	14	54	15	12	66	1.3
Peru	...	60	14	...	42	1.6
Ecuador	10	51	18	10	56	1.4
El Salvador	10	64	13	9	57	0.5
Bolivia	8	68	20	7	32	2.0
Guatemala	8	75	11	6	29	0.1
Nicaragua	...	71	15	...	38	0.7
Dominican Republic	...	70	11	...	43	1.2
Honduras	4	76	7	4	35	0.7
Haiti	3	77	5	2	11	0.7

Stages 1 and 2. Predominance of the Traditional Social Structure. Formal National Independence and Civil Wars

The common trait of these first two stages of Latin American development is the persistence of the "traditional" society which maintained its essential features throughout the political upheaval and radical changes in formal political organization.

Stage 1. Revolutions and Wars for National Independence

At the time when they gained their independence (in most cases *circa* 1810) the Latin American countries may be said to have approximated the "ideal type" of the "traditional society": subsistence economy marginal to the world market and a two strata system characterized by little or no mobility and caste-like relationships. The Spaniards and Portuguese were the ruling group, and immediately below them we find the small élite of the *créoles,* of European descent and mainly urban, who while deprived of political power still belonged (subjectively as well as objectively) to the higher stratum and retained a dominant position from the economic and cultural point of view. It was this creole élite who brought about the revolutions and achieved national independence with support of the lower strata, including the *Mestizos* and even part of the outcast group of the Negroes and the Indians who filled the armies of the independence wars. The creoles were inspired mainly by the American model, the French revolution, and seventeenth century illuminism. They attempted to establish modern democratic states with their corresponding symbols: the "constitution," the "parliament," the elected rulers, and so on. There were, however, two basic limitations to their action. The first may be found in the creole élite itself: it was the expression of a traditional structure and in spite of its ideology, it still perceived itself as an aristocracy widely separated from the popular strata. The democracy they dreamed of was the "limited" democracy of the wealthy, the educated, the well-bred of proper descent. On the other hand, the prevailing state of the society was scarcely adequate to the establishment of a representative democracy: powerful geographical as well as ethnic, cultural, and economic factors made such an undertaking simply utopian.

Stage 2. Anarchy, "Caudillismo," and Civil Wars

The outcome of such a situation was simply that, even before the end of the long and cruel wars of independence against the Spaniards, the constitutional "fictions" created by the urban élites broke down. The political and institutional vacuum resulting from the disappearance of the colonial administration and the failure of the "constitutional fictions" resulted in the geographical fragmentation of political power: the rise of local "caudillos" often of *mestizo* or even Indian origin, frequent local wars, and a rapid succession of military coups.

The army of the "caudillos" was seldom anything more than an armed band, under the leadership of a self-appointed "general." At this stage we do not find in Latin America any professional army, but the political rule of the caudillos often adopted some symbols both of the army and of the democratic regimes: the geographical fragmentation took the form of a "federal" state, the absolute rule of the caudillo that of the "president" and, at the same time, "general" of the army. During this stage the social structure remained very much the same. This was especially true of the primitive state of the economy, the stratification system, and the isolation, both economic and social, of most of the population.

Stages 3 to 6. Transition of the Social Structure from the "Traditional" to the "Industrial" Pattern

While some countries show a clear succession of these four stages, in the majority of the cases there is much overlapping. Nevertheless the scheme is useful as a conceptualization of the transition towards a mature national state: that is, toward political unification and organization, attainment of certain preconditions of economic growth, changes in the social structure, and progressive enlargement of social participation (including political participation).

There is one very important and well-known feature of this process which must be emphasized here; the unevenness of the transition, the fact that some groups within the society and some areas within each country remained unchanged and underdeveloped while others underwent great changes. This is a familiar fact in most countries, but in Latin America (as in other underdeveloped areas) it acquired a particular intensity. The typical *dual* character of the countries both from the *social* and the *geographical* points of view is expressed in the contrasts between the socially "developed" higher and middle strata and the "backward," more primitive, lower strata; the cleavage between certain areas in which most of the urban population, industrial production, educated people, wealth, and political power are concentrated, and the rest of the country, predominantly rural, with a subsistence economy, illiterate, and politically inactive and powerless. The transition, in Latin America, cannot be understood without taking into full account the repercussions of this dual structure.

Social development involves first the extension of the modern way of life to a growing proportion of the people living in the most favored areas (the emergence of an urban middle class and a modern industrial proletariat in the "central" sector of a country), and second the incorporation— by way of massive internal migration or by geographical diffusion of industrialization and modernization—of the marginal population living in "peripheral" areas. The circumstances of the process, and especially its speed, are of the utmost importance for the political equilibrium of the country.

Stage 3. Unifying Dictatorships

The struggle between the caudillos within a given country was eventually replaced by the hegemony of one among them. The unity of the state was restored and a degree of order and stability achieved. However, the character of these "unifying dictatorships" differed very widely. For our present purpose they may perhaps be classified into two main categories: "regressive" dictatorships, which maintained completely intact the traditional pattern, and "enlightened" dictatorships, which introduced at least some modernizing measures. The most important difference between the two lies in the economic sphere. While the former maintained their countries isolated from the world market, and the old subsistence economy continued to predominate, the latter fostered at least a minimum degree of economic development, through the construction of means of transport and communication, some modernization of agriculture, some educational measures, organization of the public bureaucracy, and so forth.

Generally it was these relatively more enlightened authoritarian regimes, as well as the "limited democracies," which marked the beginning of the transformation of the Latin American countries into producers of raw materials and their integration into the world market. Foreign capital was introduced, the beginnings of industrialization took place, and these changes began to produce some impact on the social structure. While they left untouched the main features of the traditional pattern—the concentration of land ownership, the two class system, the isolation of the great majority of the population—they created certain dynamic factors which in time produced further changes making for transition. The integration of the country into the world market and the degree of economic modernization often fostered the emergence of new urban middle occupational strata. While they remained a relatively small proportion of the total population, and significantly, continued to be identified with the traditional upper class, these urban strata also represented an essential precondition for further changes.

One important feature of the enlightened dictatorships is the attempt at a "professionalization" of the army and the fact that while the dictators were often military men, they tried to control the army itself, submitting the unruly military caudillos to the central political authority of the state.

Stage 4. "Representative Democracy with Limited Participation"

The changes in the social structure under a "limited democracy" were often only slightly more pronounced than those induced by the "enlightened" dictatorships. In other cases, however, the modification was more substantial. This happened chiefly when the modernizing attitudes of the élites were bolder and the resulting economic and cultural changes more profound. In some cases the contribution of massive immigration from Europe—a part of the modernizing policy of the élite—was a decisive element in the transformation of the social structure.

The most significant feature of this stage is the formal functioning of democracy, the existence of a party system, the periodical replacement of the government through elections, freedom of the press and other "constitutional" guarantees. Another and no less essential feature is the "limitation" of democracy to only a fraction of the total population. This limitation is twofold. On the one hand the existing deep cleavage between developed and backward areas within a given country involved the almost complete exclusion of a substantial proportion of the population, practically all those living in the "peripheral" areas. On the other hand, a similar cleavage existed within the "central" areas, between the élites and the emerging middle strata, on the one side, and the lower groups on the other. Often the cleavage had also an ethnic basis even if we cannot speak of "racial" discrimination in Latin America. Both kinds of cleavage—geographical and social—meant the lack of a common basis for a real national identification on the part of a substantial proportion of the population, and of course a lack of cultural and economic participation. In consequence, the functioning of democracy was really limited in the sense that only the higher strata and the small newly formed middle groups (which identified themselves with the élite) living in the "central areas" did participate in one way or another in the political process (even at the lowest level of simple voting).

However, in those countries where the middle occupational strata could expand to a higher proportion of the total population and because of their immigrant origin, or their economic and cultural significance or some other causes, were able to acquire a greater psychological and social autonomy, strong political movements appeared which strove for a more real and enlarged democracy. In general such a situation was reached only in the most advanced areas of the country.

Stage 5. "Representative Democracy with Enlarged Participation"

The typical structure corresponding to this stage is still that of the dual society referred to previously, involving the geographical juxtaposition of a modern "central region" and "backward" peripheral regions. The former comprised most of the urban population, the industry, the literates, the middle strata and the modern urban proletariat, including, of course, the industrial workers. This region would contrast sharply with other regions which still remained—even though to a lesser degree—outside this development. Democracy, social, cultural and political participation, as well as national identification, included mostly people residing in the "advanced" areas. The difference from the previous stage of "limited" democracy is that now not only the middle strata would usually participate directly in the government or even control it, but the urban proletariat of the "central" region would also be included through the unions and political parties. The spread of nationalism—right and left—and of different "ideologies of industrialization" are characteristic of this phase.

Stage 6 (A). "Representative Democracy with Total Participation"

With the growing integration of previously marginal social groups and geographical areas into the cultural, economic and political life of the nation as a whole, with the acquisition of national loyalties and identification by all the inhabitants, and with the resulting higher degree of cultural and economic homogeneity of the various groups in society, we reach a new stage which we may call, for lack of a better term, that of "full nationhood." A high degree of urbanization, total literacy and a high average education, a high degree of occupational differentiation and a high proportion of the urban occupational middle strata which may now well be nearly 50% of the active urban employed population, are the other well known traits which characterize such a stage.

While in older nations, cultural homogeneity and national loyalty may not be accompanied by a high degree of economic development, in most instances "mass consumption"—that is, mass participation in the material culture of the industrial society—may also be regarded as one of the traits of the phase of "total participation democracy." From the political point of view it means effective full citizenship for the entire population, irrespective of area of residence or of socio-economic or ethnic affiliation. As a result, an important indicator of this stage is that of political participation at the level of voting of a substantial majority of the adult population of both sexes.[2]

Stage 6 (B). Total Participation Through "National-Popular" Revolutions

This pattern, which is increasingly typical of many underdeveloped countries—either under the form of communist totalitarianism or under the form of nationalistic authoritarianism—has also appeared in Latin America. It is obvious that the kind of "political participation" which takes place in the framework of such "national-popular" regimes is quite different from that of "representative democracy." However, it would be a mistake not to recognize the tremendous change involved for the marginal strata of the "dual" underdeveloped society.

While the national popular regime negates the very values which are the basis of participation in "representative democracy"—such as civil liberties—it does incorporate the marginal strata into the economic, cultural and political life of the nation. It induces their forceful "nationalization," and results in a change from passive acceptance (through internalized norms) to "compulsory participation." In Latin America, perhaps more than in other countries, "national-popular" regimes appear to be the outcome of the failure to develop into a full "representative democracy." From this point of view such an outcome appears to be connected with the failure in the formation of adequate channels of political expression for the social groups which successively emerge from the isolation and marginality in which they lived within the traditional social structure.

Such seems to have been the role of both "limited" and "enlarged" democracy: to prepare the institutional means and adequate outlets for the political pressure of the emerging larger strata of the population, within the framework of "representative democracy." Obviously, this is not only a political problem. The successful integration into such a framework also requires an expanding and modernizing economy, at least sufficient to give, even at a very modest level, an increasing degree of participation in the material culture of the industrial civilization, and this latter requirement is certainly more acute today than it was in the countries of Europe in which development occurred earlier.

If "limited democracy" is to succeed in the role we have mentioned, at least two conditions must be met. Firstly, the regime must be stable enough and last long enough to allow the establishment of a party system adequate for the expression of the increasing popular participation. Secondly, the "revolution in aspiration" must be to a certain extent synchronous with the economic and technical possibility of raising the level of living of the population. If both conditions are not satisfied, the chances are very high that political participation will be reached through one kind or another of "national-popular" revolutions. The marginality or the complete isolation of these larger strata of the population explains the greater stability achieved in the past by "limited" democracy both in Latin America and elsewhere. The chances of such stability are decreasing very sharply today and for a country whose socio-economic development has been retarded for one reason or another, political participation is more likely to take the form of a "national-popular revolution" than that of a "limited" or even "enlarged" democracy.

Considering now the present situation of the 20 Latin American republics we find examples of most of the "stages" just described, with the obvious exception of the first, and (perhaps) the second, stage. The "contemporaneity of the non-contemporaneous" certainly does apply to present Latin America, even if qualifications must be made for the peculiar historical circumstances of each country; and for the fact that certain changes would affect every country irrespective of their general socio-economic conditions. It is true, furthermore, that we do not find here a strict correlation between the political and the total social structure, or, as was pointed out earlier, with the type and extent of military intervention. But let us insist on the purely descriptive character of our typologies. They are no more than devices for introducing some order in a rather confusing and contradictory picture.

There can be little doubt that while "representative democracy" did reach—at least during certain periods of their history—a fairly high degree of stability in the countries we have classified at the top of Table 1 (Groups A and B), it never appeared or else it failed to attain a comparable duration and stability in the other two groups (C and D). But, of course, many inconsistencies both apparent and real appear all along the continuum from minimum to maximum national and socio-economic development as defined according to the criteria adopted.

With the possible exception of Colombia, and to a lesser degree and more recently, of Venezuela, Peru and Ecuador, it can be safely stated that most of the 14 countries included in the two lower groups have failed to escape the vicious circle of dictatorships, brief attempts (or none at all) at "limited" democracy, succession crises (in general under the form of military "coups"), even if at one time or another some more "enlightened" autocracy may have introduced a certain degree of "modernization," at least in opening the country to foreign capital and enterprises to exploit the local resources in raw materials. These combinations have often proved to be stable enough—small groups of big landowners, mainly military autocrats, and foreign investors. Such is clearly the case of the Dominican Republic, Haiti, Nicaragua, Honduras, El Salvador, Paraguay, and we may note that their present social structure is fairly consistent with their political history and actual situation. Of the other countries, Colombia—with a relatively high proportion of middle occupational strata—has managed to maintain for a longer time a more stable "limited democracy," but even so gravely perturbed by the chronic civil wars between political factions. Venezuela showed the first symptom of changes toward representative democracy after the long dictatorship of Gomez. Its first freely elected government (1946) had a short duration and only in recent years a new attempt at a "representative democracy" is being made. Similar processes can be seen in the other countries.

It is not surprising that it is precisely in this area that in the last decade there have been at least three "national-popular" revolutions (Bolivia, Cuba and Guatemala), and that presently the attempts at "representative democracy" of the new civilian regimes of Peru, Ecuador, Venezuela and Colombia encounter such great difficulties in the face of the growing pressure of the previously marginal strata, which the rapid urbanization and the growth in communication media are so swiftly displacing from a passive to an active role. While the ruling class may perhaps be ready to accept the functioning of a "limited" democracy, they are certainly not disposed or prepared to accept an enlarged participation with all its economic and social implications. The chances of incorporating the new strata —statistically the great majority of the population—into the framework of a representative democracy are greatly impaired not only by this opposition, but also by the relatively politically "anomic" situation in which these vast social groups find themselves because of the lack of adequate channels of expression of their political aims within the existing party system. The legitimacy of the regime is frequently at stake and its stability greatly diminished.

The six countries of the first two groups fit rather closely into our scheme of the transition. All of them had their period of anarchy, centralizing autocracies, limited democracies and, now enlarged democracies. The modern urban proletariat and the urban middle strata form the human basis of such regimes. In Mexico and Brazil, while both groups only constitute a relatively low proportion of the total population, their heavy concentration in the cities and in certain regions within each country explains their dominant role in political life. But although with many peculiarities "representative democracy" can be said to function at present in these countries, they do offer contrasts as to the degree of stability and degree of interference of the military in civilian affairs.

Perhaps the contrast between Argentina and the other countries is the most disturbing fact. While Argentina may be considered as the most "advanced" as a national state on the basis of the usual indicators, it is also the most unstable and disturbed. After more than 60 years of continued functioning of a representative democracy, and having passed from a limited to an enlarged level without major troubles, it has relapsed in the last three decades into military revolutions, a decennial dictatorship and the very uneasy democracy of the post-Peronian period. There is, however, a difference. While most of these countries are certainly to be considered as "enlarged" democracies, the situation of Argentina can be better described as one of recent transition into a—as yet unstable—"total participation" democracy. Its very instability as compared with the greater stability of the other countries can be interpreted, at least partially, as one effect of this difficult transition. The level of voting is certainly suggestive of such an interpretation. If we consider the proportion of voters in the total adult population we find a sharp contrast between Argentina on the one hand and Mexico, Chile and Brazil on the other. While in Argentina the percentage of voters in the total adult population (20 years and more) is over 80% (and if we take, according to the legal definition, persons of 18 years and older it is still 75%), in Mexico (1958) it is 48%, in Brazil (1960) 40%, in Chile (1958) 34%. We must also remember that if we discount the foreign residents, who in Argentina are around 15% (adult age groups), the proportion of participants would be even higher. In the remaining countries the foreign residents are a very low proportion and would not make any significant difference.

We are not assuming that the proportion of voters is a cause of instability; we are using it as an indicator of the level of functioning of democracy and of integration into national society: here it is sufficient to mention countries such as England (80%, 1951), Australia (86%, 1949) or Canada (74%, 1949). We have used as a uniform basis for comparison: percentage of voters in total population of 20 years and more. It cannot be denied that the low proportion of voters in countries such as Brazil, Mexico and Chile simply means that a considerable sector of the adult population is not yet integrated into the national body. The rural dweller, the peasant isolated in his small community, is certainly less politically relevant than the industrial worker in the cities, and his role continues to be more a passive than an active one. This integration is certainly a fact in contemporary Argentina and here we must take into account the historical circumstances which caused the partial failure of the "enlarged" democracy to create an institutional framework for the smooth functioning of a representative regime at a total level of participation, in order to understand the apparent "paradox" of this country, relatively so advanced (within the Latin American continent) and still in the grip of continuous military intervention.

While it would not be safe to make any prediction, it is reasonable to think that the greater stability enjoyed by both "limited" and, later on, "enlarged" representative democracy in Chile, the strong traditions which have been formed through its long political experience and the more firmly established party system (in comparison with Argentina) will be great assets in the transition from the present "enlarged" participation, to the coming level of "total" participation. But, in any case, in all the five countries, with their rapid rate of urbanization and the even more rapid spread of communication, the incorporation of the still marginal groups is imminent. It will involve a great strain on the present institutions and, as the cases of Vargas and Peron show very clearly, they will not be immune from the possibility of "national-popular" solutions.

The role of the military in Latin America must be understood in this rather complex picture. If we conceive it as related both to the kind of political system and to its *degree* of stability, then we must expect everywhere in Latin America and at all levels of socio-economic and national development the possibility of some intromission of the military into civilian affairs. In fact, some degree of stability can be reached in most of the transition stages, even at the "backward" one of centralizing autocracy; and conversely instability may appear even at the most "advanced" level of "enlarged" democracy if its corresponding social and political requirements are not adequately satisfied.

nomic development, changing world ideological currents, and rapidly growing industrial urbanization. Because nowhere in Latin America—even in famed Uruguay and Costa Rica—are the institutional patterns of secular and impersonal representative democracy fully established, many civilian groups are innately revolutionary in their attitudes and predisposed to the use of force as an inherent and thus desirable part of the social pattern. Both military schisms and military adventures are encouraged by the civilian groups soliciting armed aid for their political ambitions. Even though the following quotation concerns the Spain of the 1930's, it is valid for the Latin American arena as well:

> No doubt the generals in 1936 thought they were saving Spain [. . .] The State must be capable of embodying and responding to what Maura called the vital forces of the community. Otherwise, as he warned repeatedly, the army will claim to embody the national will in order to enforce changes which political institutions are impotent to encompass. Above all, no democrat, repeating the follies of the progressive and moderate minorities, can appeal to the sword rather than to conviction, however slow the educative process may be. Though the Republic of 1931 came in on a vote, many Republicans were willing to see it come in through the army. Repeating the tactics of Ruiz Zorrilla, they systematically undermined the loyalty of the army. Some saw the danger. "I would prefer no Republic to a Republic conceived in the womb of the army." Many did not. How could they complain when other forces tampered with the loyalty of the army in 1936?[5]

The military will be reduced to their barracks and their professional functions alone only when Latin American countries develop sufficiently complicated power structures and a society sufficiently flexible and integrated; when social and geographical discontinuities have been greatly lessened and isolated or marginal masses incorporated into the national body; when economic and social conflicts have found institutionalized expression within a common framework of shared norms.

Notes

1. The table appeared in a slightly modified form in Gino Germani, "The strategy of fostering social mobility," paper prepared for the Seminar on *The Social Impact of Economic Development in Latin America* (Proceedings publ. by UNESCO). Only part of the basic data are shown in the table.

 For the main concepts used in formulating the scheme, see: G. Germani, *Integración política de las masas* (Buenos Aires, CLES, 1956); "El autoritarismo y las clases populares," in *Actas IV Congreso Latino Americano de Sociologia* (Santiago, Chile, 1957); *Politica e Massa* (Minas Gerais, Universidade de Minas Gerais, 1960); K. Silvert, "Nationalism in Latin America" in *The Annals of the American Academy of Political and Social*

Science, 334 (1961), 1–9; of the relevant bibliography on this subject we took especially into account: S. M. Lipset, *Political Man* (New York, Doubleday, 1960), and D. Lerner, *The Passing of Traditional Society* (Glencoe, The Free Press, 1958).

2. The phenomenon of "non-voting" and "political" apathy which appear in some developed countries (as the U.S.A., for instance) has a different meaning from the non-participation of the marginal and isolated sectors in underdeveloped countries.

3. For a narrower version of this typology and other suggested categorizations of Latin American politics, see K. H. Silvert, "Political Change in Latin America," in Herbert Matthews, ed., *The United States and Latin America* (New York, The American Assembly, 1959). Also refer to the March 1961 issue of *The Annals of the American Academy of Political and Social Science*, entitled *Latin America's Nationalist Revolutions*, for other pertinent and recent information.

4. Oscar Lewis, in his "Mexico Since Cardenas," in Lyman Bryson, ed., *Social Change in Latin America Today* (New York, Harper, 1960), pp. 301–302, writes:

> *A comparison of the allocations of federal funds to the various departments over the four presidential administrations from Cardenas to Ruiz Cortines reveals [. . .] some highly significant trends. Especially marked is the sharp decrease in the proportion of funds allocated to national defense, reflecting the demise of caudillismo as a serious factor in Mexican life. Adolfo Ruiz Cortines was the first president since the 1920's who did not depend heavily on either the national or a private army to maintain his control.*

Professor Lewis then points out that between 1935 and 1940 defense expenditures absorbed 17.3 percent of the national budget, dropping to 8.1 percent in the period 1953–1956.

5. A. R. M. Carr, "Spain," in Michael Howard, ed., *Soldiers and Governments: Nine Studies in Civil-Military Relations* (London, Eyre and Spottiswoode, 1957), pp. 145–46.

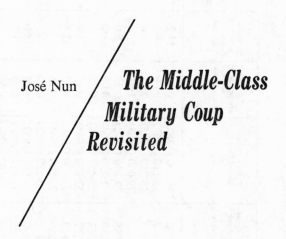

José Nun / **The Middle-Class Military Coup Revisited**

Unless a distinction is made between the structural and the circumstantial factors of military intervention in Latin American politics, important differences between countries are apt to be ignored. Table 1, for instance, shows that the number of successful coups varies independently of the degree of economic development: there were as many in Argentina as in El Salvador and fewer in Honduras than in Brazil. Evidently the intervention of the military in politics represents a different phenomenon in a country with an income per capita of $500, 70 per cent of its population living in cities, and with a large middle class, than in one where less than one-third of the population lives in cities, income per capita is only $150, and scarcely 8 percent of the population can be classified as belonging to the upper and middle classes.[1]

Interpretations which tend to ignore these differences have generally been influenced either by traditional liberal antimilitarism or by the advocacy of militarism as a dynamic force for economic development.[2]

From José Nun, "The Middle-Class Military Coup," in *The Politics of Conformity in Latin America*, ed. Claudio Veliz (London: Oxford University Press, 1967). Published by Oxford University Press under the auspices of the Royal Institute of International Affairs and reprinted by permission of the author and the publisher. [This article should not be confused with another version of the essay published in 1964. It should be noted that the article was written in 1966 and does not, consequently, incorporate subsequent events into its analysis. Ellipsis points indicate deleted text.—Ed.]

Table 1. Armed Forces in Latin America

	(a) % of urban population (1960)	(b) % of illiterates (1961)	(c) % of labour force engaged in manufacturing & construction (1960)	(d) % of upper & middle classes in total population (c. 1950)	(e) % of urban upper & middle classes in total urban population (c. 1950)	(f) GNP distributed per capita (US $ 1960)	(g) Total regular armed forces	(h) Ratio of armed forces to population	(i) % military budget of total budget	(j) No. successful military coups (1920–1966)
Argentina	68	14	29	36	38	466	108·500 (1963)	0·51	13·2	7
Uruguay	82	15	28	(33)			13·110 (1963)	0·49	1·0	
Chile	63	20	24	22	30	439	45·710 (1965)	0·62	18·0	2
Cuba	55	22	18	22	36		79·000 (1963)	1·21		4
Venezuela	62	48	15	18	27	885	22·240 (1962)	0·33	8·0	4
Costa Rica	38	21	15	22	31	310	1·230 (1964)	0·09	1·0	1
Panama	41	30	10	15	32	363	3·439 (1964)	0·32		3
Mexico	54	43	15	17	37	272	52·850 (1964)	0·15	1·0	
Brazil	39	51	17	15	35	168	263·100 (1960)	0·37	11·4	5
Colombia	46	38	17	22	28	250	22·900 (1964)	0·15		2
Ecuador	35	44	25	10	21	161	13·280 (1963)	0·30		9
Peru	36	53	18			190	44·940 (1963)	0·41	18·0	4
Bolivia	30	68	13	8	26	86	11·010 (1960)	0·31	11·0	9
Paraguay	34	34	17	14	27	129	9·100 (1962)	0·50		7
El Salvador	33	61	14	10	25	200	6·650 (1961)	0·25	12·0	6
Nicaragua	34	62	13		23	229	4·100 (1963)	0·25		1
Dominican Rep.	29	57	11			207	17·200 (1963)	0·57	26·0	4
Honduras	22	65	9	4	25	186	4·200 (1965)	0·21	7·0	2
Guatemala	31	71	10	8	16	156	8·500 (1965)	0·22		6
Haiti	13	89	7	3	14	98			23·0	5

["Sources and Explanations" have been omitted.—Ed.]

The *liberal model*, based on the experience of Europe in the eighteenth and nineteenth centuries, envisaged the army as the bastion of traditional and feudal values. Its officer corps was drawn from the aristocracy, and was antagonistic to the liberal bourgeois state. From 1815, with the Pax Britannica contributing to a decrease of militarism and the state taking deliberate measures to ensure civilian control over the armed forces, there ensued a professional revolution which reached its peak by the end of the nineteenth century. The developmentalist model conceives of the army as an intelligentsia in uniform, dedicated to progress and development and peculiarly suited to achieving them. It is based on the experience of the Afro-Asian countries, where the officer corps was mostly drawn from the popular sectors. There is a Nasserist version of this model which will be discussed later. Finally, the socialist model, which, from a rejection of militarism similar to that espoused by the liberals, has progressed to an acceptance of the integration of the military in the body politic as a means both of strengthening it and of lending additional prestige to the civilian leadership.

These three ways of approaching the problem imply that the armed forces are an independent sector, or at least that they are hardly at all integrated with the rest of society. Thus, according to one such theory, the traditional army is a step behind the modern society which is forming around it; according to another, the modern army is a step ahead of the traditional society which is disintegrating. In fact both these theories presuppose an inverse relationship between militarism and the consolidation of the diversified social structure typical of a developed country. As one writer asserts: "Army officers in politics are typical of pre-industrial nations lacking a strong middle class."[3] How then is one to explain the military coups in countries such as Argentina or Brazil, which have strong middle-class sectors, and such a high degree of industrial growth that in the former country one-third of the labour force is employed in manufacturing industry or construction, while in the second domestic production accounts for two-thirds of the capital goods the country requires?[4]

An objective analysis shows that Latin America is lacking in two of the basic elements of the liberal model: in the first place, its armies were generally formed after the professional revolution; and, secondly, the greater part of their officers are recruited from the middle class and not from the aristocracy.

Merle Kling has proposed an interesting modification of this model. His argument may be summarized as follows: in Latin America, the oligarchy and foreign capital maintain a rigid control over the conventional bases of economic power and prevent the rise of other social groups; the government therefore appears as the only base of economic power, the ownership of which can change; and from this situation there arises the privileged position of the military in the ruthless struggle to take possession of this coveted source of potential power; instability is therefore "a function of the contradiction between the realities of a colonial economy and the political requirements of legal sovereignty among the Latin American states."[5]

Even if one ignores the economic emphasis of this theory and concedes that the personal ambition of military leaders is the basic driving force behind military interventions, it is obvious that this interpretation is only valid for very undeveloped countries, characterized by a bi-polar social structure (oligarchy/masses), and a very low degree of mobility and institutional differentiation—conditions which can hardly be said to be prevalent in the more advanced countries of Latin America.

Similar objections can be raised to the "developmentalist" model—largely based on the experience of the Afro-Asian countries—which analyses "the political implications of the army as a modern institution that has been somewhat artificially introduced into disorganized traditional societies."[6] It is applicable, in other words, to countries of very recent formation, where the civil and military bureaucracies are the only alternatives, in almost entire absence of modern institutions. It is unnecessary to emphasize the difference between such societies and those of Argentina or Brazil.

This lends added interest to an examination of instability in the more-developed countries of Latin America. In the two already mentioned—Argentina and Brazil—military coups are features of the present-day situation. In the other three[7]—Uruguay, Chile, and Mexico—the last quarter-century has been marked by political stability. Is it possible, by means of an analysis of the experience of these countries, to isolate structural factors capable of explaining interventionism in situations remote from those envisaged in the traditional models? Over twenty years ago it was observed that "a government which cannot rely upon its middle classes will, almost certainly, be unable to rely upon the unbroken loyalty of its army."[8] Is this the situation? And, if so, why?

This essay attempts to analyse certain structural elements that have not generally been considered in previous interpretations of this phenomenon. For at least two reasons it makes no claim to be exhaustive; first, it excludes the very important circumstantial factors, which cannot be dealt with here; and, secondly, because a model of this nature does not claim to be an exact reflection of reality, but only to place some emphasis on certain important aspects that are not immediately obvious.

The Middle-Class Professional Army

To understand the problem of political instability, one must look behind the military façade (just as, to understand Latin American inflation, one had to look behind the monetary façade). With this end in view, both the social basis of the officer corps and some of the consequences of its recent professionalization must be considered.

(a) Social Basis

Although statistical information on this subject is still scarce, most authorities are agreed in admitting that, since the end of the nineteenth century, the majority of Latin American officers have been recruited from the middle class.[9]

In his study of generals, brigadiers, and admirals in Argentina, José Luis de Imaz found that only 23 per cent of the sample examined were descended from the traditional families. He estimated that 73 per cent of the brigadiers and generals interviewed came from families belonging to the wealthy bourgeoisie, 25 per cent from the lower middle class, and only 2 per cent from the working class.[10] Although the category "upper middle class or wealthy bourgeoisie" is excessively large, and includes everybody from landowners to professional men, and even supposing that all the fathers concerned who were landowners, businessmen, or industrialists belonged to the upper class—which is certainly an exaggeration—this survey does indicate that two-thirds of the officer corps is of middle-class origin. Moreover, contrary to what is generally believed, the data provided by Imaz indicate that "[Argentine] generals, today just as much as formerly, come from an urban background, half of them from the capital and the Greater Buenos Aires area."[11]

John Johnson reached similar conclusions with regard to the middle-class origin of Brazilian officers,[12] even though in this case the greater part came from the small towns in the interior. . . .

In Chile, where the officer corps represents a more typical cross-section of the urban population as a whole,[13] there has been, ever since the war of 1879, a continuous penetration of the military profession by the sons of middle-class families.[14] A similar trend has been evident in Uruguay and Mexico since the turn of the century. In the case of Mexico, it is possible that recruitment has taken place from even lower social strata: for example, an examination of the applications for admission to the Military College in 1955 reveals that 14.64 per cent of the candidates were the sons of workers and 2.98 per cent the sons of peasants.[15]

This description does not imply that the class situation of the officer corps entirely explains its political behaviour. It does, however, restrict the field of investigation, and makes possible an assessment of the importance and relative autonomy of outside factors inhibiting or determining the behaviour of this group.[16] It is, after all, not entirely fortuitous that the liberal model which prevailed in the nineteenth century should have paid particular attention to the basis of recruitment of those destined for military command: "After all, their origins constitute the source of the 'non-Armed Force' opinions of the armed force organizations."[17]

In the countries under discussion, there are other factors which presumably tend to strengthen this class affiliation, owing to continual contact between the civil and military spheres. Among these are the lack of a tradition of active warfare, which diminishes the separation between the daily life of the officers and that of the rest of the population. Another factor that has still not been investigated is the mediating role fulfilled by retired officers: the available data do, in fact, indicate a tendency towards "rejuvenation" among the higher ranks of the armed forces,[18] which means that the retirement—voluntary or enforced—of the officer occurs when he is still fully active and capable of embarking on a civilian career, while at the same time keeping in touch with his old comrades in arms. Moreover, whereas in technologically backward societies the increasing technical specialization of the army tends to link the officer more closely to foreign sources, in societies of a higher cultural development, such as those we are analysing, the same phenomenon leads to increased contacts between the officer and his civilian colleagues.

Finally, it is worth pointing out an obvious fact which is too often forgotten, namely the "civilianization" of the officers that is a direct consequence of their continual political activity. Although one should not exaggerate the importance of such contacts, which in any case are limited to certain social sectors, this is nevertheless an argument against the traditional conception of the army as an institution completely isolated from its social context, and the consequent exaggeration of the uniqueness of the armed forces' attitudes and behaviour. It would, of course, be absurd to deny the existence of characteristics peculiar to the army as such but so far no attempt has been made to determine how important these are in determining an officer's behaviour.[19] Several studies devoted to this question apply to the military establishment the concept of the "total institution" formulated by Goffman.[20] However, such studies pay less attention to the distinctions drawn by the same writer with regard to methods of recruitment and the permeability of the institution to the influences surrounding it,[21] and ignore his assertion that "total institutions do not really look for cultural victory,"[22] which explains the relative ease with which its members are able to become reintegrated into the society outside the institution.[23]

(b) Organization

While it is true, on the one hand, that the greater part of the officer corps comes from the middle class, the military establishment can, on the other hand, count on a degree of cohesion and institutional solidity which is entirely lacking in the Latin American middle class.

The tendency to consider social phenomena in isolation and in the abstract has led some writers to suppose that professionalization *per se* induces officers to withdraw from politics, by placing a barrier between them and the rest of society. Oddly enough, Mosca argued with equal conviction, and for well-founded reasons, that the contrary was true and, more recently, Finer has supported his arguments.[24] With regard to the Latin American armed forces, one observer asserts: "On the contrary, in those countries in which they have been most highly professionalized, they seem to have become even more closely linked with the rest of society than formerly."[25]

What happens in reality is that every system of domination attempts to internalize violence by the means most suited to its values and interests. Thus professionalism became generally accepted in European armies only at the end of the nineteenth century and as a result of deliberate government policy. The bourgeois state had experimented with various formulae for the control of the armed forces—examples of which are the unsuccessful French and American attempts to have the highest posts of command submitted to popular election—until the logic of capitalist society eventually dictated the solution. In the framework of a general tendency towards fragmentation and division of labour, the exercise of violence was also converted into a specialized field calling for high professional qualifications, and became part of a series of particular sub-systems enjoying a relative degree of autonomy. In this way "military institutions have taken on more and more the characteristics common to civilian large-scale organizations."[26] Professionalization is therefore the means by which the armed forces are incorporated into a determined place in the structuralization of society as a whole, and it is this, and not professionalism as such, that explains the apparent political neutrality of the army in the Western democracies.

This process of professionalization was bound to produce different results in Latin America, since it not only took place in armies at different stages of development but did so in the context of pre-industrial societies with structures based on the hegemony of the oligarchy and not that of the bourgeoisie.

In Europe "military organization had established its form centuries before professionalization definitely began."[27] This explains in part the successful establishment of organizational controls designed to counteract the possible centrifugal tendencies which might result from increased professionalization. In Latin America organization and professionalization take place almost simultaneously, increasing the probability of discrepancies leading to open conflict.[28]

This early professionalization had two important social consequences: first, as has been indicated above, the middle class was admitted to the career of arms through the creation of military academies; and, secondly, in contrast to its own organizational weakness,[29] this class was now allied to a sector with a remarkable degree of institutional cohesion and articulateness. In other words the armed forces became one of the few important institutions controlled by the middle class.[30]

This relationship partly explains political instability due to military intervention but it is open to two important criticisms: first, from those who consider that the profession of arms conditions its followers so thoroughly that one may ignore any other variable in seeking for explanations of their behaviour; and, secondly, from those who maintain that the middle class, by its very nature, is dedicated to the support of political stability and democratic institutions.

I have already given some of the reasons why I consider the first objection to be valid only in a relative sense. With regard to the second, it will be necessary to touch briefly on some of the factors that lead the middle class to associate with military intervention in politics.

Middle Class and Bourgeoisie

Hitherto I have deliberately used the expression "middle class" rather than "bourgeoisie." G. D. H. Cole has drawn the distinction:

> Bourgeois, to any historically-minded person, calls up at once the image of a body of citizens asserting their collective, as well as their individual, independence of a social system dominated by feudal power based on landholding and on the services attached to it; whereas the words "middle class" call up the quite different image of a body of persons who are placed between two other bodies—or perhaps more than two—in some sort of stratified social order.[31]

The same writer goes on to say that the bourgeoisie as such is not in the middle of anything, at least not consciously so.

At this point it is necessary to consider the degree of relative independence of the rural and urban sectors of the same national society; it is on this supposed independence that the hypothesis of structural dualism, so frequently met with in studies concerned with Latin America, is based. The concept of a middle class implies, by definition, a system of unified vertical stratification. But the application of the hypothesis of dualism to the Latin American situation admits of two different interpretations; in the first, the traditional and modern "poles" are analysed as if they were relatively independent entities, with the result that some writers speak of "two countries within the same territory." Hence the tendency to transfer mechanically to the Latin American situation a technologically determinist hypothesis like Ogburn's "cultural lag." The observer "isolates" São Paulo from the North-East, for example, and assumes that for the latter to attain the level of development of the former, all that is required is to transform the North-East without considering whether such a transformation would involve equally profound changes in São Paulo. On the other hand, the dialectic interpretation finds the key to the situation in the internal unity of a historically determined system of domination. This is the unity explaining the frustration of a middle class which is prevented from fulfilling the role of a bourgeoisie. In order to analyse such an interpretation, it is necessary to distinguish between two principal stages in the evolution of the system: that of the unity of the oligarchy and that of its crisis.

The Hegemony of the Oligarchy

[Due to] characteristics associated with the process of colonization, in the case of the urbanization of Latin America, . . . there was never any real dissension between the urban centres and the nascent landowning aristocracy. "Colonization was in large part an urban venture, carried out by urban-minded people,"[32] and the city represented both the point of departure and the residence of the owners of land. . . .

This initial "unitary" characteristic becomes even more pronounced in the second half of the nineteenth century, with the rapid integration of the Latin American national economies into the world market. As Celso Furtado has observed, "the entrepreneurial attitude that made the rapid development of lines of export possible had its origin within the merchant groups which operated from the urban centers."[33] Instead of a divergence developing between the interests of the dominant groups in the cities and those in the rural areas, the urban mercantile sector consolidated its position as a landowning and capitalist oligarchy.[34]

[Generally speaking,] it was thus that the great Latin American capitals became the places of residence of the privileged sectors during the era of "outward" economic growth. Beside them there developed the middle class, of the primary-products export model, composed of the exporters and importers, small industrialists, professional men, and civil servants, all integrated into the hegemonic system of the oligarchy.

This did not mean that the state was simply the expression of the subjective will of one social class, as if the underlying unity of the hegemonic structure were given by the ideology of the dominant group. On the contrary, this unity must be sought in the total structure of society, in which this ideology was only one element among many. The function fulfilled by the state—providing a framework for the oligarchy—must not be obscured by being forced into the nineteenth-century liberal model imported from Europe. In Latin America there was no question of the *status quo* being challenged; *laissez-faire* was in practice the political instrument which consolidated the economic system, and its application constituted "a deliberate measure consciously designed to achieve specific ends and not the spontaneous and automatic expression of an economic situation."[35] Structure and super-structure thus became fused into an extremely solid historical block, and found their expression in an advanced juridical and institutional system. Marx asserts that a particular class can only maintain its supremacy by exercising it in the name of the general rights of society. On the basis of a particular economic system, this "conquérante" oligarchy was able to evolve a systematic justification of its dominant position by means of a normative structure which defined those general rights in terms which applied to the existing internal relationships among social groups. The fundamental reason for its success was undoubtedly the high degree of efficacy of the system itself: the bonanza arising from the export of raw materials convinced all its beneficiaries—direct and indirect—that Argentine meat, Brazilian coffee, Uruguayan wool, and Chilean minerals guaranteed permanent economic expansion. To be optimistic, it was enough to conceive of the future as an extension of the present, and the middle class enthusiastically adopted that conservative outlook which takes no account of the future or the vicissitudes it may bring. It was members of the oligarchy, not of the middle class, who were responsible for the first industrial expansion of any importance, and it was they who organized the new industrial and commercial enterprises, in which the middle class participated only as a second-rate but acquiescent partner. . . . Since the basic principles of the system were never called into question, commercial or industrial collapse was regarded as a problem affecting only the individual concerned, or, at most, held to be the result of corruption of a system that, in its uncorrupt state, was considered unsurpassable.

The expanding middle class made no attempt to change the system as a whole: it merely demanded recognition of its legitimate right to play a part in it. Its aspirations were limited to a desire for participation in political affairs and for revendication of its moral status.[36] The most interesting features of this process were the speed with which these aspirations were satisfied and the instrumental role of the military.

This process began in Uruguay, with the election in 1903 of José Batlle y Ordóñez. This chronological priority undoubtedly reflects the very early development of the Uruguayan middle class: at the turn of the century, it already constituted between 25 and 30 per cent of the population of the Republic, and *Batllismo* was "the political movement which most exactly reflects [its] rise."[37] The great leader of the *Colorados* came to power in the middle of a civil war fought against the landowning groups connected with the Blanco Party. Whereas the armed forces of the latter were basically composed of peons recruited from the big estates, the regular army gave its support to *Batllismo* and made it possible for Batlle to establish himself in power.[38]

In Argentina, a military lodge was formed as early as 1890, under the influence of the *Unión Cívica,* the immediate predecessor of the *Unión Cívica Radical,* the middle-class party which carried Hipólito Yrigoyen into the presidency in 1916. In the intervening period there were increased contacts between the Radicals and the officer corps—some of the officers played an active part in the 1893 and 1905 rebellions—and this was one of the factors which eventually induced the oligarchy to allow free elections. As Puiggrós observes: "They feared the democratic revolution, and at the same time they realized that they could not continue to monopolize political power with the immense majority of the people against them and with Radicalism increasingly influencing the army, the police and the civil service."[39] This also explains the failure of the coup planned at the last minute by the oligarchy-dominated Senate, designed to force the resignation of President Sáenz Peña, suspend the elections, and return to the system of restricted suffrage.

In Chile, the aspirations of the middle class found expression in the *Alianza Liberal* which, in 1920, put Arturo Alessandri in the presidency. "The 'revolution of 1920' was never envisioned by most of its instigators as anything more than a program of mild palliatives; but it was unable to furnish even the palliatives."[40] Among the most obvious reasons for its failure was the systematic opposition of the Senate, still controlled by the oligarchy. As Gil observes, "the majority of the Chilean armed forces, composed of middle-class members in the officer corps and of men of proletarian origin in the rank and file, were sympathetic to the national cry for reform."[41] When, after the parliamentary elections of 1924, even the new Congress—in which Alessandri already commanded a majority—postponed the implementation of the President's programme, the army took action, overthrew the ministerial cabinet and "in an hour and without debate, the 'suggestive rattling of army sabres in the congressional galleries' obtained approval of a complete program of social legislation which had been pending for years in the Congress."[42] Although the movement was initially commanded by a group of officers identified with the upper class, "the majority of the armed forces' officers opposed the restoration to power of a discredited oligarchy."[43] Thus in January 1925 another coup, this time engineered by young officers led by Carlos Ibáñez and Marmaduke Grove, eliminated the conservative faction, brought Alessandri back to the country, and drew up a new constitution which, in the words of a liberal commentator, "although it was the work of a *de facto* government and was imposed by force of arms, has stood the test of time, and has lasted with minor modifications until our own day."[44] Thus the armed forces ensured the establishment in power of the middle class, whose programme was put into practice by Colonel Ibáñez who, as a result of military pressure, became president in 1927. One should not forget, therefore, in considering the subsequent political stability of Chile, that "the institutional structure that has governed Chile down to the present day was fashioned by Ibáñez between 1927 and 1931."[45]

In Brazil, the continuous expansion of the armed forces since 1864 made them a stronghold of the incipient middle class, to which the Empire offered few occupational opportunities. "That middle-class army, which to a certain extent formed a body outside the organizational structure of the Imperial state, would eventually overthrow it."[46] "Florianismo," however, marked the failure of the premature attempt of this sector to establish control over the state.[47] Although the solidarity of the Old Republic (*Republica velha*), rendered the process slower in the case of Brazil, events subsequently followed a path similar to those in Argentina and Chile: "The middle-class revolutions that took place between 1922 and 1937 represented the efforts made by that class to achieve, by military means, a power that always eluded it."[48] The first step towards the final achievement of this objective was the revolution of 1930, which brought Getulio Vargas to power, thanks to the decisive part played by the *tenentismo* movement. The support of the military for the régime was reaffirmed in 1932, with the defeat of the attempt to restore the oligarchy. The new groups soon realized, however, that adherence to the 1934 constitution and the effective implementation of the basic principle for which they had struggled—universal and secret suffrage—would result in their defeat at the hands of the paternalistic ballot-rigging practised by the landowners.

> Thus the middle class found itself in the peculiar position of wishing to control the state without altering the existing social and economic structure, and of being compelled by considerations of *Realpolitik* to jettison its political principles with the anti-democratic coup of 1937 and the setting up of the *Estado nôvo*.[49]

Although several circumstantial factors make it exceptional, the case of Mexico nevertheless partially confirms the pattern outlined above. The limited nature of the political aspirations of the middle class was summed up in the well-known *Maderista* slogan, "Effective suffrage and no re-election." The emphasis was, above all, political: "Madero wanted wider participation and more democratic processes in politics in an effort to end the *continuismo* of the Díaz régime."[50] This explains the timidity of the agrarian measures contemplated in Article 3 of the Plan of San Luis Potosí, which nevertheless was enough to mobilize Emiliano Zapata and his followers:

> He and his men soon threw themselves into the Revolution, not because they were excited by the magic words "effective suffrage and no re-election," as this political document [the Plan of San Luis Potosí] suggests, but because they believed in the agrarian measures promised in Article 3.[51]

The complete ineffectiveness in this respect of the thirteen and a half months of Madero's government provoked the insurrection of the Southern leader and his proclamation of the Plan of Ayala, which gave contemporary expression to the slogan of Flores Magón: "Land and Liberty." It was this peasant unrest that forced the middle class to support the reforms which, albeit with great hesitation, Venustiano Carranza was introducing; so much so that the domination of the oligarchy was in fact broken only in the following decade, under the government of Obregón, whose work was completed by Lázaro Cárdenas. As for the army, its situation was slightly different from that described in the countries discussed above. In his successful attempts to establish control, Porfirio Díaz had considerably weakened it. Gradually he forced the retirement of a quarter of the hundred generals in the army, and dismissed about four hundred more junior officers.[52] Also the professionalization of the armed forces was much slower than in the other cases quoted: "Although there was a perceptible French influence and part of the equipment was German, Mexico did not invite any foreign military mission, and rarely sent officers to study abroad. Consequently, the army was backward in both military techniques and equipment."[53] For this reason, as Edwin Lieuwen points out, the army was no more than a "fragile shell" when the 1910 revolution broke out. Nevertheless as soon as the revolution began, a number of officers, steadily increasing, "deserted the régime and joined the revolutionary forces, impressed by their power and popular support."[54] In other words, in Mexico too a sizeable part of the regular army supported the attempts of the middle class to seize power.

All this highlights the relative speed with which the middle class achieved the satisfaction of its claims; and the decisive role played by the armed forces in this process. But what must be emphasized above all is the limited nature of those claims. Except in the case of Mexico, the political events did not constitute one of those "cathartic" moments when the ascent to power of a new social group leads to profound structural changes. It was the very reverse of that process: the middle class had no need of time to develop a characteristic outlook, because it merely adopted that of the oligarchy. It accepted its heroes, its symbols, its culture, and its laws. (It is significant that both Yrigoyen and Alessandri decided to play with "loaded dice," assuming the presidency at a time when the parliamentary majority was in the hands of the oligarchy.) The middle class did not question the economic basis of the system, but formulated the conflict in terms of "equality of opportunity," that is to say equality of access to the alternatives defined by that system; for this reason the two sides eventually agreed on the socialization of the political conflict, leaving the economic one on a purely private plane. In contrast to this, the exceptional merit of the Mexican Revolution lay in its handling of the agrarian problem.

Two points are worth making. First, a description of the integration of the middle class into a historical situation dominated by the oligarchic hegemony need not be interpreted as a moral accusation levelled against that class, on the grounds that it failed in its historic mission, since in fact its behaviour was governed by the limited framework of its "possible consciousness," bearing in mind the conditions surrounding its formation. Secondly, this is a process and not a static phenomenon. Important political changes such as these cannot be explained simply in quantitative terms. The very expansion that was the result of the ascent and social integration of the middle class began, in fact, to weaken the hegemony of the oligarchy, making it especially vulnerable to the vicissitudes of the period that followed and leading it towards its definitive crisis.

The Hegemonic Crisis

After the 1929 depression, exports in the countries under discussion ceased to constitute the axis of the economic system, and internal investment replaced the external sector as the dynamic growth factor.

In the favourable conditions of a highly protected internal market—as an indirect consequence of measures taken to prevent catastrophe for the exporting groups—there took place a process of totally unplanned industrial development. The peculiar characteristic of this process of substitution of imports[55] was that it made possible industrialization without an industrial revolution, and without necessarily antagonizing the landowning oligarchy. These considerations are of the utmost importance in the interpretation of the behaviour of the new middle-class groups[56] that emerged during this period because the aspirations of these groups found expression within the framework of the hegemony of the oligarchy; the conditions of their development did not result in a fundamental conflict with that system. This is the reason for the essentially conservative nature of its political consciousness, in so far as it never transcended the limits of a corporative-economic interest and was incapable of reaching the level of "universality" attained by the oligarchical system.[57]

This makes it easier to understand, in the first place, the apparent ambiguity of outlook manifested by these new sectors, which caused so many unfounded speculations about the emergence of a national bourgeoisie: its reformist impulses have invariably originated and exhausted themselves on the level of immediate economic interests. It is therefore quite logical, for example, to assert that "the state that helps 'my industry' has nothing to do with the more abstract state which, legislating and acting, participates in the economic life and becomes the eternal symbol of the anti-enterprise."[58] In the same way an industrialist can be protectionist in outlook with regard to his own products, and an advocate of free trade with regard to the materials that such production requires.[59]

Moreover, it would be erroneous to consider as a lack what is a negation. The particularism of this class consciousness really means that the new group finds appropriate, or rather that it appropriates, the existing normative structure. The repeated failure of the developmental theorists, who have eventually become convinced of the sociological weakness and artificiality of their hypotheses,[60] shows that it is not just a question of supplying what is lacking but of contending with something actually in existence.

It would be wrong to suppose, however, that the factors in this situation have remained invariable: on the contrary, the very emergence of those sectors and the growth of the urban proletariat have undermined the hegemony of the oligarchy, as happened in Brazil and Argentina after the second world war. It is interesting to examine both cases because they represent two typical variants of the model of industrialization based on import-substitution, and also because these countries have continued to be potentially Bonapartist, in so far as the crisis of the domination of the oligarchy has resulted from the action of social groups without a vocation for exercising hegemony. In such conditions there exists a basic tendency to instability, which the Roman-style[61] military coup tries unsuccessfully to correct.

The Brazilian Variant

During the *Republica velha,* federalism and parliamentarism were the principal expressions of the oligarchic political formula, which established the Federal States as the exclusive domains of various landowning groups.
. . . The middle class came into power in 1930: there followed an intensive campaign to integrate the political life of Brazil at the national level, accompanied by an increasing utilization of the urban masses as an element of manoeuvre in the confrontations that ensued. The old agrarian sectors were, however, successful in preserving the federal and parliamentary structure. . . .[62] As Brandão Lopes asserts,

> the essential point to remember is that during this period (1945–64), Brazil became a composite state in which differing types of interests (instead of the almost unchallenged domination exercised by the agrarian interests in the past) develop agreements and compromises; and in which the "people," in the sense of the lower and middle urban sectors (though still lacking in a definable class-consciousness and ideological outlook) must be taken into consideration, even though it in no way participates in the power structure.[63]

The Bonapartist content of the *Estado nôvo* consisted, in precise terms, of the replacement of the traditional hegemonic system by an "adaptation of the formula of socialization of losses and division of profits to the terms of the new social reality emerging in the country and, simultaneously, its institutionalization."[64] It is worth while emphasizing that there was no question of the middle class ingenuously falling into an ideological trap. In the first place, as I have already pointed out, the suspension of the system of political representation, caused by the establishment of the *Estado nôvo,* served its interests. In the second place, *cartorialismo* appeared to be the functional solution of the problem of its lack of occupational opportunities. Above all, however, as far as the industrial sector was concerned, there were no basic causes of conflict between it and the oligarchy. . . .

"[T]he success that Brazil had in the substitution process is the counterpart of the fact that it was in this country that development benefited a smaller number of people and begot the sharpest social tensions."[65] The correlative of a high level of capital accumulation in the framework of a highly protected but limited market was a constant tendency "to find oneself unexpectedly with idle capacity and to divert investment into new channels, a situation which resulted in the dilemma expressed by the slogan: 'Grow rapidly or perish!' "[66] The first of these alternatives was possible as long as the dynamic impulses underlying the import-substitution process were maintained, but these have exhausted themselves without the country being able to find a pattern of self-sustained development. The result is the tendency to stagnation.

In one sense, this might lead one to suppose that the foundations have been laid for an agrarian-industrial conflict that would transform the middle class into a genuine bourgeoisie. Such a hypothesis is now more plausible than formerly; but the course of events so far makes it necessary to introduce at this juncture two considerations.

One is the extreme heterogeneity of this middle class. I am not referring solely to the fact that in Brazil, as everywhere else, it constitutes the "occupational salad" of which Mills wrote, but also to the already mentioned particularism of its outlook which has prevented it from transcending that heterogeneity and achieving a more general consciousness of solidarity, and which has also made it especially vulnerable to the influence of the upper class.

The other factor—intimately connected with the preceding one—has been the entry of the urban proletariat into the political arena. *Varguismo* was instrumental in establishing control over the explosive character of the first stage of this process, and Brazil's prosperity made it possible to gratify the aspirations of the new working class, a process undoubtedly facilitated by the low level of expectations resulting from the pre-capitalist background of the labour force. But what is happening now is a curiously regressive development: as the maturity of the working class increases—leaving out of consideration its evidently reformist outlook—the rate of economic growth of the country is diminishing for the reasons outlined above, and there is also a steadily diminishing possibility of gratifying its demands without a structural transformation of the system.

It was much to Vargas's credit that in his later years he partially realized that this situation had developed, and tried to redefine the power-system of the country. But although the army had allowed him to take over the presidency in 1930 as the representative of the middle class, and to reaffirm the establishment of the latter in the government by means of the 1937 coup, that same army, in October 1945 and August 1954, expressed the fears of that same class in the face of the more popular orientation the régime was beginning to acquire.

> In both cases, Getulio Vargas was overthrown by the armed forces, who acted on both occasions as the spokesmen and instruments of the Brazilian middle class. In both cases the middle class, which could no longer impose its own orientation on the politico-social development of the country, took a reactionary stand in the face of the government's looking to the proletariat for support and moving towards a Left-Wing solution.[67]

This is also the principal characteristic of the most recent military coup, which was preceded by an intensive press campaign and street demonstrations by middle-class groups demanding the intervention of the armed forces. Goulart had consolidated his position in the government thanks to the general strike of September 1962, and the labour movement "for the first time organized for independent action, became more conscious of its power."[68] Moreover the organization of peasant forces was progressing in the North-East. At the same time, the rate of growth of the economy was slowing down, in the midst of galloping inflation. Unable to identify the structural basis of this process and to give articulate expression to a programme capable of mobilizing the popular sectors, the middle class opted for the radical Right and, frightened by the populist measures of the government, allied itself with the traditional defenders of the *status quo* and gave encouragement to the coup.

> The movement of April 1964 thus united all the property-owning classes of society: the agrarian sectors out of fear of land reform, the industrial sectors out of fear of losing their mechanisms of security, the middle classes panicked at the prospect of a closing of the social distance separating them from the masses, and all of these sectors were moved by the even greater fear of the emergence of a process of development diverging from the classical pattern of American democracy, to which they are all culturally linked.[69]

The Argentine Variant

A fundamental characteristic of the Argentine case—as well as of the Uruguayan—is the early absorption of the agrarian pre-capitalist sector and the consequent unification of the domestic labour market. For this reason, and viewing the problem in comparative terms, it makes less sense to refer to a dualistic structure. Another consequence of this is that the process of industrialization took place in a context of a limited supply of labour, which constituted a permanent threat to the profit margins of the rural producers, in contrast to the position in Brazil, "making difficult their recovery when favourable conditions appear in the export markets."[70] Despite this, and notwithstanding the presence of peculiar factors, here too the middle class has shown itself unable to break away from its tacit agreement with the landowning sector.

In order to understand the situation, it is necessary to insist on the great efficacy of the system during the era of the hegemony of the oligarchy. At the end of the last century Argentina was already predominantly urban and was undergoing a rapid process of modernization, in which immigration played an important part. The future of the land of cattle and wheat appeared definitely assured: "A powerful tide carried everything upwards and everyone thought that the ascent would never stop until it reached the clouds, that it would never stop at all."[71] For this reason, the principal task of Yrigoyen consisted in ensuring the participation of the middle class in the project inaugurated by the generation of 1880, not of changing that project.

So true was this that when setbacks occurred in the 1920s, it was not the middle class which blamed the raw-material-exporting system established by the oligarchy, but the oligarchy which condemned the system of parliamentary democracy defended by the middle class: "The Yrigoyen government was a proof, in the eyes of many people, of the definitive failure of universal suffrage."[72]

This remarkable subordination of the middle class—combined with the fact that it was their representatives who were in power during the 1929 crisis (in contrast to the situation in Brazil)—partly explains the oligarchical character of the coup of 6 September 1930. As Dardo Cúneo observes:

> If the military rebellion was in fact just a walk through the city, this was not due to the ability of the army conspirators; it was principally due to the weakness of the middle class, to its forgetting its historic role as a class. So great was its inactivity in this respect that, although the army was officered by members of that same middle class, it served the interests of the oligarchy against theirs. The Radical government was incapable of expressing any inspiring message or of rallying its supporters.[73]

In 1928 Yrigoyen had failed to seize the opportunity of liquidating the San Martín Lodge, the nucleus of the movement that would overthrow him two years later; once the coup had occurred, the *Unión Cívica Radical,* controlled by Alvear, refused to assume the political leadership of the officers who were prepared to rise against the oligarchical restoration.[74] Although these circumstances do not alter the fact that—to a certain extent —the 1930 coup was an exception to the pattern that I have been describing,[75] they at least serve to emphasize the fact that the military coup was not carried out against the opposition of the middle class, and the representatives of the latter did little or nothing to modify its course.

Thus, in a political climate the most salient characteristic of which is "the weakness of all the political attitudes that are not the expression of the interests of the traditional privileged classes,"[76] Argentina carried out the first stage of the process of industrialization based on import-substitution. By the middle of the 1940s the contribution of the manufacturing sector to the national product was already greater than that of the agricultural sector. After the end of the war Perón not only consolidated this industrial growth, but also gave concrete satisfaction to the political rights of the urban and rural workers. The coup of June 1943 thus led to the adoption of populist measures, to the direct benefit of the new middle-class groups, whose partial opposition to the régime revealed, nevertheless, the persistence of traditional ideological tendencies.

Peronismo marked the definitive crisis of the hegemony of the oligarchy; but in Argentina, as in Brazil, it was not succeeded by the setting up of the hegemony of the bourgeoisie, but by a series of alliances and compromises which constituted the essence of a Bonapartist system.

The prosperity of the early post-war years made it possible for the

Unable to consolidate themselves as a bourgeoisie, the most that the progressive sectors of the Latin American middle classes have been able to do has been to offer the popular sectors programmes based on fundamentally quantitative goals, mobilizing them to seek the satisfaction of their demands within the existing structural framework. This is the essential ingredient in the populism of Perón, Vargas, and Ibáñez; and it provides one of the clues to its unique character: whereas elsewhere—e.g., the United States or Canada—populist movements have had an agrarian basis and arose in periods of depression, in Latin America these movements were fundamentally urban and were associated with periods of prosperity.

For this reason economic stagnation fixes the limits of such movements, as is shown by the change of orientation of Perón's régime around 1950, and the swing of Ibáñez to conservatism which coincided with the falling-off of the Korean War boom.[89]

It has often been alleged that the Latin American middle class was progressive as long as it needed popular support to achieve power and, once established there, became reactionary.[90] Although this observation is more or less valid as a mere description of actual events, the formula is dangerous on account of the class-subjectivism to which it may lead: it can tempt the observer too easily to make a metaphorical association with a psychological "vertigo" supposedly felt by that class when it reaches the heights of power.

If this analysis is correct, it is its internal composition and the manner in which it has achieved power within the framework of the hegemony of the oligarchy which is beginning to disintegrate that explains the behaviour of this middle class. Moreover, if we employ for a moment the hypothetical representation of history recommended by Weber, it is probable that if the process of import-substitution had been accompanied by opportunities of exploiting an external colonial market, these countries would have achieved self-sustained growth without radical internal changes and with a Fabian-style working-class participation in political affairs.

What actually happens is quite different, and tends to aggravate the instability of the middle class. In the first place, it lacks the internal cohesion of the upper class, which not only still dominates strategic sectors of the economy but has firm control over the symbols of prestige. Secondly, it can no longer fulfil the only promises it is able to formulate to the masses whose organization is now increasing dangerously, in contrast to the middle class's own institutional weakness.

It is necessary at this point to introduce a word of warning—even though this is not the place to go more fully into the matter—in view of the tendency of many interpreters to refer to the *"massification"* of the Latin American societies which we are considering;[91] one must be careful to distinguish between the points of view of the observer and the person observed, even though they may use similar terminology. It is in this case that the observation of Raymond Williams is particularly appropriate: "There are in fact no masses; there are only ways of seeing people as masses."[92] To the oligarchies at the turn of the century, the "masses" were the rising middle classes, just as for the latter the "masses" are now the rural and urban workers: "If you disapprove of the changes you can, it seems, avoid open opposition to democracy as such by inventing a new category, mass-democracy, which is not such a good thing at all."[93]

In these conditions, and in spite of the objective indicators of "massification" that the observer may detect, the concept of the masses does not express a general tendency towards levelling but merely identifies the proletariat, conceived as such by the propertied classes regardless of the degree of internal solidarity that those masses have been able to achieve.

If we concentrate our attention on the low level of class-consciousness of the new working class, we are apt to forget that an essential ingredient in a social class, as T. H. Marshall has emphasized, is the way in which a man is treated by his neighbour. I do not mean by this that the Latin American political struggle will assume the form of the nineteenth-century conflicts: both the context and the protagonists have changed greatly. Nevertheless, as the populist atmosphere wears off, the central contradiction takes visible shape in somewhat similar terms. For this reason, even though Furtado may be right in emphasizing the differences in revolutionary potential between the urban and the rural workers,[94] it is worth remembering that the continued existence of such differences is a function of the ideological vigour of the dualistic structure as a confusing form assumed by Latin American capitalist development. On the economic plane, the underlying unity of the process is increasingly revealed by the chronic tendency to stagnation; on the political plane, it is the alliance of the middle class with the oligarchy that fully reveals that unity.

The Middle-Class Military Coup

Schumpeter maintained that "without protection by some non-bourgeois group, the bourgeoisie is politically helpless and unable not only to lead its nation but even to take care of its particular class interest. Which amounts to saying that it needs a master."[95] He was obviously referring to Great Britain, in view of the "protective" flexibility with which the aristocracy managed to adapt itself to the rise of the bourgeoisie. Moreover, in the case of France, the disintegration at the time of the Revolution of the traditional "protecting strata" was responsible for the high degree of instability that characterized the nineteenth century. However, in order to understand the peculiar synthesis achieved by the Third Republic—which "was throughout, in spirit and operation, middle class rather than either aristocratic or peasant or proletarian"[96]—it must be borne in mind that in France too there existed a "protecting stratum," namely, the civil service, the pre-revolutionary organization of which was maintained almost intact, and which established an element of continuity which has lasted through five republics and two empires.[97]

If Schumpeter's proposition is valid for a *"bourgeoisie conquérante,"* it must be even more so in the case of a class fragmented by the particularism of its outlook and formed in a context of bargaining and compromises. For this reason, translated into the terms of this theory, my thesis is that in the Latin American countries we are considering, owing to the absence of an English-style adaptation facilitated by a remarkable economic development, and also of a French-style bureaucracy capable of absorbing the shocks originating from political conflict, it is the armed forces which assume the responsibility of protecting the middle class. It was with their support that the middle class achieved, at the beginning of the century, political recognition from the oligarchy; it was with their protection that it later consolidated itself in power; and now it is with their intervention that it seeks to ward off the threat posed by the popular sectors that it is incapable of leading.

This explains the continuous civilian pressure in favour of military intervention, which a mere chronicle of the events rarely reveals.[98] Although he does not draw all the possible conclusions from his assertion, Imaz observes:

> Thus, the appeal to the armed forces as a source of legitimation—quite apart from all the other explanations given—has become a tacit rule of the Argentine political game. It is a rule that no one explicitly invokes, but from which all political groups have benefited at least once. Publicly they would all deny the existence of such a rule, but in reality it can never be ignored by Argentine politicians, who, at one time or another during this quarter of a century, have all gone to knock on the door of the barracks.[99]

The oligarchy, of course, has recourse to this expedient, and attempts to influence the military in its favour. However, the history of the coups that have taken place in the twentieth century shows that the military have only exceptionally shown a tendency to act as the representatives of the oligarchy. In other words, if the connexion between the upper class and military interventionism serves to explain an exceptional case such as the overthrow of Yrigoyen advocated also by the middle class, nevertheless, it is the connexion between the army and the interests and values of the middle class which explains most of the remaining interventions.

Thus, failure to emphasize and distinguish between the structural factors that cause the chronic instability of this class and its *penchant* for interventionism can be doubly misleading; first, because it prevents a full understanding of the peculiar characteristics of Latin American political development, and thus fails to relate to their historical context the very concepts of parliamentary democracy and of the middle class;[100] and, secondly, because it leads the observer to treat the armed forces as external factors, who interfere with the supposed normal evolution of a political process, either through personal ambition or because they have been beguiled by the upper class into serving its interests. The problem is inevitably reduced to psychological terms, and the political development of Latin America comes to be interpreted as depending less on social transformation than on a change of mentality on the part of the army officers.

Provisional Stability

We must now make brief reference to the cases of Uruguay, Chile, and Mexico. Although, as I pointed out above, the army in these countries supported the rise to power of the middle class, their apparent political neutrality since that event seems to constitute an objection to my main argument, which up to now has been principally illustrated by reference to the cases of Argentina and Brazil. I believe, however, that it can be seen to corroborate my argument, if we identify certain peculiar characteristics on which this apolitical behavior is based.

In Uruguay, the civil war at the beginning of the century resulted in the triumph of the middle class through a tacit pact with the oligarchy. . . . In this context, most middle-class aspirations have been connected with the obtaining of better government employment, and the patronage system of the political parties and state paternalism have been appropriate instruments for the satisfaction of these demands.

These and other factors which have helped to make the case of Uruguay exceptional have become less operative in recent years. First, the reduced size of the internal market resulted in a rapid exhaustion of the process of import-substitution; and, secondly, as in the case of Argentina, the persistence of an agrarian structure based on big estates has caused a fall in productivity in the rural sector, to such an extent that since 1943 there has been no increase in the volume of the essential exports of meat and wool. The result is complete economic stagnation, and the gross product per capita has remained practically stationary for the last twenty years. This has coincided with a period of intense rural migration, accompanied by the familiar "revolution of rising expectations." Once again the public sector has tried to canalize these pressures: the numbers of people employed by it grew between 1955 and 1961 at a rate of 2.6 per cent per year, and the private sector by only 0.9 per cent. As Solari observes, "It is now a question of how long the state can continue to fulfil this function."[101] One of the first symptoms of the disintegration of Uruguay's *aurea mediocritas* was the victory in 1958 of the *Blanco* Party, which replaced the *Colorados* who had enjoyed ninety-three consecutive years of power.[102] In this decade, industrial conflicts have become more frequent, and some civilian sectors have significantly begun to urge a military intervention to thwart the "Communist menace."

In the case of Chile, the expansion of the foreign-owned nitrate and copper concerns resulted in a rapid increase in the public sector, since owing to the system of taxation "it was the government and not the native owners of the exporting sector which was the agent administering, spending and distributing a considerable proportion of the revenue generated by foreign trade."[103] To these elements—which lend the Chilean case some of the characteristics previously mentioned of the French and British cases—there were added two circumstances that are especially relevant to this discussion: first, the reduced size of the Chilean political arena—until 1946, the number of voters never exceeded 8–9 per cent of the population;[104] secondly, and for this very reason, the fact that the system made it possible to pass on the benefits derived from mining and the first stage of industrialization to those popular sectors which participated in political life, thus facilitating their acceptance of the rules of the game. It is worth noting, for instance, that "Chile is probably the only country in the world that instituted a legal minimum salary long before a minimum wage."[105] In other words, the military interventions of the 1920s consolidated the power of the middle class *vis-à-vis* a particularly flexible oligarchy; this régime integrated a limited proportion of the population into the national political system ("probably about a fifth to a quarter of all Chileans live in what we think of as a modern society")[106] and, at the same time, gave it access to its benefits.

It is not necessary to emphasize that I have pointed out only a few of the factors that explain Chile's stability: despite everything, it may be noted that every broadening of the political framework has been accompanied by the threat of its complete breakdown: between 1946 and 1952 the number of voters increased by 75 percent, and in the latter year, in a context of open rejection of the parties of the Establishment, Carlos Ibáñez was elected; between 1958 and 1964 the electorate increased by a further 78 percent, the entire political spectrum was displaced Leftwards, and the Christian Democrats were elected on a platform which can certainly be described as populist. Moreover, the Chilean economy has been virtually stagnant since 1954. In these circumstances, it seems safe to assume that, in the short term, stability will be maintained as long as the government succeeds in preserving a compromise with the higher levels of the urban wage-earning sector. However,

> the political significance of these groups as spokesmen for the working class as a whole has . . . been small and has probably been decreasing, especially since the stagnation of the Chilean economy during the last decade began to reduce the opportunities of employment and to endanger the standards of living which these groups had gained for themselves.[107]

It is, therefore, probable that the pressures exercised by the lower strata of the urban and rural proletariat will become stronger in the future and—if the government fails to satisfy their demands—may cause breakdown of the stability which a limited degree of democracy has made possible in Chile. Thus conditions would again favour a middle-class military coup, the possibility of which was widely rumoured when an electoral triumph of the *Frente de Acción Popular* was feared.

Finally, with regard to Mexico, as we have already observed: "Apart from the important peasant group of Zapata's followers which remained politically marginal until the assassination of Carranza, the Mexican Revolution from the outset had middle-class leanings."[108] The historical importance of the movement—and what made it exceptional in the Latin American context until the Bolivian and Cuban revolutions occurred—lies in its elimination of the landowning oligarchy. It thus opened the way to the formation of an authentic bourgeoisie, with an original normative structure and a collective sense of direction capable of mobilizing the politically active part of the population. As a further illustration of the difference between the form and the content of social institutions, in this case it was not a liberal state but an interventionist one that organized the hegemony of the bourgeoisie, while at the same time the atmosphere of the revolution lent a "universality" to its particularist aspirations. This explains the misgivings expressed by a decided supporter of the movement:

> This bourgeoisie has realized its potential, has become strong and becomes stronger with every day that passes, not only in the national sphere but in the international as well . . . and, like every bourgeoisie, it tends not only to become independent of the force that created it, the government, but to convert the latter into a mere instrument of its interests; the government thus ceases to be a mediator, capable of balancing the interests of the bourgeoisie against those of the rest of the nation.[109]

In this process, the armed forces played a decisive role, and their present neutrality is in fact a function of the consolidation of the hegemony of the bourgeoisie: "The military element is the permanent reserve of order; it is a force which acts 'in a public way' when 'legality' is threatened."[110] The greatest problem facing this "legality" is the fact that at least 50 per cent of the population has been denied the benefits of development:[111] "The selfsame people who made the agrarian revolution, or their descendants, have little but poverty for their reward now that the revolution has passed into the industrial stage because it has been channelled through the capitalist system."[112] The stability of Mexico, therefore, depends much less on the good humour of its generals than on the ability of its bourgeoisie to incorporate these internal colonies into the life of the nation.

The External Factor

Up to this point I have avoided referring to external pressures in favour of military intervention because it is these internal factors that determine the efficacy of any external pressure that may be brought to bear.

I mean by this that the density of social relationships in the countries under discussion is such as to make highly improbable a military coup pure and simple, in the sense that a group of officers supported by the United States Embassy seizes control of the government at midnight. The size and complexity of the military establishment, combined with the frequent divergences of opinion among the officers themselves, tend to make relatively impracticable a *putsch* that does not enjoy a relatively high degree of consensus.

With this consideration in mind,[113] two points must now be emphasized. The first directly concerns the armed forces: namely, the extent to which their outlook is influenced by the strategic revolution closely linked to the development of the Cold War and the rise of national-liberation-front movements. It is in this sense that Horowitz is right when he affirms that "United States policies of military globalism tend to make obsolete earlier efforts at a standard typology of Latin American military styles and forms based exclusively on internal political affairs."[114] Here we are not only considering the greatly expanded programmes of military aid, but the fact that, since 1961, the United States has reappraised the basic policy underlying such aid, replacing the principle of Hemispheric defence—for which it assumes sole responsibility—by that of internal security.[115]

What is most important to remember is that, by definition, the counter-insurgency operational projects blur the distinction between the military and the political spheres of action. In the context of the *guerre dans la foule*—a permanent war, which need not be declared—there is no longer any sense in the classical distinction according to which the civil power was responsible for the direction of the war and the military power for the conduct of military operations. In such a war, since the enemy is not immediately recognizable, his identification depends on the military operations themselves; this limits considerably the sphere of civilian decision.

In other words, political intervention has now become, for the Latin American officer, a matter of professional interest. In this connexion, it would be interesting to study the probable increase of the potential conflict of loyalties already mentioned: to the organization and to their profession. The tactics of imperialism may affect one more than the other, in so far as it may concentrate on the sending of missions to the country concerned, or on inviting selected officers for training in its own establishments. One may hazard a conjecture that the second alternative will be preferred in the case of the more advanced countries of the continent, where direct manipulation of the military establishment as such would not be so easy. This accounts for the increased importance attributed by the United States military academies to the political indoctrination of their Latin American guests.

I said above that I would draw the reader's attention to two points. The second of these is, in fact, essential to an understanding of the first. I refer to the particular vulnerability of the Latin American middle class in the face of the strategies used during the Cold War. This corresponds exactly to the worsening of its relations with the popular sectors, and thus systematic anticommunism appears as the kind of rationalization most appropriate to its interests. Moreover as a correlative of the absence of any vocation for hegemony among its various component fractions, the middle class only achieves a precarious unity on the basis of negative principles. It is opposed to corruption and to communism, without realizing that the former is a function of the irrationality of the system that the middle class helps to perpetuate, while the latter is merely the name that its own fears give to the aspirations of the popular sectors. This sufficiently explains why, in the five countries under discussion, it is in those where the middle class is least stable and feels most threatened that this type of outlook most flourishes. It was a Brazilian officer, General Golbery do Couto e Silva, who formulated the "ideological frontiers" doctrine, and an Argentine officer, General Onganía, who demonstrated enthusiastic adherence to it.

Some Conclusions

Precisely because the military establishment is inseparable from the society surrounding it, it is legitimate to infer in these cases a different pattern of civil-military relations from those described at the beginning of this essay. Military interventionism does not threaten the middle class (as in the liberal model), nor is it a substitute for its absence (as in the developmentalist model); it tends to represent that class and compensate for its inability to establish itself as a well-integrated hegemonic group.

Several consequences follow from this interpretation.

1. The ideologists of the middle class—whose interests, according to one partisan observer, coincide not only with those of Latin America but also with those of humanity in general[116]—would be wrong to interpret my analysis as a justification of interventionism; I have, on the contrary, tried to demonstrate why the middle class is not in a position to contribute to the development of these countries. Moreover, in its present form military interventionism tends to prevent rather than favour the possibility of certain sectors of that class ever transcending their profoundly traditional outlook.

In this connexion, the observation of Gramsci is perfectly valid when he distinguishes between "progressive" and "regressive" varieties of Caesarism.[117] Despite its compromising and its limitations, the first variety does assist the consolidation of new social groups, whereas the second tries to preserve the elements of a social order that has exhausted its possibilities of development. This is the fundamental difference between a Vargas and a Castello Branco.

Just at the moment when the loss of the dynamic impulse of the import-substitution model is creating the objective conditions for ending the agrarian-industrial pact, free elections are becoming an essential instrument of political bargaining, which makes possible the gradual union of the progressive groups. This possibility is, however, eliminated by the fears of the upper and middle classes; it is for this reason that both the Brazilian and the Argentine military governments have lost no time in suspending the electoral process, and are tending to search for forms of functional representation which avoid the risk inherent in normal elections.

We are not concerned here with advocating territorial representation in the abstract, nor must corporativism in general be identified with one of its manifestations, i.e. fascism. However, given the present degree of development of the societies I am considering, the danger inherent in projects of this kind is that they constitute an institutional "freezing" of a system of relationships which must be changed. For this reason, the price that is paid for reducing the electoral influence of the popular sectors is the maintenance of the self-same structure that has led to the crisis. Therefore, not only is this a transitory solution, since it does not deal with the fundamental causes of the problem, but it already reveals what it leads to in the long term: as the tendency to stagnation increases, so will popular discontent, and the corporativist system will develop an increasingly Rightwards bias. This will happen even though, in the short term, fortuitous movements of economic expansion—due, for instance, to a temporary fluctuation in the foreign market—may favour compromises with trade union organizations of a reformist outlook.

2. The other point worth mentioning is the possibility of a "Nasserist" variant; this is a frequent theme in present-day Latin American writing.

There are, of course, two possible meanings of the term Nasserism. One of them, on an extremely vague and theoretical level, applies the term to any military group whose objectives are "a mixture of radical independence, the reconquest of national identity and emphasis on social progress."[118] According to this interpretation, Kemal Ataturk and Perón were Nasserists *"avant la lettre."* Obviously, this greatly reduces the scientific usefulness of the concept, because what it gains in general applicability it loses in precison.

The other meaning, however, is specific, and refers to one prototype of national development—the Egyptian—and is the only one that appears relevant to a concrete analysis. From this point of view, I believe that the Nasserist variant as such is inapplicable in the context of these countries. I will give briefly some of the reasons on which I base this assertion, leaving out of account obvious ethnic and religious differences between the two contexts.

In the first place—as in the Afro-Asian model in general—the degree of integration of the Egyptian army into the society around it was considerably less than in the case of Latin America. . . . In addition to this lack of integration of the Egyptian officer into the context of the influential sectors in the country, there was also the impact of the immediate colonial situation and, later, the "experience of the concrete Fatherland"[119] as a result of the disastrous Palestine campaign.

In addition to these peculiar characteristics, it is necessary to take into account the circumstances of the country. In 1952 Egypt was an essentially agricultural country, with nearly 70 percent of the population consisting of *fellahs*,[120] a per capita income of under $120, nearly 80 percent illiteracy, and an industry contributing only 10 percent of the gross national product.[121] At the same time, as a consequence of underdevelopment and foreign control over important sectors of the economy, there was an absence of national bureaucratic and entrepreneurial cadres.

Finally, the degree of popular participation in the system was extremely low. . . .

It will be observed that we have here the characteristics peculiar to the developmentalist model, with the addition of the colonial factor, which tended to increase the nationalism of this first generation of Egyptian officers drawn from the popular sectors. Given this context, it is understandable that, after the 1952 movement, the army should become, in theory and in practice, "the real backbone of the state,"[122] and that the degree of mobilization of the urban and rural workers should be very limited. At the same time it explains the extreme economic liberalism which characterized the first phase of the Revolution (1952–6), when desperate efforts were made to attract foreign capital and thus encourage the incipient industrialization process.

. . . In other words: the previous absence of popular participation, to which I referred above, and an especially favourable international situation—due, above all, to Soviet support—made it possible to liquidate the aristocracy and the foreign interests " 'from above,' bureaucratically, without the bourgeois revolution being obliged to resolve the problem of democracy and that of the rural sector."[123] It is this specific development of Nasserism that establishes the limits of the movement. . . .

It is obvious, even from this brief outline, that there is a great difference between the Egyptian case and that of the Latin American countries under discussion, as regards the integration of the military into civilian society, a much higher degree of popular participation, and the absence of an immediate colonial experience. The most important factor, however, is the greatly superior level of development as compared with Egypt in 1952; in the Latin American countries under discussion, therefore, the chief problem is not that of introducing technical innovations but of organizing rationally and establishing social control over those that already exist. . . .

At the risk of over-simplifying the problem, it can, therefore, be asserted that these countries have already passed the Nasserist stage as far as their industrial expansion is concerned—and also as regards the degree of popular mobilization—though not as regards the confrontation with the oligarchy and the foreign interests. The immediate task facing the continent is the appropriation for social ends of the potential economic excedent, through a radical transformation of its existing structures.[124] However, both the level of development and of institutional complexity, and the vulnerability of various sectors of the army to pressures exercised by the beneficiaries of the *status quo* would appear to condemn to failure a revolution "from above" directed by the armed forces. It must be remem-

and 6/4, pp. 351–80. The particular interest of the Brazilian case lies in the fact that rarely has an ideology been so self-conscious: an example of this is the objectives and work of the Instituto Superior de Estudos Brasileiros. See Frank Bonilla, "A National Ideology for Development: Brazil," in Kalman H. Silvert, *Expectant Peoples—Nationalism and Development* (New York, 1963), pp. 232–64.

61. I am referring to temporary military dictatorship, acting as an interregnum between two civilian governments. In Argentina and Brazil, the last decade has seen a number of coups of this type; the two most recent military movements have the declared aim of ending this situation.

62. For a perceptive analysis of this point, see Furtado, in Veliz, pp. 154 ff., and Glaucio A. Dillon Soares, "El sistema electoral y la reforma agraria en Brasil," *Ciencias políticas y sociales*, 8/29, 431–44.

63. Juarez R. Brandão Lopes, "Étude de quelques changements fondamentaux dans la politique et la société brésiliennes," *Sociologie du travail*, 2 (1965), p. 245.

64. Luciano Martins, "Aspectos políticos de la Revolución brasileña," *Revista latinoamericana de sociología* (1965), p. 398.

65. Furtado, *Development & Stagnation*, p. 36.

66. Ignacio Rangel, *A inflação brasileira* (Rio, 1963), pp. 35–36.

67. IBESP (*Cadernos do nosso tempo*, 3 (1955), p. 4).

68. Neuma Aguiar Walker, "The Organization and Ideology of Brazilian Labor," in Irving L. Horowitz, ed., *Revolution in Brazil* (New York, 1964), p. 252.

69. Martins, p. 410.

70. Furtado, *Development & Stagnation*, p. 36.

71. Francisco Romero, *Sobre la filosofía en América* (Buenos Aires, 1952), p. 25.

72. Tulio Halperín Donghi, *Argentina en el callejón* (Montevideo, 1964), p. 23.

73. Dardo Cúneo, *El desencuentro argentino 1930–1955* (Buenos Aires, 1965), p. 168.

74. For an account by one of the protagonists, see Teniente Coronel Atilio Cattáneo, *Plan 1932—Las conspiraciones radicales contra el General Justo* (Buenos Aires, 1959), especially pp. 25 ff., 228 ff. Also Puiggrós, p. 321.

75. For an analysis of the institutional antecedents of the 1930 coup, see Darío Cantón, "Notas sobre las Fuerzas Armadas argentinas," *Revista latinoamericana de sociología*, 3 (1965), pp. 290–313.

76. Halperín Donghi, p. 32.

77. Compare Juan Carlos Esteban, *Imperialismo y desarrollo económico* (Buenos Aires, 1961), pp. 44–50.

78. Gramsci, *Notas sobre Maquiavelo*, p. 94.

79. Cf. Torcuato S. Di Tella, *El sistema político argentino y la clase obrera* (Buenos Aires, 1964), p. 90.

80. See *Confirmado*, 2/55 (7 July 1966), p. 65.

81. Mariano Grondona, "Definiciones," *Primera plana*, 4/184 (July 1966), p. 11. The "superstructural emphasis" of the coup becomes evident when, on the one hand, its representatives insist on the thoroughgoing renewal

84 *José Nun*

that it implies, and, on the other, the economic team selected by the "new" government is formed by the same people who have exercised these functions for the last decade or others closely connected with them.

82. See, for example, Gino Germani, *Política y sociedad en una época de transición* (Buenos Aires, 1962), pp. 153 f.

83. Trygve R. Tholfson, "The Transition to Democracy in Victorian England," *International R. of Social History,* 6/2 (1961), p. 226.

84. Ibid. p. 232.

85. For an excellent analysis of this subject, see E. J. Hobsbawm, *Labouring Men—Studies in the History of Labour* (London, 1964), pp. 272–315.

86. Cf. Royden Harrison, "The 10th April of Spencer Walpole: The Problem of Revolution in Relation to Reform, 1865–1867," *International R. of Social History,* 7/3 (1962), pp. 351–97.

87. R. A. J. Walling, ed., *The Diaries of John Bright* (New York, 1931), p. 297.

88. Cf. Stein Rokkan, "Mass Suffrage, Secret Voting and Political Participation," *European J. of Sociology,* 2/2 (1961), 132–52. Even in Great Britain it has been estimated that around 1913 no more than 17 percent of the population had the right to vote.

89. In the case of Brazil, observers have recently noted the tendency towards the adoption of an ideology on the part of the politician operating the patronage system, as his possibilities of immediately satisfying the demands of the electorate become increasingly restricted. It is obvious that this transition from being "Saviour of the Poor" to being "Saviour of the Fatherland" implies, eventually, the negation of the patronage system and as such represents a risk that the dominant groups do not seem prepared to take. See Carlos Alberto de Medina, *A favela e o demagogo* (São Paulo, 1964), pp. 95–96.

90. See, for example, ECLA, *The Social Development of Latin America in the Post-War Period* (Santiago, 1963).

91. Thus, Torcuato S. Di Tella and others, eds, *Argentina, sociedad de masas* (Buenos Aires, 1965).

92. Raymond Williams, *Culture and Society* (London, 1958), p. 300.

93. Ibid. p. 299.

94. Cf. Furtado, "Reflections on the Brazilian Pre-Revolution," in Horowitz, pp. 62–73.

95. Joseph A. Schumpeter, *Capitalism, Socialism, and Democracy* (London, 1947), p. 138.

96. David Thomson, *Democracy in France* (London, 1958), p. 58.

97. Compare Charles Frankel, "Bureaucracy and Democracy in the New Europe," in Stephen R. Graubard, ed., *A New Europe?* (Cambridge, Mass., 1964), p. 541. See also Stanley Hoffman, "Paradoxes of the French Political Community," in Hoffman and others, *In Search of France* (Cambridge, Mass., 1963), pp. 1–117.

98. The reader has only to glance at the Argentine or Brazilian press in the months before the recent military coups. An analysis of the contents of such publications as *Confirmado, Primera Plana,* or *Estado de São Paulo* would be extremely revealing.

99. Imaz, p. 84.

100. This is the fundamental mistake made by studies which attempt to describe in the abstract the developmentalist strategy of a middle-class élite. Compare Clark Kerr and others, *Industrialism and Industrial Man* (Cambridge, Mass., 1960), ch. iii. One thus loses sight of the essentially relational nature of the notion of social class. Compare Stanislaw Ossowski, *Class Structure in the Social Consciousness*, tr. S. Patterson (London, 1963), p. 133.

101. Solari, p. 156.

102. See Carlos M. Rama, "La crisis política uruguaya," *Ciencias políticas y sociales*, 5/16 (1959), pp. 233–42.

103. Aníbal Pinto, *Chile, una economía difícil* (Mexico City, 1964), p. 160.

104. See Gil, p. 213.

105. Albert O. Hirschman, *Journeys towards Progress* (New York, 1965), p. 264. The law establishing minimum salaries for employees was passed in 1937, whereas this measure was extended to the workers only in 1955.

106. Silvert, "Some Propositions on Chile," in Robert D. Tomasek, ed., *Latin American Politics* (New York, 1966), p. 387.

107. Osvaldo Sunkel, "Change and Frustration in Chile," in Veliz, p. 129.

108. Moisés González Navarro, "Mexico: The Lop-Sided Revolution," in Veliz, p. 226.

109. Leopoldo Zea, "La Revolución, el gobierno y la democracia," *Ciencias políticas y sociales*, 5/18 (1959), p. 543.

110. Gramsci, *Notas sobre Maquiavelo*, p. 81.

111. Cf. Pablo González Casanova, *La democracia en México* (Mexico City, 1965), p. 81.

112. González Navarro, in Veliz, p. 228.

113. It is important to relate this consideration to the new forms assumed by imperialist activities, especially the growing tendency to replace direct investment by various types of association with local concerns. This is even more valid in the case of the relatively advanced countries such as those we have been describing, and it is symptomatic of the internalization of the external influence to which I have referred in the text. See Hamza Alavi, "Imperialism, Old and New," in John Saville and Ralph Miliband, eds, *The Socialist Register* (London, 1964), pp. 116 ff.

114. Irving L. Horowitz, *The Military of Latin America* (mimeo) p. 45. Horowitz analyses in detail the incidence of the external factor, and I therefore refer the reader to his work "The Military Elites," in S. M. Lipset and Aldo Solari, eds., *Elites in Latin America* (London, 1967), pp. 146–189.

115. Cf. Lieuwen, *Generals vs. Presidents*, pp. 114 ff.

116. Víctor Alba, "La nouvelle classe moyenne latinoaméricaine," *La Revue socialiste*, 133 (1960), p. 468.

117. Gramsci, *Notas sobre Maquiavelo*, pp. 84 ff.

118. Anuar Abdel Malek, "Nasserismo y socialismo," in R. García Lupo, ed. 1, *Nasserismo y marxismo* (Buenos Aires, 1965), p. 186.

119. Jean Ziegler, *Sociologie de la nouvelle Afrique* (Paris, 1964), p. 294.

120. Abdel Malek, *Égypte—société militaire* (Paris, 1962), p. 26.

121. Charles Issawi, *Egypt in Revolution* (London, 1963), pp. 46–47.

122. Ziegler, p. 347.

123. Hassan Riad, "Las tres edades de la sociedad egipcia," in García Lupo, pp. 38–107.
124. For an analysis of the concept of "potential economic excedent," see Paul A. Baran, *The Political Economy of Growth* (New York, 1957). . . .
125. The idea of "revolutionary reformism" is discussed by, among others, André Gorz, *Stratégie ouvrière et néo-capitalisme* (Paris, 1965), and Lucio Magri, "Le modèle de développement capitaliste et le problème de 'l'alternative' prolétarienne," *Les Temps modernes,* nos. 196–7 (1962), pp. 583–626.
126. Alexis de Tocqueville, *De la démocratie en Amérique* (Paris, 1963), Bk ii, ch. 26, p. 349.

Robert D. Putnam / *Toward Explaining*
Military Intervention
in Latin American Politics

I. Introduction

Military intervention in politics is extremely common. Outside the North
Atlantic area, the armed forces are more likely than not to be among the
most important power contenders in any political system, and military
regimes are at least as widespread as either totalitarian or democratic ones.
It is surprising, therefore, that until recently this phenomenon has attracted
little attention from students of politics. Though there has been some speculation about the causes of military intervention, our actual knowledge of
the subject is meager indeed.

The preeminence of the military in politics in Latin America has long
been recognized, but, even in this case, as recently as 1960 George Blanksten could complain that "political studies of the Latin American armed
services are sorely needed."[1] Aside from a few vague remarks about

From Robert D. Putnam, "Toward Explaining Military Intervention in Latin
American Politics," *World Politics,* 20, no. 1 (1967): 83–110. Copyright © 1967 by
Princeton University Press and reprinted by permission of the author and of Princeton University Press. [Table I of the original article has been omitted from this edition.—Ed.]

Author's Note: I should like to thank the following individuals for their help in
the preparation of this research note: Hayward R. Alker, Jr., Karl W. Deutsch, Robert H. Dix, Richard Simeon, and Rosemary Putnam.

"Hispanic heritage" and "backwardness," virtually no empirically based explanations of Latin American militarism have been offered. Since Blanksten wrote, of course, Johnson and Lieuwen have undertaken excellent analyses of this topic, but both authors' works have been primarily historical studies of the development and extent of military intervention in various countries, rather than verified, general explications of the causes of this phenomenon.[2]

A study of the factors that account for the varying political role of the military in Latin America would thus be useful both for students of Latin American politics and for students of comparative politics generally. Latin America constitutes in many respects an ideal "laboratory" for analyzing militarism. The range of military involvement is great—from "pure" military regimes, such as Argentina's present regime, to "constitutional" military regimes, such as El Salvador's, to military "protectorates," such as Brazil's, to civil-military coalitions, such as Argentina's under Perón, to regimes in which the military is merely one among numerous important "power groups," such as Mexico's, to regimes in which the military is virtually nonpolitical, such as Costa Rica's. In this "laboratory," certain independent variables are held constant—colonial background, nature of the struggle for independence, length of independence, religious background, cultural authority patterns.[3] This means that we cannot examine the impact of these constants on the propensity for military intervention, but it does allow us to focus more clearly on other possible explanations. The purpose of this research note is to investigate in this Latin American "laboratory" some of the more important speculations about the sources of military involvement in politics.

II. Theoretical Propositions

A survey of the literature on military intervention in politics discloses four broad categories of factors suggested as causes of, or conditions for, intervention or abstention: (1) aspects of socioeconomic development; (2) aspects of political development; (3) characteristics of the military establishment itself; and (4) foreign influences. I shall here present and explicate the relevant hypotheses and shall refrain from setting out the broader theoretical perspectives of the various authors.[4] In particular, I shall limit my attention to propositions that answer the question, What accounts for the varying incidence of military intervention in politics? (There are many other interesting questions in this general area, concerning the political and ideological orientations of military regimes, the political, social, and economic consequences of military intervention, and so on, but these will be ignored here.)

One of the most common hypotheses links the propensity for military intervention with social and economic underdevelopment. Samuel Finer argues that *the propensity for military intervention is likely to decrease with increased social mobilization.*[5] The concept of social mobilization refers to such developments as urbanization, the rise of mass education and mass communications, the development of a money economy, and increased mass participation in social and political activities and associations. Social mobilization increases the number of potential political actors and diffuses increased political resources to these actors. The assumption underlying this hypothesis is that these actors will be willing and able to sustain civilian political institutions.[6]

Finer and others have also argued that *economic development, especially industrialization, diminishes the propensity for military intervention.*[7] This effect of economic development stems partly from the increased socio-technical complexity that puts public administration beyond the skills of the armed forces, partly from the civilian opportunities for social mobility which economic development opens up, and partly from greater wealth, which allows and encourages stable, civilian government.[8] Germani and Silvert have articulated a hypothesis hinted at by others, namely, that *military intervention is inhibited by the rise of middle strata in the social structure,* since these middle strata have in especial measure both the motivation and the ability to create and sustain stable civilian political institutions.[9] These same authors also argue that *the likelihood of military intervention is greater, the greater the cleavages and the less the consensus in a society.* (This proposition is related to the proposition discussed below linking military intervention and political violence.)

A second set of variables, correlated with but distinct from those involving social mobilization and economic development, may be grouped under the heading "political development." The most obvious hypothesis, as stated by Finer, is that *"where public attachment to civilian institutions is strong, military intervention in politics will be weak. . . . Where public attachment to civilian institutions is weak or non-existent, military intervention in politics will find wide scope—both in manner and in substance."*[10] Though this proposition is important, it is also somewhat unsatisfying, for it fails to take our search for explanation very far from the phenomenon that we are trying to explain. A more interesting hypothesis, suggested by Finer, Johnson, and others, is that *the propensity for military intervention in politics decreases with increasing popular attention to and participation in politics.*[11] Another set of hypotheses relates military intervention to weaknesses in civilian political institutions: *military intervention decreases with increasing strength and effectiveness of political parties, of political interest groups, and of civilian governmental institutions.*[12] Huntington's theory of political development and decay stresses the importance of "the institutionalization of political organizations and procedures." "Political decay"—of which a notable symptom is military intervention—

arises out of an imbalance between social mobilization and political institutionalization. Therefore, *the greater the social mobilization and the less the
political institutionalization, the greater the likelihood of military intervention*.[13] A final aspect of political development that is relevant here concerns the role of violence. Lieuwen and Needler have argued that *the
tendency toward military intervention increases with increasing political
violence*.[14] Obviously, the military have an important advantage in a political game where violence is trump, for that is their strong suit.

The third set of hypotheses concerns the way internal characteristics of
a military establishment affect its predisposition to political intervention.
*"Professionalization" of the military is linked with decreased military inter-
vention* (Huntington) *and with increased military intervention* (Finer).[15]
This apparent contradiction can perhaps be resolved if we consider a few
of the possible components of "professionalization." Many students of
civil-military relations have suggested that *military intervention decreases
with the development within the military of a norm of civilian supremacy*.[16]
As with the proposition linking military abstention with the legitimacy of
civilian institutions, the proposed explanatory factor in this hypothesis is
"too close" to the phenomenon to be explained. On the other hand, if the
hypothesis is given a historical focus, it is rather more interesting. Thus,
with respect to Latin American armies it is commonly asserted that military intervention is the prevailing norm because of the Hispanic heritage.[17]
Similarly, it is argued that *the propensity for military intervention increases
with the habituation of the military to intervention,* or more simply, that
intervention breeds more intervention.[18]

The larger and more sophisticated the armed forces, the more likely that
they will have the administrative and technical skills necessary for running
a government and that the military will have a preponderance of armed
power over civilians. Thus, some have argued that *the size and sophistication of the military establishment are positively related to the propensity
for intervention in politics*.[19] Janowitz has discussed a variety of other
internal characteristics of the military establishment which he sees as related to the propensity for political involvement, such as political ideology,
social and political cohesion, and career and recruitment patterns. I shall
not pursue these propositions here since I do not have the data necessary
to test them.

Two final factors often adduced to explain military intervention,
especially but not exclusively in the Latin American context, involve
foreign influences. First, it is often alleged that *military training missions
from foreign nations inculcate attitudes favorable or unfavorable to military intervention in politics*. Edelmann echoes many others in arguing that
"the influence of German, Italian, and certain other military missions" has
been among the "most important" causes of military intervention in Latin
America,[20] while Johnson argues that the effect of U.S. missions is to
transmit norms of civilian supremacy along with their tutelage in military

techniques.[21] Second, it is often argued that by a kind of "demonstration effect" *military intervention in one country encourages intervention by the armed forces of other countries in their own political systems,* or more simply, that coups are contagious.[22]

III. Methodology

There is no dearth of suggestions about what factors are causally related to military intervention in politics. The problem is to subject this array of propositions to some kind of empirical testing. The primary method used here is correlational analysis. For each Latin American country an index is constructed representing the extent of military intervention in politics over the last decade. This is our "dependent variable." This index will be correlated with a variety of other data intended to represent or reflect some of the suggested independent variables. The strength of the empirical relationships will be summarized by the standard Pearsonian correlation coefficient r.[23]

This technique is a powerful one for testing hypotheses such as those outlined above, for it allows us to weigh and summarize all the relevant evidence. In particular, we can go beyond mere lists of illustrations and exceptions. This technique is, of course, not the only possible one—other complementary techniques are the case-study method and the comparative historical method. Nor is it without its limitations. First, the present analysis is "synchronic," rather than "diachronic"; that is, it compares information on military intervention and, for example, social mobilization at the present time in the various Latin American countries. With one important exception, we shall not compare data that would allow us to examine changes in the degree of intervention and mobilization in one country over time.

Second, as already suggested, we shall not examine all the factors that might be linked theoretically to military intervention. In particular, two classes of factors are beyond the scope of this investigation. First, we cannot examine propositions involving variables that are virtually constant throughout the Latin American area, such as religion, colonial background, length of independence, and the like. However, it is precisely these factors that could not possibly account for the wide variation among these countries in military intervention.[24] Second, a number of theoretically interesting and relevant variables must be ignored here because we lack the data necessary to test them. We lack direct information on the political allegiances of the populations, on the extent of social cleavage and consensus in the various countries, and on the internal characteristics and norms of the military, such as those discussed by Janowitz. For a few of these factors we can make some attempt to use indirect indicators, but these attempts must be especially tentative. On the other hand, the relative success or failure of attempts to explain military intervention with the factors for which data are available will give us some indication of how much variation is left to be explained by *other* factors.

Before proceeding further, the term "military intervention" must be more precisely defined. In doing so, I shall borrow Robert Gilmore's definition of militarism: "The military institution is concerned with the management and use of controlled violence in the service of the state according to terms laid down by the state. When the military institution veers from this role to participate in or to influence other, non-military agencies and functions of the state, including its leadership, then militarism exists in greater or lesser degree."[25]

Obviously, the persuasiveness of this study depends on the validity of the index of military intervention used as the dependent variable. The heart of this index, which I shall call the "MI index," is a rating assigned to each country for each year of the decade 1956–1965, based on the extent of military intervention in the political life of that country for that year. This rating is on a scale from zero to three, from least to most intervention. Thus, for the decade, a country's MI score could range between zero and thirty.

The ends of the scale are easiest to define. A rating of zero is given to a country in which the armed forces were essentially apolitical, their role restricted to that of a minor pressure group on strictly military matters. Latin American examples of this level of intervention during the period studied were Uruguay and Costa Rica, as well as Bolivia during the years just after the 1952 revolution. A country that was ruled directly by a military regime, either individual or collective, and in which civilian groups and institutions were reduced to supplicants or tools of the military, is rated three. Examples of this level of intervention were Paraguay and (after the coups of the early 1960's) Brazil, Ecuador, Guatemala, Honduras, and Bolivia. Ratings of one and two are assigned to levels of intervention falling between these two extremes. A rating of two is given when a country was ruled by a military-civilian coalition in which the civilian elements had some real influence, or by civilians subject to frequent demands from a powerful military establishment, or by a dictatorship (often of a personalistic variety) based on force of arms, but not solely responsible to the armed forces.[26] Examples of this level of intervention in Latin America during the last decade were Brazil and Argentina (except for periods of direct rule by military juntas), Venezuela after Pérez Jiménez, and Nicaragua (a "familistic" dictatorship in which the armed forces played an important, but not predominant, role). A rating of one is given when a country was ruled by essentially civilian institutions, with civilian power groups preeminent, but with the armed forces still a significant political force in nonmilitary matters. Examples of this level of intervention were Mexico and Chile, and Colombia after Rojas Pinilla.

This rating method explicitly excludes from consideration certain polit-ical characteristics of related interest. I have not considered the degree of "democracy" in a country, apart from the extent of military intervention. Thus, for example, Castro's Cuba, despite its quasi-totalitarian character, is rated only one, since the available evidence suggests that the military play only a minor role in contemporary Cuban politics. Nor have I considered the ideological complexion of the military establishment; both the reac-tionary Paraguayan regime and the reformist regime in El Salvador are rated three. . . . [Sources for data are available in Appendix I.]

The data on the independent variables for each country are of three general types. In the first place, certain standard statistics, such as extent of urbanization, measures of economic development, and literacy rates, have been gathered from a number of statistical handbooks. Second, some variables based on rankings by informed observers have been drawn from *A Cross-Polity Survey* by Banks and Textor.[27] Finally, information on several dichotomous characteristics, such as the incidence of German mili-tary training missions, has been compiled from standard treatments of Latin American politics. Sources for data on all these variables are given in Appendix II.

The data on the independent variables involve problems of reliability and validity. "Reliability" refers to the accuracy of the statistics in measur-ing whatever it is that they measure. How accurate, for example, are the data on per capita GNP? As is well known, statistical data from Latin America are often not of the highest quality, and the reader is referred to the sources listed in Appendix II for discussions of this problem in particular cases. It is important to understand that in general the effect of unreliability in measurement of variables is to *reduce* the obtained correlation co-efficients slightly below the values that would be expected if there were no such measurement error.[28] "Validity" refers to the accuracy of the statistics in measuring the concepts in which we are interested. How well, for example, does per capita GNP or the proportion of the GNP derived from agriculture indicate "socio-technical complexity"? We cannot resolve these problems; we can only use appropriate caution in interpreting the results.[29]

IV. Results

Socioeconomic Development

The correlations between the MI index and various statistical indicators of social mobilization and economic development are given in Table I. Five variables measure social mobilization: (1) percent of population in cities over 20,000, (2) percent of adults literate, (3) newspaper circulation per 1,000 population, (4) university students per 1,000 population, and (5)

Table I. Military Intervention as a Function of Social Mobilization and Economic Development

Variable Number	Variable Content	Correlation With MI Index
1	Percent of population in cities over 20,000	—.49
2	Percent of adults literate	—.47
3	Newspaper circulation per 1,000 population	—.57
4	University students per 1,000 population	—.45
5	Radios per 1,000 population	—.44
6	Per capita GNP (1957)	—.30
7	Percent of GNP derived from agriculture	.26 (.18)
8	Percent of labor force in agriculture	.24
9	Percent of population in the primary sector	.39
10	Percent of labor force earning wages or salaries	—.42 (—.32)
11	Percent of labor force employed in industry	—.29
12	Percent of population in middle and upper [social] strata	—.48 (—.45)

Sources: See Appendix II. For Variables 7, 10, and 12, the correlation coefficients are based on data including "best guess" estimates for two or three countries for which precise data are not available. Coefficients in parentheses are based on data *not* including these estimates. See note 29.

radios per 1,000 population. As one might expect, these variables are highly intercorrelated: the mean intercorrelation is .81. They are also fairly closely correlated in the expected direction with military intervention: the mean correlation is —.48.[30] To simplify subsequent analysis, I have added together each country's (standardized) scores on these five indicators to form a single index of social mobilization, or "SM index." This index represents very accurately the factor common to these five indicators—all of the intercorrelations among the five components and all of their individual correlations with the MI index can be accounted for in terms of covariation with the SM index. This index itself correlates —.53 with the MI index. The conclusion must be that social mobilization is fairly strongly, and negatively, related to military intervention. More than one-quarter of the total variance in the MI index can be accounted for by covariation with social mobilization. (The square of a correlation coefficient, termed the "coefficient of determination," indicates what proportion of the variance in one variable is accounted for by covariation with the other. Here, for example, —.53 squared equals .28 or 28 percent.)[31]

Six of the variables are closely related to economic development: (1) per capita GNP, (2) percent of GNP derived from agriculture, (3) percent of the labor force in agriculture, (4) percent of the population in the primary sector, (5) percent of the labor force earning wages or salaries, and (6) percent of the labor force employed in industry. Again, these variables are highly intercorrelated: the average intercorrelation among them is .72. Each is moderately correlated with military intervention in the expected direction: the mean correlation of the six with the MI index is −.32.[32] As in the case of social mobilization, to make subsequent discussion simpler I have added together each country's (standardized) scores on these six indicators to form a single index of economic development, or "ED index." Like the SM index, the ED index represents very accurately the factor common to its six components. This ED index correlates −.37 with the MI index.

Before we can decide definitely on the relationship between economic development and military intervention, however, we must take into account their joint correlation with social mobilization. This procedure, in fact, produces a most remarkable result: if we remove the effect of social mobilization, economic development itself turns out to be *positively*, not negatively, correlated with military intervention! The pattern of simple, or zero-order, correlations among these three variables is given in Figure 1. Since the ED index and the SM index are very highly intercorrelated, the partial correlation between economic development and military intervention, controlling for social mobilization, becomes +.26. The explanation of this finding is that the SM-MI and SM-ED correlations are so strong that they "mask" the real, positive ED-MI correlation.

A more sophisticated procedure for analyzing this pattern of interrelations is provided by causal path analysis.[33] This technique allows us to calculate "causal weights," or "path coefficients," indicating the nature and importance of the causal relationships among a set of variables, provided (1) we are willing to posit some particular pattern of causal relations among the variables, and (2) we are willing to ignore (at least temporarily) the possible effects of variables not included in the set being considered. In our present case, the first of these conditions can be met by assuming that military intervention is a result, rather than a cause, of social mobilization and economic development. As a first approximation, this is probably true; later in this research note I shall explore this point further. (Path analysis does *not* require us to decide which way(s) the causal

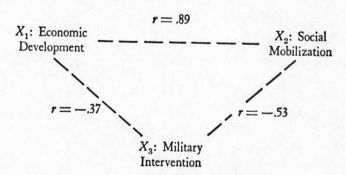

Figure 1. Intercorrelations among economic development, social mobilization, and military intervention.

arrow joining development and mobilization should point.) If we can make the assumption implied in the second condition—that there is no fourth variable intruding—we can calculate from the correlation coefficients given in Figure 1 the causal weights, or path coefficients, given in Figure 2.[34] These weights imply that the direct effect of social mobilization on military intervention is strongly negative and that the direct effect of economic development on military intervention is moderately positive. Path analysis also allows us to estimate the proportion of the variance in a dependent variable which remains unaccounted for by a system of independent variables.[35] Social mobilization and economic development together account for about thirty-three percent of the variance in the MI index, leaving sixty-seven percent yet to be explained.

The remaining hypothesis linking socioeconomic development and military intervention refers to the rise of the middle strata. Accurate information on the class structure of the Latin American countries is difficult to obtain, but Germani and Silvert present data on "the percentage of the population in middle and upper [social] strata."[36] The correlation of this variable with the MI index is −.48, supporting the notion that the rise of the middle strata is associated with a decline in military intervention. However, because this measure of class structure is almost perfectly correlated with the SM index ($r = .94$), it makes virtually no *independent* contribution toward explaining variance in levels of military intervention.

In sum, then, there seems to be good evidence that both social mobilization and economic development affect a country's propensity for military rule. Social mobilization definitely inhibits military intervention in politics, as predicted. The direct effect of economic development seems to be to encourage military intervention, although there is also a strong indirect effect linking economic development and military abstention, by way of social mobilization. The implications of this complicated pattern of find-

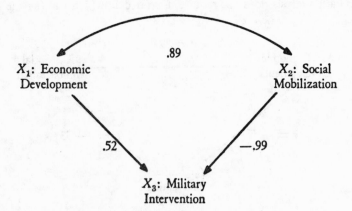

Figure 2. Path coefficients for relationships among economic development, social mobilization, and military intervention.

Table II. Military Intervention as a Function of Political Development

Variable Number	Variable Content	Correlation With MI Index
13	Constitutional restrictions on the military	—.18
14	Percent of voting-age population voting	—.13
15	Interest articulation by parties	.04
16	Interest articulation by associations	—.19
17	Stability of party system	—.36
18	Interest aggregation by parties	—.63
19	Log_{10} ($10 \times$ deaths from domestic group violence per million population)	.20
20	Weighted Eckstein "instability" index	—.08

Sources: See Appendix II.

ings can be brought out by several examples. Colombia and El Salvador are, in terms of the ED index, equally developed economically, but Colombian society is considerably more mobilized, as measured by the SM index. For the period under consideration, the Colombian military were much less involved in politics than were their Salvadoran counterparts. On the other hand, Venezuela and Costa Rica are about equally mobilized socially, but Venezuela is considerably more developed economically. As the preceding analysis would have predicted, Venezuelan politics in the period studied were much more subject to military intervention. Altogether the variables examined in this section account for about one-third of the total variance in the incidence of military intervention in Latin American politics.

Political Development

Data on political development are much less readily available than data on socioeconomic variables. The correlations between military intervention and the political variables for which we can obtain data are given in Table II.

First, let us consider briefly the question of public commitment to civilian rule. Alexander Edelmann argues that among the most important influences counteracting military intervention in Latin America are "constitutional and legal restrictions imposed on members of the military regarding political activity. . . . Written not only on paper but also in the aspirations of liberty-loving citizens, they serve notice on the military of what their fellow countrymen expect."[37] If Edelmann is right that constitutional restrictions reflect popular norms and that these popular norms inhibit military intervention, then there should be a high correlation between constitutional restrictions and military abstention from politics. In fact, the correlation between military intervention and constitutional limits on military political activity is only −.18. The mean MI score for the four-teen nations that as of 1959 had some constitutional restrictions on polit-ical activity by the military is 17.4, while the mean MI score for the entire region is 18.4. The evidence clearly fails to confirm Edelmann's hypothesis. The explanation may be either that constitutions and popular aspira-tions are unrelated or that these aspirations do not affect military inter-vention.

A frequent hypothesis is that popular political participation inhibits military intervention. The best available indicator of such participation is the proportion of the adult population that votes in national elections.[38] Table II shows that the correlation between electoral turnout and military intervention, though in the predicted direction, is quite low. As a matter of fact, if we control for the level of social mobilization, the remaining partial correlation between turnout and military intervention is virtually zero.

In assessing the hypotheses linking military intervention to the weakness of political parties and pressure groups—the political infrastructure—we are forced to rely almost exclusively on the judgments compiled for the *Cross-Polity Survey*. Four scales presented there are relevant: (1) extent of interest articulation by political parties, (2) extent of interest articula-tion by associations, (3) stability of the party system, and (4) extent of interest aggregation by political parties. The correlations of the two vari-ables involving interest articulation are, in fact, negligible, viz., .04 for parties and −.19 for associations. Judging by these statistics, strong and articulate parties and pressure groups do not necessarily inhibit military intervention, nor do weak parties and pressure groups necessarily en-courage intervention.[39] The stability of the party system is somewhat more strongly related to military intervention, and the extent of aggregation by political parties is quite strongly related, with coefficients of −.36 and −.63 respectively. These figures, especially the latter one, strongly suggest that in contemporary Latin America political parties and military regimes represent mutually exclusive mechanisms for reaching political decisions. On the other hand, these relationships are hardly surprising, because they approach being tautological. In any country where a military regime was in power most experts would be likely *ipso facto* to rate as insignificant the role of parties in aggregating interests and resolving political problems.

The final proposition to be considered in this section on political devel-opment links military intervention to the role of violence in politics. Two different indices of political violence in the Latin American countries are available. Harry Eckstein compiled from the *New York Times Index* an enumeration of violent events occurring in every country in the world in the period 1946–1959 and tallied these in ten categories ranging from civil wars to police roundups. I have computed for each Latin American country an index based on five of his categories, with "warfare" and "tur-moil" weighted by a factor of four, "rioting" and "large-scale terrorism" weighted by two, and "small-scale terrorism" weighted by one.[40] (These were the only categories dealing with mass violence.) The other index of political violence is based on the variable "Deaths from Domestic Group Violence per Million Population, 1950–1962" presented in the *World Handbook of Political and Social Indicators*. To reduce the skewing effect caused by the great variance in this variable (from 2,900 for Cuba to 0.3 for Uruguay), I have used a logarithmic transformation to "squash" the distribution. (Given the nature of the distribution, the effect of this transformation is to raise the correlation coefficient obtained with the MI index.) The first index of political violence, based on Eckstein, is virtually unrelated to military intervention. The second index is slightly related in the expected direction, with $r = .20$, but this relationship disappears when controls are introduced for socioeconomic development.

Our conclusions about the hypotheses linking military abstention and political development must be cautious because of the limitations of the data available. With this qualification in mind, we can conclude that (apart from the trivial relationship between rule by the military and rule by political parties) there is very little evidence linking political development to military abstention in any straightforward way. Widespread participation in elections, strong parties and pressure groups, and freedom from political violence are neither necessary nor sufficient conditions for military abstention.

The Military Establishment

Several students of military intervention have stressed the importance of internal characteristics of the military establishment in determining the extent and nature of military intervention. Unfortunately, data are available for only a few, very gross, characteristics of the armed forces of the Latin American countries. Table III shows the relationships between the MI index and these characteristics—military expenditures as a proportion of GNP, military personnel as a proportion of the adult population, and total military personnel.

The strong positive relationship between military intervention and military spending is hardly surprising and is probably the result of circular causation. Interestingly, militarism in the sense of intervention in politics does not seem to be linked to militarism in the sense of the proportion of

Table III. Military Intervention as a Function of Internal Characteristics of the Military

Variable Number	Variable Content	Correlation With MI Index
21	Defense spending as a percent of GNP	.55
22	Military personnel as a percent of adults	.07
23	Military personnel in thousands	—.24

Sources: See Appendix II.

men in arms. Still more interesting is the *negative* correlation between absolute size of the military establishment and extent of military intervention. This finding directly contradicts the proposition relating intervention to the size and sophistication of the armed forces. The finding cannot be attributed to the spurious effects of either simple population size (for the correlation between population size and the MI index is virtually zero) or socioeconomic development. Possibly the negative correlation reflects an inhibiting effect of either greater "professionalism" or lower internal cohesion in larger military establishments. Of course, the relative weight of this variable in determining military intervention is not great, for it accounts at best for only about six percent of the total variance in the MI index.

Foreign Influences

One of the most common explanations of military intervention in Latin America is that German military training missions during the late nineteenth and early twentieth centuries "infected" Latin American officers with ideas of military involvement in politics. As it turns out, this is a good example of a proposition that has been "tested" by time rather than evidence. The correlations between the MI index and the incidence of German, French, Chilean, and U.S. missions are given in Table IV.

The two most notable figures are the slight *negative* correlation between German influence and military intervention and the moderate *positive* correlation between Chilean missions and military intervention. The average MI score for the countries that had German missions is 15.2.[41] The average score for those that had French missions is 18.7, and for those with Chilean missions, 23.0. (It will be recalled that the mean score for the area as a whole is 18.4.) Neither the negative finding involving German missions nor the positive one involving Chilean missions can be attributed to spurious correlations with socioeconomic development. The explanation for the German finding seems to be simply that a plausible hypothesis has been repeatedly affirmed without adequate testing. Without more detailed

Table IV. Military Intervention as a Function of Incidence of Foreign Military Training Missions

Variable Number	Variable Content	Correlation With MI Index
24	German military training missions	—.20
25	French military training missions	.03
26	Chilean military training missions	.36
27	U.S. Mutual Defense Assistance Agreements	.06

Sources: See Appendix II.

Table V. Number of Countries with Military Coups in Half-Year Periods, 1951–1965

	NUMBER OF PERIODS	
NUMBER OF COUNTRIES	*Obtained Distribution*	*Random Distribution*
0	8	10.3
1	13	11.0
2	8	5.9
3 or more	1	2.8
	30	30.0

Source: The Annual Register (London 1951–1966).

information about the Chilean missions, that correlation will have to go unexplained.

The data on U.S. military missions refer to the twelve countries having Mutual Defense Assistance Agreements with the U.S. as of 1960 and are included only for general interest. The fact that the correlation of U.S. missions with military abstention is at present negligible need not imply that over a period of several decades such contacts will not affect the political orientations of the Latin American armed forces.

The other major foreign influence often alleged to affect military intervention is the "demonstration effect" of military coups in other countries. Historians of particular instances of military intervention have from time to time apparently uncovered some direct evidence of such influence, but the question to be considered here is to what extent this kind of "coup contagion" is a general phenomenon. The technique to be used is a familiar one in mathematical sociology.[42] I first listed all the successful military coups in Latin America from 1951 to 1965. The number of countries experiencing coups in each half-year period was then tallied.[43] Essentially, the technique consists of comparing the obtained distribution of coups with the distribution that would be expected if the incidence of coups were random across countries. If coups are contagious, we would expect more periods during which there were either *no* coups or *many* coups than we would expect if coups were distributed randomly throughout the fifteen-year span. Table V compares the obtained distribution with the distribution that would be expected if the thirty-two coups of this period had been distributed randomly. (This random distribution is given by the formula called Poisson's distribution.) The evidence clearly disconfirms the contagion hypothesis. If anything, the data suggest that coups are slightly *more evenly* distributed (not less evenly, as the contagion hypothesis suggests) than chance alone would imply, although overall the differences are rather small.

These findings conclusively disconfirm several widely repeated proposi-

Table VI. The Incidence of Military Intervention in Four Five-Year Periods

Period	Mean MI Index Per Annum
1906-1915	1.53
1951-1955	2.02
1956-1960	1.87
1961-1965	1.81

tions about military intervention. Neither German military missions nor "coup contagion" can be blamed for military involvement in Latin American politics.

Historical Trends and Influences

I have already described the construction of the MI index for the period 1956–1965. Exactly the same procedures were used in compiling MI scores for the periods 1906–1915 and 1951–1955 (see Appendix I). Taken together these data allow us to examine the relative incidence of military intervention at selected periods over the last half-century. Table VI gives the relevant data. The average levels of intervention show that although the extent of intervention since 1950 has been somewhat higher than it was a half-century earlier, the general trend within the later period has been downward.[44] The intercorrelations among the scores for the most recent five-year periods, given in Figure 3, illustrate the not surprising fact that the extent of military intervention in the various countries tends to be quite constant, at least over this fifteen-year period.

Hypotheses linking military intervention or abstention to traditional norms in the military establishments imply that there will be a significant correlation between past and present levels of intervention. The simple correlation between the MI scores for the period 1956–1965 and the period exactly a half-century earlier is .47, thus moderately confirming this prediction. Perhaps, however, this correlation merely reflects the fact that the countries predisposed to military intervention by socioeconomic conditions in 1906–1915 were at the same relative level of socioeconomic development at mid-century. Perhaps, that is, continuities in socioeconomic development, rather than continuities in traditions of militarism, account for the association.

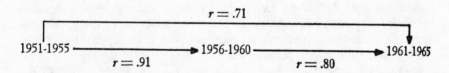

Figure 3. Intercorrelations among MI indices for three recent five-year periods.

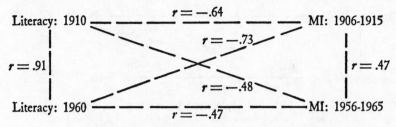

Figure 4. Intercorrelations among literacy rates, 1910 and 1960, and military intervention scores, 1906–1915 and 1956–1965.

Precise information on earlier levels of socioeconomic development in all twenty Latin American countries is impossible to obtain. Fortunately, for one indicator of social mobilization—literacy—we can make some reasonable estimates. Among those seven countries for which 1910 literacy rates are available, these rates correlate almost perfectly ($r = .98$) with the 1950 literacy rates for inhabitants of sixty-five and over—the generation who were young adults in the earlier period. Relying on this fact, we can use the 1950 rates for those sixty-five and over—which can be closely estimated for all the countries—as indicators of the levels of social mobilization a half-century ago.

Figure 4 displays the intercorrelations among our four variables: literacy in 1910 and 1960 and military intervention in 1906–1915 and 1956–1965. Of the several hundred possible causal models that might be used to fit this set of correlations, all but four can be eliminated as inconsistent with the pattern of correlations obtained or with the temporal ordering of the variables.[45] The four possible causal models are shown in Figure 5. If we assume that military intervention in 1906–1915 could not have significantly influenced literacy rates in 1910 (even though it might have influenced *later* literacy rates), we can eliminate Models A and B. If, in

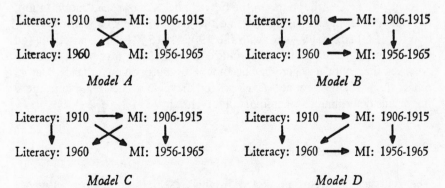

Figure 5. Four causal models consistent with intercorrelations shown in Figure 4.

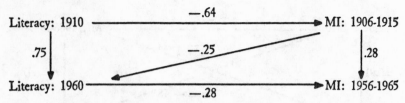

Figure 6. Path coefficients for relationships among literacy rates, 1910 and 1960; and military intervention, 1906–1915 and 1956–1965.

addition, we assume that 1910 literacy rates do not affect 1956–1965 military intervention directly, but only indirectly through their influence on 1960 literacy rates, we can also eliminate Model C.

Having decided on a particular causal model, we can apply the technique of causal path analysis to examine the interrelationships among social mobilization and military intervention for the two periods. The results of this analysis, given in Figure 6, show that both contemporary literacy rates and earlier levels of military intervention make independent contributions toward explaining present levels of military intervention. The figure also reveals that military intervention itself has a deleterious effect on subsequent levels of literacy. One implication of this pattern of findings is that part of the strong correlation earlier noted between social mobilization and (contemporary) military intervention can be traced to the impact of earlier military intervention on both contemporary levels of mobilizaticn and contemporary levels of intervention.[46]

Another surprising fact revealed by this historical analysis is that levels of socioeconomic development were relatively much more important determinants of military intervention a half-century ago than today. As shown in Figure 4, the correlation between 1910 literacy rates and 1906–1915 military intervention was −.64, while a half-century later the analogous correlation was −.47. In terms of variance explained, the impact of literacy on military intervention dropped from forty-one percent to twenty-two percent. We lack earlier data on the other indicators of social mobilization, but it is interesting and significant that the overall index of social mobilization for 1960 correlates −.67 with the 1906–1915 MI index, as compared to −.53 with the 1956–1965 MI index. Over the last fifty years in Latin America the political sphere has become more autonomous; that is, factors other than socioeconomic development have become relatively more important determinants of military intervention.[47]

V. Conclusions

The statistical analyses presented in this research note have answered some questions about military intervention. Social mobilization clearly increases the prospects for civilian rule. Traditions of militarism play an important role in accounting for contemporary military intervention. Neither foreign training missions nor foreign examples of successful intervention seem to have any impact.

But some of the findings call for further reflection and inquiry. How can we account for the fact that the direct effect of economic development seems to be to encourage, rather than to inhibit, military involvement in politics? What are we to make of recent speculations linking political institutionalization and military abstention, in the light of the present negative findings?[48] What are the implications of the declining (although still important) strength of the relationship between military intervention and levels of socioeconomic development?

Overall, the independent variables we have examined here account for somewhat less than half of the total variance in contemporary military intervention.[49] One way of beginning the search for other significant factors is to examine so-called "deviant cases," that is, countries with MI scores considerably higher or lower than would be predicted on the basis of the variables examined here. Let me illustrate this technique.

Figure 7 displays a "scattergram" of the relationship between military intervention and social mobilization. Obviously, a few countries are widely out of line with the relationship characterizing the remaining countries. Argentina has a much higher MI score than would be expected on the basis of its social development, while Bolivia and Costa Rica have MI scores much lower than would be expected. The effect of these deviant cases is to lower substantially the obtained correlation coefficients. If we

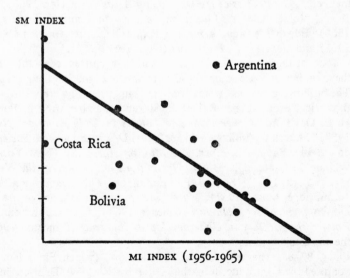

Figure 7. Scattergram of relationship between social mobilization and military intervention.

remove Argentina from the analysis, the coefficient rises from −.53 to
−.67, and if we remove Bolivia and Costa Rica as well, the coefficient
rises to −.79. The proportion of variance explained has risen from twenty-
eight percent to sixty-two percent. Similar analyses could be presented
using the other independent variables discussed in this research note.

Let me be clear that the import of this discussion of deviant cases is *not*
that these variables "really" explain the higher amounts of variance, for
obviously we cannot "write off" countries like Argentina, Bolivia, and
Costa Rica. Rather, this analysis focuses our attention on the countries
that are most anomalous when analyzed in terms of the variables considered here, as well as on the characteristics that might explain their
deviance. In the case of Bolivia, the 1952 revolution drastically reduced
(temporarily, at least) the role of the military to a level below that which
might have been expected for a country at its level of socioeconomic development. From this perspective, the events of 1964–1965 in Bolivia might
be interpreted as a "return to normalcy." The "Argentine paradox" is a
familiar one to students of Latin America; the present study graphically
reveals once again the extent of this paradox. The case of Argentina and,
by contrast, the case of Costa Rica suggest the importance of pursuing the
suggestions of Germani and Silvert that military intervention is related to
the extent of cleavage or consensus in a society.

Notes

1. "The Politics of Latin America," in Gabriel A. Almond and James S. Coleman, eds., *The Politics of the Developing Areas* (Princeton 1960), 502.
2. John J. Johnson, *The Military and Society in Latin America* (Stanford
   1964); Edwin Lieuwen, *Arms and Politics in Latin America* (New York
   1961) and *Generals vs. Presidents* (New York 1964).
3. Certain of these variables are, to be sure, not entirely constant throughout
   the area, but they are so nearly so as to warrant ignoring their effects.
4. The following works were consulted in preparing this inventory of
   theoretical propositions: Robert J. Alexander, "The Army in Politics," in
   H. E. Davis, ed., *Government and Politics in Latin America* (New York
   1958); Stanislaw Andrzejewski, *Military Organization and Society* (London 1954); Samuel E. Finer, *The Man on Horseback* (New York 1962);
   William F. Gutteridge, *Military Institutions and Power in the New States*
   (New York 1965); Samuel P. Huntington, *The Soldier and the State*
   (Cambridge, Mass., 1957); Morris Janowitz, *The Military in the Political
   Development of New Nations* (Chicago 1964); John J. Johnson, ed., *The
   Role of the Military in Underdeveloped Countries* (Princeton 1962); and
   the works cited in note 2.
5. Finer, 87–88. The term "social mobilization" (which Finer himself does
   not use) was introduced in this sense by Karl W. Deutsch in "Social
   Mobilization and Political Development," *American Political Science Review*, LV (September 1961), 493–514.

6. Huntington's counterhypothesis linking social mobilization with *increased* military intervention is discussed later in this section.
7. Finer, 113–15; Alexander, 158.
8. Janowitz's attack on this proposition (pp. 18–20) is weakened by his failure to distinguish the military-civilian dimension from the democratic-authoritarian dimension and by his failure to recognize that a correlation can be important without being perfect.
9. Gino Germani and Kalman Silvert, "Politics, Social Structure and Military Intervention in Latin America," *European Journal of Sociology,* II (Spring 1961), 62–81, [reprinted in this volume].
10. Finer, 21.
11. Finer, 87; John J. Johnson, "The Latin-American Military as a Politically Competing Group in Transitional Society," in Johnson, ed., *Role of the Military,* 127.
12. Finer, 21, 87–88, 115; Alexander, 157.
13. Samuel P. Huntington, "Political Development and Political Decay," *World Politics,* XVII (April 1965), 386–430.
14. Lieuwen, "Militarism and Politics in Latin America," in Johnson, ed., *Role of the Military,* 132–33; Martin C. Needler, *Latin American Politics in Perspective* (New York 1963), 76.
15. Huntington, *The Soldier and the State,* 84; Finer, 24ff.
16. For example, Finer, 32.
17. For example, Alexander, 153.
18. *Ibid.,* 154–55.
19. Janowitz, 42.
20. Alexander T. Edelmann, *Latin American Government and Politics* (Homewood 1965), 189.
21. "The Latin American Military," in Johnson, ed., *Role of the Military,* 129.
22. Lieuwen, "Militarism and Politics," *ibid.,* 134.
23. See Hubert M. Blalock, Jr., *Social Statistics* (New York 1960), 273ff.
24. Obviously, this study can consider only the range of variation in the independent variables which occurs in Latin America. For example, levels of social mobilization above or below the level achieved in Latin America might have effects on militarism which could not be detected in this study.
25. Robert L. Gilmore, *Caudillism and Militarism in Venezuela* (Athens, Ohio, 1964), 4–5.
26. In this connection it may be helpful to note Gilmore's distinction between "militarism" (as defined above) and "caudillism": "Caudillism is a political process in which violence is an essential element. . . . [It] may be defined as the union of personalism and violence for the conquest of power" (pp. 5, 47). Caudillist regimes, such as Haiti's, are rated two.
27. Arthur S. Banks and Robert B. Textor, *A Cross-Polity Survey* (Cambridge, Mass., 1963).
28. See George A. Ferguson, *Statistical Analysis in Psychology and Education* (New York 1959), 289. Given the probable error margins for the data used here, reliability coefficients in the range .8–.9 would be expected. This would mean, for example, that an obtained coefficient of .20 understates the actual correlation by about .02–.05 and that a coefficient of .60 understates the actual correlation by about .06–.15. For error estimates, see

Bruce M. Russett and others, *World Handbook of Political and Social Indicators* (New Haven 1964). For a detailed analysis of GNP error and a calculation of an approximate reliability coefficient, see Hayward R. Alker, Jr., "The Comparison of Aggregate Political and Social Data . . . ," *Social Sciences Information,* v (September 1966), 1–18.

29. For a few of the variables, data were not available for all twenty Latin American countries. In some cases, I have estimated the missing data and calculated coefficients including this "best guess" data. Unless these "guesses" are *wildly* off (and I do not believe that they are), the error introduced by including them is probably less than the error that would be introduced by ignoring the countries they represent. Precise data on Uruguay, for example, are often missing; yet it would be quite misleading to ignore the fact that this country fits many of our hypotheses remarkably well. Coefficients based on "best guess" data are indicated as such, and in all cases coefficients have also been presented without this "best guess" data.

30. There is considerable debate about whether tests of statistical significance are appropriate in cases, like the present study, in which we have not a random sample from a larger universe but a complete universe, viz., all contemporary Latin American countries. Strictly speaking, significance testing is merely a way of checking inferences from a random sample to the universe from which that sample is drawn. On the other hand, Blalock and Gold have argued that significance tests may help us sift important from unimportant findings, even when there is no question of inferring to a larger universe. See Blalock, 270, and David Gold, "Some Problems in Generalizing Aggregate Associations," *American Behavioral Scientist,* VIII (December 1964), 16–18. Gold, however, adds the qualification that when one is dealing with small *N*'s (as we are here), "judgments of importance that can be made reasonably from the *size* of associations should take precedence over tests of significance." Keeping in mind the problems associated with significance-testing in this situation, one may find the following figures helpful: assuming a one-tailed test and an *N* of 20, an $r \geq .38$ is significant at the .05 level; an $r \geq .31$ is significant at the .10 level; and an $r \geq .23$ is significant at the .33 level. These significance levels are derived from the *World Handbook,* 262.

31. See Blalock, 295–99.

32. In calculating this mean correlation and in compiling the ED index that follows, I have reversed the scoring for Variables 7–9, so that a large positive number always refers to a high level of development.

33. The discussion that follows is not intended to be a complete presentation of the logic and methodology of causal path analysis. For introductions to this recently developed technique, see Hubert M. Blalock, Jr., *Causal Inferences in Nonexperimental Research* (Chapel Hill 1964); Raymond Boudon, "A Method of Linear Causal Analysis . . . ," *American Sociological Review,* XXX (June 1965), 365–74; and Otis Dudley Duncan, "Path Analysis: Sociological Examples," *American Journal of Sociology,* LXXII (July 1966), 1–16. For a readable and comprehensive introduction for political scientists, see Hayward R. Alker, Jr., "Causal Inference in Political Analysis," in Joseph Bernd, ed., *Mathematical Applications in Political Science,* 2nd Series (Dallas 1966).

34. The equations for calculating the path coefficients (or p's) in this case are quite simple:

$$r_{21} = p_{21}$$
$$r_{32} = p_{32} + r_{21}p_{31}$$
$$r_{31} = p_{31} + r_{21}p_{32}.$$

This is a simple algebraic system of three equations and three unknowns. For the general equation of path analysis, see Duncan, 5.

35. The equation for calculating the residual variance is quite simple:

$$p_{3u}^2 = 1 - p_{32}^2 - p_{31}^2 - 2p_{32}r_{12}p_{31}.$$

See Duncan, 6.

36. R. Vekemans and J. L. Segundo present numerically identical data under the heading "Percent of population at intermediate and senior grades of employment," in "Essay on a Socio-economic Typology of the Latin American Countries," in E. de Vries and J. M. Echavarria, eds., *Social Aspects of Economic Development in Latin America,* Vol. 1 (Paris 1963).

37. Edelmann, 192–93.

38. It is true that the accuracy of electoral turnout as an indicator of participation is limited by variations in the social and institutional context of the act of voting. Voting does not have the same meaning in the U.S. and the USSR, in the Netherlands and Uganda. Restriction of our attention to the Latin American countries minimizes this problem. For a fuller discussion of the problem, see Germani and Silvert.

39. Edelmann argues that one particular sort of interest group is especially likely to inhibit military intervention: "The most serious threat of all to the power of the military is that posed by the labor unions . . ." (p. 194). Actually, the correlation between military intervention and the proportion of union members is −.07. Huntington argues that political decay varies directly with the extent of party fragmentation. The comparable *Cross-Polity Survey* variable is called "Party System: Quantitative"; this correlates .23 with the MI index; controlling for social mobilization reduces this to .16.

40. I have borrowed this weighting technique from Eldon Kenworthy, "Predicting Instability in Latin America" (unpublished).

41. This negative finding is independent of the particular period during which the various missions were in residence. The mean MI score for only those countries that had German missions in the nineteenth century—generally the period referred to in this connection—is lower still: 13.6.

42. See James S. Coleman, *Introduction to Mathematical Sociology* (Glencoe 1964), 288–311.

43. Attempted but unsuccessful coups were ignored, partly for the conceptual reason that the definition of an "attempted coup" is problematic, partly for the practical reason that adequate information on attempted coups is lacking. The period of a half-year is chosen as representing about the optimum length of time during which contagion might be expected to operate. An analysis using one-year intervals produced results exactly comparable to those reported. I tallied countries rather than coups so as to exclude the effects of "contagion" within a single country.

44. The lower level of intervention in the earlier period probably reflects (1) the fact that after the turn of the century civilian government enjoyed a period of considerable success in Latin America and (2) my decision (see

note 26) to distinguish "caudillism" from "military intervention."

45. This elimination process follows the technique suggested by Herbert Simon and Hubert M. Blalock, Jr. See Blalock, *Causal Inferences,* 61–94 and *passim.*

46. Perhaps an analogous explanation would apply to the relationship between economic development and military intervention. We lack the data necessary to carry this analysis further.

47. Huntington argues that one aspect of political development is an increasing autonomy of politics from other social spheres. See "Political Development and Political Decay," 401–30.

48. Huntington's theory of political development (*ibid.*) implies that social mobilization leads to military rule and that civilian rule depends on strong political institutions; neither of these propositions is confirmed by the present study. It would be worth further investigation to determine whether the propositions do apply to other underdeveloped areas.

49. Among the other independent variables considered and rejected in the present study were (1) total population ($r = .02$), (2) racial composition ($r = .16$), and (3) rates of social change (for urbanization, $r = -.18$).

Appendix I. Year-by-year Military Intervention Scores

Country	1906	1907	1908	1909	1910	1911	1912	1913	1914	1915	1951	1952	1953	1954	1955	1956	1957	1958	1959	1960	1961	1962	1963	1964	1965	MI INDEX 1906-15	MI INDEX 1956-65	NEEDLER'S RANKINGS*
Costa Rica	1	1	1	1	1	1	1	1	1	1	0	0	0	0	0	0	0	0	0	0	0	0	0	0	0	10	0	0
Uruguay	1	1	1	1	1	1	1	1	1	1	0	0	0	0	0	0	0	0	0	0	0	0	0	0	0	10	0	1
Bolivia	1	1	1	1	1	1	1	1	1	1	3	0	0	0	0	0	0	0	0	1	1	1	1	1	3	10	9	1
Chile	1	1	1	1	1	1	1	1	1	1	1	1	1	0	0	1	1	1	1	1	1	1	1	2	1	10	10	1
Mexico	2	2	2	2	2	2	2	2	2	2	1	1	1	1	1	1	1	1	1	1	1	1	1	1	1	18	10	1
Colombia	2	2	2	2	1	1	1	1	2	2	1	1	1	1	1	1	1	2	1	1	1	1	1	1	1	14	15	1
Cuba	1	1	1	1	1	1	0	0	0	0	2	2	3	3	3	3	3	3	1	1	1	1	1	1	1	10	16	4
Panama	0	0	0	0	0	0	2	2	2	2	3	3	3	3	3	3	3	3	1	1	1	1	1	1	1	0	20	2
Nicaragua	1	1	1	1	1	3	1	2	2	2	2	3	3	3	3	2	2	2	2	2	2	2	2	2	2	17	20	4
Peru	1	1	1	1	1	2	1	1	2	3	3	3	3	3	2	2	2	2	2	2	2	2	2	2	2	14	21	2
Brazil	3	3	3	3	3	2	2	2	3	3	2	3	3	3	3	3	3	3	2	2	2	2	2	2	3	16	22	2
Haiti	3	3	3	3	3	3	3	3	3	3	2	3	3	3	3	3	3	3	2	2	2	2	3	3	3	30	22	3
Ecuador	2	2	2	2	2	2	2	2	2	2	2	2	2	2	2	3	3	3	2	2	2	2	3	3	2	20	23	2
Honduras	2	2	2	2	2	2	2	2	2	2	2	2	2	2	2	3	3	3	2	2	3	2	3	3	2	20	23	2
Argentina	1	1	1	1	1	1	1	1	1	1	2	2	2	2	2	3	3	3	2	2	3	2	3	3	2	10	23	3
Venezuela	2	2	2	2	2	2	2	2	2	2	3	3	3	3	3	3	3	3	3	3	3	3	3	3	3	20	23	3
Guatemala	2	2	2	2	2	2	2	2	2	2	2	3	3	3	3	3	3	3	3	3	3	3	3	3	3	20	26	3
El Salvador	2	2	2	2	2	2	2	2	2	2	3	3	3	3	3	3	3	3	3	3	3	3	2	3	3	20	27	4
Dominican R.	2	2	2	2	2	2	3	2	2	1	2	3	3	3	3	3	3	3	3	3	3	2	3	3	3	21	28	3
Paraguay	2	2	2	2	2	2	2	1	1	1	2	2	3	3	3	3	3	3	3	3	3	3	3	3	3	16	30	4

* Martin C. Needler, Latin American Politics in Perspective (New York 1963), 156-57. Rankings of "Normal Political Role of Military": 0="None"; 1="Limited"; 2="Intervene"; 3="Veto Power"; 4="In Control."

SOURCES: The Annual Register (London 1951-1966); Frank Brandenburg, The Making of Modern Mexico (Englewood Cliffs 1964); H. E. Davis, ed., Government and Politics in Latin America (New York 1958); John E. Fagg, Latin America: A General History (New York 1963); Robert L. Gilmore, Caudillism and Militarism in Venezuela (Athens, Ohio, 1964); John J. Johnson, The Military and Society in Latin America (Stanford 1964); Edwin Lieuwen, Arms and Politics in Latin America (New York 1961) and Generals vs. Presidents (New York 1964); John Martz, Central America (Chapel Hill 1959); Dana G. Munro, The Five Republics of Central America (New York 1918) and The Latin American Republics: A History, 2nd ed. (New York 1950); Martin C. Needler, ed., Political Systems of Latin America (Princeton 1964); Franklin D. Parker, The Central American Republics (New York 1964); J. Fred Rippy, Latin America: A Modern History (Ann Arbor 1958); Robert E. Scott, Mexican Government in Transition (Urbana 1959); William S. Stokes, Latin American Politics (New York 1959); Theodore Wyckoff, "The Role of the Military in Latin American Politics," Western Political Quarterly, XIII (September 1960), 745-63.

Appendix II. Sources of Data for Independent Variables

Variable Number	Variable Content	Source Number and Page
1	Percent of population in cities over 20,000	I, 228
2	Percent of adults literate (1960)	XI
3	Newspaper circulation per 1,000 population	II, 108
4	University students per 1,000 population	I, 228
5	Radios per 1,000 population	II, 118
6	Per capita GNP (1957)	II, 155
7	Percent of GNP derived from agriculture	II, 172; III, 70
8	Percent of labor force in agriculture	II, 177
9	Percent of population in the primary sector	IX, 64
10	Percent of labor force earning wages or salaries	III, 38
11	Percent of labor force employed in industry	X, 90
12	Percent of population in middle and upper [social] strata	IX, 64
13	Constitutional restrictions on political activity by military	VIII, 132
14	Percent of voting-age population voting	II, 84
15	Interest articulation by parties	V, 37
16	Interest articulation by associations	V, 33
17	Stability of party system	V, 43
18	Interest aggregation by parties	V, 38
19	Log_{10} (10 $\times$ deaths from domestic group violence per million population)	II, 99
20	Weighted Eckstein "instability" index	IV, Appendix I
21	Defense spending as a percent of GNP	II, 79
22	Military personnel as a percent of adult population	II, 77
23	Military personnel strength in thousands	III, 41
24	German military training missions	VI
25	French military training missions	VI
26	Chilean military training missions	VI
27	U.S. Mutual Defense Assistance Agreements	VII, 201
28	Percent of adults 65 and over literate (1950)	XII
29	Percent of adults literate (1910)	XIII

SOURCES: *I.* Gino Germani, "The Strategy of Fostering Social Mobility," in E. de Vries and J. M. Echavarria, eds., *Social Aspects of Economic Development in Latin America,* Vol. I (Paris 1963). *II.* Bruce M. Russett and others, *World Handbook of Political and Social Indicators* (New Haven 1964). *III.* Center of Latin American Studies, *Statistical Abstract of Latin America* (Los Angeles 1962). *IV.* Harry Eckstein, *Internal War: The Problem of Anticipation,* a report submitted to the Research Group in Psychology and the Social Sciences, Smithsonian Institution (Washington 1962). *V.* Arthur S. Banks and Robert B. Textor, *A Cross-Polity Survey* (Cambridge, Mass., 1963). *VI.* John J. Johnson, ed., *The Role of the Military in Underdeveloped Countries* (Princeton 1962), 108, 163; John J. Johnson, *The Military and Society in Latin America* (Stanford 1964), 69-71; William S. Stokes, *Latin American Politics* (New York 1959), 129-32. *VII.* Edwin Lieuwen, *Arms and Politics in Latin America* (New York 1961). *VIII.* Stokes, *Latin American Politics. IX.* Gino Germani and Kalman Silvert, "Politics, Social Structure and Military Intervention in Latin America," *Archives Européennes de Sociologie,* II (Spring 1961), 62-81. *X.* R. Vekemans and J. L. Segundo, "Essay on a Socio-economic Typology of the Latin American Countries," in de Vries and Echavarria, eds. *XI.* United Nations, *Compendium of Social Statistics* (New York 1963). *XII. Ibid.;* United Nations, *Demographic Yearbook* (New York 1955, 1964); UNESCO, *World Illiteracy at Mid-Century* (Paris 1957). *XIII. Ibid.;* UNESCO, *Progress of Literacy in Various Countries* (Paris 1953).

Philippe C. Schmitter / **Military Intervention, Political Competitiveness, and Public Policy in Latin America: 1950-1967**

Chronic military intervention and erratic party competitiveness have been considered hallmarks of Latin American politics. Understandably, they have been the object of a good deal of theoretical speculation, detailed description and even systematic analysis on the part of scholars studying the region. Surprisingly, these efforts have focused exclusively on the *causes* of either military intervention (MI) or political competitiveness (PC) and have neglected almost entirely their *consequences*. They leave us with the generals (or colonels as the case may be) battering down the gates to the presidential palace or with a peaceful transfer of office by open, contested election and tell us very little about what these triumphant groups do with their newly-acquired power. In short, intervention by the military and competition by political parties have been treated exclusively as dependent variables—the objects rather than the subjects of analysis.[1]

This essay inverts our attention and treats military intervention and party competitiveness as independent variables. It asks the central question: What, if any, changes in public policy may be plausibly and prob-abilistically attributed to rule by the military or by competitively selected

From Philippe C. Schmitter, "Military Intervention, Political Competitiveness and Public Policy in Latin America: 1950–1967," in Morris Janowitz and Jacques van Doorn, eds., *On Military Intervention* (Rotterdam: Rotterdam University Press, 1971). Reprinted in edited form, by permission of the author and publisher. [Acknowledgments omitted. A significant proportion of the graphic and tabular material included in the original paper has had to be omitted from this edition.—Ed.]

civilian elites in Latin America since 1950? Have we any grounds for asserting that another politically dominant group might have pursued different policies? And, if so, in what specific issue areas are these differences most likely to be found?

We begin with relatively simple bivariate and cross-sectional instruments of analysis, cross-tabulating a classification of the twenty Latin American republics by regime type with a set of policy indicators for the period *circa* 1960. Subsequently, multivariate indicators will be introduced, in effect to control for possible environmental determinants. Finally, in the last half of the essay, we will check the observations and findings already obtained by switching to longitudinal or serial data for the period 1950–1967. This will permit us to overcome some of the objections often leveled at cross-sectional analysis, at the same time amassing evidence from several data bases and manipulating it with a variety of analytical techniques—all of which may contribute to the plausibility of our findings.

Regime Types in Latin America

The two dimensions we have used to describe and categorize regimes in Latin America, extent of military intervention in politics and degree of competitiveness prevailing between political parties,[2] are (rather surprisingly) not very highly correlated with each other. As figure I demonstrates, a cross-tabulation of the two reveals a rather scattered pattern of distribution. To characterize military intervention as of 1960, I have utilized the tripartite classification scheme of Edwin Lieuwen (Group I: Countries in which the armed forces dominate politics; Group II: Countries in which the armed forces are in transition from political to non-political bodies; Group III: Countries in which the armed forces are non-political) which has the virtues of being based on an extensive monographic comparative analysis and of dividing the twenty units according to almost even cell frequencies.[3] As an indicator of competitiveness I have calculated the percentage difference between the winning and second running party in the national (presidential) election closest to 1960. Where the two leading contenders were less than 14 percentage points apart, I have considered the system as highly competitive. Countries with a spread of 14 to 40% I have classified as moderately competitive and those with over 40% differences have been assigned to the non-competitive cell. While this respects the natural distribution of scores rather well (only Argentina might seem out of place), it does result in a less even pattern of distribution: eight regimes in the highly competitive category; five in the moderately competitive one and six in the non-competitive one.[4]

Seven regimes are bivariantly "consistent." Chile, Uruguay and Costa Rica are both highly competitive and civilian dominated; Paraguay, Nicaragua, El Salvador and Haiti are simultaneously non-competitive and

| | | Degree of Military Intervention | | | |
		Non-Political	Transi-tional	Dominant	N
	Highly competitive (Less than 14% difference)	Chile Uruguay Costa Rica	Brazil Peru Ecuador Guatemala	Panama	(8)
Compet-itive-ness of Party System	Moderately Competitive (14 to 40% difference)	Colombia	Venezuela Argentina	Honduras Dominican Republic	(5)
	Non-competitive (more than 40% difference)	Bolivia Mexico	Cuba*	Paraguay Nicaragua El Salvador Haiti	(6)
	N	(6)	(7)	(7)	

* Due to lack of data for this period due to revolutionary upheaval, Cuba has been omitted from most of the following tables. Haiti and Uruguay have also frequently been left out due to missing information.

Figure I. Regime types in Latin America ca. 1960

military dominated. Brazil, Peru, Ecuador and Guatemala managed (ca. 1960) to maintain a very competitive party system despite considerable military intromission in political life; Honduras and the Dominican Republic were moderately competitive despite the dominant presence of military actors. Several of these "systemic incompatibilities" were subsequently removed by coup in the succeeding years, but for the period under analysis they, along with Argentina and Venezuela, had structurally hybrid systems. Bolivia, Mexico and to an extent Colombia exhibit a more stable sub-type: the civilian, non-competitive regime. Panama represents the only case of the extra-ordinary combination of high party competitiveness and a domineering military. This "incompatibility" was also removed in subsequent years.

For the time series analysis a slightly modified set of categories was used. Both variables were dichotomized, resulting in four modal regime types: the civilian, competitive (CC); the civilian, non-competitive (CNC); the military, non-competitive (MNC); and the military, competitive (MC).*

* Figure II, "Frequency of regime types in Latin America 1950–67," has been omitted.

Working Hypotheses

Despite their tendency to treat intervention and competitiveness exclusively as dependent variables, previous students of Latin America have occasionally provided certain clues or hints as to their probable impact upon such broad issues as inflation, social reform, industrialization, nationalization, income redistribution, etc. Virtually all observers seem convinced of the relevance of regime types for predicting and understanding the scope and nature of public policy in Latin America. The notion that political outputs and outcomes are determined primarily, if not exclusively, by such conditions as the level of economic development, the degree of social mobilization, the nature of ethnic stratification, the extent of external dependence, the relative size, density or natural resource base of the society has rarely been entertained by scholars of the region. Even those activists who tend to see virtually all national policies as dictated by a cabal consisting of the United States State Department, the Pentagon, the CIA and the International Monetary Fund would probably hesitate to claim that such basic dimensions of the domestic regime were completely irrelevant to understanding who gets what, when and how.

Perusal of the general political development literature and especially of works dealing specifically with Latin America discloses substantial disagreement over the impact of both military intervention and electoral competitiveness upon public policy. Since these scattered observations are rarely accompanied by evidence, we can treat them as speculative contradictory hypotheses (although they are rarely presented as such). Stating their positions in a way that admittedly does some violence to the subtlety of their respective arguments, it does seem possible to reduce them to three competing statements of probable relationship for each of the two sets of independent variables. In short, we can examine the ranges of distribution of policy indicators with a positive, a negative and a null hypothesis in hand.[5]

MI_1: Military establishments are dedicated organizationally and ideologically to the preservation of order. Changes in public policy tend to disrupt existing distributions of benefit and to modify previous levels of expectation which leads to disorder and are therefore likely to be resisted by the military. "Moreover, a military establishment depends for its form, status, emoluments, and privileges on the social order that gave it existence."[6] Particularly in Latin America where they have historically acquired exclusive control over decisions relating to their rank, salary, promotion, welfare and retirement benefits, defence spending and national security policy, these military elites will seek to insure by pressure or seizure of power that these "rights" are not jeopardized by other competing groups. Given severe budgetary constraints such demands conflict with the priorities established by social and political reformers and provide an additional motive for military resistance to increases in welfare spending, public investment and other "progressive" measures. Other observers have added that, despite the shift in recruitment to middle sector origins,[7] Latin American military officers tend to marry into the ranks of provincial elites, to seek entry into the clubs and social institutions of the upper class and otherwise to exhibit a strong desire to imitate and be accepted by the traditionally dominant social and economic sectors of the society. Again, this should provide them with more motives for opposing such outputs as more egalitarian tax systems, land reform, income redistributing welfare schemes, enfranchisement of illiterates, spending on popular education, transfers of revenue from the agricultural and commercial to the industrial sector and inflation creating budgetary imbalances.[8]

MI$_2$: The military in developing countries (*y compris* Latin America) form a cohesive elite sensitive to national performance and dedicated to national developmental goals. They alone, in the absence of articulated party structures, possess the requisite internal discipline and organizational coherence to follow policies aimed at concentrating and wisely investing political resources while containing the fissiparous tendencies of regional, class or clan conflict. Granted that they value order above all other "system virtues," they nonetheless have learned that the preemptive promotion of "progressive" measures is the most efficient means to that end, given the pervasiveness of popular demands for modernization.[9] Professionalization in training and task has given them new technical skills and ideological aspirations and this "has induced Latin American armed forces to support technological progress, industrialization, and economic development in general."[10] Shift in recruitment has led them increasingly to favor middle-sector or middle-class objectives, which if not radical do at least imply important increments in the role of public authority in such areas as investment, health and education, income redistribution, industrial management, etc. The fact that military officers live in a thoroughly bureaucratized environment under heavy public subsidization inclines them naturally to favor statist or socialist solutions to developmental dilemmas. "In short, a new type of military man is coming to the fore and often becoming a major force for constructive social change in the American republics . . . The new military man is prepared to adapt his authoritarian tradition to the goals of social and economic progress."[11]

MI$_3$: The military in Latin America is only one among several groups competing for hegemony over the political system. As regards internal cohesion, ideological purpose, basis of recruitment or technical knowledge, it possesses no special skills or resources which are not available elsewhere. Hence, military political activists are incapable of ruling alone or of permanently legitimating their domination of the political system.[12] They must seek out and strike up alliances with diverse civilian groups. In so doing, they are more likely to continue policies already initiated or advocated by their civilian allies than to introduce startling innovations which might upset coalitional support.[13] On the other hand, whether or not they openly occupy the top executive and administrative positions, the military establishment is likely even in civilian regimes to play an important decisional role. This null hypothesis, therefore, predicts that the substance of policy-making in Latin America is relatively indifferent to military or civilian hegemony. Dichotomous treatment ignores the extent of interpenetration in such complex political systems "sin elite dirigente."[14] The hypothesis is even more convincing when the class interests and origins of the two, presumably exclusive, groups become identical.[15] Overt military rule becomes epiphenomenal, an emergency interim device for conserving the policies of a given social group when its hegemony is threatened by aspirant classes or masses. While the regime style may change when the generals take over, especially as regards such "regulatory" issues as freedom of expression, distributional and redistributional policies may continue unaltered.[16]

PC$_1$: Competition between political parties insures a high degree of accountability on the part of dominant elites to subordinate groups by organizing the political process in such a way as to provide structured alternatives.[17] Where such groups have high aspirations for development *cum* modernization (and this seems to be the case in Latin America), policy-makers will be compelled out of fear of losing their tenure in office to respond to these demands. They will tend to create new public resources and power to meet them and to channel existing resources in such a way as to maximize their developmental impact. Information is high and relatively costless in such systems; hence, leaders are well supplied with data on the distribution and intensity of opinion and can move in response to these articulated desires before they reach crisis proportions. They are also less likely to make gross errors of calculation based on poor information.[18] Followers also tend to be better informed on the performance of decision-makers and this may provide important internal checks on waste, corruption and other distortions to serve private ends. Competitiveness is usually associated with higher levels of popular participation and, subsequently, a stronger sense of identification with the political system. Such regimes can count upon greater voluntary compliance with norms and more willingness to forego immediate material gain in favor of differed symbolic payoff.[19] Their greater legitimacy in other words permits them to maintain policy continuity in the face of a short term decline in effectiveness.

PC$_2$: Non-competitive regimes are more effective developmental agents due to their greater internal coherence, discipline and continuity. They tend to have more centralized decisional structures which permit both a more efficient extraction and allocation of resources. Unlike competitive regimes, these can afford to override special clientelistic dependencies demanding immediate payoffs and resisting sacrifices in the name of the general good. Single party or dominant party systems are thus more likely to engage in rational, long-term planning and to focus their efforts on slowly maturing "basic" investments.[20] They can also sustain higher rates of gross investment by coercive limitation of current consumption and by better resisting pressures for a "premature" egalitarian distribution of benefits. By lessening dependence upon fickle shifts in public opinion and by diminishing the importance of certain strategically placed electoral groups—e.g. the manipulated voting blocs of rural oligarchs or urban populist demagogues—decision-makers in such systems have much greater role security. They can count on being in office for longer periods of time and are more likely to carry out policy innovations, since they can be better assured that these will not be wiped out by erratic variations in electoral favor or opportunistic shifts in coalitional support. Concentration of power and security in office when combined with a diffuse elitist orientation toward defensive "modernization from above" provides the most effective political base for overcoming the resistance of entrenched interests to change and the exacerbated desires of popular masses for immediate and unproductive gratification.[21]

PC$_3$: The degree of partisan competitiveness is irrelevant for understanding policy outputs in Latin America. On the one hand, existing parties (with a few notable exceptions) lack the requisite internal organization, ideological or programmatic consistency and sense of member identification to perform the beneficial functions implied in PC$_1$.[22] There is no reason to anticipate their insuring accountability in the Latin American context. A restricted and/or manipulated franchise coupled with an oligarchic, narrow-based, professionalized *cadre* of party leaders greatly reduces the party system's capacity for eliciting a sense of legitimacy or for aggregating reliable information. Far from enhancing the citizen's sense of participation in the political process, existing party systems stand as a barrier to it. Far from providing an effective check on waste and corruption in public spending, they have become the primary means for channeling and distributing such practices. On the other hand, non-competitive systems in Latin America do not seem to possess the guarantees of internal coherence, discipline and continuity indicated in PC$_2$. Closer examination reveals, as V.O. Key might have predicted, considerable internal factionalism on personalist, regionalist and functionalist lines. Far from being overridden, special clientelistic dependencies rooted in immediate payoffs and exemptions become the means for insuring order and continuity.[23] Policy changes in response to slight shifts in personal and group fortune and sporadic extra-systemic uprisings of public opinion are at least as frequent and consequential as those due to variations in electoral support. Coercion is used more to insure tenure in office than as an instrument for systematic extraction of resources and their most efficient long-term allocation. This security in office and greater concentration of power seem to result in a rigidification of the policy-making process and an unwillingness to experiment when faced with a changing schedule of demands once the original "modernization from above" impetus has been spent. In short, competitiveness or the lack of it may also be epiphenomenal in the Latin American setting. In the absence of specification of other environmental or systemic

characteristics, we have no reason to anticipate that the margin of difference between contending political groups will be associated with any particular pattern of outputs—more modernizing or more traditional, more
state-expanding or state-contracting, more public or more private, more
efficient or more wasteful, more leftist or more rightist, more consistent or
more erratic.[24]

For purposes of exposition, the above propositions have been stated in a
parsimonious manner which often distorts the original thought. Many who
have advanced speculations on these relations have hedged their comments
with references to intervening and/or concomitant conditions held to be
necessary or helpful in explaining a particular policy output or outcome.
Most frequently, authors have engaged in primitive periodization as a
means for specifying their hypotheses, e.g., "On the whole, at any rate
until the rise of communism and Castroism in Latin America, political
interventions by the military had aimed at change rather than at maintaining the *status quo*."[25] With the time series data in the latter half of this
essay, we will be able to document—for a restricted number of issue
areas—whether such a dramatic reversal has in fact occurred after 1960.
   Confused, contradictory and ill specified as the working hypotheses
may be, their most frustrating aspect is their vagueness as concerns the
dependent variable: public policy. We are told that the military in Latin
America favor or do not favor "change," "development," "modernity,"
"stability" or "*the status quo*." Competitive party systems allegedly promote or fail to promote "corruption," "equality," "responsible government," "decentralization" or just plain "progress." As we turn to a brief
discussion of operational indicators of public policy, we find that it is
difficult indeed to measure such political outputs and systemic outcomes.

Indicators of Public Policy

Policies are actions of authority groups taken to implement their decisions.
They are attempts by a political system to cope with and occasionally to
transform its environment by deliberate measures. These measures may involve the commitment of physical (money, men) and/or symbolic (verbal
encouragement) resources or "non-acts," decisions not to respond or even
not to take up the issue. Such policies of benevolent or malevolent neglect
have proven least amenable to measure and often pass undetected, as they
will in this essay.
   Of course, policies differ greatly in their effectiveness at accomplishing
their desired ends. For this purpose it is analytically important to distinguish between a *policy output* which is a deliberate act (or non-act) of a
public authority to allocate resources for a determined purpose, e.g., to
derive a certain proportion of its revenue from the progressively scaled

taxes upon income and property, and a *policy outcome* which reflects the indirect impact (intended or not) that the policy has had, e.g., greater equality of income:[26] Often the two dimensions will covary; for example, large proportional expenditures in education are likely to be associated with low levels of illiteracy and a greater percentage of youths attending school. Elsewhere, the linkage may be more tenuous. Sustained high rates of gross national investment may not be associated with high aggregate increases in GNP due to such intervening factors as varying capital output ratios, time leads and lags and sheer mismanagement and wastage. Such crude monitors of system performance as economic growth, "social progress," stability and absence of violence are usually the product of a concatenation of policy outputs, rarely a single one, and of environmental forces beyond the control of domestic policy-makers. Hence, in the following, as we differentiate outputs and outcomes across the 18 republics our general orienting hypothesis is that policy outputs should be easier to predict with single indicators and that the influence of regime-type upon them should be proportionately greater than in the case of the more complex, "concatenated," outcomes.

Policies can be classified, measured and evaluated according to numerous criteria.[27] One thing becomes clear, however, as one contemplates the impressive range of activities which can be called public policies and then consults the burgeoning efforts of social scientists at quantifying them. These attempts tap only that proportion of the total range which has been labeled *allocative policies,* "decisions which confer direct [material] benefits . . . upon individuals and groups."[28] Allocations of symbolic benefit and so-called *structural or regulatory policies* "which establish authority structures or rules to guide future allocations" have not been subjected to the same sort of rigorous analysis in the literature and this essay is no exception. Confinement to indicators of policy which are "naturally quantifiable," e.g., monetary expenditures, enrollment ratios, rate of annual growth, etc. is particularly serious when intuitively we have reason to suppose that a great deal of the difference between living under military or civilian rule, with or without a competitive party system, is felt primarily in such structural policies as freedom of expression and assembly, corporatism in interest group behaviour, restricted enfranchisement, concentration of decisional authority, etc. The decision to restrict our purview at this stage of the analysis to allocative decisions and their eventual (inferred) outcomes should be recognized as a distortion, motivated by practical and not normative concerns, and one which purposively underplays the probable policy differences between the regime types we are considering.

With some irregularity due to variations in data availability, we shall be examining a series of policy indicators or monitors as dependent variables. The *outputs* (ca. 1960) begin with total public revenue and expenditures, the balance between the two and the extent of centralization in governmental resources. Next we shall look into the structure of the respective tax systems, the extent of public involvement in economic investment and patterns of expenditure for social welfare, education, health and defence. The *outcomes* (ca. 1960–65) cover annual increase in GNP and industrial production, gross national investment, export and import performance, rates of inflation, school enrollment, and violence. Hence, despite their failure to reflect changes in the rules of the game, the indicators do monitor a wide range of system performance. Forearmed with our competing positive/negative/null hypotheses let us first examine them bivariately to discover whether there exist significant differences in the mean value of these indicators in military/civilian and competitive/non-competitive regimes and, if so, in what direction the differences run.

A Bivariate, Cross-Sectional Analysis

In table I,* the independent regime variables are trichotomized, as discussed above, and run against several policy indicators. For example, the average total governmental revenue for countries with a non-political military was 18.2% of GNP. Units with a military establishment in transition to a less politically active status had proportionately "wealthier" governments (21.6%); those with a domineering military were by far the poorest (14.2%). The statistical test for the significance of such a difference in mean values (F-test), which takes account of the number of units involved and the ever existent overlap in minimum and maximum values for each category, tells us that there are only 16 chances in one hundred that such a distribution could be due to chance. As suggestive as this finding is, the adjacent one is even more convincing. Competitiveness has an even greater impact. There are only three chances in one hundred that countries with highly contested party systems would not have a mean value for public revenue higher than the moderately competitive systems, which in turn, have more resources than the non-competitive variety. Contrary to the expectation that regimes must limit internal competitiveness in order to squeeze more resources from their economic systems, in Latin America those where electoral competitiveness is highest are most successful at extracting scarce resources from their environment.

The sheer quantity of data on military intervention, party competitiveness, and public policy outcomes makes it impossible to analyze each relationship in detail. Many are clearly insignificant. Regime type seems to bear little direct relation to such outcomes as the budgetary balance (although non-competitive and outright military regimes are noticeably more ortho-

---

* Table I, "A bivariate, cross-sectional analysis of military intervention, party competitiveness and selected indicators of public policy in Latin America ca. 1960," has been omitted.

dox spenders) and extent of public investment. In general the degree of competitiveness is much the more relevant predictor. Military rule has little impact on welfare expenditures of various sorts (social services, education or health) while the differences in mean value are quite significantly related to competitiveness. Interestingly, the highest levels of social spending are attained by the extremely competitive systems followed closely by the completely non-competitive ones. Where the dominant party has a 14 to 40% margin, public welfare-mindedness seems to be at its lowest.[29]

We find out why when we look at the distributions on defense expenditures. These intermediately competitive regimes are big and steady military spenders, while the most competitive ones easily devote less of their scarce resources to pacifying their defence establishments.[30] Those ruled directly by the military spend more of their budget on themselves (but less of their GNP) than the transitional regimes, have the lowest levels of expenditure per soldier—but the highest rates of increases in their defence budget!

It is important to note the differing nature of taxation systems under the differing regimes. Contrary to the view that competitive regimes are so shot through with special class and sectional dependencies that they cannot impose more egalitarian, i.e., more direct, tax obligations upon their citizens, these score by far the highest in mean value. Even more impressive is the impact of militarism. Direct taxes fall; indirect taxes (especially taxes on exports and imports) rise as a percentage of central government revenue with each successive increment in military intervention.[31] Competitiveness has much less of a differentiating impact.

When one switches to such "outcome" indicators of general system performance as GNP increase, rise in industrial production, exports or imports, rate of inflation and investment, relative increase in school enrollment, our regime typology becomes markedly less significant. The overlap in the range of values is such that even where differences in means are large they could be due to random chance. In short no regime type seems to be exclusively linked with developmental success, as measured by such gross indicators of performance. Military-dominated and non-competitive systems do—on the average—seem to have grown a bit faster economically (especially in industry)[32] and have been better at increasing their foreign trade earnings and at curtailing inflation. Not a bad recommendation for them were it not for the fact that the overlap is considerable and that these regimes generally start from a lower productive base.

Ceteris paribus, we have discovered some very important bivariate relationships between regime-type and the nature of public policies pursued. And we have unmasked certain areas which seem to be indifferent to these dimensions. These findings do not massively confirm either of the three competing hypotheses regarding intervention, but they do hint that politics may not be irrelevant or epiphenomenal in Latin America.

A Multi-Variate, Cross-Sectional Analysis

Of course, all other things are not equal and our findings thus far can easily be challenged as spurious—as demonstrating not the relevance of either military intervention or party competitiveness—but the importance of some prior, "environmental," factor which establishes such rigid parameters on decision-makers that they are compelled to adopt certain regime-types as well as certain public policies. The most likely candidate for compelling-ness is the level of economic development. Several scholars have observed that in Latin America (and elsewhere) military intervention is negatively and party competitiveness positively related to higher per capita income, economic productivity or urbanization.[33] In our typological scheme, all the consistent occupants of the MNC cell (Paraguay, Nicaragua, El Salvador and Haiti) are among the least developed countries of the region, although in the "transitional" and upper ranks of non-militariness and competitive-ness a good deal of overlap occurs.

A simple and direct means for controlling for the possible effect of economic development is to correlate an indicator of it (in this case, $ income per capita ca. 1961) with the various policy indicators.[34] Where no significant correlation emerges, the initial finding is sustained. Where one does occur, we can analyze the residuals from the regression to dis-cover the probable marginal impact of regime-type upon these patterns of public spending and accomplishment.

The first significant finding is that very few of the policy indicators correlate more than .500 (approximately significant at the .05 level) with per capita income. The outcomes of total government expenditures, budget balance, centralization of revenue, public investment, social and welfare expenditures, defence spending and all the indicators of gross outcomes[35] are *not* that closely linked to levels of economic development.

Only three significant correlations emerge which merit closer scrutiny: (1) Total government revenue as % of GNP (+ .652); (2) Indirect taxation as a % of total government revenue (− .537); (3) $ expenditures per soldier (+ .630). Here, we must reexamine the relation between regime type and policy output while controlling for the level of develop-ment.

Figure III and table II* demonstrate both the overall relation of total government revenue and per capita income and the breakdown of the residuals from the regression by regime-type. For example, the equation predicts that Chile should have a total government revenue of 20.4% of its GNP while El Salvador is expected to have 15.5% of its GNP going to public authorities. The actual, or better observed, value for Chile is 25.7%—5.3% more than predicted—while El Salvador had 14.2%—

* Figure III, "Plot of government revenue from all sources as a % of GNP (ca. 1961) by per capita gross national product (ca. 1961)," and table II, "Total govern-ment revenue and per capita income," have been omitted.

1.3% less than anticipated. Brazil has an extraordinary, positive 10.3% residual and Mexico an extraordinary, negative 10.1% residual.[36]

Grouped by MI and PC, the greater differentiating impact of the latter is readily apparent. All the low competitive regimes (with the marginal exception of Bolivia [+ 1.0%]) are getting less resources than predicted while the highly competitive ones are predominantly above the regression line. Costa Rica and Panama are very slightly below it and only poor Guatemala is markedly "out of line" (− 5.1%) with its level of economic development. There is little doubt from the pattern of residuals that decreasing MI tends to be associated with positive residuals, but there are more exceptions and overlaps: Colombia and Mexico in the low intervention category and Brazil, Peru and Ecuador at the intermediate level. Nevertheless, the regression provides supplemental evidence that, regardless of level of development, the more competitive and less military regimes are more capable of extracting resources for the pursuit of public policies. Mythology to the contrary notwithstanding, enlarged participation and voluntary compliance seem to be more effective for this purpose than enlightened autocracy and governmental coercion.

Indirect taxation,* especially through levies on exports and imports,[37] has historically been the major source of government revenue. Economic development has brought a diversification of resources and a decline in the importance of this regressive tax—hence there is a high negative correlation with per capita income. The residuals seem to indicate, however, that militarism may be a key intervening variable in this transformation. Again with the exception of Costa Rica, all the countries with quiescent military establishments get much less of their revenue indirectly. Some of those with "transitional" establishments (Ecuador, Peru and Venezuela) also have followed suit. Only Panama (− 5.7%) and Paraguay (− 8.5%) seriously challenge our finding that military regimes prefer or retain indirect taxation schemes. Competitiveness has no such regular an impact.

For the last issue arena in which economic development seems to play a partially determinant role, $ expenditures per soldier,** no clear pattern emerges from the residuals. Countries at intermediate levels of competitiveness seem to have a noticeable propensity for spending more on the capitalization of their military establishments (especially, Venezuela, with a positive residual of $4,258!). This observation doesn't hold for Argentina (− $2,017) or for those highly competitive regimes which may be bribing their respective militaries a bit (Chile [+ $253]; Ecuador [+ $241]; Costa Rica [+$136]). By and large the non-competitives seem more self-confident and less lavish in bestowing favors on their defence forces, except for Nicaragua. Nevertheless, the pattern is only suggestive, hardly conclusive.

But, one may quite legitimately interject, level of development is not the only environment condition which might conceivably reduce the signifi-

---

* Table III, "Indirect taxation and per capita income," has been omitted.
** Table IV, "Expenditure per soldier and per capita income," has been omitted.

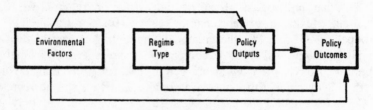

Figure IV. A model of the "rigid environmental determination" of policy outputs and policy outcomes

cance of the bivariate relationships we have uncovered between regime-types and such outputs as total resources, tax systems, welfare and defence spending to spuriousness. Other antecedent variables beyond the control of actors could be exerting a determinant impact upon both sets of apparently related variables. Controlling for these might make intervention and competitiveness as epiphenomenal as the "cynical" hypotheses suggested.

To test for this possibility, I propose we adopt the "extreme" theoretical posture of "rigid environmental determinism." Conditions antecedent to the political system and beyond its short-term control are accepted as independent givens, establishing strict parameters upon decision-makers. All the variation in outputs and outcomes which we can find associated probabilistically with such parametric elements are considered to have been "caused" by them. The influence of the political system (in this event, as operationalized by the regime typologies) is strictly marginal. Once the environment has been given maximum and exclusive credit for determining outputs and outcomes, we will ask: What variation is left which might be linked to the characteristics of the political system? And how does this vary according to regime-type?

The technique for operationalizing this primitive and extreme theory of policy-making is merely an extension of the one already utilized above. Instead of just a single environmental control (per capita income), we will enter a large number of possible determinants into a multiple regression with the outputs and outcomes as the dependent variables. First, we shall see how well this battery of factors manages to predict public policies in Latin America, i.e., we will discover if there, indeed, remains some "elusive" residual variance for politics to explain. If it does appear that the environment is not omnipotent as a predictor, we may then ask how the residuals cluster by regime-type.

To render the environmental data more manipulable (and to transform them in a manner compatible with the multiple regression causal model), some 126 variables from the cross-sectional data bank were factor analyzed and given a varimax orthogonal rotation to facilitate interpretation.[38] This "pool of variance" produced eight orthogonal or uncorrelated factors.

Deletion of variables, various rotational options, independent manipulation of two ten-unit subsets (Central America and Caribbean vs. South America) and a replication with 1950 data resulted in essentially the same structure of relationships, so I propose to consider them as the principal components of the contemporary Latin American social, economic and cultural environment and to use the factor scores obtained for the twenty units as the independent variables in the following regressions.

The eight factors I have labeled: (1) Modernization/development; (2) Commercial dependence upon the United States; (3) Size; (4) Dependence upon United States private capital, especially in petroleum; (5) *Hispanismo* or catholic-mestizo culture; (6) Client dependence upon United States economic aid; (7) Amerindian; (8) Density. For the variable loadings from which these labels were derived see appendix II of this essay.

Table V. Environmental Factors (8) and the Prediction of Policy Outputs and Outcomes ca. 1960

		Multiple R	Percent of unexplained variation	Single best predictor*	Partial R
I.	**Outputs**				
I.1.	Total government revenue from all sources/GNP (1961)	.818	33%	DEVT	+.671
I.2.	Total government expenditures (average 1960-65)	.681	54	HISPANO	+.532
I.3.	Balance between central government expenditures and revenues (average 1960-63)	.749	44	COMERCE	+.493
I.4.	Central governmental revenues as % of total government revenues (1960)	.944	11	HISPANO	+.600
I.5.	Direct taxes as % of total central government revenue 1960)	.800	36%	DEVT	+.484
I.6.	Indirect taxes as % of total central government revenue (1960)	.870	24	DEVT	−.567

128   *Philippe C. Schmitter*

		Multiple R	Percent of unex-plained variation	Single best predictor	Partial R
I.7.	Taxes on exports and imports as % of total central government revenue (1960)	.910	17	SIZE	−.746
I.8.	Public investment as % of GNP (1960)	.731	47	CAPITAL	+.620
I.9.	Capital outlay as % of total central government expenditures (1961)	.854	27	CAPITAL	+.604
I.10.	Social expenditures as % of central government expenditures (1960)	.570	68	COMMERCE	+.342
I.11.	Social expenditures as % of central government expenditures (1960)	.434	81	CAPITAL	+.299
I.12.	Educational expenditures as % of central government expenditures (1960)	.680	54	SIZE	−.432
I.13.	Educational expenditures as % of GNP (1959)	.889	21	COMMERCE	+.632
I.14.	Health expenditures as % of central government expenditures (1960)	.575	67	COMMERCE	+.436
I.15.	Defence expenditures as % of central government expenditures (1960)	.696	52%	CLIENTS	−.398
I.16.	Defence expenditures as % of GNP (1960)	.461	79	DENSITY	+.391
I.17.	Defence expenditures per soldier (1960)	.976	5	CAPITAL	+.846

	Multiple R	Percent of unexplained variation	Single best predictor	Partial R
I.18. Average annual increase in defence spending (1960)	.583	66	COMERCE	−.379
II. Outcomes				
II.1. Per capita average annual increase in GNP (1960-65)	.729	47	COMERCE	+.418
II.2. Average annual increase in industrial production (1960-65)	.776	40	COMERCE	+.617
II.3. Average annual rate of gross national investment as % of GDP (1960-65)	.858	26	DENSITY	−.466
II.4. Average annual percentile increase in export earnings (1960-65)	.823	32	INDIO	+.484
II.5. Average annual percentile increase in imports (1960-65)	.739	45	DEVT	−.466
II.6. Average annual rate of inflation (1960-65)	.818	33	SIZE	+.650
II.7 Total increase in primary and secondary school enrollment (1960-65)	.851	28	CAPITAL	+.657
II.8. Total increase in university enrollment (1960-65)	.846	29%	HISPANO	+.673
II.9. Total magnitude of civil strife (1961-65)	.659	57	CAPITAL	+.515

* Coded abbreviations for eight factors: DEVT = modernization and development; COMERCE = commercial dependence; SIZE = size; CAPITAL = dependence on foreign capital and investment; HISPANO = catholic, hispanic culture; INDIO = amerindian population; CLIENT = dependence upon United States aid; DENSITY = density of population and transport.

In table V, these eight factors combine in a linear additive manner to predict the output and outcome indicators. The multiple R column shows that some relatively high levels of prediction are obtained, although there often remains an ample margin within which regime-types may make their contribution. The percent of unexplained variance is a rather crude index of this, derived by subtracting R^2 (proportion of explained variance) from 100. A perusal of this column provides an interesting confirmation of a speculative point advanced earlier. The combined battery of environmental factors does an impressive job of predicting the gross aggregative outcomes (multiple R's from .851 to .729), except for the total magnitude of civil strife. Politics seems to have more to do with this outcome. The environment is a bit less proficient in estimating the total level and balance of government resources. The very high multiple correlation (.944) with the extent of centralization of government revenue calls into question our earlier inference, that military intervention might be responsible for such a concentration. Also the relatively high levels of prediction concerning the nature of the tax system (.800, .870, .910) suggest that regime-type may be less important in determining this output than we had earlier supposed through bivariate analysis.

Where the environmental factors do a poor job is in the prediction of patterns of public expenditure. Except for educational spending as % of GNP and $ expenditures per soldier, Latin American governments seem to be exercising considerable actor discretion in how they allocate their resources—either as a percent of the budget or of GNP. From 52 to 81% of the total variance is left unaccounted for, even assuming complete environmental determinism. This, to me, is evidence of a strong impact of political system characteristics in these issue areas. Below, we shall concentrate on the analysis of the residuals from these predictive equations.

Another confirmation of a previous inference comes from examining the policy outcomes in table V. The eight factors, by and large, do well in estimating the dependent values while as we noted above, there are few significant differences between regime-type as concerns these variables. As I hypothesized above, political system characteristics are more clearly related to outputs—those deliberate attempts to cope with or transform the environment—and much less clearly associated with concatenated indicators of global success or failure. The direct arrow in figure IV from the environment to policy outcomes, bypassing both the regime and its outputs, is an important line of determination. Governments in Latin America seem only very marginally capable of modifying their overall system performance given the strong "parametric" relevance of such factors as external dependence, ethnic stratification, size and density.

The indicator of total magnitude of civil strife, however, is not as environmentally determined. Here, regime-type, especially in the case of those semi-competitive, "transitionally" militaristic countries, may be significant, as we observed above.

Table VI. Social Welfare Expenditures as a % of GNP and Environmental Factors: An Analysis of the Residual Effect of Regime-Types ca. 1960

	Military intervention	*Party competitiveness*	
Low	CHI + .15% UGY No data (assumed +) COS + 2.20 COL − 2.26 BOL − 1.31 MEX − 2.09	CHI + .15% UGY no data (assumed +) COS + 2.20 BRA + .59 GUA + .40 PER + 2.75 PAN + .71 ECU + .31	High
Trans- itional	BRA + .59 PER + 2.75 ECU + .31 GUA + .40 VEN + .17 ARG + .84 CUB − 2.62	VEN + .17 ARG + .84 COL − 2.26 HON − .37 DOM − 1.82	Moder- ate
High	PAN + .71 HAI + .30 NIC + 1.10 ELS + 3.08 PGY − 2.14 HON − .37 DOM − 1.82	HAI + .30 NIC + 1.10 ELS + 3.08 PGY − 2.14 BOL − 1.31 MEX − 2.09 CUB − 2.62	Low

Table V also reveals why our previous use of per capita income as a control variable was so ineffectual. The Modernization/Development factor (per capita incomes loads + .889 on it) is not the best partial predictor among the eight factors. Except in those areas we already discussed (total government revenue and direct vs. indirect taxation), allocative policies in Latin America seem relatively insensitive to variation in this complex of interrelated conditions.[39] *The most impressive environmental determinants of how resources are extracted and distributed are those related to external dependence*—above all commercial dependence upon the United States followed closely by private capital dependence. In these "penetrated political systems," the most severe constraints upon public policy-makers seem to be imposed not by internal political structures or the overall level of economic development, but by outside actors and actions. No understanding of policy-making—at least not in this region of the world—can be complete without the systematic consideration of external dependence (in all its three forms: commercial, capital and clientelistic) as an independent variable.[40]

Again, limitations of time and space preclude our analyzing the residuals from each of the multiple regressions. Let us concentrate on that range of outputs which our analysis has pinpointed as providing regime-types with their greatest margin for manoeuvre: public expenditures on social welfare, education and defence.

The residuals from the regression on social welfare spending show a pattern which was only weakly discernible by bivariate analysis of variance. Military intervention has an almost randomizing effect, with some tendency to concentrate higher than predicted welfare expenditures in transitional regimes. Partisan competitiveness has, on the contrary, a striking impact. Every single one of the highly competitive regimes ca. 1960 had a positive residual, i.e., was spending more than it "should have" on welfare! The noncompetitive regimes had predominately negative residuals with the interesting exceptions of Nicaragua (1.1% more than expected or 2.8%) and El Salvador (3.1% above its predicted value of 3.9%).[41] Polities with moderately competitive party systems were rather sharply divided between two with positive errors of prediction (Venezuela and Argentina) and three with negative errors (Colombia, Honduras and the Dominican Republic). The latter three were decidedly less competitive than the former two ca. 1960, although reversals have since occurred. From table VI, it can be affirmed that, all things being equal, the more competitive regimes in Latin America do tend to spend more of their resources on social welfare than the less competitive.

With educational expenditures the pattern is much less clear.* For one thing, this is the only expenditure policy which the environmental factors predicted quite well, leaving little residual variance for regime-types to explain. The original bivariate observation that competitiveness accounted for a greater significance of difference than military intervention continues valid—the MI residuals are quite scattered—but so are the PC residuals. There is a cluster of highly competitive countries which are spending more than anticipated. However, the three most competitive Central Americans (Costa Rica, Guatemala and Panama) spend less, while that subregion's least competitive regimes (Nicaragua and El Salvador) spend more! Another interesting cluster is formed by Mexico and Colombia, both civilian non-competitive regimes at that time, and both with large negative residuals. Perhaps, Bolivia would join this group were the data available. In summary, the evidence suggests that, all things being equal, neither MI or PC has a major impact on overall educational spending which seems to be determined mostly by the respective environmental contexts of the countries.[42]

The residual pattern as regards defence expenditures is, however, unambiguous.** Those Latin American countries with a politically quiescent

---

* Table VII, "Educational expenditures as a % of GNP," has been omitted.
** Table VIII, "Defence expenditures as a % of GNP," has been omitted.

military spend less on defence even after all other factors have been considered. The big spenders are (with the exception of the Dominican Republic) grouped in the "transitional" category. In their moves in and out of political life, the military seem to be driving up costs—perhaps as the civilian elites competing for their support attempt to buy them out (or in). Puzzlingly, two countries which were just beginning to experience an armed insurrectionary, guerrilla effort in 1960 (Venezuela and Guatemala) were spending less than the general equation predicted.[43]

Before switching to the analysis of longitudinal data, let us look at the two issue areas in which we have found some evidence of a more satisfactory developmental performance for military regimes. The distributions were not different to a statistically significant degree, but the "high" military regimes did have the highest mean value for average annual rates of industrial growth and the lowest mean value for average annual rates of inflation (both 1960–65).*

The distribution of residuals does provide some confirmation of the earlier bivariate finding. Only Chile and Costa Rica among the "low" MI countries had more industrial growth than one would have predicted from their environment alone; whereas such solidly military-ruled countries as Nicaragua, El Salvador, Paraguay, Panama and Honduras did even better proportionally. The coercive-restrictive formula is not infallible, however, as the Dominican Republic (− 4.5%!) and Haiti (− 1.3%) testify. Those with on-again, off-again military rules are rather evenly split. Partisan competition has a much less predictable effect. Nevertheless, before we leap to the conclusion that, despite their consistently inferior record on the promotion of "progressive" policy outputs and the absence of any significant differences in rates of investment, public or private, somehow the military manage to be associated with better overall rates of growth, we must observe that the possible marginal effect is very slight. Environmental factors seem to set very strict parameters, regardless of who occupies the roles of formal executive sovereignty. Countries commercially dependent upon the United States, with a stronger catholic and mestizo background and larger in population and area grew faster, more-or-less regardless of who governed them or how.

Control of inflation and the suppression of "demogogic" spending are frequently cited as motives by *golpistas* and, by the mean values of table I, those countries overtly run by their military establishments did have the lowest annual rates of inflation from 1960–65 (and the most balanced budgets 1960–63). But through the analysis of residuals, their performance becomes less impressive. The environmental characteristics in fact predict a deflationary economy for four of them: El Salvador, Honduras, Panama, and the Dominican Republic and a very low rate of increase for

---

* Tables IX, "Average annual rate of industrial growth and environmental factors," and X, "Average annual rate of inflation and environmental factors," have been omitted.

Nicaragua (+ 0.4%). Their smaller size, lesser development and high commercial dependence upon the United States all contribute significantly to lowering their "natural" propensity for inflation. Given the lower pressures for driving up costs, we are entitled to be a bit sceptical about giving their military rulers all the credit. In fact those who did exceptionally well in controlling price levels were Mexico, Argentina, Colombia and Ecuador —they had a very unfavorable context within which to make policy and managed to make it effectively. Brazil, Uruguay and Chile also had a series of similar structural impediments, but got more than they "deserved." This suggests that too competitive a party system can be a liability in contemporary Latin America, although Ecuador, Costa Rica and Peru have not done badly.

A Bivariate, Longitudinal Analysis

Sectioning the Latin American republics at a single point in time, we have uncovered a series of interesting and suggestive associations between different regime-types and different patterns of public policy. First and foremost, we have shown that certain basic dimensions of the structure of authority in these systems, i.e., their "civilianness" and their degree of partisan competition, are relevant to predicting policy *outputs*—although they are less capable of contributing to our understanding of overall system performance, or *outcomes* as they have been labelled here. Even when controlling for a very inclusive set of possible environmental determinants, the residual or marginal impact of regime-type persists in key areas of public expenditure.

So far we have deliberately avoided making two types of inferences. We have not interpreted our cross-sectional findings as "proving" that such associations persist over time, "causing" the contemporary low scorers to advance along some regression line established by the more developed or more autonomous units. For example, we have established (ca. 1960) that the percent of total government revenue obtained from indirect taxes tends to decline with an increase in per capita gross national product. In fact for each $100 increase in the latter, there is a 4% decrease in the former. The cross-sectional data provides us with no grounds for inferring that as, say El Salvador, moves from its present (1960) per capita income of $267 to $367, it will concomitantly be propelled by some unspecified process mechanism to reduce its present 76% dependence upon indirect taxes by 4%, regardless of regime-type.[44] As James Coleman has pointed out, to make such an inference from data at a single point in time "assumes, either implicitly or explicitly, that the causal processes have resulted in an equilibrium state. That is, the implicit assumption in regression analysis is that this is a stable relationship, which would give the same value for the regression coefficients in a later cross section unless an exogenous factor disturbed the situation."[45] Leaving aside the general issue of natural equilibria in systems with rapidly changing parameters, we have shown rather convincingly that, in such penetrated societies as those of Latin America, exogeneous variables—especially the level of commercial and financial dependence on the United States—do determine a wide range of outcomes, including the rate of GNP increase. We have, therefore, even less grounds for accepting such an assumption in this area of the world than among more developed and less externally vulnerable political systems.

By rerunning some of our cross-tabulations (where data was available) for 1965, we have introduced a pseudo-time dimension—another cross-section five years later. Although space limitation precluded presentation of all the data, it may be gleaned from the probabilities reported in table I that most of the relationships stood the test of time. Despite the fact that a large number of regimes switched from civilian to military during this period (and, in the process, became much less electorally competitive) similarly significant distributions emerged, evidence that maybe it is not so hazardous as we believed to make longitudinal inferences from cross-sectional analyses.

The second inference we have avoided is to assert that relationships present within the universe of all Latin American countries will explain causality within every subsample of these countries or within each country.[46] Hence, even if El Salvador were to decrease its dependence upon indirect taxes in the predicted direction and by the predicted amount, this does not necessarily imply that the same causal agents or processes were at work as in the rest of Latin America. Inversely, just because a country does not change as predicted does not prove that identical causal agents were not at work. These might have been effectively present but neutralized by the impact of unspecified parametric conditions not present in the whole universe.[47]

Serial or longitudinal analysis of data for each unit across time provides a means for overcoming some of these limitations. In addition, it has a number of other advantages. Serial data tends to be more reliable and comparable in that within unit variations in record-keeping are minimal compared with the problems involved in assuring equivalence across units. Most importantly, its use permits us to escape from the assumption of simultaneity, i.e., that relationships between social and political processes have an immediate effect. Examination of changes over time within each unit permits us to search for lags (and leads) in the timing of relationships.[48]

One primitive way of analyzing longitudinal information is simply to plot it over time for each unit. By superimposing regime changes (by *golpe, imposición* or *elección*) upon the plot, we can get a visual impression of the evolution of public policy under the aegis of different types of political actors. We can also get an image of the general trend of spending in that issue area as it responds to such structural or environmental conditions as increases in economic development, inflows of private foreign capital and increments in United States economic and military aid—irrespective of such "epiphenomenal" or "superstructural" occurrences as regime changes.

Again, limitations of space make it impossible to examine all of our outputs and outcomes over time. Therefore, I have had to be selective in terms of both indicators and units. We will focus our attention on those policy areas in which the cross-sectional analysis demonstrated the greatest sensitivity to political system characteristics: total public expenditures, direct taxation, education and defence spending and, for contrast, on one output where no significant relationship was discovered: public investment.* As for units of analysis I propose to examine four "pairs" of countries which have had a somewhat similar history of regime-types.

Chile and Venezuela

Chile has had a consistently civilian and competitive regime for the entire period; Venezuela has had the same only since 1958.[49] In both cases, executive power has been peacefully transferred to an opposition party by means of open electoral competition. Venezuela's per capita GNP is higher, but the size, complexity and extent of external dependence of the two societies can be considered roughly comparable.

The pattern of total government expenditures shows contradictory trends in the two countries. Rapid increase in Venezuela was associated with military non-competitive rule (November 1952–January 1958). The ensuing years of competitive civilian rule have produced a secular proportional decline in the role of government as measured by total spending. In Chile, from the depths of Ibañez's reign (1952–58), competitiveness has been associated with the inverse. Interestingly, the conservative regime of Alessandri (1958–64) increased government revenues from 16 to 25% of GNP. Frei's subsequent appearance again drove them up significantly during his first year in office.

Both countries clearly have had problems with military spending. The wide fluctuations in values are particularly great in the Chilean case, despite its reputation for having a quiescent and apolitical military (a reputation somewhat tarnished by the quasi-*golpe* of 1969). Populist civilian rule there and military rule in Venezuela brought with them large injections

---

* For the paired cases which follow, only graphs on defence expenditure have been included. Figures V, VII–XI, XIII–XVI, XVIII–XXI, and XXIII–XXIV have been omitted.

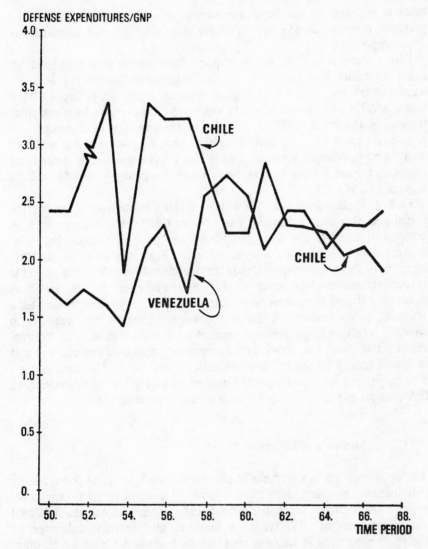

Figure VI. Defence expenditures as a % of GNP from 1950–1967—Chile and Venezuela

of funds for the military. In Chile, there has come a subsequent secular decline, especially since 1961; whereas Venezuela remains trapped in a stalemated series of cyclical variations around a constant mean of 2.25% of GNP.

Educational spending in both follows a more even, incrementalist, pattern of gradual increase—with, however, somewhat greater cyclical variation in Chile. The impact of competitiveness after 1958–9 in Venezuela is apparent in the large increases in education expenditures. The previous military dictatorship of Pérez Jiménez followed diametrically opposite policies.

Direct taxation in Chile seems trapped (admittedly, at a high level for Latin America) in a pattern of cyclical stagnation. Its returns wax and wane rather independently of regime changes, never exceeding 44% of total central government revenue. In Venezuela, however, we have evidence, replicating the cross-sectional findings, of the capacity of a competitive regime to extract not only more resources from its populace, but to do so in a more egalitarian manner. Direct taxes have risen consistently and cumulatively since the end of the Pérez Jiménez regime—except for a slight setback in 1961–62.

Earlier we failed to establish any significant relationship between the magnitude of public investment (as a % of GNP), and regime-types. A comparison of Chile and Venezuela shows one possible reason why. Allocative policy in this area seems very erratic, especially in Chile, and exhibits neither the incremental pattern we found in education nor the cyclical stalemate which seems to characterize defence spending or direct taxation. Perhaps in systems lacking an effective commitment to long-term planning, public investment becomes a residual category very sensitive to windfall surpluses in government revenue or to the availability of external credit. Venezuela's less erratic investment policy may be a reflection of that country's strong budgetary position and its low level of dependence on foreign public grants and loans. In neither case have we much evidence to link changes in public investment with system competitiveness.

Mexico and Colombia

Similar as they are in a number of parametric conditions, the communality that interests us particularly is that both have civilian, non-competitive regimes; Mexico for the entire period and Colombia since the National Front agreement of 1957. There is, however, an important difference. In the former, rotation in office takes place between factions of a well-organized, well-entrenched party; in the latter, two separate parties have agreed to exchange the spoils of executive office periodically (*alternación*) and evenly (*paridad*). They continue, however, to compete with each other at other levels of the political system as well as with a rising number of opposition parties left out of the original deal.

The total expenditures of Mexico's central government are a model of consistency. Except for slight spurts, linked perhaps to presidential successions,[50] the proportion of GNP extracted for public purposes has remained constant—while, of course, GNP was increasing rapidly. Colombia's total spending has been much more erratic, before *and* after 1958. Like

Mexico, the proportion is low by Latin American standards, e.g. they have large negative residuals, but unlike Mexico it has been marked by cyclical irregularity and a secular trend toward higher values. As was earlier the case with Venezuela, the initial spurt towards greater political penetration of the economic system came under the aegis of authoritarian military rule. A second spurt began nine years later, this time during the Liberal regime of Lleras Camargo (1958–62). It seems clear that *alternación* in Colombia means significant proportional changes (back and forth) in overall government spending; whereas *continuación* in Mexico does not.

In education, Mexico has followed a more evenly incremental policy than Colombia, again evidence that its non-competitive system has been providing the political coverage for an essentially bureaucratic decision-making process. The latter's educational spending was apparently more subject to the vagaries of politics—declining under military dictatorship (1957) and rising rapidly in the years of Liberal rule (1960–62). Since then Colombia's pseudo-competitiveness has been associated with the by now all too familiar pattern of a cyclical stalemate—rises and falls above and below a more or less constant mean.

The extraordinary consistency of Mexican policy-making is nowhere better illustrated than by defence spending—a standard deviation of only .08 around a mean of .71% of GNP. For Colombia, we find confirmation that military rule tends to bring with it and in its wake higher levels of military expenditures. Shortly after the spending linked to the Rojas Pinilla regime[51] had returned to normal, the level rose again—not, one may hypothesize as a side product of revived, if controlled, party competitiveness, but as an indirect result of the emerging guerrilla threat. The subsequent leveling off does suggest that this regime-type may be the most successful at limiting military purchases, particularly when compared with the continued erratic fluctuations of Chile which has never had to face such an armed threat.

Finally, we find some evidence of possible policy irregularity in Mexico, albeit in a regressive direction. Direct taxes declined rapidly during the Alemán and Ruiz Cortines regimes (1946–1958), rose under Lopez Mateos (1958–64), only to fall again in the first year that Diaz Ordaz was in office. The relation of these trends to regime periods does suggest that they reflect deliberate policy rather than the vagaries of income distribution and tax collection. The cross-sectional relation between GNP and direct taxation merely recorded the static fact that Mexico's attained level was high (it had a residual of +7.4% in 1960) and ignored the dynamic fact that reliance on these presumably more egalitarian sources of revenue had been declining steadily since 1951 with increases in per capita income.

Colombia's record with direct taxation is more similar to that of Chile, albeit with greater fluctuations about a constant mean. The level is high, the highest in Latin America to be exact, and the variations seem more

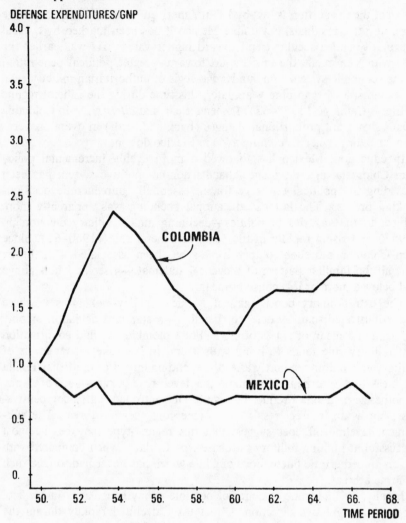

Figure XII. Defence expenditures as a % of GNP from 1950–1967—Mexico and Colombia

related to "super-structural" cycles of evasion and amnesty than to more structural determinants such as regime-type, development or prosperity due to external trade. Only a detailed case-study can confirm or reject this supposition, however.

Data on public investment in Colombia (comparable Mexican data were not available) controvert our earlier hypothesis that policy in this area was likely to be quite erratic due to the residual and episodic manner in which such investments were made. The role of the Colombian government has been modest but it shows a clear relation to regime changes and demonstrates (after 1960) that civilian regimes, if quasi-competitive, tend to effect more sustained policy changes than do military regimes. We find a "peak" clearly associated with the Rojas Pinilla regime (we have found similar ones in the plots on total expenditures, defence spending and educational spending [inverted]). This is an instance of what might be called a pattern of "demagogic policy"—a remarkable, rapid (and presumably well-publicized) effort in certain policy areas, followed by an almost equally rapid return to the *status quo ante*. The Venezuelan data show Pérez Jiménez doing the same thing. Edwin Lieuwen has caught the essence of this particular policy cycle and associates it with certain forms of military rule:

> Even in those few cases in the past when the military were in the vanguard of the forces of change, their leaders nearly always perverted or distorted the original aims of the revolution. Reform-minded military leaders generally came to power with a majority of the people behind them. For a short time, they drew upon a reservoir of popular support, launched ambitious projects for economic development, and enacted social-welfare measures. Yet, somehow, these regimes became more totalitarian and eventually stopped their drive for reform. It appeared at times as though the new military rulers were psychologically unprepared to accept authentically popular solutions to their national problems.
>
> The record shows that the military leader's ardor for reform generally cools rapidly in the aftermath of victory, slowing any program of social advancement.[52]

These spurts of pseudo-reform under military sponsorship, while they may leave an important residue of inflated expectations and exacerbated rancor, do seem to return the political system more-or-less to where it started from the aggregate perspective of public revenue and expenditures.

El Salvador and Nicaragua

Two military-dominated polities with rigged systems of party competition, the former with a reputation for progressive policy-making, the latter frequently taken as the model of an atavistic traditional dictatorship, El Salvador and Nicaragua offer attractive comparative possibilities. Size and level of development differ only by the relativistic criteria of Central America and both have thoroughly dependent economies although admittedly in different products.

The impact of El Salvador's reformist military rulers, Osorio (1950–56) and Lemus (1956–60), is immediately apparent from the data on government expenditures. In this case not only did government expenditures rise dramatically but they were consolidated at this level and did not collapse when they were overthrown in 1960–61. Since then, expenditures have varied around a constant norm. Nicaragua, on the other hand, is a

model of incrementalism. Despite a few fluctuations in the aftermath of
Anastasio Somoza's assassination in 1956, it subsequently followed the
gradualist path we have come to associate with tight oligarchic, non-competitive rule.

Again, in educational spending, Nicaragua has been consistently incrementalist. El Salvador's pattern also parallels that of its total expenditures:
rapid rise associated with military reformism and subsequent consolidation. This is a pattern which we have not encountered before and one
which conforms *grosso modo* to the speculations of Charles W. Anderson
concerning the policy-making process in Latin America. According to
him, change occurs by cooptation of those who have demonstrated a certain command over one of a variety of power resources and by a renego-
tiation of the distribution of benefits which, however, protects as much as
possible existing statuses, subsidies, privileges and exemptions—corporate
and individual. Policy changes then by sedimentation: rapid innovation as
a new coalition is being formed (usually by the expanding-sum expedient
of creating new public resources) and then a stable *plateau* of more-or-less
constant expenditures—perhaps punctuated by shallow cycles as contending coalitional "partners" test each other's strength. Some countries like
Mexico attained this *plateau* before our data series started. El Salvador
attained it during the series. Consistent incremental change such as we
have found in Nicaraguan, Chilean and Mexican educational expenditures,
stale-mated fluctuation with large cycles as in Venezuelan and Chilean
defence spending, Chilean public investment or Colombian direct taxation,
or "demagogic" boom and bust cycles as in Colombia and Venezuela are
incompatible with such a sedimentary process of policy formation.

Defence spending in El Salvador is quite stable over the long run, belying
the cross-sectional inference that protracted and overt military rule is
associated with high average annual increases in defence budgets from
1960 to 1963. The Nicaragua trend line is upward with an enormous bulge
coming immediately prior to Anastasio Somoza's *continuista* efforts and
assassination in 1956. Defence spending never returned to the low 1951–
52 norm and has shown a tendency to increase in recent years—perhaps
a reflection of sporadic guerrilla opposition rather than regime-related
pressures.

For Nicaragua the pattern is clear—no interest in increasing direct taxation regardless of possible parametric pressures.[53] For El Salvador the
pattern is equally clear—frustration of reformist measures instituted early
in the "revolutionary" Osorio regime followed by sporadic efforts in the
late 1950's and 1960's at "modernizing" the country's tax base.

In public investment both countries show a generally positive trend line
probably reflecting societal and market forces rather than deliberate policy
—*except* for the startlingly great increase in Nicaragua from 1955 to 1957.
Cynically, one might note its coincidence with the spurt in military spending
and assume that the public investment went into tanks, machine guns and

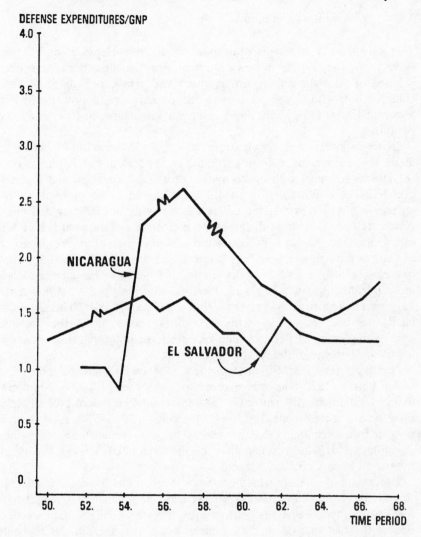

Figure XVII. Defence expenditures as a % of GNP from 1950–1967—El Salvador and Nicaragua

officers' salaries, but Charles Anderson assures us that most of it went into road building, electric power, commodity stabilization, industrial loans and a new social security system.[54] Public investment fell off sharply after 1957 (it is doubtful that given its resource base and penetrated economy, Nicaragua could have sustained such *étatisme* without major structural reforms in property relations), but never regressed to its *status quo ante* level and has since expanded cyclically.

Argentina and Peru

This may seem a rather disparate pair (in size, development and dependence) but they do share one important communality: both have been plagued by sporadic military intervention and erratic periods of partisan competitiveness until recently, when the military seized power with the apparent intention of ruling both countries for a more-or-less protracted period.

In total government expenditures, Peru would seem to be trying to attain the sedimentary pattern suggested by Anderson, but failing to consolidate its advances with the formation of a stable coalition and distribution of benefits. Whether this should be attributed to the problems of incorporating APRA within the policy apparatus due to military and elitist resistance or to conditions dictated by the external environment is an interesting potential subject for a case-study. Nevertheless, the global pattern of central government spending is one of frustrated sedimentation. Also one cannot help but observe that the major increases have been associated with military rule: 1951–56, 1962–63 and presumably, although the data are not reported, the present Velasco regime (1968–). This definitely challenges both our cross-sectional findings and some of the previous longitudinal ones. In Peru, civilian regimes have not noticeably expanded the financial power of the central government.

Nor have they done so in Argentina. The major increase took place under Perón (1955—he was overthrown in September) and Aramburu in 1958. Otherwise, the pattern is the by now familiar one of cyclical stalemate with a recent tendency toward stagnation (1961–67). Also there is no evidence here that GNP increases (however erratic) are propelling governments to take a larger piece of the expanding pie—as one might infer from Peru, Chile and Nicaragua.

Except for the beating that education took under Perón, spending in this arena for Argentina has been cyclical but gradual and cumulative, less I would hypothesize the consequence of regime changes, than a reflection of the fact that of all the countries examined Argentina is the only one with a substantially literate population, a developed educational system and a low birth rate. In this context policy innovation is more likely to be structural than allocative, hence not easily measured by changes in the gross rate of sectoral expenditures.

Peru, however, shows an extraordinary pattern of cumulative increases in educational spending coinciding with the election of Prado in 1956 and continuing unabated and unaffected by regime changes thereafter, until in 1965 and 1966, it had attained the highest level in Latin America. Rolland Paulston in his excellent monograph on Peruvian educational policy, however, provides us with the sort of detailed case study with which it is essential to complement these cruder aggregate analyses. He argues with convincing evidence that despite such rises in expenditure, "the social class-linked education structure reflects and perpetuates the hierar-

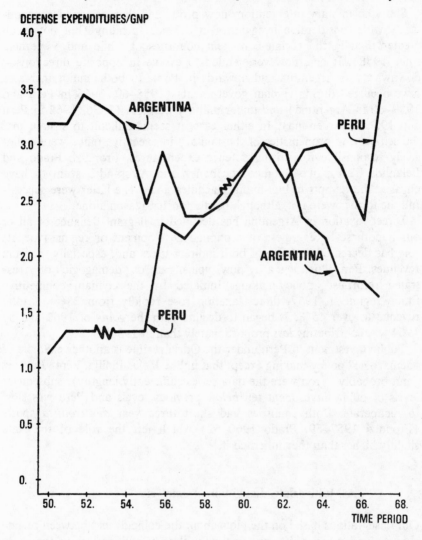

Figure XXII. Defence expenditures as a % of GNP from 1950–1967— Argentina and Peru

chical social system and in so doing obstructs educational rationalization and development." Among other things, he observes that 95% of total expenditures goes for teachers' salaries and that a good bit of the remaining 5% is paid as rent to private individuals who own a substantial proportion of the classrooms.[55] This certainly suggests that we exercise great caution before interpreting apparently comparable aggregate findings as evidence of relative "development," "progress," "equality" or "welfare." Simply spending more, even on such a desirable public good as education, may not facilitate the accomplishment of "a better life for all."

Sporadic military intervention, now protracted, has occurred concomitantly with considerable irregularity in defence spending (but not much greater than in the regime-consistent countries of Chile and Venezuela since 1958). It has, however, tended to evolve in opposite directions—downwards in Argentina and upwards in Peru. In both, major increases have occurred during civilian governments (1958–60, 1966 in Peru and 1959–60 in Argentina) *and* under military auspices (1956, 1962 in Peru and 1956 in Argentina). In either case, it seems difficult to sustain that the self-serving propensities of the military in executive office were exclusively responsible for raising defence expenditures. Frondizi, Prado and Belaunde Terry, like Betancourt, Ibañez and Alessandri, seem to have engaged in attempts to buy military acquiescence. The latter were successful; the former were not, although hardly for that reason alone.

Direct taxation in Argentina has declined in flagrant defiance of all of our hypotheses. Regardless of economic development or regime-type, its role has decreased in favor of both indirect taxes and, especially, non-tax revenues. Peru illustrates a by now typical case of "demagogic" or "frustrated reformist" policy-making. Initiated by the civilian, competitive Prado regime in 1957, direct taxation rose rapidly from 23% of total revenue to over 45%. It began to decline with the *golpe* of 1962 and by 1964 was contributing *less* proportionately than in 1956!

Public investment in Peru under the Odria regime is another example of "demagogic" policy-making except that unlike Rojas Pinilla, Pérez Jiménez (and probably Perón were the data series sufficiently lengthy), subsequent levels of public investment fell *below* previous levels and Peru was slow to recuperate. Both countries had short three year *desarrollista* spurts (Frondizi 1957–59, Prado 1960–62) which left the role of the state slightly higher than they inherited it.

A Multivariate, Longitudinal Analysis

Our observations based on the plots about the coincidences between regime changes and policy shifts were actually already multivariate in the sense that we superimposed political discontinuities upon the relationship between spending and time. Nevertheless, despite occasional asides referring to levels of development or degrees of external influence, we could easily be accused of ignoring a large number of concomitant changes. We cannot possibly introduce all of these here, but we can insert the most obvious control of all: economic development.

By shifting from the country as the unit of analysis to the country/year and correlating the annual values for various policy indicators with the $ per capita income for the same year we can not only check our original cross-sectional associations, but also test for the persistence of relations over time within specific subsets.

The most important general observation is that the patterns of association ca. 1960 and 1950–67 are quite similar. Not only are the correlation coefficients of similar direction and magnitude but even the intersects and slopes nearly the same. For example, the correlation between direct taxation and per capita income was +.303 in 1960 and +.312 for the entire 1950–67 period. The comparable regression equations were: for 1960 $y = 20.30 + .022x$; for 1950–67 $y = 16.94 + .023x$. The much larger number of cases in the latter regression makes the pattern of association more statistically significant, but it is still very much the same pattern.[56] This does not mean that running cross-sectional regressions is in all respects an adequate substitute for longitudinal ones, but it does suggest that for many descriptive purposes the potential discrepancies may have been exaggerated.

The real test comes when we start fitting lines to subsamples of this mass of data.* By calculating the regressions for all the country/years in each of our regime types (excluding military, competitive ones due to their infrequency—ten cases), we may be able to pinpoint secular trends over time in which differing systems of political rule affect the relation between economic development and public policy.

In the first place, there emerge few statistically significant correlations. This, of course, is merely a confirmation of what we have already discovered: level of economic attainment is not a very good predictor of what sort of policies a Latin American government will follow.[57] Where some significant relation does exist, one can, however, discern interesting differences between military, non-competitive, civilian, non-competitive and civilian, competitive regimes. For example, among all Latin American regimes since 1950, total government expenditures correlate +.357 with per capita income. For civilian, competitive regimes, the relationship is much tighter (+.607). Successive increases in aggregate income are associated with a greater increment of government spending in this type of government than in military regimes. Non-competitive civilian regimes actually seem to decline proportionately in financial strength with economic development! These findings replicate those from the bivariate analysis of variance, the multiple regressions and some of the inferences drawn from the plots across time.

The regression with direct taxation as a dependent variable shows regime-linked differences, both of a distinct nature. The slopes are rather similar, but the intersects differ. At equivalent levels of development civilian, non-competitive regimes collect more from this source, civilian, competitive less and military, non-competitive least of all. This order is a bit surprising in that greater competitiveness in 1960 was found closely linked

* Figures XXV, "Total government expenditures as a % of GNP by per capita gross national product," XXVI, "Direct taxes as % of total government revenue by per capita gross national product," and XXVII, "Public investment as a % of GNP by per capita gross national product," have been omitted.

to higher mean values in direct taxation but the reluctance of military rulers to shift from more traditional sources of revenue to ones which depend heavily on voluntary citizen compliance is manifest. For all three regime-types, however, increments in national income "produce" approximately the same increment in direct taxation.

We must interpret this global plot of public investment as a % of GNP by per capita income cautiously. The country plots showed this to be an indicator of highly erratic performance, full of "opportunistic" or "demagogic" rises and falls. Nevertheless, the clusterings do confirm our earlier scattered comments in that military regimes emerge as high public investors (and getting more so the more developed they are) while the comparatively resource-poor, non-competitive civilian regimes have been much less active in this regard.[58]

Conclusion

Merging observations from such a variety of types of data and techniques of analysis is a difficult and hazardous task. Despite the general encouragement given "multimethodological approaches" there are, in fact, few precedents for such a synthesis. Nevertheless, I believe we can make some tentative empirical generalizations which are, at the least, not controverted by our various juxtapositions and manipulations of data, cross-sectional or longitudinal.

1. Indicators of overall system performance (*outcomes*) are much less predictably affected by regime-type or changes in regime-type than are indicators of direct governmental allocations (*outputs*). How much Latin American countries invest, industrialize, increase their GNP, raise their cost of living, increase their school enrollment and/or engage in foreign trade seems more the product of environmental or ecological factors than the willful acts of politicians grouped according to their competitiveness or civilian/military status.[59] The cross-sectional analysis suggests that the level of external dependence (on trade, finance and/or aid) is a more important setter of parameters than level of economic development, size, density, cultural heritage or ethnic stratification. But this has yet to be confirmed with serial data.

2. Political structural variables are, however, significantly associated with various indicators of how much Latin American polities can extract from their environments (i.e., total government expenditures and revenues), upon whom the burden of this extractive process will fall (i.e., taxation), how much of these scarce resources will be plowed back into the system to develop it (i.e., public investment) and which social groups will be benefited by these efforts (i.e., sectoral expenditures). In short, politics or in this instance military intervention and party competitiveness are

relevant to an understanding of the nature of public policy in this region of the world, definitely more so than in the more limited, homogeneous area of North American state politics.

2a. The military in power definitely tend to spend more on themselves —on defence spending—above all, when they are on-again, off-again rulers. Under equivalent conditions, they seem to spend less on social welfare than either type of civilian regime. Their "track record" on total expenditures and public investment has been erratic. Prior to 1960, they were occasionally responsible for rapid increases in both—followed by equally rapid returns to the *status quo ante*. Since then they seem to have been more associated with the reverse—a tendency toward increasing privatization of the economy and society.[60] Unfortunately, the recentness of the Peruvian, Bolivian and Panamanian military experiences has excluded them from our analysis. They may herald a reverse trend which might be spreading by contagion.

2b. Civilian regimes definitely spend less on defence (where they are not plagued by frequent military interruptions and threats) and more on welfare. The more consistently competitive among them have also been more successful in expanding the role of public institutions, although their investment record has been erratic—probably due to vagaries in resource availability more than the internal dynamics of competition. Most significant has been the greater propensity for civilian regimes to have shifted their resource extraction to a more egalitarian base through direct taxation. In several of these cases, e.g. Chile and Colombia, however, they seem to have reached the upper limit of voluntary compliance with this policy.

In summary, no regime-type seems to be exclusively responsible for "developmental success" in Latin America. Competition and with it, less coercion and more participation and voluntary compliance, seems in the long run to have promoted a greater "publicization" of the development process and greater equality in the distribution of its benefits,[61] but with certain "overhead" costs in terms of wider and more rapid policy fluctuations and higher rates of inflation and budgetary imbalance. Military regimes have occasionally been more spectacularly successful in altering the established, and usually stagnant pattern of policy, but their longer term effect has often been ephemeral—with a marked propensity for systems to return to some pre-established level after their "demagogic" excesses.[62] More often than not, the military themselves have promoted this return to "normality."

3. The patterns of public policy in Latin America over time rarely resemble that which is considered normal or modal for the United States. Only in a few well-organized, consistently authoritarian regimes, e.g., Mexico and Nicaragua, and in a very few policy arenas, e.g., educational spending, have we found evidence of incrementalism—of policy being based on a stable calculus composed of the previous year's expenditures plus ar

estimate of total resource availability for the coming year.[63] Instead, we have identified several other, quite distinct, patterns: the demagogic boom-and-bust, the cyclical stalemate, and the sedimentary consolidation. This suggests, to me, that policy-making in Latin America is a volatile (but not necessarily unpredictable) process, more vulnerable to the constriction of external circumstance and more sensitive to the clash of internal contradiction, than in the more stable, bureaucratized and perhaps dehumanized polities of the developed world.

Customarily an exploratory article such as this concludes with a lament about the quality of its data and a repetition of Lord Bryce's plea for "Facts, facts and more facts." This will be an exception. I think the data are about as good as we have any right to expect and I do not believe that further compilation and manipulation of aggregate data will do more than improve our capacity to describe. As for our capacity to analyze, to understand causality and process in complex systems, this article has approached and perhaps exceeded the limit of tolerable inference. Hopefully, it will stimulate not massive data gathering across a large number of units but the careful selection of individual cases or pairs of cases, conforming to or deviating from the modal pattern. These should be subjected to a "disciplined, configurative analysis" sensitive to actor perceptions and motives, the qualitative as well as quantitative dimensions of choice and the multiplicity of intervening conditions including, if necessary, *virtú* and *fortuna*.

Notes

1. An important exception to this generalization, indeed the only systematic comparative inquiry into public policy-making in Latin America, is Charles W. Anderson's *Politics and Economic Change in Latin America* (Princeton: Van Nostrand, 1967), esp. pp. 203–366. For a single case study, see James W. Wilkie, *The Mexican Revolutions: Federal Expenditure and Social Change Since 1910* (Berkeley: University of California Press, 1967).

2. MI and PC are admittedly not the only relevant dimensions for differentiating regime-types in Latin America or elsewhere—despite their prominence in the literature. Future research could well focus on how such political system characteristics as centralization, bureaucratization, party organization, ideological militancy, corporatism in interest group relations, legislative strength, administrative efficiency, judicial independence, leadership commitment to modernization or just plain honesty affect public policies. Typologies and scoring systems for several of these variables can be found in Arthur S. Banks and Robert B. Textor, *A Cross-Polity Survey* (Cambridge: MIT Press, 1963), and Irma Adelman and Cynthia Taft Norris, *Society, Politics and Economic Development* (Baltimore: The Johns Hopkins Press, 1967).

3. *Arms and Politics in Latin America* (New York: Praeger, 1960), pp. 154–172. It should, perhaps, be noted that many of the regimes Lieuwen considered tending toward a withdrawal of the military from politics have moved in the opposite direction since 1960 or remained stably transitional. To introduce some time perspective into the cross-sectional analysis, I have attempted where possible to replicate my juxtaposition of 1960 data with information from 1965. For this purpose, I have used the typology presented in Martin C. Needler, *Latin American Politics in Perspective* (Princeton: Van Nostrand, 1963), pp. 64–71. Collapsing Needler's time categories into three and classifying the information as of 1965, I obtained the following, roughly comparable, classification of regime-types by degree of military intervention: "Minimal involvement/pressure group" (Costa Rica, Uruguay, Chile, Bolivia, Colombia, Mexico); "Constitutional Guardians" (Argentina, Venezuela, Guatemala, Dominican Republic, Haiti); "Veto power/Rulers" (Brazil, Paraguay, Peru, Ecuador, Panama, Nicaragua, Honduras, El Salvador, Cuba). For a more recent typology (1966) see Edwin Lieuwen, "The Latin American Military" in U.S. Senate Subcommittee on American Republics Affairs, *Survey of the Alliance for Progress* (Washington: GPO, 1967), p. 15.

4. Again, I recalculated the competitiveness scores for elections closer to 1965. Using a slightly more restrictive definition of highly competitive (0–10% difference) I got the following tripartite distribution: HIGH (Argentina, Uruguay, Peru, Panama, Costa Rica); MEDIUM (Brazil, Chile, Ecuador, Colombia, Venezuela, Honduras, Guatemala, Dominican Republic); LOW (Paraguay, Bolivia, Mexico, Nicaragua, El Salvador, Haiti, Cuba).

5. Actually, existing hypotheses linking regime types to policy outputs often tend to confuse the military and competitive dimensions. Military rulers are held to pursue certain policies because they can afford to ignore the demands of competing parties. This tells us little about those few military regimes which tolerate party competitiveness and leave us in doubt about what sort of policies civilian noncompetitive regimes are likely to follow. I have tried in the above to differentiate between those elements uniquely associated with the two regime-type dimensions.

6. Lyle N. McAlister, "The Military" in John J. Johnson, ed., *Continuity and Change in Latin America* (Stanford: Stanford Univ. Press, 1964). This and the same author's "Recent Research and Writings on the Role of the Military in Latin America," *Latin American Research Review*, vol. II, no. 1 (1966), pp. 5–36 are very valuable and suggestive propositional inventories.

7. But, "An alternative hypothesis . . . is that the recruit or officer of poor or modest background considers himself lucky to achieve the rewards of military life and tends to give strong support to the system that provides them . . ." Daniel Goodrich, "Panama" in Martin C. Needler, ed., *Political Systems of Latin America* (Princeton: Van Nostrand, 1964), p. 138.

8. The most insistent proponent of this "pessimistic" interpretation of military rule has been Edwin Lieuwen. See his *Arms and Politics in Latin America; Generals vs. Presidents—Neo-Militarism in Latin America* (New York: Praeger, 1964); "The Latin American Military" (1967). Lieuwen's view is,

however, *nuancé*. For example in the latter study he observes that "Sometimes [the military] intervenes to foster social change and reform, at other times to enforce social stability" (p. 1). By periodization he identifies a brief decade of "military activism" (1945–53), but subsequently he tends to regard military intervention as "counterrevolutionary" and anti-reformist: "there is not a single military establishment in Latin America today that advocates rapid social reform" (p. 14). Martin Needler presents a less *nuancé* and more pessimistic view: "What is [the function of the military coup] in relation to social and economic change? Clearly, its purpose must increasingly be to thwart such change because the point of the coup is to prevent from happening what, it is assumed, would happen in its absence." *Political Development in Latin America* (New York: Random House, 1968), p. 64. This presumably rules out military intervention as a response to civilian *immobilisme* or stalemate, or as the agent of populist authoritarian change. Cf. Samuel Finer, *The Man on Horseback* (New York: Praeger, 1962), pp. 47 *et seq.* for an interpretation which stresses the military's self-seeking propensies.

9. Cf. Charles W. Anderson, "El Salvador" in Martin C. Needler, ed., *op. cit.*, p. 60, also his *Politics and Economic Change in Latin America*.
10. Lyle N. McAlister, *op. cit.*, p. 140.
11. *The Rockefeller Report on the Americas* (Chicago: Quadrangle Books, 1969), pp. 32–3. This "optimistic" hypothesis linking the military to modernization and/or development has been most convincingly argued by observers of the new nations of Africa, Asia and the Middle East. Cf. Manfred Halpern, *The Politics of Social Change in the Middle East and North Africa* (Princeton: Princeton University Press, 1963); Edward Shils, "The Military in the Political Development of the New States" in J. J. Johnson, ed., *The Role of the Military in Underdeveloped Countries* (Princeton, Princeton University Press, 1962); Lucian Pye, "Armies in the Process of Modernization," in *ibid.;* Lucian Pye, *Aspects of Political Development* (Boston: Little Brown, 1966), p. 173; Morris Janowitz, *The Military in the Political Development of New Nations* (Chicago: University of Chicago Press, 1964), p. 42 *et seq.* For Latin America, the most persuasive spokesman for this point of view (although again not without reservations) has been John J. Johnson. See especially his *The Military and Society in Latin America* (Stanford: Stanford University Press, 1964), pp. 93 *et seq.*
12. "The more complex the government, the more likely it is that the coup involves an alliance between the military and some bureaucratic and political elements," Keith Hopkins, "Civil Military Relations in Developing Countries," *The British Journal of Sociology*, vol. XVII, no. 2 (June 1966), p. 179.
13. "At best, the new militarists have merely continued programs conceived or initiated by the civilian regime they overthrew," Lyle McAlister, *op. cit.*, p. 156. Also Wilson C. McWilliams, ed., *Garrisons and Government* (San Francisco: Chandler, 1967), p. 20.
14. Cf. José Luis de Imaz, *Los Que Mandan* (Buenos Aires: EUDEBA, 1964), pp. 236–50.
15. "Despite differences in their approach to politics, the military and civilian components of the middle sectors tend to agree on their broad social and

economic objectives," John J. Johnson, *Political Change in Latin America* (Stanford: Stanford University Press, 1958), p. 14.

16. This "cynical" null hypothesis seems implicit in the work of José Nun. See his "The Middle-Class Military Coup" in Claudio Veliz, ed., *The Politics of Conformity in Latin America* (London: Oxford University Press, 1967), pp. 66–118, [reprinted in edited form in this volume]. For a more general discussion, see Henry Bienen, "Introduction" to Henry Bienen, ed., *The Military Intervenes* (New York: Russell Sage Foundation, 1968), p. xvii.

17. Cf. V. O. Key, Jr., *Southern Politics* (New York: Vintage Books, 1949), p. 307. Key, however, specified that in order to perform this function party competition had to be associated with high levels of organization such that dependent groups ("have-nots") were presented with clear sets of structured alternatives.

18. Cf. David E. Apter, *The Politics of Modernization* (Chicago: University of Chicago Press, 1965), pp. 238–240.

19. Cf. Lucian Pye, *Aspects of Political Development* (Boston: Little Brown, 1966), p. 73.

20. Cf. David Apter, *op. cit.;* Karl de Schweinitz, Jr., *Industrialization and Democracy* (New York: The Free Press, 1964), *passim;* Warren F. Ilchman, "Productivity, Administrative Reform, Antipolitics: Dilemmas for Developing States," in Ralph Braibanti, ed., *Political and Administrative Development* (Durham, N.C.: Duke University Press, 1969), pp. 506 *et seq.*

21. An interesting propositional inventory (without the cynical null hypotheses) which proved very useful for the above discussion is Eric A. Nordlinger's, "Governmental Structures and Responsiveness to Popular Aspirations: Some Notes, Hypotheses and Cross-National Data," unpublished MS, Center for International Affairs, 1969 (?). Nordlinger uses a universal compilation, classification, and correlational analysis on a few aggregate outcome variables, but asks many of the same questions as this essay.

The recent American State politics literature has, of course, devoted much attention to the impact of partisan competitiveness upon public policy. Although I use rather different instruments of analysis, I have found the following books and articles of seminal importance in inspiring and structuring my inquiry: Richard E. Dawson and James A. Hofferbert, "Inter-party Competition, Economic Variables and Welfare Policies in the American States," *Journal of Politics,* vol. XXV (1963), pp. 265–289; Thomas R. Dye, *Politics, Economics and the Public* (Chicago: Rand McNally, 1966), especially pp. 15–18; Ira Sharkansky and Richard I. Hofferbert, "Dimensions of State Politics, Economics and Public Policy," *American Political Science Review,* vol. LXIII, no. 4 (1969), pp. 876–879; Charles Cnudde and Donald McCrone, "Party Competition and Welfare Policies in the American States," *American Political Science Review,* vol. LXIII, no. 4, (1969), pp. 858–866.

22. Latin America would, then, be an exception to V. O. Key's proposition that competition was associated with higher levels of party organization. On the institutional amorphousness of most of the region's parties, consult Alan Angel, "Party Systems of Latin America," *Political Quarterly,* vol. XXXVII,

no. 3 (July–September 1963), pp. 309–23; John D. Martz, "Dilemmas in the Study of Latin American Political Parties," *Journal of Politics*, vol. XXVI, no. 3 (August 1964), pp. 509–31; Jean-Pierre Bernard *et al.*, *Tableau des Partis Politiques en Amérique du Sud* (Paris: Armand Colin, 1969), especially the "Introduction" by Leslie F. Manigat.

23. For an extended discussion of the role of *clientelas* in Brazilian politics, see my *Interest Conflict and Political Change in Brazil* (Stanford, California: Stanford University Press, 1971), pp. 302–306. Also John Duncan Powell, "Peasant Society and Clientelist Politics," *American Political Science Review*, LXIV, 2 (June 1970), pp. 411–425.

24. Cf. Gudmund Hernes, "On Rank Disequilibrium and Military Coups d'État," *Journal of Peace Research*, no. 1 (1969), pp. 65–72.

25. Jacques Lambert, *Latin America* (Berkeley: University of California Press, 1963), p. 239.

26. Cf. Ira Sharkansky, "Environment, Policy, Output and Impact: Problems of Theory and Method in the Analysis of Public Policy," in Ira Sharkansky, ed., *Policy Analysis in Political Science* (Chicago: Markham, 1970), pp. 61–79.

27. Cf. Theodore Lowi, "American Business, Public Policy, Case-Studies and Political Science," *World Politics* (July 1964), pp. 677–715; Robert Salisbury and John Heinz, "A Theory of Policy Analysis and Some Preliminary Applications" in Ira Sharkansky, ed., *op. cit.*, pp. 39–60.

28. *Ibid.*, p. 43.

29. The significance of difference for the 1965 data tends both to confirm and intensify the observed relationship between competitiveness and social welfare expenditures. In only one case, educational spending, do the 1965 figures show a markedly more significant association with military intervention. Health expenditures seem to have evened out across regime types from 1960 to 1965.

30. This relationship holds up even when controlling for such "provocations" as border incidents. These bear little observable relation to military spending. Cf. Joseph S. Loftus, *Latin American Defense Expenditures, 1938–1965* (Santa Monica: The Rand Corporation, Memorandum RM-5310-PR/FSA, January 1968).

31. The observation remains valid as concerns the proportion of direct taxes in 1965, but becomes less significantly different for indirect taxes. This seems due to the rise in other (non-tax) revenue for those semi-militarized countries. The mean importance of such revenue (mostly from welfare institutes and semi-public agencies) reached 20.4%, an increase of 2.6% over 1960.

32. One key to understanding this better performance is the remarkably greater propensity for overtly military regimes to be associated with increases in electric production: + 74% as opposed to + 51% for the quasi-military regimes and + 49% for the civilian ones.

33. Cf. Seymour Martin Lipset, *Political Man* (Garden City, NJ: Doubleday, 1959), pp. 27–63; Martin C. Needler, "Political Development and Military Intervention in Latin America," *American Political Science Review*, LX (September 1966), 616–26; Robert D. Putnam, "Toward Explaining Military Intervention in Latin America," *World Politics*, vol. XX (October 1967), pp. 83–108, [reprinted in this volume].

34. Multiple cross-tabulation and analysis of variance were more-or-less ruled out by the low number of cases.

35. Only the average annual increase in imports (1960–65) correlated significantly (and negatively) with per capita income (− .569). An analysis of the residuals revealed that military regimes did engage in more international trade, an indirect indicator that they are most likely to follow liberal economic policies.

36. Mexico's governmental expenditure is, then, startlingly low as a % of its GNP. One possible distortion may come from the underreporting of expenditures of decentralized agencies and mixed (semi-public) corporations —which get reported in other countries' compilations. According to Wilkie, *op. cit.*, pp. 5–6 these "supplemental" expenses were about equal to the regular ones.

37. The correlation of per capita income and taxes on foreign trade as a % of total tax revenue is − .566. I will not discuss this regression since it is to some extent subsumed under the indirect taxes *rubrique*.

38. I have discussed these eight factors in the complete version of my essay published in English as "New Strategies for the Comparative Analysis of Latin American Politics," *Latin American Research Review,* vol. II, no. 2 (Summer 1969). This has appeared in full as "Nuevas estrategias para el analisis comparativo de la política latinoamericana," *Revista Latinoamericana de Sociologia,* no. 4 (1970).

39. But as a rule the "modernization/development" factor was a better single predictor than the more orthodox per capita income.

40. I have analyzed the influence of these three dimensions of external dependence (commercial, capital and clientelistic) upon patterns of political structural change, especially the emergence of authoritarian rule in my "The Ecology of Political Change in Latin America," unpublished MS, Center for International Affairs, Harvard University, 1970. Cf. Douglas Chalmers, "Developing on the Periphery: External Factors in Latin American Politics," in James Rosenau, ed., *Linkage Politics* (New York: The Free Press, 1969), pp. 67–93.

41. Haiti with its positive residual of 0.3% is too close to the regression line to seriously challenge the generally poor record of non-competitive regimes for welfare spending.

42. Of course, military/civilian, competitive/non-competitive regimes may spend proportionately similar aggregate amounts on education, but for very different things under this *rubrique,* e.g. technical vs. liberal education, primary vs. secondary or university education.

43. In 1965, the residuals on defence spending for Venezuela and Guatemala were still negative (− .4% and − .8% respectively), while Colombia with its *violencia* and rural guerrillas continued spending from .4 to .5% more than predicted. Peru and Cuba, however, had become by far the largest "residual" spenders.

44. In fact, El Salvadorian dependence on indirect taxation did decline from 75.4% in 1961 to 67.9% in 1968 while per capita income increased by $42. The 7.5% decrease brought the country to a position much closer to its predicted position on the regression line. We repeat, however, this cannot be used to infer causality of a system equilibrating nature.

45. "The Mathematical Study of Change" in Hubert M. Blalock Jr. and Ann B. Blalock, eds., *Methodology in Social Research* (New York: McGraw-Hill, 1969), p. 444.

46. Cf. for an insightful discussion of this "contextual" fallacy and several others, Hayward R. Alker Jr., "A Typology of Ecological Fallacies" in Mattei Dogan and Stein Rokkan, eds., *Quantitative Ecological Analysis in the Social Sciences* (Cambridge: MIT Press, 1969), pp. 69–86.

47. "Unexplained variance and inaccurate parameter estimates indicate that while empirical summaries of cross-system patterns can be derived from data on a sample of systems, they cannot be expected to explain the behavior of individual countries," Ron Brunner, unpublished manuscript in process, Center for International Affairs, Harvard University, 1970.

48. Cf. Robert Burrowes, "Multiple Times-Series Analysis of Nation-Level Data," *Comparative Political Studies,* vol. 2, no. 4 (January 1970), pp. 465–480.

49. Uruguay or Costa Rica might have made better "partners" for Chile but data on the former was too incomplete and the latter was discarded on the grounds of a considerable disparity in size and societal complexity.

50. Cf. Raymond Vernon, *The Dilemma of Mexico's Development* (Cambridge: Harvard University Press, 1963), p. 118.

51. It should be noted that defence spending was already on the rise before Rojas Pinilla seized power, presumably as a reflection of the *violencia* which began in 1948.

52. "The Military: A Force for Continuity or Change" in John J. TePaste and Sydney N. Fisher, eds., *Explosive Forces in Latin America* (Columbus, Ohio: Ohio State Press, 1964), p. 77.

53. I have discussed these pressures for tax reform as they have affected the process of Central American regional integration in my "La Dinámica de contradicciones y la conducción de crisis en la integración centroamericana," *Revista de la Integración,* No. 5 (November 1969), pp. 119–125.

54. "Nicaragua" in Martin C. Needler, ed., *op. cit.,* pp. 108–9.

55. "Social Stratification, Power, and Educational Organization: The Peruvian Case," Centro Intercultural de Documentación, Cuernavaca, Mexico, December 1969/156. A draft version of the paper was presented at the Interdisciplinary Conference on Power, Policy and Education: Studies in Development held at the State University of New York on November 16, 1968.

56. There were two exceptions. Total government revenue as a % of GNP correlated +.652 with per capita income in 1960. With the longitudinal data, this fell to +.388, almost the same as total government expenditures. Public investment as a % of GNP had almost no relation to per capita income in 1960 (+.093) but, examining the relationship over a longer time period, it became a highly significant +.356.

57. This, of course, is a finding quite contrary to that stressed in the aggregate data literature on American state politics where urbanization, per capita income or industrialization have been good predictors of various policy indicators. Cf. the works mentioned above in note 21, especially Thomas Dye, *op. cit.,* pp. 282–292.

58. The correlation in CNC regimes is a very weak +.138 indicating a very

scattered pattern of association. Note also that while the correlation within MNC regimes and CC regimes is quite similar (+.437 and +.473), the intersect and slope reveal a quite different relationship. For an intelligent methodological comment which emphasizes the "pitfalls of correlation" in hiding very different distributions, see Edward R. Tufte, "Improving Data Analysis in Political Science," *World Politics* (July 1969), pp. 641–54.

59. As noted above, total magnitude of violence was an exception to this generalization and the only system outcome in which regime-type seemed to play a key role.

60. A supplementary indicator of this was the "better" performance of overtly military regimes in expanding foreign trade, especially imports, and in balancing national budgets. This suggests their greater support for development along the lines of the classic capitalist model which stresses limited public intervention, orthodox fiscal policy and reliance on the international division of labor.

61. Admittedly, the exclusion (due to problems of data comparability) of revolutionary Cuba which has promoted these same policies much more *a fundo* by non-competitive means limits the range of applicability of this generalization.

62. El Salvador, we have noted, is an interesting exception to this as may be some of the current military populist regimes.

63. For an excellent summary of the literature which stresses incrementalism as the predominant mode of politico-administrative decision-making, see Ira Sharkansky, *Spending in the American States* (Chicago: Rand McNally, 1968), pp. 12–17.

Appendix I. Regime Types in Latin America—1950–1967

	1950					1955					1960					1965		1967
1. Arg-	CC	CNC	CNC	CC	MC	MC	CC	CC	CC	MC	MC	CC	CC	MC	MC	CC	MNC	MNC
2. Bol-	CC	CC	MNC	CNC	CNC	CNC	CNC	CC	CNC	CNC	CNC	CNC	CNC	MNC	MNC	MNC	MNC	MNC
3. Bra-	CC	CC	CC	CC	CC	CC	CC	CC	CC	CC	CC	CC	CC	CC	CC	CC	CC	CC
4. Chi-	CC	CC	CC	CC	CC	CC	CC	CC	CC	CC	CC	CC	CC	CC	CC	CC	CC	CC
5. Col-	CC	CNC	CNC	MNC	MNC	MNC	CNC	CNC	CNC	CNC	CNC	CNC	CNC	CNC	CNC	CNC	CNC	CNC
6. Cos-	CC	CC	CC	CC	CC	CC	CC	CC	CC	CC	CC	CC	CC	CC	CC	CC	CC	CC
7. Dom-	MNC	MNC	MNC	MNC	MNC	MNC	MNC	MNC	MNC	MNC	MNC	MNC	MC	CC	CC	MNC	CC	CC
8. Ecu-	CC	CC	CC	CC	CC	CC	CC	CC	CC	CC	CC	CC	MNC	CNC	CNC	CNC	CNC	CC
9. Els-	MC	CC	CC	CC	CC	CC	CC	CC	CC	CNC	CNC	MNC	MNC	MNC	MNC	MNC	CC	CC
10. Gua-	CC	CC	CC	CC	MNC	MNC	MNC	CC	CC	CC	CC	CC	MNC	MNC	MNC	MNC	MNC	CC
11. Hon-	CNC	CNC	CNC	CNC	CC	MC	CC	CC	CC	CC	CC	CNC	CNC	CNC	CC	MNC	MNC	MNC
12. Mex-	CNC	CNC	CNC	CNC	CC	CNC	CNC	CNC	CNC	CNC	CNC	CNC	CNC	CNC	CNC	CNC	CNC	CNC
13. Nic-	MNC	MNC	MNC	MNC	MNC	MNC	MNC	MNC	MNC	MNC	MNC	MNC	MNC	MNC	MNC	MNC	MNC	MNC
14. Pan-	MNC	MC	CC	CC	CC	CC	CC	CC	CC	CC	CC	CC	CC	CC	CC	CC	CC	CC
15. Pgy-	CNC	CNC	CNC	CNC	MNC	MNC	MNC	MNC	MNC	MNC	MNC	MNC	MNC	MNC	MNC	MNC	MNC	MNC
16. Per-	MNC	MNC	MNC	MNC	MNC	MNC	CC	CC	CC	CC	CC	CC	CC	CC	CC	MC	CC	CC
17. Ugy-	CC	CC	CC	CC	CC	CC	CC	CC	CC	CC	CC	CC	CC	CC	CC	CC	CC	CC
18. Ven-	MNC	MNC	MNC	MNC	MNC	MNC	MNC	MNC	MNC	MNC	MC	CC	CC	CC	CC	CC	CC	CC

Appendix II. Latin American Ecological Factors

*Factor # 1: 'Modernization/Development'**

1. Percent Population in Primary Occupations	−.977
2. Percent Population in Non-Manual Occupations	.974
3. Telephones per 100 population	.950
4. Percent Population in Non-Agricultural Occupations	.941
5. Doctors per 1,000 Population	.938
6. Hospital Beds per 1,000 Population	.935
7. Newspaper circulation per 1,000 Population	.933
8. Urbanization in Cities over 2,000	.929
9. Percent Population in Middle and Upper Sectors (1950)	.927
10. Urbanization in Cities over 100,000	.925
11. University Students per 1,000 Population	.921
12. Percent Population in Tertiary Occupations	.914
13. Radios per 100 Population	.896
14. Per Capita $ Income	.889
15. Newsprint Consumption in Kilos per Capita	.889
16. Mortality Rate per 1,000 Population	−.887
17. Matriculation in Secondary School as % of age eligibles	.867
18. Dentists per 1,000 Population	.867
19. Percent Population in Secondary Occupation	.855
20. Percent Population Literate	.852
21. Vehicles per 100 population	.843
22. Television sets per 100 population	.838
23. Cement consumption per capita	.835
24. Percent of Housing with Running Water	.835
25. Percent of Population Foreign Born	.834
26. Per Capita Electricity Consumption	.828
27. Caloric Intake per capita	.826
28. Diversification of Labor Force Index	.819
29. Percent of Economically Active in Manufacturing	.800
30. Concentration of Urban Population in Capital City and Suburbs	.769
31. Percent Economically Active in Factories employing more than five workers	.765
32. Percent of Population which is salaried	.741
33. Petroleum-Gas Consumption per capita	.740
34. Minifundio, farms with less than 5 hectares as % of total number of farms	−.717
35. Agriculture as % of GDP	−.716
36. Total School Enrollment as % of age eligibles	.713
37. Primary School Enrollment as % of age eligibles	.710
38. Manufacturing as % of GDP	.685
39. Concentration of Urban Population in Capital City	.641
40. Average Number of Persons per House	−.618
41. Ratio of Urban to Industrial Employment Growth	.617
42. Average Annual Urban Growth Rate (1955–60)	−.607
43. Percent of Consensual Unions	−.587
44. Percent of Industrial Workers who are female	−.566
45. Marriage Rate	.515

Sum of Squares   41.36

* Only variables with loading >.500 reported.
All data unless otherwise noted ca. 1960.

Factor # 2: Commercial Dependence Upon U.S.

1. Exports to the US as % of Total Exports .... .833
2. Per Capita US Private Investment (1950) .... .822
3. Ratio of Workers in Industry and Services .... .774
4. Law Students as % of Total University Students .... −.651
5. Ratio of Employment Increase in Industry and Services ..... .618
6. Cinema Attendance per capita [A] .... .612
7. Per Capita Economic Growth (1955–60) .... .582
8. Per Capita Industrial Growth (1955–60) [B] .... .579
9. Ratio of Occupational Opportunities in Non-Manual Employment to Secondary School Graduates .... .576
10. Total Population Growth from 1950–60 .... .530
11. Imports from the US as % of Total Imports .... .503
12. Latifundismo – % of total land cultivated in holdings over 1,000 hectares ... −.500

Sum of Squares   10.09

A This variable also loads .601 on Factor # 1.
B This variable also loads −.524 on Factor # 6.

Factor # 3: Size

1. Total Population .... .951
2. Total US Economic Aid (1950–60) .... .906
3. Number of Radio Stations .... .898
4. Number of Newspapers .... .871
5. Area in Km² .... .863
6. Total Gross Domestic Product .... .853
7. Percent of US Private Investment in Manufacturing .... .842
8. Exports and Imports as % of GNP .... −.637
9. Exports as % of GDP[A] .... −.540
10. Percent of Houses with Sewage .... .526
11. Percent of University Students Matriculated Abroad ..... −.519

Sum of Squares   11.92

A This variable also loads .540 on Factor # 4.

Factor # 4: Dependence Upon U.S. Private Capital, Especially in Petroleum

1. Energy Production per capita[A] .... .709
2. Concentration of Benefits by Economic Sector .... .689
3. Foreign Profit Remittances as $ of total Exports .... .686
4. Total US Private Investment (1950) .... .685
5. Net Private Capital Inflow .... .681
6. Percent Increase in School Enrollment (1950–60) .... .657
7. Exports as % of GNP .... .540
8. Petroleum-Gas Consumption per capita .... .523

Sum of Squares   8.91

A This variable also loads .621 on Factor # 1.

Factor # 5: Hispanismo

1. Percent of Population which is Catholic .900
2. Percent of Population which is Black (1950) −.843
3. Private School Enrollment as % of Total −.743
4. Percent of Priests who are native-born .699
5. Percent of Population which is Protestant −.696
6. Inhabitants per hectare of cultivated land −.690
7. Racial Heterogeneity .578
8. Growth Rate of Capital City (1950–60)**A** .541
9. Percent of Population which is Mestizo .512

                                                Sum of Squares   7.74

A This variable also loads −.501 on Factor # 6.

Factor # 6: Client Dependence on U.S. Economic Aid

1. Per Capita US Economic Aid (1950–60) .873
2. External Dept as % of Exchange Earnings (1964) .827
3. External Dept as % of GDP (1964) .785
4. GINI index of Concentration in Land Holdings (1950) .691
5. Average Annual Rate of Inflation (1955–60) .669
6. Ratio of Industrial to Total Growth −.621
7. Per Capita Industrial Growth (1955–60) −.524
8. Per Capita Economic Growth (1950–60) −.501

                                                Sum of Squares   9.05

Factor # 7: Amerindian

1. Percent of Population who Speak Major Language −.783
2. Percent of Population which is Amerindian .692
3. Divorces per 1,000 Population −.641
4. Percent of Farms of Subfamilial Size .548
5. Percent of Farms Owner Operated −.542
6. Faithful per Priest .500

                                                Sum of Squares   6.27

Factor # 8: Density

1. Railroad Trackage (per Km^2) .849
2. Road Density (per Km^2) .658
3. Population Density (per Km^2) .600

                                                Sum of Squares   6.08

III
Case Studies

Liisa North / *The Military in Chilean Politics*

On September 11, 1973, the attempt to create a democratic socialist society in Chile was brought to a violent end by a coup d'état. Contrary to the expectation of Allende and the Unidad Popular (U.P.) leadership and mass base, organization of the coup did not precipitate a division in the armed forces significant enough to provoke a civil war. Since the coup, an increasingly large number of analyses have appeared probing the fundamental causes and reasons for U.P.'s inability to remain in power. Those analyses have documented (1) the role of the United States in damaging the Chilean economy through credit boycotts, dumping of copper reserves, etc.; (2) the economic chaos created by the lockouts, black markets, and speculation organized by entrepreneurial associations (the *gremios*); (3) the attenuation of the government's power to contain ever increasing economic and social disorder as a consequence of Christian Democratic and National party obstructionism in Parliament; and (4) the internal divisions within the U.P. coalition itself which made it difficult for the government to act consistently and decisively.[1] Certainly the fundamental

From Liisa North, "The Military in Chilean Politics," *Studies in Comparative International Development*, 11, no. 1, copyright © 1976, by Transaction, Inc. Reprinted by permission of the author and Transaction, Inc.

Author's note: Many thanks to Antonio Bandeira, Claudio Duran, J. P. Farrell, Steve Hellman, Abraham Lowenthal, and Herbet de Souza, who provided me with invaluable criticism and comment on the first draft of this paper.

causes of the coup are not to be found in the armed forces. However, to the extent that the analyses of the coup have been made in a lacunae of information concerning those institutions and their interaction with the U.P. government, Allende and his advisors have been faulted with a generally weak and naive policy vis-à-vis the armed forces.

Errors were obviously made by the U.P. government in formulating a general strategy that would have permitted it to remain in power and accomplish the transition to socialism. And errors were made in the tactics pursued vis-à-vis the armed forces. Suggestions concerning the organization of popular militias and dismissal of officers suspected of disloyalty, however, ignore the realities of the Chilean military organizations: their capacity, organization, and zealously guarded professional autonomy concerning promotions, assignments, and dismissals, as well as their monopoly over arms.[2] The formulation of a strategy to prevent professional military organizations from successfully intervening to end a revolutionary process was and is extremely difficult.

The U.P.'s strategy vis-à-vis the armed forces was, of course, part and parcel of its overall strategy to maintain power and implement the transition to socialism. It was generally premised on the possibility of working through the existing institutional structures of the state, given their strength and relative autonomy within the democratic political system of Chile. According to the analysis of Allende's personal political advisor, Joan Garcés, it was more specifically premised on the U.P. government's adherence to constitutional norms, and its capacity to maintain public order and a reasonable amount of economic stability, if not actual growth (Garcés, 1972: 27–50; Martner, 1972: 135–47). The maintenance of these conditions, along with the broad guarantees and numerous benefits promised to the country's large middle class in the U.P. program,[3] were perceived as necessary for winning over or at least neutralizing that powerful and well-organized sector of the population. Neutralization, of course, signified the prevention of an alliance of the middle class with the large landowners and bourgeois industrialists, who would be spearheading an aggressive opposition in their attempt to maintain control over the means of production. This strategy, heavily dependent on a supportive or neutral middle class, implied the necessity of controlled and disciplined working-class and peasant mobilization in support of the government. Spontaneous and "illegal" mass action would threaten public order and, at a minimum, provide material for powerful antigovernment propaganda to which both the middle class and the armed forces would be very responsive.

Garcés' analysis and the U.P. literature in general demonstrated an acute awareness of the instruments of control available to the state, and the importance of the middle class in the political system. While these issues were extensively and carefully examined, the forms that a disciplined working-class and peasant mobilization would have to take were rather sparsely elaborated. In fact, Garcés limited "social pressure from the bottom" to "specific cases or very concrete objectives" (Garcés, 1972:35). This suggests that the mobilization of the mass base for a socialist transformation was not perceived as a continuous process that had to be initiated from the moment that the U.P. ascended to power.[4] The implications of this orientation will be taken up after the analysis of the U.P.'s strategy vis-à-vis the military has been completed.

The conditions identified as necessary for obtaining the support or neutrality of significant sectors of the middle class were also those considered necessary for maintaining the loyalty of the officer corps of the armed forces, or at least a large enough number of officers to prevent a successful right-wing coup. In addition, the armed forces shared certain institutional norms and problems which the U.P. government could attempt to utilize for maintaining their loyalty. In any event, a policy of direct confrontation was to be avoided. Although the possibilities of gaining some support within the officer corps and neutralizing the majority were fundamentally dependent on the success of the overall strategy, my primary objective here is to analyze the U.P. strategy vis-à-vis the armed forces.

In order to carry this out, it is necessary to review the known facts concerning the history, officer recruitment patterns, and capacity of Chile's armed forces, among which I include the Carabineros (a militarized national police force), as well as the army, navy, and air force.[5] Given the tradition of nonintervention enjoyed by Chile's armed forces, none has been the object of extensive study. There are only two major works available on their contemporary structure, both limited in scope and information (Joxe, 1970; Hansen, 1967), and many of the key events in the Allende government's interaction with the armed forces remain to be clarified. Of necessity therefore, the analysis presented here is tentative.

Political History of the Chilean Military

Unlike most Latin American military institutions, the Chilean armed forces have had a historical tradition of nonintervention in the political process. Or more precisely, interventions had been infrequent enough to permit the development of a myth, shared by both the military and civilian populations, concerning the neutrality and apoliticism of the armed forces. The last coup prior to September 11, 1973, occurred on September 13, 1932; its goal was the organization of elections to reestablish normal democratic procedures following a period of instability, dictatorship and military conspiracies and interventions which had begun in 1919.

The armed forces' overt political involvement during the period extending from 1919 to 1932 was basically related to the acute economic problems and intense and frequently violent social conflicts which Chile was experiencing at that time. With the spectacular expansion of the nitrate export industry in territories conquered from Peru and Bolivia in the War of the Pacific (1879–83), and the growth of the copper export industry following the turn of the century, Chile experienced a rapid process of social change and capitalist economic development. Domestic industries were established, the size of the state bureaucracy grew quickly, and people moved into cities. By 1920, 46.4 percent of the population lived in urban centres of 2,000 or more; 28 percent lived in cities of 20,000 or more (Germani, 1971; Rouma, 1948). Concurrently, both a significantly large middle class and a working class came into being. Particularly during the second decade of the twentieth century, both classes began to organize (often in conflict and independent of each other) and demand social and political reforms from what were extremely corrupt governments, governments which represented the interests of an oligarchy composed of large landowners, wealthy financiers, merchants, and native mining entrepreneurs allied with foreign investors. The workers' struggle was particularly bitter: in December of 1907, 2,000 men, women, and children were gunned down by the army during a nitrate miners' demonstration at Santa Maria de Iquique; between 1911 and 1920, there were 293 strikes, many of them violently repressed. In addition, the struggle for reform, particularly after World War I, took place in an increasingly deteriorating economic situation, a consequence of the development of synthetic nitrate production elsewhere and the postwar slump.

In this situation, the military organizations (the army in particular) began to conspire seriously in 1919 and finally intervened on September 5, 1924, to support reform programs backed by the middle class and important sectors of the working class.[6] The situation, in a number of superficial respects, paralleled that of the Allende years. The reform candidate who had won the presidency in 1920 was unable to obtain the passage of his program in a Parliament controlled by an oligarchic opposition. Unlike 1973, 1924 saw young army officers intervene to force passage of the reform proposals of the president.[7]

The effect of the military intervention of 1924 and its sequels was to advance the process of middle-class participation and increase representation of its interests in the state apparatus. For the protagonist of the political process which began with the presidential election of 1920 was the middle class; the working class participated in a subordinate role. As middle-class demands were at least minimally satisfied, the governments of the late twenties and early thirties engaged in the repression of working-class organizations and of the Communist party in particular. It was not until the mid-thirties that working-class organizations began to gain full freedom of operation.

Significantly, the interventionist military institutions of 1919–32 already enjoyed a tradition of apolitical professionalism. And indeed the officers intervened in the political process in 1924 only at the point when a significant number were convinced that civilian politicians were incapable of resolving the crisis. Army officers were particularly concerned about the effects on discipline and morale of the repression in which their institution was repeatedly called to engage. In 1924, these officers therefore requested Parliament to "dispatch the laws demanded by the working class in order to end their anguish which . . . affects the troops who should not be brought into contact with popular agitation" (Bicheno, 1972: 106). Shortly after this intervention, the Carabineros (a part of the army cavalry) were reorganized "into a national police force by integrating the old Carabineros with city police forces" (Hansen, 1967: 88).[8] The army was thereby relieved of duties related to the maintenance of internal order except in major emergencies.

The military conspiracies and interventions of the period extending from 1919 to 1932 were, therefore, fundamentally a response to acute economic, social, and political conflicts. The younger army officers in particular, who since the 1880s had been recruited to an increasing extent from the middle class, intervened to back up the reform demands of the class of their origin in order to establish social peace.

A secondary but nevertheless significant reason for at least the 1919 conspiracy and the open intervention of 1924 related to a number of problems specific to the military institutions. Many officers were mobilized into political action primarily on the basis of professional complaints. These included: the violation of professional military principles of merit and seniority on the part of politicians and members of the elite who had maneuvered to obtain promotions and privileged assignments for their friends and relatives; neglect on the part of politicians in providing funds for equipment; and low salaries as well as the nonpayment of salaries during the months immediately preceding the 1924 coup (Nunn, 1963: 145; Saez Morales, 1934: 19).[9]

Between 1932 and 1970 social conflict in Chile never became acute enough to elicit military intervention. The middle class was fully integrated into the state apparatus during the thirties and forties. The left organizations of the working class (the Communist party, the Socialist party, and the labor organizations) lacked unity until the fifties and engaged primarily in electoral politics, never seriously threatening the power and privileges of the upper and middle classes. In this situation of orderly political competition, some economic growth, and relatively attenuated social conflict, the tradition of military professionalism and apoliticism, of respect for the constitution and democratic process, could be reinstituted and fortified.

During the 41 years prior to Allende's election, the Chilean armed forces did reestablish a strong professional culture which was apolitical to the extent that officers subordinated their own political views to the professional norms of the military institutions, which were legally bound to respect the constitution. According to Hansen, summarizing the statements of 37 retired army generals, "Any breach of the norm of nonparticipation in partisan politics resulted in early retirement. The officer had not only to have no contacts with organized political groups but also had to present an image of political neutrality" (Hansen, 1967: 191). Toleration of deviance from the norm varied, however, depending on whether the deviance was toward the left or the right. While a "strong manifest commitment to any political philosophy . . . endangered an officer's career," overt "radical left" commitments were particularly frowned upon (Hansen, 1967: 191).

The reestablishment of a strong professional culture within the military institutions and the application of sanctions against officers with overt political commitments were, in fact, given particular impetus by three coups which took place in 1932 (North, 1967: 34–37, 74–75; Bicheno, 1972: 115–20). The application of political criteria in promotions and assignments, an unavoidable concomitant of interventions, naturally destabilized career expectations and created resentments. Furthermore, one of the 1932 coups was particularly offensive to the upper- and middle-class public: on June 4, Air Force Colonel Marmaduke Grove led a coup which established the "Socialist Republic of Chile." Although Grove and his associates were quickly deposed in another coup (June 16), even his ephemeral success appeared a shocking threat to the propertied classes. By late 1932, the officer corps wanted re-isolation from politics as institutional chaos approached an all time high, and prestige descended to an all time low: "For a matter of weeks, officers were socially ostracized and openly taunted by the public. Large numbers of officers were retired and the military budget for 1933 was drastically cut. In addition, to insure against further intervention, a civilian militia was organized and remained active until 1936" (Hansen, 1967: 59). This militia was formed by the sons of the upper and middle classes, and it was designed to keep officers with radical political perspectives as well as the civilian left in line.

Fundamentally, it was the exercise of strong civilian leadership, capable of moderating social conflict by meeting the major demands of the middle class and by making limited concessions to the working class, that precluded military interventions between 1932 and 1973. However, the internalization of professional norms of political neutrality on the part of officers was also important. It can be argued that the officer corps' ideology during this period was primarily constitutional and professional, although that is a relatively fragile ideology in any society experiencing acute class conflict. Nevertheless, a professional military culture was a reality, i.e., it had significant behavioral consequences.

Although there were no open military interventions into politics between 1932 and the election of Allende, there were a number of conspiracies within the military organizations, primarily in the army. Significantly, those conspiracies were largely based on institutional grievances, which is not to say that the conspiracy leaders (in contrast to most supporters) were lacking in political motivation. A conspiracy in 1939 was definitely fascist oriented, being directed against the Popular Front government, which was supported by the Socialist and Communist parties and led by the Radical party (Bicheno, 1972: 126–27; Joxe, 1970: 78). An incipient conspiracy in 1946 was inspired by Peronism and included some type of participation by a number of Socialist political leaders (Joxe, 1970: 79). A conspiracy in 1948 was inspired by a mixture of corporatist-type claims and Peronist nationalism (Joxe, 1970: 79–80). Peronist ideology again surfaced in conspiracies organized in 1951 and 1955.[10] (The 1955 conspirators were court-martialed in 1956, "accused of conspiracy, lack of discipline and violation of the principle of hierarchy as well as of the principle of apoliticism of the Army" [Joxe, 1970: 81]). The leader of a conspiracy which concluded with a rebellion in 1969, Army General Roberto Viaux, manifested his extreme right-wing political position later; however, in 1969 the support and considerable sympathy that he received within the armed forces was largely based on institutional professional claims (Bicheno, 1972: 133).[11] The numbers of officers involved in most of these conspiracies were apparently small, and upon discovery, the military organizations themselves administered punishment.

The institutional complaints which surfaced in these conspiracies, and particularly in the army, were not mere fabrications to camouflage political goals. After the Second World War, the percentage of the national budget devoted to the armed forces continued to decline, with few interruptions. While all branches of the armed forces felt the squeeze, the army apparently suffered the most as its share of the defense budget dropped from 41/42 percent to 35 percent. "As a result of this double squeeze, the Army's portion of the 1964 budget was only about 40 percent of the pre-war level" (Hansen, 1967: 196). This trend had an obvious negative impact on the capacity to maintain equipment and train recruits, as well as on officers' salaries. In the mid-sixties, in comparison to other professional groups, the salaries of army officers

> were extremely low, and were perceived so, not only by officers, but also by middle and upper class civilians. . . . The salary of sub-Lieutenant was as low as that of common laborers. The wives of lieutenants, captains and majors without independent means were generally forced to work to supplement the family income. Often wives employed as secretaries earned more than their officer husbands. The economic difficulties faced by the officer, especially in the lower ranks, were not a question of luxuries, but of decent housing, clothing and an education for their children (Hansen: 1967: 200).[12]

The situation of Carabineros officers was substantially the same, while air force and navy officers' salaries may have been somewhat higher (Duran, 1974).[13]

In 1970, what generalizations might be drawn from this history about the possibilities of military intervention? First, acute economic problems coupled with social and political conflict could very likely set the stage for a military intervention. Second, the major part of the officer corps was apparently constitutionalist, and therefore it could be expected that before the armed forces could agree to intervene, social and political conflict would have to reach crisis proportions. Third, military conspirators, historically, were able to recruit support for themselves not only on the basis of political claims, but also on the basis of institutional professional claims. Fourth, conspiring officers had been "progressives" as frequently as they had been right-wingers. The rationale for calling Peronist-nationalist conspirators "progressive" lies in the fact that significant sectors of Chilean Socialism passed through a Peronist ideological period in the forties and fifties, and as was indicated earlier, Socialist leaders were in contact with Peronist officers.

These generalizations did not apply equally to all branches of the armed forces. Progressive tendencies were significant in the army and the Carabineros; but for reasons to be developed later, they were weak in the air force and almost absent in the navy. Nevertheless, the history of the Chilean armed forces provided a cogent foundation for the U. P. leaders' belief that nationalist and progressive elements existed within the officer corps, and that it would be difficult to provoke the constitutionalist majority into intervention, particularly if U. P. policies responded to the major institutional problems of the armed forces. In other words, there was room for maneuver.

Social Recruitment and Social Relations of the Officer Corps

From the last decade of the nineteenth century, the officer corps of the Chilean army was increasingly recruited from the middle class. By the forties, middle-class dominance in the corps was complete, and during the fifties and sixties, given the declining prestige of the institution, cadets began to be recruited from the lower-middle class also (Hansen, 1967: 210).[14] The only survey data on the social recruitment of army officers, however, are limited to 37 generals retired between 1952 and 1964. Their fathers were businessmen (20 percent), professionals and managers (26 percent), military officers (26 percent), farmers (20 percent), and white collar employees (9 percent) (Hansen, 1967: 172). If the occupations of the fathers of these generals are at all representative of the army officer corps as a whole, the majority were recruited precisely from those social categories which by late 1972 were inviting military intervention to depose Allende, through actions such as their participation in, or support for, the October "bosses' strike."

The officer's class origin, of course, is not the only class factor in his experience. He, as an officer, occupies a middle-class position, and he most frequently marries into his own class or higher. In Chile, as elsewhere, the typical first assignments of officers are in the provinces.

> *Most of the officers' informal contacts . . . were with members of the rural upper class:* landowners, professionals, businessmen and those people in the provincial towns with "means." . . . Officers in the provinces were accepted as members of the set. They were invited to their social functions and were looked upon (and looked upon themselves) as potential husbands for their daughters.

> [Since] the great majority of military posts were located in the provinces [and] as all officers were required to spend a specified period in each rank in a command position, *periodic contacts with the rural upper class were maintained throughout their career.* This continuing association was reflected in the relatively high percentage of the . . . [generals'] in-laws . . . who were engaged in occupational pursuits typical of the rural upper class: agriculture and business (Hansen, 1967: 170, italics added).[15]

More precisely, it was particularly in southern Chile that officers established contacts with the rural upper class, or in other words, members of the country's landowning aristocracy. In the desert north, the professional and business classes with whom the officers interacted, although upper class in local terms, formed part of the middle class in national terms.[16] At the higher ranks an officer spent more time in and around Santiago, where the advanced schools, key garrisons, and headquarters of the army are located. There his civilian social contacts and friendships were established primarily among members of "the new urban middle class: professionals, managers, and bureaucrats" (Hansen, 1967: 177).[17]

In summary, the typical army officer is a member of the middle class in terms of his own occupation and his father's occupation. His close civilian social contacts include the middle class and, to the extent that the data summarized above are representative, the provincial upper class. Even limited systematic information on the social origins of the officer corps of the Carabineros, air force, and navy is lacking. However, observers familiar with Chilean political history and social structure tend to agree that Carabineros officers, to a greater extent than army officers, are the sons of lower-middle-class families, and even working-class families, while the air force and the navy recruit more officers from the upper-middle class. These two latter branches of the armed forces apparently enjoy more prestige, given their more advanced technology, the possible transferability of the technical training to attractive civilian occupations, and perhaps greater possibilities for travel. The navy, in particular, has an aristocratic tradition, and even today recruits quite a few of its officers from the upper class.

While the differences in the social origins of the officers in the four branches of the Chilean armed forces are not dramatic (all essentially recruit from the middle class), they may be significant enough to produce variations in fundamental social and political attitudes, especially if parallel differences in marriage patterns and civilian social contacts also exist. It is probably not pure coincidence that Allende found least support among navy and air force officers, although class alone may not provide a complete explanation.

With increasing political tension, social conflict, and economic chaos, especially after the October 1972 "bosses' strike," both the Unidad Popular and the opposition began to identify the struggle taking place in Chile as a class war (De Souza, 1973a: 61–82: 1973b: *passim*).[18] In this situation, the conflict within the officer corps between fundamental social and political orientations (which, of course, correspond with the predominant orientations of the officers' class of origin and social contact) and professional norms of nonintervention was bound to become acute. Thus the U.P. strategy of wagering on the constitutionalism of the armed forces, of attempting to neutralize and/or win over the officer corps to permit the dismantling of the capitalist system, was problematic.

However, to argue that the September 11 coup was inevitable due to the class nature of the officer corps is precisely to ignore the acuteness of the conflict which did take place inside the armed forces. Professional norms of nonintervention were strongly established, and despite the significance of the social-class relationships described, most officers spent most of their time with other officers and/or recruits. Among the 37 retired generals studied by Hansen, friendships with other officers far outnumbered those with civilians. Asked to identify the occupations of their five best friends during their final years of active service, they named 192 fellow officers compared to 36 civilians (Hansen, 1967: 178). While the friendship pattern indicates relative isolation from civilian social contacts, it did not imply isolation from the general, or even a particular, ideological environment: officers were not constrained in their choice of reading material, but until sometime in the sixties, only *El Mercurio,* the newspaper which articulated the position of Chile's landowning and industrial elite, was available in the officers' clubs. Subsequently the Radical Democratic *La Tercera,* popularly identified as a "minor *Mercurio,*" was ordered (Duran, 1974). The friendship pattern did, however, imply the officers' relative isolation within a particular type of institution with its own traditions and norms, and therefore the possibility of maintaining some distance between a unique professional culture and civilian social conflict and debate.

Furthermore, during their careers officers experienced significant contradictions which could attenuate class loyalties. In the army, the first assignments in the provinces

> placed young officers in intimate and continuous social relations with members of the lower class. . . . Often the conscripts looked upon him as a patron or father, and strong interpersonal ties developed. The young officer noted that in many cases *the new conscripts had been badly treated.* Many were *undernourished, unkempt and ill. Most had little edu-*

cation. . . . Contact with conscripts and other lower class personnel continued throughout the career, although generally on a progressively less direct and intimate basis (Hansen, 1967: 170, italics added).

These experiences, of course, could produce within the officer merely a sense of superiority and contempt for the lower classes. However, in the context of underdevelopment, coupled with increasing political debate concerning problems of "modernization" and reform, they could also lead to some questioning of a system which brought into the army recruits who could hardly be expected to perform well as soldiers.

Military participation in national development programs also brought army officers into direct contact with problems of economic growth, manpower training, social problems, etc. Military civic action programs were controversial within the army officer corps. At least a significant minority was opposed to them on the grounds of their incompatability with the military's unique defense functions. However, a majority of the retired generals interviewed by Hansen favored increasing the army's participation in national development programs, and almost half of those in favor could be described as politically progressive (Hansen, 1967: 236).[19]

The contradictions and both real and potential divisions within the army were therefore significant. A similar situation apparently existed within the Carabineros, whose officers, often as a function of their repressive role, were also in frequent contact with the day-to-day problems of the poorer sectors of the population. The air force and the navy, with their greater isolation from the social and economic problems of the country, experienced fewer internal conflicts. (The officer corps of the navy, in particular, was practically united in its opposition to Unidad Popular.)

Thus the cumulative impact of a number of relatively minor differences in social origins, civilian social contacts, and career experiences apparently created significant differences in sociopolitical attitudes among the officer corps of the four branches of the armed forces and within each branch.[20] The Unidad Popular leaders were aware of these differences, as were the officers themselves. The U. P. strategy of attempting to neutralize and/or win over the officer corps was therefore not only based on reliance on the armed forces' constitutionalism. It was also based on an analysis of the actual and potential cleavages within and among the armed forces.

Military Preparedness and U.S. Military Aid

There are some discrepancies in the data concerning the size of the Chilean armed forces, which may result from differences in the base years used. According to two reports published in 1967 and 1968, the number of men and officers integrated into the army, navy, and air force totalled 46,000. According to two other reports published in 1967 and 1973, the total for the three services reached 60,000 (Joxe, 1970: 95; IDOC, 1973: 12). The strength of the Carabineros is variously reported as 24,000 and

30,000 (Joxe, 1970, 97; IDOC, 1973: 12). Whether the 46,000 or 60,000 figure is taken as the correct one, the ratio of military personnel to total population in Chile is among the highest in Latin America, second or third to Cuba (Joxe, 1970: 95). If the Carabineros are included in the calculation, Chile definitely ranks second (Joxe, 1970: 98). Given the professional military training and organization, as well as the level of armament of this national police force, there are legitimate grounds for their inclusion, although it must be remembered that a part of Carabineros personnel are engaged in activities such as traffic control. Whatever the precise figures and ratios may be, the evidence argues for a relatively high level of military strength, particularly in view of the fact that Chile (unlike Cuba) has not been faced with a foreign threat in recent times, or (unlike her continental neighbors) with a domestic guerilla problem.

In addition to the relatively high manpower strength, the military institutions of Chile are well organized, well trained and well disciplined. Those institutions, for example, could hardly be compared to the corrupt, disorganized, and demoralized armed forces of Batista's Cuba (Gonzalez, 1974: 89–90).[21] And despite the institutional complaints of the army officers, the military organizations as a whole are quite well equipped, having a strong counterinsurgency power and high degree of mobility. For example, the air force is well equipped with troop and materiel transport craft, and its light bomber squadron of B–26 Invaders is particularly suited for low-level tight-pattern bombing, in urban areas if necessary (IDOC, 1973: 12).[22]

The high level of training and equipment was to a significant extent maintained through the United States Military Assistance Program (MAP). In 1952, Chile signed a bilateral mutual defense assistance pact with the United States, thereby becoming eligible for MAP aid under the Mutual Security Act of 1951 (Klare, 1972: 276–77). Until the Cuban Revolution, MAP aid, in the logic of the cold war, was "made available for the modernization of Latin American armies in order to strengthen the hemisphere's defenses against external aggression" (Klare, 1972: 276). With the review of U.S. military strategy following Castro's victory and the radicalization of the Cuban revolutionary government, "funds for counterinsurgency training and equipment were first made available to Latin American armies in . . . 1963" (Klare, 1972: 279). Thus in 1968, for example, 76 percent of the military aid the Department of Defense requested for Latin America was to be spent "on hardware and services related to counterinsurgency" (Klare, 1972: 279). Between 1953 and 1966 Chile, a peaceful country, ranked "second only to Brazil among Latin American countries as a recipient of U.S. military aid . . . both in terms of military grants and delivery of surplus stocks" (*Monthly Review,* 1971: 10; NACLA, 1972: 53; Joxe, 1970: 99–110). And on a per capita basis, Chile received more U.S. military assistance than any other Latin American country. During the same period, this aid amounted to 9.7 percent of Chile's total defense expenditures (Joxe, 1970: 103, Klare, 1972: 281).[23] After 1963, although precise figures are lacking, it can be assumed that most of this aid, in line with the general pattern of military aid to Latin America, was directed toward increasing the counterinsurgency potential of the Chilean armed forces.

The United States has also invested heavily in the training of Chilean military personnel, primarily officers.[24] Between 1950 and 1968, 2,064 Chileans were trained in the United States and 549 on Canal Zone bases (Joxe, 1970: 101),[25] and during the sixties, the U.S. maintained an annual average of 48 military personnel in Chile (NACLA, 1972: 53). In line with the post–Cuban Revolution U.S. military strategy, the "training programs [were] designed . . . to emphasize the importance of counterguerilla operations" (Klare, 1972: 298).

There were variations in the amount of U.S. aid and training provided to the different branches of the armed forces. During a five-year period in the sixties, the favored aid recipients were the navy and the air force (Hansen, 1967: 203). From 1959 to 1969, the average annual percent of total armed forces personnel programmed for training on U.S. bases was .3 for the army, 1.1 for the navy and 1.4 for the air force (Kemp, 1970: 4). Although "during the 1960s the proportional amount of army training given to Chile by the United States [was] one of the lowest in Latin America" (Kemp, 1970: 29) and considerably lower than air force and navy training, the Chilean army benefited from the presence of a large number of U.S. Mobile Training Teams (MTTs). In fact, from 1961 to 1967 "the levels of MTTs remained considerably higher by overall Latin American standards than the levels of direct training" (Kemp, 1970: 29).[26] Also, the number of army personnel programmed for training in the United States rose steeply in 1968, and although it declined somewhat in 1969, that year's figure remained above the levels of 1959–67 (Kemp, 1970: 29, 31).

What is the significance of these trends in U.S. training and assistance? Over the decade 1959–69 the greatest continuous impact of U.S. aid and training was apparently felt by the air force and the navy. Since this was the case, the already-identified antipathy toward the U.P. and the reactionary attitudes of navy officers, in particular, as well as sectors of the air force officer corps, could easily have been fortified by more extensive interaction with their U.S. counterparts.[27] The steep rise in the training of army personnel during 1968 and 1969, which was also accompanied by the purchase of helicopters,[28] may well have been based on a political calculation on the part of U.S. military advisors as well as Chilean officers. For by 1968 it was becoming clear that the 1970 presidential elections might produce a left-wing victory, given the increasing conflict between the Christian Democratic and National parties, and the consequent improbability of their unity behind a single candidate. And after all, it was primarily the ground forces that would have to deal with a popular revolt.

(In this respect, the United States also had helped to prepare the Carabineros. During the sixties, the United States began to provide significant amounts of aid to this militarized police force, which received 2.4 million dollars between 1961 and 1970 through the Public Safety Program [NACLA, 1972: 53; Joxe, 1970: 98]. The Carabineros, of course, had been the main instrument of internal repression since the 1920s.)

The rather impressive level of preparedness of the Chilean armed forces has led several observers to argue that the hybrid middle-class/elite Chilean governments of the last decades have maintained a particularly large, and well-equipped and trained military apparatus as the last line of defense against a revolutionary threat, a threat based on the increasing electoral and organizational power of the working class. The same reasoning, the argument continues, underlies U.S. policy (*Monthly Review,* 1971: 12; Joxe, 1970: 110–11). There is little doubt concerning the validity of this argument vis-à-vis the United States. However, the argument is somewhat problematic vis-à-vis the post World War II governments of Chile.

Certainly the middle class and elites expected the armed forces to defend them in the case of a revolutionary threat. But apparently they felt secure enough in their capacity to control the political process and the state to reduce military spending, and not to respond to the institutional complaints concerning salaries and equipment which kept emerging from the army, in particular. In terms of manpower, since the forties, "the long-term growth of the military has not even kept pace with that of the general population" (Hansen, 1967: 198).[29] The share of defense (army, navy, and air force) in the national budget went down from 18 percent in 1948 to 9 percent in 1968 (Joxe, 1970: 87–88). Joxe presents a table on military spending over a five-year period which covers four years of the Conservative Alessandri administration and one year of the Christian Democratic Frei administration. (See Table 1.) Although military spending as a share of the national budget continued its downward trend, given the rapidly increasing amount of state spending (particularly under the Christian Democratic administration), Frei, at least during the first year of his government, significantly increased the absolute amounts of military expenditure. The Carabineros and police were particularly favored, the army least so. During the last year of his government, Frei was, in fact, confronted with a mutiny over salaries in the army. As late as May of 1973, Joxe still argued that the evolution of the military budget prior to 1970 had "certainly not contributed to aligning [at least] the army strongly to the forces of the traditional right" (Joxe, 1973: 20, 22).[30]

The U.P. was thus faced with highly professional armed forces with an impressive capability for internal repression. Their ideological formation throughout the sixties had been strongly influenced by U.S. counterinsurgency training. In general, this training no doubt reinforced anticommunist and antisocialist attitudes within the officer corps. However, the constitutionalist tradition was also strong; the majority of officers, like the

Table 1. Military Spending 1961–1965 (base 100: 1961)

	1961	1962	1963	1964	1965
Police and Carabineros	100	103.7	90.4	90.6	109.2
Defense (total)	100	97.3	89.0	87.4	97.8
Army	100	96.3	83.0	82.1	82.9
Navy	100	98.5	97.1	92.3	107.1
Air Force	100	96.3	79.2	84.2	99.3

Source: Joxe, 1970: 97.

civilian population, believed and took pride in Chile's uniquely democratic history in Latin America. In addition, there was dissatisfaction with the manner in which both the Conservative Alessandri and Christian Democratic Frei administrations had dealt not only with the internal problems of the military institutions, but also with the social and economic problems of the country (Farrell, 1974).[31]

The U.P. Strategy vis-à-vis the Armed Forces in Theory

Summarizing from the information presented above, it is possible to identify the factors that allowed U.P. strategists to believe that a rightist military intervention might be prevented. They were: (1) the constitutionalist professional norms of the majority of the officer corps (to repeat, this is not to say that the officers were apolitical, but to emphasize that historically they had tended to subordinate, and perhaps would continue to subordinate, their political predilections to principles of constitutionalism and nonintervention); (2) the presence of nationalist and progressive officers, particularly within the army, and therefore the difficulty of organizing a right-wing coup without precipitating a split in the armed forces; (3) the possibility of using the satisfaction of institutional demands as a tactic for reducing pressure for intervention.

Operating against the above were the following factors: (1) the middle-class social affiliations and fundamentally conservative or centrist political attitudes of the majority of officers, which acute social and economic conflict had historically brought to the surface; (2) the ideological implications of professional military training and education with their emphases on order, hierarchy, and authority; (3) the presence of clearly reactionary elements in the officer corps; (4) the ideological influence of U.S. training and continued association of Chilean officers with their U.S. counterparts.

In terms of their general political analysis of the military, Allende and his advisors were also convinced (and I believe correctly so) that any attempt on the part of the government to organize armed militias of workers and peasants, or otherwise clearly step outside the bounds of legality, would have quickly resulted in giving the upper hand to the reactionaries in the officer corps. For it must be stressed that the progressive officers who supported and cooperated with Allende were also constitutionalist, and it was on the basis of *legalistic and professional arguments* that they could influence officers with no sympathy for the U.P. government to remain neutral. This fact had another implication: any abnormal interference by the executive in military promotion and assignment patterns would also redound to the benefit of reactionaries, for such interference could easily be identified as an assault on the professional integrity of the military. Within normal accepted routine, however, Allende could exert limited influence on promotions; generals were nominated by the president and "political reliability was thus an important [and accepted] criterion at this level" (Hansen, 1967: 191).

Respect for the legality of the existing system and the internal autonomy of the military institutions were identified as a fundamental, but by no means sufficient condition for maintaining the loyalty of the armed forces. Public order and a modicum of economic stability were also required, as the strategy vis-à-vis the military was part and parcel of the strategy toward the middle class. The officer corps could hardly be expected to repress middle-class protest (no matter what forms it took) over a sustained period. And neither the middle classes nor the officer corps could be expected to easily countenance a lengthy economic crisis or repeated disturbance of the public order through illegal takeovers of land or factories, or for that matter, mass demonstrations calling for the destruction of the existing legal order. Therefore, the necessity of controlled and orderly mass mobilization, and the discouragement of spontaneity (Garcés, 1972, *passim*).[32] Thus, among the reasons for not encouraging continued mobilization on the basis of the popular organizations which spontaneously emerged as a response to the October 1972 "bosses' strike," military pressure figured.

The holding of mass mobilization in check, for which the U.P. has come under severe scrutiny by its critics on the left, formed an integral part of the strategy. It was a part of the attempt to retain the support of progressive officers, to hold the effective allegiance of the professional constitutionalist majority, and to isolate the interventionist right. The U.P. wanted to avoid engaging in any action that might throw the majority constitutionalist center of the officer corps into the arms of the reactionary right. Conversely, the Allende government expected to be able to maintain the loyalty of the constitutionalists if illegal or violent action was instigated by reactionary officers and political leaders.

In general terms I believe that U.P. analysis of the situation within the armed forces was sound. It required a great degree of flexibility and decisiveness in its implementation, rapid adjustment in response to the quickly deteriorating social, political, and economic situations, particularly after the October 1972 crisis and the attempted coup of June 29. Unfortunately, U.P. policy manifested a certain "inflexibility" and a serious lack of decisiveness: as it became clear that most of the middle class had moved into opposition, the U.P. was not able to agree on an alternative strategy that faced up to this fact.

The U.P. Policy vis-à-vis the Armed Forces in Practice

The analysis of the military made by U.P. strategists and Allende led them to take action to satisfy the institutional demands of the armed forces (including the retention of close ties with the U.S. military establishment), to respect the internal promotions and assignment patterns, and to integrate the armed forces (the army in particular) not only into a few national development projects, but into the day-to-day operations of vital sectors of the public administration and the economy.

The U.P. government approved salary increases for the armed forces, the largest for the lower and middle ranks. The armed forces also benefitted from new housing projects and the acquisition of new equipment, and top-ranking officers acquired cars specially imported for them (*Latin America,* 1972b: 386; Joxe, 1973: 2029). Figures on military spending under Allende are not available. However, there is no doubt that it went up. In addition, the Chilean armed forces continued to receive grants, equipment, and training from the United States. Military aid was, in fact, the only type of aid that the United States gave to Chile during Allende's presidency. In 1971, for example, the United States granted the air force five million dollars for the acquisition of transport aircraft and paratroop equipment (NACLA, 1972: 53). The United States also continued to participate in various joint maneuvers with the Chilean armed forces and attend their celebrations. This policy of building up the armed forces, of course, involved serious risks, since increased strength could be used to destroy the U.P. government as well as uphold it.

While respecting formal regulations concerning promotions, Allende had "safe generals" as commanders of all the branches of the military by the beginning of 1972 (Joxe, 1973: 2029). Joxe describes them rather intriguingly as "favorable to the U.P., or rather to the class alliance which attempts to restore an essential role to the non-monopolistic bourgeoisie" (Joxe, 1973: 2029). The meaning and implications of this characterization of "safe generals" are not entirely clear in Joxe's analysis; in fact, some of these generals supported the September 11 coup, while others opposed it.

Finally, the U.P. government integrated members of the armed forces into the planning and management of key sectors of the economy.

For the first time in Chilean history, representatives of the military participate[d] directly in the production of goods and services. Brigadier General Pedro Palacios Cameron was named (December, 1970) director of the Chuquicamata Copper Company, and representatives of the Army, Navy and Air Force [were] on the national production boards of the copper, iron and nitrate companies. Military representatives [were] part of Odeplan, the National Planning Organization, which . . . [had] cabinet status. Further, the U.P. . . . . included the military in its development activities in the four southern provinces of Cautin, Malleco, Valdivia and Osorno. Military men participate[d] in the distribution in the "one-half liter of milk" program; in the planning of the Third U.N. Conference on Trade and Development, which [was] held in April 1972 in Santiago; and in the government agency responsible for developing national sports (NACLA, 1972: 52).[33]

This account of military participation in economic management and administration in general could be much extended.

What were the consequences of this policy? Little accurate information is available. However, some observers have argued that on the whole it had a positive effect on the armed forces' support for U.P. Officers involved in the food distribution program, for example, became acutely aware of the ways in which the black market operations of the middle class and the political right were sabotaging the economy. In one exceptional case, a young officer who had been involved in the government's economic programs resigned from the army in order to better aid in the achievement of U.P. goals by helping to organize the *cordones industriales* (Bandeira, 1974). The overall effects of officer integration into economic management and public administration, however, were contradictory. Certainly some progressive officers already favorable to expanding military civic-action programs responded positively, but officers adamantly opposed to expanding military participation outside very narrowly defined limits were not lacking, even in the army. Their reaction was highly negative. In particular, "stories of army officers being actively engaged in the mass mobilization movement" were seen "as an attempt by the extreme left wing of the Allende government to seriously violate . . . professional norms" (Farrell, 1974). Anxiety concerning the U.P. government's capacity and commitment to maintaining the professional integrity of the armed forces even affected "officers who were neutral or, indeed, supporters of Allende" (Farrell, 1974). Furthermore, the participation of officers in public administration and economic management not only acquainted them with the negative consequences of the black market, U.S. actions, etc.; it also brought them into immediate touch with the "administrative inefficiencies and ineptitudes" (Farrell, 1974) of the government. Finally, it remains to be clarified whether it was not primarily the progressive officers who were incorporated into national development programs, thereby leaving officers neutral or opposed to U.P. in command of troops.

Whatever the effects on officers were in terms of increased support or withdrawal of support from Allende, it is certain that the incorporation policy gave control, or partial control, of important enterprises and activities to military personnel, and provided them with experience that would make the future institution of a military government easier. Thus, this policy also had its double edge.

Military penetration into the state apparatus also took forms not foreseen in the original strategy. As conflict between the U.P. and various opposition groups reached crisis proportions, becoming violent in various provinces (e.g., over land reform), those provinces were declared Emergency Zones (De Souza, 1974). According to Chilean law an Emergency Zone was a virtual mini–military dictatorship: the military commander of the area took over all normal civilian political functions and could name military personnel to manage critical sectors of the local administration. As the number and duration of the Emergency Zones increased in the course of Allende's presidency, more and more officers had to confront and deal with the entire range of economic, social, and political problems and conflicts in their areas of operation. The military takeovers in the Emergency Zones were "qualitatively similar to a coup" (De Souza, 1974): the military could use all means necessary to maintain public order.

Furthermore, whereas the president could choose the officers to be appointed to nationalized industries, planning agencies, etc., the commanders of units in particular provinces were designated by the military, and the executive's control over their manner of operation was severely limited. Thus the military in many areas became increasingly autonomous in the exercise of power. It should also be remembered that there were extensive social contacts between officers and members of the landed rural upper class in the southern provinces, and between officers and members of the business and professional middle class in the northern provinces as well as Santiago. As landowners in particular, and business and professional groups to a lesser extent, became increasingly threatened by U.P.'s reform measures, to act within the confines and spirit of U.P. policies must, of necessity, have become increasingly problematic for large numbers of officers; in fact, they increasingly acted in contradiction to those policies, particularly in the south, where the postcoup repression was especially harsh (*Latin America,* 1974: 149).

In addition to the military presence in the national bureaucracy and in the Emergency Zones, following the October 1972 "bosses' strike," the military entered the cabinet. In fact, "the key . . . which . . . ended the strike that . . . brought the country to the brink of paralysis, was the appointment to . . . [the] cabinet of senior officers from the three branches of the armed services" (*Latin America,* 1972a: 353). Officers, although not the same ones in all ministries, remained in the cabinet until the parliamentary elections of March. They again reentered the cabinet in August with the second middle-class/entrepreneurs' strike, which was begun by the truck owners on July 26.

Thus by September 1973, the Allende government was virtually a captive of the armed forces, which were or had been involved at all levels in the country's crisis as managers of enterprises, as bureaucrats in the national administration, and as political leaders in the Emergency Zones and in the cabinet. By September political debate in the officer corps had been open for months, and divisions were profound. Allende and the U.P.

leadership still calculated on a split within the armed forces if a right-wing coup were attempted. They expected support from army and Carabineros officers in particular.

The Strategy of the Opposition vis-à-vis the Armed Forces and the Breakdown of the Constitutionalist Majority

The extreme right had been attempting to provoke a military coup from the moment that Allende was elected. Before Allende's inauguration, extreme right-wing elements kidnapped and, through a blunder, assassinated the army's commander-in-chief, General René Schneider, in the expectation that the left would be blamed for the attack and that the officer corps would unite to prevent Allende's ascension to power. Despite the participation of the commanders-in-chief of the navy and the air force, the commander of the Santiago division of the army and the director of the Carabineros, the plot failed. Although General Schneider's personally strong constitutionalist commitment, well known as the "Schneider Doctrine," was important in defusing the plot, his views would not have prevented an extension of the conspiracy if the majority of the officer corps had not shared his position (Garcés, 1974a: 20–23). The conditions for a successful right-wing coup did not yet exist within the armed forces or within the civilian political arena. In terms of the objectives of the right, the assassination backfired. For the moment at least, it solidified the majority of the officer corps' resolve to respect the election mandate, for military investigators were able to ascertain the culpability of the extreme right. It also allowed the government to eliminate a few militant reactionaries from the officer corps, although by no means all. Several other conspiracies were discovered during Allende's presidency.

With the failure of the initial attempts to provoke a coup, the opposition to the U.P. turned to all forms of parliamentary and legal obstructionism to prevent the implementation of the U.P. program. It also turned to the systematic organization of economic chaos, a task in which it was aided by U.S. policy, to prepare the ground for an eventual coup. The "bosses' strike" of October 1972 had the overthrow of the government as its ultimate objective. However, with the entrance of the military into the cabinet, opposition tactics were toned down as both the National party and the Christian Democrats began to prepare for the March parliamentary elections. They expected to obtain a two-thirds majority, which would have allowed them to impeach Allende. Instead, the U.P. gained seats in Congress, its popular vote (despite the extremely difficult economic situation) reaching 44 percent, an increase of approximately 8 percent over the 1970 vote for Allende. With the possibility of electorally defeating the government eliminated, the opposition turned again to tactics intended to provoke a coup, of which the strikes beginning on July 26 were the last major and successful act.

Prior to this last assault on the U.P., a premature coup took place on June 29. It was premature in the sense that its right-wing organizers in the armed forces were not yet fully prepared; they did not have enough officers from the increasingly diminishing and wavering constitutionalist sector willing to support them, and (probably most important) Allende supporters still remained in key positions in the military hierarchy, particularly in Santiago. Most prominent and respected among them was General Carlos Prats, commander-in-chief of the army. However, by that time the officer corps was rapidly becoming more and more willing to support a right-wing coup, or at least not to oppose one.

The attitude changes taking place in the officer corps were fundamentally related to the general intensification of class conflict following the March elections. A total stalemate had been reached. Within the existing parliamentary system, the U.P. could not fully implement and rationalize its social and economic reforms without non-U.P. support. The opposition could not legally remove the president, but it could continue to maintain a chaotic situation in which class polarization would become more and more acute as the economy, already in a critical state for more than a year, continued to deteriorate. Furthermore, U.P. reforms in the process of implementation or discussion were seriously menacing the economic and social status of petit bourgeois sectors: agricultural marketing and purchasing cooperatives of necessity implied the elimination of middle men —small and medium as well as large merchandising operations; a state-operated trucking corporation implied the elimination of significant numbers of private operators. Those sectors of the middle class not adversely affected by U.P. reforms were ready to be convinced that they would be in the near future. In the logic of this process, the Christian Democratic party, the most important middle-class political organization, which had already been calling for and organizing "civil disobedience" since early 1972, redoubled its opposition with, of course, the aid of the United States. Thus by May and June of 1973 not only the landowners and the bourgeoisie, but also most of the middle class were neither supportive nor neutral; they were in strident opposition to the government. This, of course, had a profound impact on the officer corps.

In addition to the intensification of class conflict, the officer corps was particularly agitated by two phenomena which, although manifestations of the basic class conflict, were not intrinsic to it. One, the U.P.-proposed educational reform, was also agitating the middle class. The other, MIR (Movimiento de Izquierda Revolucionaria) and left Socialist proselytization among soldiers, was specific to the military institutions. The educational reform was identified by the opposition as a totalitarian move to control the minds of *their* children: the text of the proposal, with its avowed commitment to the creation of a new man, fed and inflamed the fears of the upper and middle classes, and along with them, the officer corps (Farrell, 1974).[34] The opposition press (*El Mercurio* in particular) organized a veritable propaganda war against the U.P. government on this issue.

However, it was left-wing attempts at the penetration of the armed forces that produced reactions among officers that "ranged from extreme unease over to substantial anger, if not outright fear" (Farrell, 1974).[35] Since not only the MIR but left-wing Socialists, who formed part of the U.P. coalition, were identified by the military as responsible for proselytizing among conscripts, by extension the president was also held responsible. But neither the impact of the educational reform nor left-wing proselytizing should be isolated as "explanations" for the coup (Alexander, 1974: 4).[36] They must be analyzed in the context of the generalized and increasingly violent class conflict that permeated Chilean society by mid-1973, and the lack of coherent and unified political direction on the part of the U.P. government and leadership. Officers were not only becoming convinced that Allende would or could not maintain the professional integrity of the armed forces, but also that he could no longer control the political, social, and economic process underway.

A Reactionary Coup: Was It Inevitable?

Despite the already weak position of the government within the officer corps at the time of the June 29 attempted coup, its failure created a situation in which the U.P. could possibly have taken the type of offensive action that would either have preserved and solidified the government, or provoked a split within the armed forces leading to a civil war, but not to the massacre of the left which has taken place. For high-ranking officers within the progressive group then argued that the moment was appropriate for purging the active right-wing elements from the military institutions. In addition, the attempted coup had provoked a resurgence of popular mobilization and organization. The U.P. masses were demanding, and willing to support forceful action on the part of the president. Progressive officers, for their part, were willing to receive support from the unions: although a workers' military *organization* hardly existed, many workers were, in fact, armed by June (De Souza, 1974; Garcés, 1974a: 31–54; 1974b).

The September 11 coup organizers themselves have indicated that the situation following the June 29 uprising was critical for them (Kandell, 1973: 24). During the coup attempt, hundreds of officers indicated their willingness to support the government. And within the U.P.'s strategic analysis of military policy, the purge would have been appropriate; i.e., the attempted coup was an illegal, unconstitutional act on the part of the right and as such provided grounds for offensive action.[37]

The events following the June 29 revolt, and the reasons for not attempting a purge are not entirely clear. Allende's own politically cautious attitude and his profound fear of civil war were certainly a factor. Divisions within the U.P. coalition also played their role. Apparently, for some time before the June 29 uprising, Allende and his advisors had been considering the necessity of developing structures that would have allowed loyal officers to coordinate their actions with workers' organizations. However, this required a tactical unity which did not exist in the U.P. (Garcés, 1974a: 43). In particular, the left in the coalition distrusted the officers and argued for relying on armed workers. Thus the lack of structures for coordinated action that would have channeled effective and directed mass support to loyal officers may have inhibited Allende from taking the risks of forceful action against what was by then a fairly large group of officers involved in conspiracy.

The lack of forceful action at that time, however, gave the initiative to the right, both inside and outside the armed forces. As a consequence, both the military and civilian supporters of the U.P. were demoralized. And the demoralization became worse in the following weeks as both groups were essentially left without political direction (Touraine, 1973; *passim*). Some factories were converted to the production of armaments, and Communist party members, at least, were directed to obtain arms.[38] However, U.P. action during the months of July and August, on the basis of available descriptions, appears to have been particularly uncoordinated, indeed, even chaotic.

Meanwhile, the actions of the military and civilian right were increasingly well coordinated. Key U.P. supporters in the armed forces, General Prats most important among them, were maneuvered into resignations and retirements (Garcés, 1974a: 48–51). The military searched factories and working class districts for arms—apparently well informed about where to find them. The coup organizers coordinated their actions with civilian fascist and right-wing groups, while the economy was brought to virtual chaos through strikes organized by businessmen's associations and by hundreds of violent acts of sabotage. Finally, Christian Democratic leaders began to openly invite military intervention.

At the end of August, Allende personally decided to implement his earlier proposals involving structures to coordinate the actions of loyal officers and workers' organizations (Garcés, 1974a: 44). But it was too late. The U.P. no longer had control over the situation, the group of officers involved in the organization of coordination with workers was infiltrated, and the majority of the officer corps could now be convinced to support the coup, or at least not to oppose it.

Miliband has summarized well the military dynamic following the June 29 coup:

> People who are thus and thus at one time, and who are or are not willing to do this or that, *change* under the impact of rapidly moving events. . . . Thus conservative but constitutionally-minded army men, in certain situations, become just this much more conservative-minded; and this means that they cease to be constitutionally-minded. The obvious question is what it is that brings about the shift. In part, no doubt, it lies in the worsening "objective" situation; in part also, in the pressure generated by

conservative forces. But to a very large extent, it lies in the position adopted, and seen to be adopted, by the government of the day. . . . The Allende administration's weak response to the attempted coup of June 29, its steady retreat before the conservative forces (and the military) in the ensuing weeks . . . all this must have had a lot to do with the fact that the enemies of the regime in the armed forces . . . grew "more and more numerous." In these matters, there is one law which holds: the weaker the government, the bolder its enemies, *and* the more numerous they become day by day (Miliband, 1974: 463).

Even in the crisis situation of August, it was apparently not an easy task to convince officers to support the coup. According to officers engaged in the plotting,

The greatest obstacle . . . was the armed forces' 40-year tradition of political neutrality: "I would have pulled my hair out for teaching my students for all those years that the armed forces must never rebel against the constitutional government," said an officer who formerly taught history at a military academy. "It took a long time to convince officers that there was no other way out" (Kandell, 1973: 23–24).

In fact, many officers were never convinced. During the day and night before the coup, the right-wing officers carried out their own purge within the armed forces. According to their initial declarations, only 50 officers were arrested (Kandell, 1973: 24), a statement belied by the fact that 57 air force officers alone have been tried for resisting the coup. And the air force officer corps had fewer U.P. supporters within it than the army. According to other sources, "several hundred" officers were executed or arrested in the purge; "some sources speak of between 2,000 and 3,000 members of the armed forces and police losing their lives in the coup before the coup" (*Latin America,* 1973: 357).

In summary, military involvement in the process set into motion with the election of Allende was unavoidable, but a successful reactionary coup on September 11 was by no means inevitable. In the light of the history of the Chilean armed forces and factors related to their organization and strength, the strategy vis-à-vis the military of those within the U.P. who most consistently supported Allende was certainly problematic but basically sound: the conditions for a civilian armed uprising simply did not exist in Chile, and the government therefore had to maintain significant support and neutrality within the officer corps in order to maintain itself in power. While the strategy vis-à-vis the military was basically sound, it was tied to an overly inflexible general strategic orientation, involving the maintenance of middle class support and a lack of emphasis on mass organization. Because the necessity of forceful and continuous mass organization was not recognized by important sectors within the U.P. coalition, the coalition was incapable of arriving at a tactical unity that would have permitted it to counter the right-wing and fascist offensive. Allende's proposals concerning the coordination of loyal officers with workers' organizations could have been a step in the right direction. But in order to be successful, it needed forceful parallel action in the civilian political arena. In this respect, Miliband's critique concerning the lack of "a network of organs of power, parallel to and complementing the state power, and constituting a solid infrastructure for the *timely* 'mobilization of the masses' and the effective direction of its actions" is apropos (Miliband, 1974: 472).

In order to have effective structures of parallel power when the system reached a crisis, it was necessary to consistently pursue their organization from the moment that the government was inaugurated. I believe that this could have been done in ways that would not have precipitated a coup. In other words, a somewhat different overall strategy did not necessarily imply abandoning the policies identified as necessary for maintaining a maximum of military support. Mass organization did not have to involve unconstitutional action, disturbance of public order, or immediate arming of workers, the conditions identified by Allende and his advisors as the precipitators of a coup by a united officer corps. The actions of loyal officers after June 29 also indicate that when a crisis was reached, they were willing to act with and arm workers' organizations *to defend the system as it was legally constituted*. The possibility of pursuing this strategy, however, was made difficult by the divisions within the U.P. For the left in the coalition it would have involved abandoning unrealistic assumptions about soldiers with arms deserting en masse, and accepting the necessity of close cooperation with the progressive sector of the officer corps, as well as the fact that the armed forces could not be confronted by a mass insurrection in the conditions that prevailed in Chile (Garcés, 1974a: *passim*). For the moderates it would have involved an acceptance of the fact that in the long run a major portion of the middle class would *not* remain neutral —the logic of U.P. reforms in favor of the working classes, both urban and rural, of necessity involved a negation of the interests of significant sectors of the middle class, which would not be willing to compromise on what they identified as the sine qua nons for maintaining their social and economic status. If this had been recognized, the need for structures of parallel power would have appeared more urgent.

Of course, it can also be argued that the U.P. made serious political and propaganda errors which unnecessarily alarmed the middle class and the officer corps (e.g., the proposed educational reform), and that these relatively marginal factors were crucial in tipping the scales against the U.P. in a situation where the balance of forces was about even; that the fundamental causes of the coup inhere in Chile's status as a dependent nation and the international policy of the United States in particular; that Allende personally could not provide the kind of leadership that the situation demanded. Mistakes were certainly made and the international situation was clearly unfavorable. Both problems, as well as Allende's leadership, need to be more thoroughly analyzed and evaluated. However, the analysis of problems related to the role of the middle class and mass organizations, and strategy vis-à-vis highly professional and capable military institutions, remain fundamental for any discussion of socialist transformation not only in Chile, but anywhere in the "Western democracies."[39]

Notes

1. Among the best analyses of the fundamental causes for the success of the fascist coup of September 11 are Miliband (1974: 451–73) and Garcés (1974a: 11–54). For an insightful day-to-day account and analysis of the events preceding the coup, see Touraine (1973).
2. For analyses critical of the U.P. policy vis-à-vis the armed forces, see Sweezy (1973) and Plotke (1973).
3. The Popular Unity's "Program of Government" is available in a large number of publications; among them are NACLA (1972: 130–42) and Allende (1973: 23–51).
4. Garcés argued that this strategy did not "exclude the thought of resorting to social pressure—from the bottom—in specific cases or for very concrete objectives." However, for him, it was "the opposite of political realism and a deformed vision of the political process to affirm: 'We suggest to the Unidad Popular and to the Government that to rely on the *real protagonists* of the social process underway would have been more serious and more courageous on their part: between February and October of this year (1971) 345,000 industrial workers, peasants, settlers and students have participated in strikes and illegal take-overs. . . .' The maintenance of public order is not only a requirement of every government; it always favours whoever controls the government" (Garcés, 1972: 35).
5. Since the coup, the Carabineros have been formally recognized as the fourth branch of the armed forces—they were integrated into the Ministry of Defense whereas formerly they formed part of the Ministry of the Interior.
6. The reforms proposed included social security legislation, state control of banks and insurance companies, the separation of church and state, and direct election of the president. For more information on this period, as well as on Chilean political history in general, see Gil (1966) and Petras (1970).
7. For a very good brief discussion of this period, see Bicheno (1972: 97–134). Although the progressive officers gained control of the situation in the armed forces, there was also a strong reactionary sector in the officer corps, particularly in the navy (Pike, 1963: 178–81).
8. The effects of internal repression were also demoralizing for the army officer corps, who had directed two successful international wars during the nineteenth century, and thought of themselves as the protectors of the nation against external aggression.
9. General Saez Morales, who lived through these events, discusses favoritism particularly bitterly in his memoirs (Saez Morales, 1934: 19).

10. The name the 1951 conspirators gave their group was "Por Una Mañana Auspiciosa" or PUMA. The 1955 group was known as the "Linea Recta," and it was a reconstituted version of the PUMA (Joxe, 1970: 80).

11. Already a year before Viaux's rebellion, there was considerable disturbance within the army concerning salaries and other institutional problems: the minister of defense was removed and replaced by a general who was supposed to deal with the institutional problems. His inaction provoked further resentment and therefore sympathy among officers for Viaux's movement, which received considerable support from the navy and air force as well as the army. Viaux obtained the removal of the minister of defense as well as salary increases and new equipment for the army from Frei's government. No serious charges were brought against Viaux: he was simply dismissed. Viaux was probably already involved with civilian right-wing political groups, but the full political implications of his 1969 rebellion remain to be clarified (Duran: 1974).

A good summary of the conspiratorial activities of Chilean officers by Nef (1974: 59–63) has come to my attention since the completion of this summary analysis. Nef stresses the conservative and reactionary tendencies within the Chilean armed forces. There is no doubt that those tendencies existed. However, my reading of the available evidence convinces me that the political situation in the armed forces was more contradictory and complex than Nef's analysis suggests. Nef, for example, points out (1974: 62) that Viaux attempted to present himself as a "peruanista," i.e., a progressive. To me, this indicates that Viaux was convinced that he could not obtain widespread support within the officer corps on the basis of a right-wing position.

12. Hansen (1967: 295) also reports widespread dissatisfaction with the military as a career choice for their sons among upper- and upper-middle-class respondents in Santiago.

13. Professor Duran, for example, indicated that his uncle, who was an army officer, gave up his military career in 1968 for economic reasons. Duran also remembers meeting an officer's wife who was driving a taxi to supplement the family income.

14. Hansen (1967: 211) writes: "The basis of the present trend toward incorporation of lower middle class elements appeared to rest upon the decline in the prestige of the career. Talented youth from the upper and middle class were no longer attracted to the military as a career. As a result, the base of recruitment had been broadened in order to provide sufficient officer candidates." Hansen writes broadly of the military; however, he provides data only on the army. Therefore, in using his thesis, I take all references to the military (unless he specifies air force, etc.) as limited to the army.

15. The fathers of the 37 officers' wives were businessmen (31%), professionals and managers (17%), military officers (14%), farmers (31%), and white collar employees (6%) (Hansen: 1967: 172).

16. These regional variations were pointed out to me by Duran (1974).

17. Concerning the 37 retired generals' organizational affiliations, Hansen (1967: 177, 179) writes: "All retired generals interviewed had belonged

to at least one military association, and over a third to only military associations. Of civilian affiliations, middle class organizations such as Rotary, Masons, various historical societies, and sporting clubs predominated. Only one general belonged to Santiago's elitist Club de Union, and another four to various provincial equestrian clubs which were likely to have a large proportion of their members drawn from the traditional elites."

18. On September 2, 1973, Eduardo Cruz Mena, president of the striking College of Physicians said: "It is certain many people will die as a result of the lack of medical attention; in wartime one has to kill." Quoted in *Last Post* (1973: 26).

19. Hansen (1967: 248) writes: "In general, our data suggested a close connection between political views and an officer's orientation toward military participation in civic action programs. Officers who held leftist political sentiments were more favorable to civic action than rightists. Eighty-nine percent (N = 9) of those who identified themselves as 'leftists' favored an increase in civic action programs as compared to 52% (N = 21) of 'somewhat leftist' and 17% (N = 6) of 'rightists' and 'somewhat rightist.' " Hansen indicates that "somewhat leftist" could be considered a basically "centrist" position (p. 301) and therefore I have chosen to consider the "leftists" only as politically progressive.

20. Given air force and navy recruitment of their officers from the better off sectors of the middle class, and even the upper class in the case of the navy, the professional political culture of the two institutions may include more elitist values than those to be found in the army and Carabineros.

21. Gonzalez (1974: 89–90) has described the Cuban army thus: "To begin with, the Cuban army had a low level of professionalism. Staffed in large part with Batista's cronies who had joined him in the 'Sergeants' Revolt' of 1933, the army was shot through with senior officers who had distinguished themselves only by their personal corruption and attachment to the dictator. The top leadership, therefore, was generally deficient in many of the hallmarks of military professionalism—strong constitutional commitment as opposed to personal attachments, career advancement on the basis of military merit rather than political criteria, adherence to military doctrine, and a distinct sense of military mission. . . . Such an army was capable of an internal police function, of quashing Moncada-like assaults. But it was incapable of sustaining a counterinsurgency campaign. . . . Corrupt at its very core, the Batista army was susceptible to bribery by the *fidelistas*, who were sometimes able to buy their way through enemy lines. . . ."

22. The potential military use of the B-26 Invaders was pointed out to me by an ex-officer of the U.S. army who was involved in training Latin American officers at Fort Sill, Oklahoma in 1967.

23. It is not clear whether the figures used by Joxe (1970: 103) and Klare (1972: 281) include the cost of training Chilean officers on U.S. bases.

24. For a discussion of U.S. military training programs and institutions for Latin America, see Klare (1972: 295–307). Enlisted men as well as officers are trained at U.S. bases. For example, courses on "aircraft maintenance, electronics, radio, instrument training and repair," etc., are available for

enlisted personnel at the Inter-American Air Force Academy in the Canal Zone (Klare, 1972: 302).

25. Between 1959 and 1969, the "average annual number of Chilean military personnel programmed for training" for the U.S. and Canal Zone bases was 370. (Klare, 1972: 298).

26. There were also air force and navy MTTs in Chile (Kemp, 1970).

27. It would also be interesting to know at which ranks of the Chilean officer corps U.S. training had been most extensive, and whether or not there were significant differences in strongly anti-U.P. attitudes from rank to rank.

28. Between 1965 and 1969, the Chilean army purchased 26 helicopters from the U.S. (Kemp, 1970: 32).

29. Since Chile in the 1960's still had one of the highest ratios of military personnel to civilian population, this indicates that the level of militarization in Chile before the forties must have been remarkably high.

30. In his earlier work, Joxe (1970: 113) also discussed the possibilities of "military populism"; but that he considered a possibility only in a situation in which middle-class living standards were not threatened by the left.

31. Farrell (1974) became acquainted with a group of air force officers in Santiago while he was acting as a consultant to the Ministry of Education from January 1970 to July 1971. He paraphrased the officers' attitudes: "Well, in '58, we tried Alessandri, and nothing important happened to the country. In '64, we tried Frei, and he coudn't get things moving either. We might as well try this fellow Allende, and see if maybe he can get something going. If he doesn't do anything, we can try someone else six years from now."

32. Of course, there were important differences within the U.P., but the above summary reflects what I perceive as the position of Allende and those politically closest to him.

33. See also issues of *Latin America* for 1972 and 1973. For Allende's views on the question of military participation, see Allende (1973: 135–137).

34. Farrell (1974) wrote: "To explain their reaction, I should note a very general feeling about the Allende regime which I observed amongst many middle class Chileans who were either supporters of Allende or at least neutral, i.e., prepared to tolerate him. It could be characterized by a comment I heard one friend make at a party, which comment was roundly seconded by all of those others who heard him make it. 'They can play around with the economy if they like; they can fiddle about with the political and social systems if they like; but they had better keep their damned hands off my kids.' "

35. The negative impact of proselytization among conscripts was also noted by Bandeira (1974) and Duran (1974).

36. Alexander emphasizes the proselytization and "provocation" by left-wing elements inside and outside the U.P. as "decisive" in provoking the September 11 coup (1974: 4–5). He fails to refer to the destabilization campaign coordinated by the civilian right (including sectors of the Christian Democratic party) in collaboration with the United States. That is, he does not situate left wing "provocation" in the overall context of class conflict, and the limitations under which the U.P. government was operating.

37. Nef has pointed out that one of the factors inhibiting intervention by professional bureaucratic military organizations is "the fear or uncertainty on the part of the officer corps that intervention may not be successful and therefore harmful to the institution" (1974: 67). He also emphasizes the importance of institutional leadership. These two factors in fact could have redounded to the benefit of the U.P. government in the days immediately following the aborted June 29 uprising. Given the support of the commander-in-chief of the army, General Prats, as well as of other high-ranking officers (particularly in the army and the Carabineros), a rapid purge of right-wing officers could have produced the "uncertainty" that would have inhibited another right-wing attempt. Nef's analysis tends to overdetermine the success of a right-wing military movement, and to leave almost no room for maneuver on the part of the U.P. government vis-à-vis the military. In this respect, it would be interesting to compare the Chilean situation with the recent events in Portugal.

38. Information provided by Chilean refugees who prefer to remain anonymous.

39. For a more general analysis of the development of Chilean society, with a focus on persistent and underlying historical "authoritarian corporatist" tendencies, see Kaufman (1974).

References

Alexander, Robert J. 1974. "Chile a Year After the Military Coup." *Freedom at Issue* (no. 28): 4–19.

Allende, Salvador. 1973. *Chile's Road to Socialism.* Middlesex: Penguin Books Ltd.

Bandeira, Antonio. 1974. Series of interviews and discussions. Ph.D. candidate, Department of Political Science, York University. Formerly a student at FLACSO, Santiago, Chile.

Bicheno, H.E. 1972. "Anti-Parliamentary themes in Chilean History." In *Allende's Chile,* ed. Kenneth Medhurst. London: Hart-Davis MacGibbon.

De Souza, Herbet. 1973a. *Acerca del problema del doble poder en Chile.* Santiago: FLACSO.

————. 1973b. *Las elecciones parlamentarias de Marzo de 1973.* Santiago: FLACSO.

————. 1974. Series of interviews and discussions. Ph.D. candidate, Department of Political Science, York University. Formerly at the Planning Office of the President (ODEPLAN), Santiago, Chile.

Duran, Claudio. 1973. "Chile: Revolution and Counter-Revolution." *Social Praxis* 1 (no. 4): 337–58.

————. 1974. Series of interviews and discussions. Lecturer, Division of Social Sciences, York University. Formerly of the University of Chile.

Farrell, J. P. 1974. Letter (June 25). Chairman, Department of Educational Planning, The Ontario Institute for Studies in Education, Toronto. Consultant to the Ministry of Education, Chile, January 1970 to July 1971.

Garcés, Joan E. 1972. "Chile 1971: a Revolutionary Government within a Welfare State." In *Allende's Chile*, ed. Kenneth Medhurst. London: Hart-Davis MacGibbon.

———. 1974a. *El Estado y los Problemas Tácticos en el Gobierno de Allende*. Madrid: Siglo XXI.

———. 1974b. "Chile: how they killed a democratic revolution." *Manchester Guardian Weekly* 110 (no. 1): 15.

Germani, Gino. 1971. *Sociologia della Modernizazione*. Barri: Editori Laterza.

Gil, Federico G. 1966. *The Political System of Chile*. Boston: Houghton Mifflin Company.

Gonzalez, Edward. 1974. *Cuba Under Castro: The Limits of Charisma*. Boston: Houghton Mifflin Company.

Hansen, Roy Allen. 1967. "Military Culture and Organizational Decline: A Study of the Chilean Army." U.C.L.A.: Ph.D. dissertation.

IDOC (International Documentation on the Contemporary Church). 1973. *Chile: The Allende Years, The Coup, Under the Junta*. New York: IDOC.

Joxe, Alain. 1970. *Las Fuerzas Armadas en el Sistema Político Chileno*. Santiago: Editorial Universitaria, S.A.

———. 1973 "L'Armée Chilienne." *Les Temps Modernes* 29 (no. 323): 2006–36.

Kandell, Jonathan. 1973. "Plotting the Coup." In *Chile: The Allende Years, The Coup, Under the Junta*. New York: IDOC.

Kaufman, Robert R. 1974. "Transitions to Stable Authoritarian Corporate Regimes: The Chilean Case" presented at the Inter-University Seminar on the Armed Forces & Society, at the annual meeting of the American Political Science Association, Chicago, Illinois, August 29–Sept. 2, 1974.

Kemp, Geoffrey. 1970. *Some Relationships Between U.S. Military Training in Latin America and Weapons Acquisition Patterns: 1959–1969*. Cambridge, Mass.: Center for International Studies, M.I.T.

Klare, Michael T. 1972. *War Without End: American Planning for the Next Vietnams*. New York: Vintage Books.

Last Post Staff and Latin American Working Group. 1973. "Chile Report" *Last Post* 3 (no. 6): 19–34.

Latin America, A Weekly Political and Economic Report. 1972a. "Chile: military alliance." Vol. 6 (no. 45).

———. 1972b. "Chile: military influence." Vol. 6 (no. 49).

———. 1973. "Chile: enemies within." Vol. 7 (no. 45).

———. 1974. "Chile: general power." Vol. 8 (no. 19).

Martner, Gonzalo. 1972. "The Economic Aspects of Allende's Government: Problems and Prospects." In *Allende's Chile*, ed. Kenneth Medhurst. London: Hart-Davis MacGibbon.

Miliband, Ralph. 1974. "The Coup in Chile." In *The Socialist Register*, ed. Ralph Miliband and John Saville. London: The Merlin Press.

Monthly Review. 1971. "Review of the Month: Peaceful Transition to Socialism?" 22 (no. 8): 1–18.

NACLA (North American Congress on Latin America). 1972. *New Chile,* Berkeley: NACLA.

Nef, Jorge. 1974. "The Politics of Repression: The Social Pathology of the Chilean Military." *Latin American Perspectives* 1 (2): 58–77.

North, Liisa. 1967. *Civil-Military Relations in Argentina, Chile and Peru.* Berkeley: Institute of International Relations, University of California.

Nunn, Frederick M. 1963. *Civil-Military Relations in Chile, 1891–1938.* University of New Mexico: Ph.D. Dissertation.

Petras, James. 1970. *Politics and Social Forces in Chilean Development.* Berkeley and Los Angeles: University of California Press.

Pike, Frederick B. 1963. *Chile and the United States 1880–1962.* Notre Dame, Indiana: University of Notre Dame Press.

Plotke, David. 1973. "Coup in Chile." *Socialist Revolution* 3 (no. 4): 99–124.

Rouma, Georges. 1948. *L'Amérique Latine,* vol. 1. Bruxelles: Renaissance du Livre.

Saez Morales, Carlos. 1934. *Recuerdos de un soldado: el ejército y la política,* vol. I. Santiago: Biblioteca Ercilla.

Sweezy, Paul M. 1973. "Chile: The Question of Power." *Monthly Review* 25 (no. 2): 1–11.

Touraine, Alain. 1973. *Vie et Mort du Chili Populaire.* Paris: Editions du Seuil.

Guillermo A. O'Donnell / *Modernization and Military Coups: Theory, Comparisons, and the Argentine Case*

I examine here one aspect of the political behavior of the Argentine military: the formulation of demands backed by the threat of the use of force, and especially the execution of coups d'état against national authorities. I deal with a brief period of Argentine history (1955–66). This, therefore, is not a general study of the "role of the military in developing countries," nor an analysis of "civic-military relationships in underdeveloped countries." I will attempt to demonstrate that these topics are too broad in scope to allow for more than shallow and empty generalizations. The study of the political behavior of the military[1] requires at a minimum the specification of two structural levels and their analysis along a temporal dimension: the condition of the larger national society to which the military belongs (including the so-called "external factors") and the state of the military organization itself. Each of these affects the other, both change over time, and both have an important but changing impact on the political behavior of the military. And, in turn, both can be substantially affected by the consequences of that behavior. Neither of these factors can be adequately specified when the referent is as general as "the military in underdeveloped countries," nor can they be incorporated at this level of generalization into an analytical framework capable of examining their complex interactions through time.

From Guillermo O'Donnell, "Modernización y Golpes Militares: Teoría, Comparaciones e el Caso Argentino," *Desarrollo Económico* (October–December 1972). Reprinted in translation by permission of the author and original publisher. English translation copyright © 1976 by Holmes & Meier Publishers, Inc.

In the first section of this study I consider briefly some characteristics of the Argentine social structure during the 1955–66 period. The second section focuses on the changes effected within the military organization during this period. The third section derives propositions to explain the behavior analyzed in the first two sections; it also explores the consequences of this behavior for the two structural levels—societal and organizational—which are treated as independent variables in the first stage of analysis. Additionally, these propositions provide a basis for critically analyzing certain theoretical conceptions about the political role of the military in countries characterized by "high modernization." The fourth and final section formulates more specifically important aspects of the analysis.

I. First Structural Level: The Argentine Social Context, 1955–66

The period 1955–66 marked the worsening of a crisis which embraced— and embraces—numerous facets of Argentine society. The complex manifestations of this crisis make it impossible to attempt a satisfactory summary within the confines of this study. I will limit myself to stating briefly those factors which appear to have exerted the most significant and direct influence on the political behavior of the military. Thus, the criterion used is somewhat arbitrary, and this summary does not pretend to substitute for a detailed study of the Argentine social context during the 1955–66 period.[2]

Argentina does not fit the stereotype of the "underdeveloped country."[3] The Argentine case is one of high modernization.[4] Argentina is a dependent society, marked by an imbalanced productive structure and spatial configuration. It is subject to many social rigidities, with a high concentration of economic and political power. Innovative creativity directly applicable to productive processes is low, and the influence of more economically advanced societies on institutions, roles, and social practices is great. This influence helps determine important characteristics of the more modernized sectors (especially the large urban centers), and is expressed in important patterns of dependence, which are in turn linked to other structural characteristics of high modernization: a high degree of industrialization, high urban concentration, a high level of social differentiation and of political activity, and a relatively solid and autonomous organizational base (especially among trade unions) in the popular sector.[5]

Argentine industry operates at high cost, with multiple inefficiencies, through a combination of high oligopolistic concentration and numerous small producers, and with a growing need for raw material imports, capital goods, and technological know-how. These characteristics, combined with stagnant agricultural production, carried Argentina to a chronic deficit in its balance of payments—and along with other factors which are impossible to examine here—contributed to the limited economic growth and high inflation which characterized Argentina in the 1955–66 period. After the overthrow of Perón, the prevailing viewpoint was that controlling inflation and increasing exports were requisites for the economic growth of the country. To attain these objectives, it seemed indispensable to contain demands for goods and services in order to transfer income to the producers of agricultural exports. Because it was felt that excess demand originated in the consumption expectations of the popular sector, these socioeconomic policies tended to worsen the situation of the very same sector which maintained a strong loyalty to Peronism. Consequently, the socioeconomic cleavage between the "popular sector" and the "rest of society" tended to coincide with the political cleavage between "Peronists" and "anti-Peronists." This situation was accentuated by the vindictive nature of numerous public decisions during the period 1955–58, and by the various attempts to destroy and to weaken the unions. It was inevitably consolidated by the closing to Peronism of access to the electoral process, whether by direct and open proscription, or through the annulment of elections of Peronist candidates.

It is necessary to mention some aspects of the economic situation during the 1955–66 period. Per capita income grew at an annual rate of 1.3 percent.[6] From year to year great fluctuations occurred within this low average; as indicated in the first column of Table 1, the years 1956, 1959, 1962, 1963, and 1966 registered net losses in per capita income, some of notable amounts. The annual inflation during the period was 32.67 percent, but the average inflation in the negative growth years was 39.68 percent (see column 2 of Table 1). Only in 1958 and 1965 did the deflated wages surpass the level of 1947, but then only to fall again in the following year. After reaching a maximum of 46.9 in 1952, the percentage of the GNP represented by salaries and wages had fallen in 1965 to 39.8 (see column 3 of Table 1), despite the fact that as early as 1961 productivity per worker exceeded the rate in 1953 by 23 percent.[7] The low productivity of the agrarian sector and the deficient structure of the industrial sector determined that the years of resurgent economic activity would generate a massive demand for imported goods. This, in turn, further worsened the economic strangulation which originated in the balance of payments deficits.[8] This resulted in drastic devaluations, generally accompanied by measures designed to reduce internal demand, to eliminate "marginal" producers, and to transfer income to agrarian producers.[9] By raising the price of imports and of exportable foodstuffs intended for domestic consumption, the devaluations fed inflation, while at the same time the recessive policies markedly diminished production and demand. These were the years of negative growth which, as can be seen in Table 1, were also the years of highest inflation and of the greatest negative redistribution of income.

The devaluations were supposed to provide relief in the balance of payments through controls on internal demand and through the relative price improvement of agricultural exports. Another intended long term effect of

Table 1. Selected Socioeconomic Time-Series, Argentina 1955–66

Year	(1) Annual changes in GNP, at fixed pesos (% of previous year)	(2) Annual inflation (% over previous year)	(3) Salaries and wages (% of GNP for that year)	(4) Changes in Argentina's net position in foreign exchange (in millions of dollars, current value)
1955	5.0	12.3	43.0	− 175
1956	− 0.2	13.4	42.6	− 19
1957	3.6	24.7	41.4	− 60
1958	5.3	31.6	43.3	− 217
1959	− 7.7	113.7	37.8	113
1960	6.1	27.3	38.4	161
1961	5.1	13.5	39.9	− 57
1962	− 3.7	28.1	39.1	− 234
1963	− 5.5	24.1	39.1	202
1964	6.2	22.1	38.2	− 11
1965	6.7	28.6	39.8	139
1966	− 2.4	32.3	39.1	53

Sources: (1) Banco Central de la República Argentina, *Origen del Producto y Composición del Gasto Nacional,* Suplemento del Boletín Estadístico No. 6, 1966 and C. Díaz Alejandro, *Essays on the Economic History of the Argentine Republic.* Yale University Press, 1971. (2) C. Díaz Alejandro, *op. cit.* (cost of living in Greater Buenos Aires). (3) CEPAL, *El Desarrollo Económico y la Distribución del Ingreso en la Argentina,* 1968. (4) C. Díaz Alejandro, *op. cit.*

these measures was to improve agricultural productivity, and with that to obtain a definitive solution to external economic strangulation. But these policies meant severe losses for the urban-industrial sector, which in response actively promoted the high levels of conflict characteristic of the 1955–66 period. As a result of the effective opposition of the urban sector, the recessive policies were soon relaxed, and the expected benefits were never forthcoming. The dynamics of the situation can be summarized as follows: The devaluations benefited the agrarian producers and, to a large extent, the financial sector. But as inflation continued, as new devaluations failed to occur, and as the pressure from the urban sector intensified, the urban sector began to recoup its losses.[10] In one swift blow the recessive economic effects were quashed, the incurred inflation compensated for the effects of devaluation, and domestic economic activity increased again. This generated new pressures on the balance of payments, a new balance of payments crisis became evident, and a new devaluation occurred. One of the results of this cycle was the extreme income instability of diverse sectors, as shown in Table 2.

It is difficult to exaggerate the political consequences of these processes, especially in a context of (1) prior hostility of important sectors of the population toward the regime and the ruling officials, (2) the exclusion of the first plurality within the electorate from all real possibility of access to governmental positions, and (3) the importance of the organizational support of the social sectors ultimately destined to suffer the consequences of the economic policies already mentioned. It should be pointed out that the combination of constantly high inflation with drastic devaluations and limited economic growth meant that the maintenance of a steady income in monetary terms was equivalent to a real loss of that income of approximately one-third per year. Moreover, given the fact that the rate of inflation was higher in the negative growth years, this real loss tended to be greater in the years in which competition between social sectors was closer to conditions of zero sum. Any benefit gained had to be constantly adjusted to the rate of inflation. Each "player" was forced to run a race not only against inflation but also against other "players," because the zero-sum

Table 2. Changes of Income in Argentina by Sector, 1958–1965, in Constant Pesos (expressed as percentage of income)

Sector	*(1)* *Average absolute variation in each sector during this period (%)*	*(2)* *Year of maximum positive variation for each sector (as % of previous year)*	*(3)* *Year of maximum negative variation for each sector (% of previous year)*
Rural			
Agrarian	12.1	34.8	− 20.8
Urban			
Industrial	4.8	10.1	− 8.5
Construction	7.8	37.5	− 11.1
Transportation and Communications	4.4	12.7	− 6.7
Government	8.1	14.3	− 17.0
Electricity, Gas and Water	10.1	37.5	− 20.0

Source: Excerpted from CEPAL, *El Desarrollo Económico y la Distribución del Ingreso en la Argentina,* 1968.

conditions dictated that any benefits gained had to be "paid for" by the other players who were left in the dust in the race against inflation. Income fluctuations between the agrarian sector and the urban sector, as indicated in Table 2, are expressions of the complex processes and conflicts involved in this situation.

Inflation and zero-sum conditions also determined that for each sector the time spent "catching" inflation was of critical importance: as time passed real losses increased and it became more unlikely that one would attain sufficient new monetary income to compensate for that already lost through inflation. This situation could not fail to produce strong politicization and concentration of socioeconomic demands. Politicization occurred for two reasons: first, because it was clear that in the choice and implementation of public policies were to be found the most efficient means of influencing the reallocation of resources required by competitors; and second, because in the coercive apparatus of the state could be found the means necessary to impose these reallocations on the sectors that would have to "pay" for them with a real decline in their income levels. Likewise, strong concentration of demands could not be prevented because it was impossible to channel demands through governmental institutions (such as Parliament, the political parties, or the provincial and municipal governments) which played a very secondary role in the allocation of socioeconomic resources. For the very same reason, it became increasingly improbable that other institutions would achieve any real influence in the expression and resolution of conflicts.

This situation maximized the importance of channels of political access which allowed one to exercise power over the presidency directly.[11] Since the armed forces were the most effective channel for exercising power over the presidency, competing civilians tried to persuade military factions to articulate sectoral demands. Naturally, this severely fractionalized the armed forces.

These patterns of the formulation of demands implied for governments the explicit threat of being overthrown. The credibility of this threat was reinforced by numerous *planteos*[12] and by the various coups d'état (successful and unsuccessful) during the period 1955–66. Of course, this gave an obvious advantage in the race against inflation to those sectors that could initiate threats of coups d'état by the armed forces. These threats were made possible by direct contact with military officials, upon whom the urban and rural entrepreneurs could generally count (albeit with different factions). However, the better-organized urban workers counted on a strategy which, although more indirect and costly, could produce similar results. The promotion of high levels of social protest, such as paralyzing production by means of strikes and occupying buildings, placed governments in the position of being unable to maintain "law and order," and for that very reason, in imminent danger of being toppled. With this

the professionalization of, and in U.S. influence over, the Argentine armed forces. These factors, in turn, generated consequences of great importance.

The first and perhaps most important of these consequences was a clear recognition of the organizational achievements of the military and the need to preserve them through a high degree of internal cohesion. Still fresh was the memory of the organizational damage wrought by the type of political participation characteristic of the *golpista* period, and, in particular, of the internal fractionalization resulting from the channeling of sectoral demands through the military in the praetorian game. Consequently, the "legalist" officers insisted on adopting a position supposedly "above politics," which among other things meant that the political plots, which were so commonplace in previous years, disappeared in the period 1963–66.[29] Of course, a position "above politics" did not indicate disinterest in national politics, nor did it signify that the new military leaders entirely dismissed the possibility of new coups d'état. Rather, as General Onganía stated repeatedly, the armed forces should not interfere with the normal official activities of civilian authorities, but should and could intervene in "cases of extreme seriousness," as determined by the armed forces in each concrete case.

A second and closely related consequence was the redefinition of the position and functions of the armed forces in Argentine society. To quote General Onganía,

> [The armed forces] exist to guarantee the sovereignty and territorial integrity of the Nation, to preserve the moral and spiritual values of Western and Christian civilization, to maintain public order and domestic peace, to promote the general welfare, to sustain the enforcement of the Constitution, of its rights and essential guarantees, and to maintain the republican institutions in which they are established legally.[30]

In the same speech he added that for the attainment of these goals, two "fundamental premises" must be fulfilled: first, the maintenance of a "high level of aptitude and capacity of the armed forces to safeguard the best interests of the Nation," and second, the "socioeconomic development" of the country.

It is worthwhile to note that, in accordance with this criterion, the functions of the armed forces are much broader than those postulated by the *golpista* officers, who tended to define their role as preventing "totalitarian parties" from attaining governmental power. But more important are General Onganía's "fundamental premises": if the armed forces are to fulfill their vast "mission," their organizational power and Argentine socioeconomic development are postulated as necessary conditions. Therefore any problem that would hinder establishment of these conditions could be interpreted as an impediment to the fulfillment of the armed forces' mission. According to this concept the functions of the armed forces are so extensive and essential that any problem affecting these conditions has to be interpreted as an attack on the most "vital" interests of the nation. Since by action or inaction governments can impede the fulfillment of the "fundamental premises," it is obvious that within this conception governmental authorities can only receive a conditional loyalty.

> Military obedience is ultimately owed and directed to the Constitution and its laws, never to the men or political parties which circumstantially hold power. Were this not so, the goal to which the armed forces strive would be fundamentally destroyed: they would cease to be apolitical and become praetorian guards at the service of specific groups or persons.[31]

This conception should be understood from the perspective of a third consequence: the armed forces' adoption of the so-called "Doctrine of National Security." Its origins can be found in the decolonizing experience of the French Army,[32] but its adoption by a good many of the Latin American armed forces was largely due to an explicit political decision of the United States. There is ample evidence that U.S. authorities saw the adoption of this "doctrine" by the Latin American armed forces as the best safeguard against the impact of the Cuban Revolution and the revolutionary potential of the area.[33] According to this "doctrine," the local armed forces, in addition to the "traditional aim" of preparing for foreign wars, must include among their "specific duties" "internal warfare" against "subversive" agents who attempt to wrest the "underdeveloped" nations from the sphere of "Western civilization," and to bring them under "communist" control. Countries like Argentina are in a state of "internal warfare," as evidenced by terrorism, high levels of conflict among "important social groups" and the "breakdown of national internal cohesion."[34] "The enemy operates in all areas," and as a result "internal warfare" can be "ideological, economic or political."[35] Consequently, the "enemy" is multifaceted and multiple strategies are needed to fight him: "it is always the enemy who confuses, who disguises and masks the options. . . ." The description and definition of the enemy are not always clear. "Here is where the combat experience of the armed forces and their special preparation for warfare make them indispensable in the securing of the objective —in the characterization of the enemy, in the determination of his capabilities and modes of operation, in the selection of strategy and in assuring that the appropriate course of action is taken to achieve desired ends."[36] "Victory" in this "war" will mean the attainment of a satisfactory state of "national security"—defined as "the situation, certainly classifiable, in which the vital interests of the nation are safe from interferences or disturbances—internal or external, violent or nonviolent, open or surreptitious—that can neutralize or delay development and consequently weaken the very existence of the Nation or its sovereignty."[37]

"Subversion" flourishes "in an underdeveloped socioeconomic environment." Therefore the "subversive agents" are vitally interested in maintaining and aggravating high levels of social conflict "caused" by "underdevelopment." This is "the socioeconomic battle front," opened by the armed forces in their struggle for the attainment of "national security": without a prosperous society, highly integrated with a low level of conflict, "national security" will not be attained and the armed forces will not have accomplished one of their fundamental goals. From this it naturally follows "that development is the very essence of national security"[38] and that the latter "demands above all a complete involvement and total harmony with development which is its basic factor, which it serves and which it uses." Thus, "national security" in its most profound sense is not a purely military concept but has a much wider connotation; it is part of the national policy since it is linked with all aspects of life in the society and therefore with the "Vital Interests of Argentina."[39] It also follows that "there consequently does not exist a doctrine or a strategy of the armed forces which differs from that of the entire society."[40] "Security" is confused with "development," and both become part of the "specific functions" of the armed forces. This ideology permits, at least potentially, the militarization of any social problem which for whatever reason is considered important by the officers of the armed forces.

The persistence of the social processes alluded to in the first section of this study could be interpreted as an indication that the "fundamental premise" of "socioeconomic development" was not being fulfilled. In addition, the combination of this with high levels of social protest led to the diagnosis of the growing probability of an extensive diffusion and final victory of "subversion." According to the national security conception, poor government management and the strangulation of development interacted to facilitate "subversion." Therefore, the underlying logic of the national security conception indicated that it was part of the "specific duty" of the armed forces to eliminate these two "authentic causes" of "subversion," and that these governmental and socioeconomic factors were susceptible to attack and elimination. The connection between the new military ideology and the state of society drew a wide range of social problems (all those that could be included within the vague connotations of "attaining socioeconomic development" and "eliminating governmental inefficiency") into the very nucleus of these "specific duties."

But these conclusions are only valid if a fourth consequence has also resulted from the efforts at professionalization: the military officers must be convinced that their capabilities are clearly superior to those of the civil sectors, and that these capabilities are sufficient to solve a wide range of social problems. That conviction resulted, in part, from the continuation of socioeconomic problems and the persistence of mass praetorianism. However, it is my impression that it resulted principally from the very success of the attempt at military professionalization. As the military officers saw it, they had resolved "their" problem, even though the civil sectors and the government continued in a state of total crisis. This feeling of organizational accomplishment led to the belief, however illogical, that the military possessed a superior capacity to confront the social problems which the civil authorities evidently could not solve.[41] The armed forces were not only the "last hope" of a situation viewed as bordering on acute social crisis—this also had been claimed by the *golpista* officers—but they were also an organization which, under "legalist" leadership, had acquired technical skill, training in "social problems," and sufficient internal unity to involve themselves directly and successfully on the socioeconomic battlefront.

These seem to be the major consequences of the process of professionalization of the armed forces which began with the "legalist" triumph of 1963. This interpretation emerges from the not so rigorous basis of my conversations with military officials, but it is confirmed by the written statements, declarations, and speeches of the "legalist" leaders. A more complicated problem is posed when one asks to what degree the military's perception and evaluation of the social structure and of its own role was a consciously justificatory pretext for the plan of taking over the government. In my opinion the majority of these officers were acutely aware of their organizational accomplishments and were sincerely convinced of their superior ability to attain "socioeconomic development" and the elimination of "subversion." All civilians and, in particular, all political parties had "failed"; it was time for the "last hope," and the military was sufficiently prepared.

The legitimization of the military government and of the tremendous expansion of the social function which the "legalists" had assigned to their own organization would be the result of a final "victory" against "underdevelopment" and "subversion." The ideology of "national security" rendered these officials the important service of providing a pattern of interpretation for numerous social problems, reinforcing their sense of belonging to an organization which they felt merited a role of complete political control, and rationalizing the attempt to establish that domination. Besides engendering a feeling of organizational accomplishment, this ideology convinced the "legalists" that they could carry out their new "duties" without damaging their own institution, and with substantial benefit to society.

Another factor of great importance at the social and military level should be added to those previously mentioned. Many officials believed that their corporate interest in maintaining professionalism and cohesion would be seriously endangered if they persisted in their decision to suspend direct political participation. The state of society threatened the reintroduction of internal fractionalization. In a praetorian environment military officers, motivated by their own perception of corporate interest, can fall into a period of organizational introspection. But this same interest will lead the military officers to intervene once again as praetorianism persists, to avoid the risk of internal division and decline in the level of professionalization—a risk provoked by the praetorianism of the social context of which they are a part. But—and this is an extremely important point for the theme of this study—this new intervention has the characteristics, purposes, and social effects that reflect the changes in the military organization.

The partisan elections celebrated in 1965 showed that the Peronists still retained a plurality within the electorate. At the same time there were abundant indications that numerous civil sectors had reached the "consensus of termination" and were pressing strongly for a new military intervention. The high level of social protest, marked by strikes and the occupying of businesses, seriously worried the more established sectors. President Illía was noted for his lassitude and his ineffectiveness in making decisions, and the Parliament seemed reduced to a forum for personal quarrels. In 1967 new and more important elections were to be held, and the military continued as divided as always over the eternal problem of permitting or prohibiting the electoral participation of the Peronists. Given the stimulus from other social sectors, the internal evolution of the military, and the continuation of the processes mentioned in the first section of this study, it is no exaggeration to say that in 1965 the major question was simply the date of the new coup d'état, not its execution or its termination of the political regime of 1955–66.[42] The choice of the date seems to have been largely determined by the risk of reintroducing military fractionalization over what attitude to adopt toward the forthcoming elections. To deal with this problem effectively, the "legalist" officers had to execute the coup late enough for the risk to be clearly perceived in the military, but not so late that the electoral campaign of 1967 had already begun. In this way the "legalist" leaders optimized the probability of strong military cohesion in support of the coup d'état and minimized the possibility of civil opposition.[43]

In line with this view of the reasons for the timing of the coup is a statement made by the commander-in-chief of the army, General Pistarini, shortly before the coup was executed:

> The attainment of this situation ["efficiency, spiritual unity, and fulfilled professional capability" of the armed forces] has cost not only time but great sacrifice. Any directive operation to place the army at the service of secondary interests or identify it with political, economic or social sectors commits a crime against the armed forces in seeking its division and confrontation and therefore commits a crime against the country.[44]

On June 28, 1966, the revolutionary junta, made up of the commanders-in-chief of the three branches of the armed forces, deposed President Illía and designated General Onganía as president. In several different documents and speeches the junta and the new president enunciated the wide-ranging "goals of the Revolution," dissolved the institutions of the former political regime, and stated that they were considering staying in power for the indefinite (but doubtless long) period of time required to achieve these goals. With very few exceptions the social sectors and public opinion expressed their support for the coup.[45]

The ideology of "national security" permitted the transformation of a conception of organizational interests into an argument justifying a coup d'état which attempted the indefinite displacement of the civil government personnel. The state of society had to be improved, not only because it implied "underdevelopment" and fed "subversion," but because it threatened to reintroduce military fractionalization. From the point of view of this ideology, a return to the *golpista* period would mean that the "highest interests of the nation" would suffer, due to the inevitable deterioration of the organization which had claimed for itself total obligation and responsibility for the protection of those interests. Under the "national security" doctrine, on the other hand, not only would all the visible and important social problems remain subject to military control, but, in addition, the corporate military goals, especially the attainment of conditions considered vital for the survival and expansion of the organization, would remain indistinguishably linked to the "highest interests of the nation"—as defined by the military.

The real advance in military professionalism, the feeling of organizational accomplishment and of superior capability, the high degree of corporate identification, and the ideology of "national security," characterized a military process which produced enough objective capacity and subjective confidence to execute a coup d'état which sought a drastic and definitive change from the existing political regime. In order to do this, and despite the fact that various civil sectors had reached the termination consensus well before June 1966, it was necessary for the armed forces to have completed the process of professionalization (with the four consequences already indicated) and for the social structure to have presented new dangers of fractionalization in the armed forces. The *golpista* military officers intervened several times, but with much more specific demands and with the expressed purpose of restoring governmental power to "appropriate" civilian rule. When in 1962, the *golpistas* tried to take over the government directly and for an extended period of time, they failed because of their precarious control of the seriously divided military and the absence of a justifying ideology. In contrast, the new military leaders, who were with some historical irony named "legalists," did not intervene until, strongly united, they could take direct control of the government with the intention of maintaining power indefinitely to accomplish much more ambitious goals. For what occurred in 1966, two necessary conditions had to exist which were absent in 1962: (1) variables in the social structure which were expressed in the termination consensus, and (2) variables within the military organization resulting from its process of professionalization. The professionalization of the armed forces in a praetorian context raises the critical point for military intervention. But once the critical point is reached, military intervention takes place with more internal cohesion, with a comprehensive justificatory ideology, and with the purpose of achieving goals much more ambitious than those of the coups undertaken by less professional armed forces. Contrary to what many governing officials and experts have supposed, professionalization of the armed forces does not resolve the endemic problem of militarism. All it does is exchange a higher critical point for the probability of a much more comprehensive military intervention directed toward the establishment of much more complete domination.

What has been said up to this point permits us to propose generalizations which available information suggests should be applicable to other nations whose social structures have similar characteristics of high modernization and mass praetorianism. The next section will be devoted to comparing these propositions with prevailing interpretations in political sociology, with which they differ in several important respects.

III. Comparative Theoretical Focuses on the Political Behavior of the Military

The social and organizational processes described in the preceding sections support propositions[46] applicable to the political behavior of the military in social contexts of high modernization.[47]

Proposition 1: The "highly modernized" nations have distinct characteristics which tend to generate equally distinctive patterns of political behavior. Specifically, it is important to note: (a) a prolonged process of industrialization that fails to acquire either a sufficient level of vertical integration or a scientific-technological structure capable of generating innovations and of applying them continuously to the uneven productive processes typical of this form of industrialization; and (b) the existence of large and complex urban centers with a politically active and highly organized popular sector. Furthermore, high modernization tends to consolidate historically inherited problems (particularly external dependence and inequitable distribution of resources) and to generate high rates of inflation, irregular economic growth and limited governmental capability.

Proposition 2: If this historical legacy also includes a high level of popular alienation from the political regime and its authorities, as well as little conformity between real and institutionally prescribed behavior, it is highly probable that nations experiencing situations of high modernization will undergo prolonged periods of mass praetorianism.[48] In a situation of high modernization and mass praetorianism, political competition tends to establish inter-sectoral violence and threats against the government as the most effective means of formulating and articulating demands. This leads to a decline in the role played by formally democratic institutions, to an even greater diminution of governmental capability for resolving social problems, and to the consolidation of conditions of zero-sum competition between sectors. These consequences reverberate, aggravating mass praetorianism.

The logic of the situation of high modernization and mass praetorianism leads to diminishing socioeconomic returns and to growing political activity on the part of the urban popular sector. In turn, this heightened political activity is perceived by a substantial part of the other, more established sectors as a serious threat to their control. This perception provokes defensive reactions aimed at closing direct access to the political process for the popular sector and its leaders; this tends to be considered a requisite for the elimination of the risk and for the implementation of public policies which, by favoring an even greater concentration of resources in large public and private organizations, will supposedly generate higher and more stable rates of economic growth. But the form the defensive reaction will take depends in great measure on changes in the military organization.[49]

Proposition 3: Given the conditions specified in the previous propositions, there exists a strong probability of frequent interventions by the armed forces, as much by means of threats of force against the national government (*planteos*) as by the taking over of governmental power. The motivation, and a fundamental effect of these interventions, will be the closing of direct political access to the representatives of the popular sector and the denial of their public policy demands. In these interventions, the armed forces express and execute the defensive reaction of the more established sectors to (1) the growing levels of political activism by the popular sector, (2) the conditions of zero sum which characterize the competition for the distribution of resources, and (3) to mass praetorianism generally.

Although the preceding proposition is expressed in very general terms, it coincides with an important current in the study of the political behavior of the military.[50] In an important article, José Nun argued that in contemporary Latin America, political interventions by the military were expressions of the ambiguities and fears aroused in the middle class (from which a good part of the army officers are drawn) by processes of social change which had mobilized the working class and had placed in question the viability of capitalist development in the more economically advanced nations of the continent.[51] Much later, Samuel Huntington continued this line of argument, formulating it in more general terms: the armed forces tend to fulfill a "progressive" role in promoting the entry of the middle class into a political arena previously monopolized by traditional oligarchies; but once this objective is reached, its principal preoccupation is to impede the political participation of what Huntington calls "the lower class."[52]

With certain reservations, it seems clear that the Latin American case supports the interpretation of these two authors. In those cases (such as Argentina and Brazil) in which, through an extended period of industrialization, a substantial part of the middle sectors has secured various agreements with the traditionally dominant sectors, the motivation and effects of military interventions have been in the direction implied by this structuralist focus. In other cases—Argentina during the Perón era, Brazil under Vargas, and modern-day Peru—where the aspirations of numerous middle sectors were to a large extent blocked by still dominant traditional sectors, and where industrialization, density of urban concentration, and the degree of political activism of the urban popular sectors were considerably lower, the armed forces fulfilled the more "progressive" role also foreseen by these authors. But although the structuralist focus points in the correct direction, it leaves various outstanding problems which should be carefully considered.

First, it pays little or purely circumstantial attention to the consequences which military organizational factors can have on the political behavior of the military.[53] Accordingly, this focus refrains from studying over time empirical variations in the form and degree of the closure of political access for the popular sector which military interventions may produce. As the Argentine case illustrates, these different forms of military intervention hold different consequences for the society and for the political regime.

Second, this conception may be sufficient as a generic description of military behavior under different kinds of social structures, but it cannot in reality explain variations in this behavior in similar kinds of societies. One possible solution to this problem, which is utilized by these authors, is to postulate that the middle-class background of the majority of the armed forces officers leads them to "express" or to "represent" the attitudes and interests of the middle class. But the presumption of this linkage as the principal factor explaining the political behavior of the military ignores the factor of military organization itself. It also overlooks the ambiguity of the terms "express" and "represent," and above all, the extreme heterogeneity of the so-called "middle class" or "middle classes" or "middle sectors" in highly modernized societies.[54]

Proposition 4: The different ways in which the armed forces close political access to the popular sector, and reject its public policy demands, depend to an important extent on the nature of the military organization. The state of the military organization is a variable, whose empirical changes should be studied over time because they are a fundamental factor for explaining and predicting the political behavior of the armed forces.

This proposition should be stressed strongly. From it are derived important differences in the interpretation of military behavior that I am proposing from those that come from the "structuralist" focus and from the "neo-realist" focus that I will analyze next. Distinguishing the explanatory role of the level of organization marks one important difference with the "structuralist" authors. A second and more important difference is on the level of military organization as a variable which should be studied empirically over time.

Following the classification proposed by Alfred Stepan, I will call "neo-realist" the focus I will now analyze.[55] According to this point of view:

Distilled to its essentials, the military in developing countries is viewed as an ideologically and structurally cohesive organization capable of high levels of internal discipline and serving as a repository of technological and managerial skill, whose members share a professional belief-system combining the elements of secular rationality, puritanical asceticism, patriotic nationalism, dedication to public service, and an orientation toward the goal of modernization. These conclusions are reached by inferring what the consequences would be of transferring the organizational forms of the military in Western countries to transitional societies.[56]

On the basis of these presumed characteristics of "the military in the developing countries," one deduces that the capabilities of the military are significantly superior to those of the civilian sectors in terms of technological qualification, of possible efficient and rational decision-making and implementation, and of "modernizing" motivations. In turn, this presumed superiority endows the military with special abilities, markedly superior to those of the civilian sectors, to conduct and attain the "development" of their nations.[57] From this conception, it follows easily (although not always in an explicit way) that not only is it probable that the military will directly assume governmental power in the "underdeveloped countries" but also that they should assume it for the sake of "development."[58] The least that can be said about the evidence this interpretation offers in support of its arguments is that it is completely unsatisfactory.[59] But it is worth the effort to analyze some of its aspects and implications.

First, the "neo-realist" focus is a salient example of a futile search. Ever since the proletariat became identified as the great actor from which one could expect great and positive social changes, various ideologies and intellectual trends have tried to identify one or another "collective actor" (the bourgeoisie, the managers, the middle class, the farmers, the intellectuals) as the bearer of positive characteristics which distinguished it clearly from the other actors in its historical context. These special characteristics have been the basis for hoping that this or that "actor" was the executor or decisive vanguard of great social changes—more or less revolutionary ones according to the chosen "actor" and the ideological preferences of the author, but always in agreement with the latter. Many "Western" students of "underdeveloped countries' found that their hopes—extrapolated from the historical experience of their own countries—did not have much substance. The bourgeoisie (or the managers, or the middle class) did not play the central role in promoting "development," understood as a repetition of the patterns of change of their own societies. On the contrary, these observers found themselves faced with an unforeseen persistence of social rigidities and of developmental strangleholds, the emergence of increasing levels of social protest and political instability, the disintegration of preexisting standards of organization of social life, and the appearance of new models that could not be located in the existing conceptual pigeon-holes provided for by the historic experience of their own nations. With the possibility of new international alignments affecting their own national loyalties,[60] the agreement on expectations by these scholars brought many to the "discovery" that, after all, the military was the political actor endowed with the most suitable abilities and attitudes for directing the processes that would culminate in "socioeconomic development," with political stability and with the strong affiliation of these nations with the "Western" sphere.[61]

The simplistic conception of the social structure and of the processes of change implied by the search for the great "actor" is not of utmost importance for the thesis of this work. Rather, it is more relevant to emphasize the conceptual mechanisms that permit attributing such a role to the armed forces in the "underdeveloped" nations. Commenting on the theoretical problems created by "concept expansion," Giovanni Sartori writes:[62]

> By and large, so far we have followed (more or less unwittingly) the line of least resistance: broaden the meaning—and thereby the range of application—of the conceptualizations at hand. That is to say, the larger the world [studied by comparative politics] the more we have resorted to *conceptual stretching*, or conceptual straining, i.e., to vague, amorphous conceptualizations. . . . But the case cannot be proven by *transferring the same denomination* from one context to another. For this amounts to pure and simple terminological camouflage: things are declared alike by making them *verbally* identical.

Disregarding historical contexts, different actors inserted in different social structures receive the same names. This nominal identity permits postulating an incorrect analogy regarding the real attributes of different historical actors. And, in turn, that analogy carries the hope that those different actors will exhibit similar political and social behavior.[63] The risk of committing this erroneous extrapolation from one actor or well-known sector (generally the existing one in some "developed" nation) toward an actor or sector nominally identical, but almost completely unknown (the one existing in the "underdeveloped world") is particularly great in the case of the military. One notes that in almost all of these nations the military has tried to imitate the formal organizational characteristics of the military in the more highly developed countries; it has received training, armaments and strong ideological influence from the military in the country upon which its own nation is most markedly dependent. To theorize by extrapolation one must, at the point of departure, rely upon an impression (which in the light of recent events one can suspect is highly idealized) of what the "developmental" role of the armed forces of the more "developed" countries would be. However, if one is disposed to believe as well that the resemblance in formal characteristics of military organizations is indicative of resemblance in real characteristics, it is then possible to postulate, with some validity and without need of empirical testing, that the military in the "underdeveloped" countries have the special abilities which these authors attribute to them.

Second, only if one is disposed to believe that the formal characteristics of the military organization correspond to a high degree with its real characteristics is it possible to affirm, as the "neo-realist" authors typically do, that the military has a high degree of internal cohesion and possesses vertical patterns of authority which allow it to make efficient and expedient decisions. Further, when this is contrasted with the impression of the inefficiency, confusion and dislocation of the civilian sectors—also typical of these authors—it is possible to postulate the special "developmental" capabilities of the armed forces. But the internal cohesion of the military in the "underdeveloped" countries is one of the more persistent and more unfounded myths of contemporary social science. All the empirical studies show that the internal cohesion of the military is, in the best of cases, a difficult and precarious achievement; more typical are very frequent and very prolonged periods of profound fractionalization.[64] The Argentine case and, in general, all of Latin American history. illustrates this statement quite well.

Third, the attribution of internal cohesion, of superior technological and decision-making capability, and of a modernizing *ethos*—all areas in which the military is contrasted with civilian sectors—implies something more than the previously mentioned extrapolation from an (idealized) image of the characteristics of the military in the more "developed" countries. It also implies ignoring the differences existing in the social contexts of different "underdeveloped" countries. These nations may have in common their "underdevelopment" and the fact that their militaries exist in an "underdeveloped" society. But beyond this hardly useful level of generalization,[65] it is essential to take into account important differences in the societies to which the military belong, as much from one country to another as over a length of time within one country. This is a point upon which the "structuralist" authors have insisted: no study of the political behavior of the military can ignore differences and changes in the state of its social context. The price paid for this error consists in erroneous generalizations based upon the extrapolation from the experience of the more "developed" countries or upon the unjustified extension of the findings in one "underdeveloped" nation to the large and heterogenous whole formed by all "underdeveloped" countries.

Fourth, one can apply the term "army" to the forces in nineteenth-century Prussia, in nineteenth-century Argentina, and in present-day Argentina, but it is deceptive to imply that the concept "army" has the same meaning in these various applications. To mention only two very basic matters: (1) for most of the nineteenth century the Argentine army had no clear supremacy in the control of the means of violence inside the national territory, and (2) most of its members did not dress in a way that

armed forces. The structural position of the armed forces, especially its control over the means of organized violence, permits—if and when the professionalist impulse has been successful—the elaboration or adoption of an ideological justification for political domination in which the corporative interest is identified with "the highest interests of the Nation."

The change in the political ideology of the military officers and its close connection with the organizational changes encompassed in the shift from a low state to a relatively high state of professionalism is of utmost importance. The content of the military officers' political ideology, its changes and connections with the organizational changes, should be contrasted with a third component of the "neo-realist" attitude. This consists of the attribution of a particular *ethos* to the military, resulting from education in military institutions. This *ethos* is composed of a strong devotion to duty, intense national identity, a certain indifference toward civilian sectoral interests, a "puritan" attitude, and a tendency toward corruption weaker than that of the civilian sectors—to which the "neo-realists" impute much less favorable attitudes in all these dimensions. This third attribution of the "neo-realist" point of view again implies taking at face value an ostensible aspect of the military organization: in this case the self-image of the military officers. It is worth mentioning some aspects of this new problem.

First, since empirical data which could verify or disprove the attribution is lacking, it is impossible to know at what point the self-image coincides with real attitudes. The least one can suspect is that the degree of correspondence has important variations from one country to another and over a length of time in the same country.

Second, who holds these attitudes or predispositions? Do all military officers at all hierarchical levels? If not, who ought to hold them in order for it to be possible to affirm that such predispositions permit (together with the attributed characteristics already discussed) military officers to play a privileged "developmental" role? In this sense one can formulate a likely hypothesis: the real existence of the mentioned *ethos* is an inverse function of the degree of political participation by the military. When a group of officers attempts a takeover of governmental power (and more so when it exercises power) it must dedicate a substantial part of its energies, preparation and time to achieving developmental goals. Such actitivies are scarcely military ones.[73] They place the military in daily contact with sectors, problems, and rules for decision-making which probably cause important adjustments in the predispositions or attitudes (presumably) acquired during the interval in which they were more circumscribed by the military's internal organizational life.

Third, these supposedly "functional" attitudes are not the only ones that one might attribute to military officers. Others are strong prejudice against what is political, mental rigidity, bureaucratization, and a predominant preoccupation with order and stability. Additional attitudes could be mentioned that do not seem very adequate for carrying out the complex tasks of governing and promoting "socioeconomic development."[74] This mixture of favorable and unfavorable attitudes (presumably) would imply attribution of a complex group of predispositions. Without empirical data—almost wholly nonexistent—it is impossible to know how each one of these presumed predispositions interacts with the others to generate the attitudinal climate which presumably influences the political behavior of the military.[75]

Fourth and finally, proposition 9 suggests that it may be more useful to locate certain factors of the military's behavior at a more specifically political level. This level is that of the expressed ideologies that define the role of the armed forces in society, outline their relations with other sectors, and legitimatize their domination of governmental power. The degree of possible variations in the military's political behavior emerging from an adequate study of these ideologies will usually be much lower than that corresponding to (presumed) attitudes whose empirical reference is much more vague and isolated from political issues.[76]

Proposition 10: Given the conditions stipulated in the preceding propositions, internal cohesion of the armed forces is converted into the most highly valued organizational achievement, and its preservation into the dominant preoccupation of its members. The persistence of mass praetorianism implies an inevitable risk for the preservation of internal cohesion and/or for the very survival of the military institution. The corporate interest in guaranteeing the preservation of cohesion raises the critical point at which military intervention and the assumption of governmental power become probable. But, insofar as praetorianism is perceived as (and effectively is) a grave menace to cohesion and survival, it creates strong impulses in favor of new military intervention. In contrast to the previous ones, the coups executed by professional armed forces aim at a radical transformation of the social context, in ways which would supposedly eliminate threats to the military organization and to its professional achievements.

This proposition underscores the importance of the perception of corporate military interest as an explanatory factor in the promotion of new coups and in the ends to which they are directed.[77] The professional interests of the military officers (including involvement with their own careers), the expansion of potential political power implied by professionalism, and the emergence of justificatory ideologies cause preservation of internal cohesion and the survival of the organization to predominate in the thoughts of the military leaders. In praetorian conditions, the civilians quickly recognize the efficacy of the armed forces as a channel for their demands and seek from them limited actions to satisfy these demands. But for the professional military leaders it is clear that to continue taking frequent part in civilian conflicts fatally reintroduces fractionalization.[78] This results in a temporary withdrawal by the military from political participation, creating a "political vacuum" in the last stages of mass praetorianism and high modernization. Praetorianism continues in full force, aggravated by the persistence of social problems and by the increase in the rates of political activity of movements and sectors (particularly the popular sector) which are no longer contained by military interventions.[79] But eventually praetorianism, as well as the characteristics of growing conflict which tend to accompany the "withdrawal" of the military, ends by being perceived as the most serious threat to internal cohesion and to the survival of the military organization. Whether by means of national problems on which the armed forces cannot avoid taking positions which will divide them (the case of the electoral participation of the Peronists in Argentina) or by means of the emergence of mass movements that seem resolved to eliminate the armed forces or at least reconstruct them profoundly (the Brazilian and Greek cases), a context of mass praetorianism cannot fail to generate strong inducements in favor of a coup on the part of the professional armed forces.

IV. Some Suggestions and Projections

> Uncertainty appears as the fundamental problem for complex organizations, and coping with uncertainty, as the essence of the administrative process. . . . External uncertainties stem from 1) generalized uncertainty, or lack of cause/effect understanding in the culture at large, and 2) contingency, in which the outcomes of organizational action are in part determined by the actions of elements of the environment.[80]

These observations were not written with the military in mind. They are conclusions formulated by a student of the behavior of civilian organizations (particularly private firms). Organizations try to reduce uncertainty as it is perceived as affecting the internal state and/or viability of the organization. With this objective they attempt to negotiate, with those who appear to control the factors underlying the uncertainty, the "solutions" which will stabilize the "context" relevant to the organization.[81] In other cases, instead of negotiating, organizations may attempt a more ambitious strategy: if there is no satisfactory way to regulate the context, an organization "tries to move its boundaries—to incorporate or encircle unreliable units."[82] In both negotiation and incorporation, the organization's directors operate through concepts and strategies which reflect their bias in perception and evaluation, as well as the patterns of decision-making which result from organizational specialization in certain types of activity.[83]

There is a striking parallel between these findings of modern organization theory and the segment of political behavior studied in this paper. The military's "withdrawal" from direct participation in the praetorian political game is in good part determined by the concern to assure the survival and eventual consolidation of its organization. But, although this "withdrawal" doubtless improves the state of the organization, it resolves neither the uncertainty provoked by its praetorian context, nor the risks which that context presents for military organization. In fact, it would seem to accentuate them. The period of organizational introspection required by the transition from a low to a high level of professionalization isolates the military from its social context. But this isolation is precarious and temporary. It soon becomes evident to military leaders that if they attempt to maintain this isolation for a prolonged period, internal cohesion will be broken, and the very survival of the organization will be threatened. The social context is a source of risks which the military cannot control unless it succeeds in converting the social context into a form which (presumably) will assure that these risks will be definitively eliminated. The uncertainty emanating from the social context compounds the feeling of organizational accomplishment and superior aptitude for completing a utopian political project designed to obtain a perfectly integrated and harmonized society (that is, one which is no longer a source of uncertainty).[84] In accordance with what has been said thus far, the ways in which relevant aspects of the social context are perceived and evaluated closely correspond to the organization's biases: the "actors" in the context are "enemies" to be defeated on various "fronts"; the solution to social problems implies "battles" to be won, "operations" to complete. An essentially hostile conception of the social context and its actors, and of the means suitable for confronting them, contributes[85] to the military's implantation of authoritarian political forms, regardless of the "progressive" or "conservative" content of its projected public policies.

These analogies do not seem spurious. Their validation will permit us to subsume several aspects of the military's political behavior, until now unexplained or seemingly paradoxical, under the genus of organizational behavior oriented toward the reduction of uncertainty in the social context. In addition, these analogies serve to place in proper perspective two fundamental differences between the behavioral patterns of private organizations and those of the armed forces. First, the latter can utilize means which are only rarely at the disposal of private organizations. On the basis of its control over the instruments of organized violence and its high degree of internal cohesion, professionalized armed forces need not *negotiate* with other actors a "satisfactory" stabilization of the social context (negotiation which praetorianism suggests would be hardly successful). The armed forces can *impose* upon other political actors, through force or explicit threats of force, its own conception of the ways in which the social context should be stabilized. The second and fundamental difference is that, due to the structural position of the armed forces, their relevant social context can only be the entire national entity of which they are a part. The result is the expansion of the real and ideological "borders" of the military organization, aimed, according to James Thompson's observations, at absorbing or incorporating into the orbit of its decisions all of the social problems which seem important to military leaders. The national character of the context relevant to the military also implies that any attempt at stabilization will center on the attainment of direct control of the national government. It represents the focal point of power and legality from which the social context can most efficiently and definitively be modified.

Armed forces which are minimally professionalized tend to be a nominal aggregate of civil-military coalitions, lacking in a strong sense of corporate identity. In contrast, professionalized armed forces are acutely conscious of their distinctiveness and convinced of their superior capabilities in comparison with those of civilian sectors. This contributes to the military officers' self-image as members of an organization clearly differentiated from anything civilian and also to the adjustment of their political behavior to their perception of their corporate interests. Because of their professionalism, not in spite of it, professionalized armed forces manifest a high probability of taking upon themselves the responsibility for overcoming recurring civil-military crises by way of the installation of a new political regime. They consider the potential militarization of all salient social problems and their resolution in the direction of consensus, integration, and harmony as ideologically justified. Under conditions of mass praetorianism and high modernization, the military's public policy would consist fundamentally in suppressing social conflict and social revolutionary movements, achieving the political deactivation of popular sectors, closing all channels of direct or indirect political access to "popular" leaders, and adopting a technocratic and "apolitical" conception of "development." This conception inevitably favors the concentration of all types of resources (including economic resources, though not exclusively) in favor of large public and private organizations; and its political viability requires, among other necessary conditions, the effective deactivation of popular sectors. In addition, the fact that there is insufficient private capital and technology to undertake large-scale projects determines that private foreign capital will play a critical role in the distribution of power within the bureaucratic-authoritarian regime imposed by the professionalized armed forces.[86]

The political utopia of professionalized armed forces is a defensive reaction against the multiple tensions of high modernization and its probable concomitant, mass praetorianism.[87] Once the government has been taken over, the results fall far short of the expectations of that utopian vision. But even so, the inauguration of, and attempts to consolidate, a bureaucratic-authoritarian regime have the effect of transforming the distribution of political and economic power in the society. Large public and private organizations concentrate power and resources which in the preceding period they had had to share with leaders of political parties and mass movements, with unions and with representatives of small firms. Dependency is consolidated through foreign-owned firms which produce for the internal market and no longer for export. The accelerated diffusion of means of mass communication (facilitated by the high concentration of urban population), the preeminence of technocratic roles, and the close ties between the elite sectors of the local armed forces and those of the United States further contribute to the growth of dependency.[88]

As with all predominantly defensive ideologies, the mobilizational content[89] of the professionalized military's political utopia is weak, and its real influence over behavior tends to diminish after a relatively brief exercise of governmental power. Once the armed forces are in power, the realities of national government begin to blunt the simplistic angles of their ideology, especially when, as in the case of Argentina, the new regime fails to suppress expressions of social protest and fails to implement a technocratic conception of "development." The ideology's loss of effective force spells the reemergence of mass praetorianism, zero-sum conditions in the social context, and military factionalism.

Proposition 11: Once they are in direct control of the national government, leaders of professionalized armed forces remain preoccupied with the preservation of internal cohesion. This preoccupation permeates their criteria for decision-making and is hardly congruent with the attribution to the military of superior capabilities for rapid and efficient decision-making.

The sharing of an ideology of "national security" (or its equivalent) and a social utopia of harmony and integration does not prevent daily dissension on problems as fundamental as the criteria by which public and private goods should be allocated among diverse regions and sectors. The military's concern not to carry these disagreements to the point of provoking internal factionalism leads to dysfunctional consequences: a marked slowness in decision-making; an inhibition of initiative in governmental decision-making due to the veto power of various military strata;[90] the application of criteria of military seniority in assignments to governmental positions (including president of the nation);[91] the arbitrary allocation of certain governmental functions and areas of competence to particular service branches; immense difficulties in coordinating the actions of functionaries who are, in reality, responsible to their respective branches.[92] The classic discovery is made that governmental problems are much more complex than had been imagined and much less amenable to resolution through vertical patterns of decision-making and command.[93]

Proposition 12: Government by professionalized armed forces once again generates the serious risk of rupturing their internal cohesion. If their governance is "successful," this risk can be temporarily controlled but at the cost of high levels of repression and a marked isolation of the military government from many political actors. If their governance "fails," internal cohesion is inevitably ruptured. The principal cleavage within the military organization emerges between those who maintain that an even more right-wing radicalization is necessary ("deepening the Revolution") and those who maintain that a quick "exit" from the most salient position of power would be the lesser of evils given the circumstances.

In the case of Argentina, real social explosions demonstrated that the government had failed to politically deactivate the popular sector and its most important organizational support, the unions. The government also "failed" to guarantee "order and authority," raise and stabilize rates of economic growth, diminish inflation, alleviate balance of payments problems, and carry out other measures required by the technocratic conception of "development" which it attempted to implement and which its civilian allies demanded. In addition, the policies of high concentration typical of bureaucratic-authoritarian regimes seriously affected the interests of a large stratum of national entrepreneurs. The opposition of students and intellectuals found attentive audiences in these sectors. General Onganía was succeeded by General Levingston, who seemed inclined to "deepen the Revolution." A short time later he was deposed by General Lanusse, on the basis of the argument favoring a rapid "exit."

In 1971, a new coup, promoted by officers who saw in "exit" a "betrayal" of the "Revolution" and the promises made by the armed forces, failed. It was not yet clear, in June of 1972, whether a "continuist" position or the attempt to find an exit via elections would prevail within the armed forces. In other words, military factionalism reappeared, simultaneous with mass praetorianism and the zero-sum socioeconomic processes alluded to in the first section of this paper. The expectations built around the political utopia delineated by the military in 1966 had to be adjusted to the recognition that the regime inaugurated by that coup d'état had failed in even the most narrowly technocratic norms of performance.

Although the basis for my opinions on this matter is highly speculative, it seems clear that the principal component of the new internal cleavage remains the perception of corporate interest. But whereas in the past the effort at professionalization and coup d'état seemed the most "obvious" means of protecting that interest, today it is far from obvious which side of the option between "continuism" and "exit" can best serve it. "Exiting" implies elections—mass praetorianism has reemerged, the government is clearly unpopular and cannot obtain enough guarantees that the "appropriate" candidate will be elected. On the other hand, the indefinite continuation of the current regime presupposes a degree of military cohesion currently nonexistent. Governmental failure has eroded the military's confidence in the authority of its "developmentalist" aptitudes, and an enormous degree of governmental coercion, probably too disruptive to the interests under protection, would have to be exercised.[94]

This paper has focused on one aspect of the political behavior of military institutions: their formulation of demands via "threat" tactics and more especially, their execution of coups d'état against national governments.[95] This is also the focus of most of the literature on the military in politics, but I hope to have demonstrated the flaws in the currently prevailing emphases and the potential for alternative focuses. The Argentinian armed forces of 1960, 1965, and 1970 were nominally the same. Nevertheless, their political behavior differed in many very fundamental ways. Processes of change at the level of the larger social context and within the organizations themselves determined and were influenced by those differences in the militaries' political behavior—their objectives, their political ideologies, the means and aptitudes at their disposal (and those which they thought they had) for the attainment of objectives, the public policies which they proclaimed and, later, the public policies which they constructed and attempted to implement.

The resulting framework is one of complex interactions over time, between two structural levels, the larger social level and the organizational level, and between those levels and the military's political behavior. Simplifying, one can affirm that a high level of modernization tends, on one hand, to result in mass praetorianism, and on another, to introduce "professionalizing" changes in military organization. These, in turn, effect critical changes in the means and objectives with which militaries attempt to affect the social context of which they are a part. In a first stage, concerns centered on the military organization itself induce a successful attempt at professionalization. In a second stage, that same motivation contributes toward the execution of a new coup d'état, which inaugurates a "bureaucratic" type of political authoritarianism, characteristic of highly modernized countries which have suffered a period of mass praetorianism. This coup d'état implies a level of political participation by the military and a militarization of social problems which greatly exceed what could have been attempted by officers of a less professionalized institution. Therefore in conditions of high modernization, a relatively high level of military professionalization is achieved which in short order induces the most intense and comprehensive type of military politicization. This is a paradox built into the very logic of the situation, to which a second paradox is added: the high probability that this politicization will destroy a fundamental component of military professionalization, whose preservation powerfully contributed to the decision to assume governmental power—the internal cohesion of the armed forces. Therefore, mass praetorianism and military factionalism can easily emerge in the political regime which the military implanted precisely in the hope of eliminating both. Should this occur, "the politicians" may return to the scene, but it would be risky to guarantee them an incumbency longer than that required for the concretizing of a new professionalist attempt by the armed forces.

Notes

1. When referring to the "military" in this study, I am referring to the "officers of the armed forces." When I refer to any of the branches of the armed forces, I will specify which one I am referring to, "army", "navy", or "air force."
2. For a development of this section's theme, I recommend my book *Modernization and Bureaucratic Authoritarianism: Studies in South American Politics* (Berkeley: Univ. of California Press, 1973).
3. I am placing the terms "development" and "underdevelopment" in quotation marks. In doing this I want to register my disagreement with the concepts underlying these terms, concepts which I will discuss below.
4. In using the concept of "modernization" and its related term "high modernization," I follow David E. Apter, *The Politics of Modernization* (Chicago: Univ. of Chicago Press, 1965), and *Choice and the Politics of Allocation*, (New Haven: Yale University Press, 1971).

   According to Apter a situation of "high modernization" consists of an extended penetration of institutions, roles, and information generated in the more industrialized societies, which is not accompanied (in the society which receives these "transplants") by the rapid creation of new information and its continual application to the productive-technological processes. In my own previously cited study, I argue that despite the fundamentally derivative nature of these transplants, differences among them are indicative of different levels of modernization among nations. In turn, those different levels of modernization correspond to the basic differences in the productive structure, in the patterns of social stratification, and in the norms of political behavior of the nations being compared. Those differences become especially salient through the analysis of data related to the "centers" of each of the compared countries. In terms of this data, the South American countries can be classified as follows: Argentina and Brazil (adding Mexico if figures related to all Latin American countries are included) are the nations which have the most highly modernized "centers"; Chile, Colombia, Peru, Venezuela, and Uruguay are in an intermediate group; and Bolivia, Ecuador and Paraguay are the nations with the lowest level of modernization in their national centers. These results, attributable to the structural characteristics of the centers of each of these nations, differ from the results produced by the studies of aggregate figures current in sociology and political science. These studies use nationally averaged figures that inevitably blur the differences of intranational heterogeneity. The result is that—for example—a country like Brazil, which has one of the most highly modernized centers of the continent, is classified "far below" Argentina. In this way, the type of social structural data which

seems most useful for the study of numerous characteristics of political behavior at the national level is diluted. This note, which is a compact
summary of the first chapter of my *Modernization and Bureaucratic
Authoritarianism* underlies the theoretical discussion that I will use in the
last section of this study. It only remains to be added that the classification
of two countries at different levels of modernization does not imply, in any
way, that one country is more or less "developed" than another. In all cases,
modernization is a characteristic—observable in diverse structural levels—
of countries which are dependent and subject to numerous social rigidities.

5. For the purpose of this study, I am designating as the popular (urban)
sector that sector composed of the working class and of segments of the
middle class (principally consisting of unionized workers).

6. Statistics from Banco Central, *Boletín Estadístico*, various issues.

7. CEPAL, *El Desarrollo Económico y la Distribución del Ingreso en la
Argentina*, 1968. This is a work of primary importance for the study of
the socio-political dynamics of the period.

8. C. Díaz Alejandro (*Essays on the Economic History of the Argentine
Republic*, Yale University Press, 1970, p. 356) estimates that the income
elasticity of the demand for imported goods was 2.6. (In other words, each
unit of growth of national income caused an increase of demand of 2.6
units of imported goods.)

9. For economic analysis of these policies, see A. Ferrer et. al., *Los Planes de
Estabilazación en la Argentina* (Paidos, 1968).

10. Without considering yet how this "sector" was distributed between workers
and entrepreneurs.

11. Defined here in the sense of H. Lasswell and A. Kaplan (*Power and
Society*, Yale University Press, 1950) as the capacity to submit to severe
limitations and sanctions.

12. By *planteos* I mean demands formulated by officers of the armed forces,
which are accompanied by the threat of the use of force in the event they
are not satisfied by the national government.

13. The observation is not strictly true for the period 1963–66. During this
period the national government made a clear effort to diminish the degree
to which public decisions were subjected to the game of sectoral threats.
But apart from the fact that it is difficult—and unnecessary for the purposes of this study—to discover to what degree this was achieved, it would
seem that this aided the overthrow in which all the participants of the
praetorian game—losers and winners—played a part.

14. According to this author, "praetorianism" emerges when the levels of
political participation and mobilization markedly exceed the levels of
political institutionalization. "Mass praetorianism" tends to occur when
this disjunction occurs in highly modernized and politically mobilized
societies where large socio-political movements and complex organizations
play an important role. In various sections this author describes the
principal aspects and consequences of mass praetorianism. "In all societies,
specialized social groups engage in politics. What makes such groups seem
more 'politicized' in a praetorian society is the absence of effective political
institutions capable of mediating, refining, and moderating group political
action. In a praetorian system social forces confront each other nakedly;

no political institutions, no corps of professional political leaders are recognized or accepted as legitimate intermediaries to moderate group conflict. Equally important, no agreement exists among the groups as to the legitimate and authoritative methods for resolving conflicts. . . . In a praetorian society, however, not only are the actors varied, but so also are the methods used to decide upon office and policy. Each group employs means which reflect its particular nature and capabilities. The wealthy bribe; students riot; workers strike; and the military coup." Samuel Huntington, *Political Order in Changing Societies* (New Haven: Yale Univ. Press, 1968), p. 196.

15. I mean by "resources" all of the human and economic means available to the government for decision-making and implementation of public policies. For data on this question and others previously mentioned, see my *Modernization and Bureaucratic Authoritarianism*.

16. Expressed in its most general terms, this potential dilemma has always challenged political theory. But the probability of its emergence is particularly high in conditions of high modernization, where the persistence of several bottlenecks to development, of dependence and of social rigidities, all historically inherited, interact with high levels of political activity and organizational support within the complex group of political actors created by the high level of social differentiation characteristic of the more modernized "centers" of these nations. By "emergence" of the dilemma, I am indicating not only its detection by the observer, but also its perception by the contending actors and the resulting adjustment of their strategies to that perception.

17. The situation described in these pages agrees very well with David Apter's analysis of the unfolding of what he calls "reconciliation systems" in situations of high modernization.

18. Naturally in this type of situation the formation of coalitions follows well-defined patterns. In my *Modernization and Bureaucratic Authoritarianism*, I argue that, in a context of high modernization and mass praetorianism, the tendency is toward the formation of a winning coalition supported by large private and public organizations (including the armed forces in the latter). The personnel who occupy the top positions in these organizations tend to perceive the "solutions" to the state of the social structure as requiring a high concentration of economic and political resources which would benefit the organizations they control. This project, in turn, implies the political elimination of the popular sector, which must pay a good portion of the cost of the public decisions which further this high concentration. The forced political exclusion of the popular sector underlines the crucial importance of governmental enforcement of the public policies of the "bureaucratic-authoritarian" regime which this coalition tends to inaugurate. This, in turn, emphasizes the important role that the military sector plays within the coalition. But as I will point out further on, important changes in the structure of the military organization itself must occur so that it can play such a role, and, consequently, that the new political regime can be installed.

19. This and the following section are based on the analysis of publications and on interviews with military officers which were carried on intermit-

tently since 1957–58. Until 1963–64 I spoke with them more as a participant than as an observer of the processes which are being examined here.

20. Taken from *La Prensa,* April 9, 1959.

21. Concerning this situation see chapter 4 of my *Modernization and Bureaucratic Authoritarianism* or "Un juego imposible: competición y coaliciones entre partidos políticos en Argentina, 1955–1966," *Revista Latinoamericana de Sociología,* 1972.

22. J. M. Saravia argues that these organizational preoccupations, and not democratic convictions, were the determining factor in the "anti-coup" position of these officers (*Hacia la Salida,* Emece, 1968). This interpretation is supported by the prologue to his book, written by one of the more influential military officials, General Lopez Aufranc. The crucial significance of this organizational preoccupation was also evident in the conversations I had with military officials before and after the emergence of this internal conflict.

23. These officials were soon designated by names with positive connotations, such as "professionalists" or "legalists," which should be compared with the derogatory implications of the names given to their rivals.

24. By "professionalism-professionalization" I mean a condition of the military organization characterized by: (1) technical and organizational capacity for the management of those means of violence overwhelmingly superior to those available to civilians; (2) internal cohesion, expressed in regular obedience to the formally established lines of command; (3) corporate self-identification, expressed in "a sense of organic unity and consciousness of themselves as a group apart from laymen." This last is taken from Samuel Huntington (*The Soldier and the State,* A. Knopf and Random House, 1957, p. 10), whose definition of professionalism inspired this study.

25. After 1963 the incidents of open military disobedience to hierarchical superiors disappeared. In addition, even the *golpista* officials whom I've interviewed since 1963 agreed that the organizational changes implemented by the "legalists" included (and to a large extent were based on) a notable improvement in operating patterns of authority.

26. For more information on this point see, Robert Potash, "Argentina," in L. McAlister et. al., *The Military in Latin American Socio-political Evolution: Four Case Studies* (American University, Washington, D.C., 1970), pp. 85–126.

27. On this point and other related aspects see L. Veneroni, *Estados Unidos y las Fuerzas Armadas de América Latina* (Ediciones Periferia, 1971). This agreement and the "advisory" military missions are closely linked with the doctrine of "national security" to which I will refer later on.

28. In my conversations with "legalist" officials, a theme which appeared time after time was that the *golpistas* had turned into slaves of civil groups and "politicians," without benefit to the state of the social structure and with serious damage to the military organization. I also have the impression that after the "legalist" victory, there was an important change in the type of personal contact which the military leaders maintained. This contact tended to be progressively concentrated on technocrats and "apolitical" civilians in such a way that personal and institutional links with people in control of large organizations (above all private) were consolidated; this alliance constituted the nucleus of the coalition which executed the coup

d'état of 1966. But, and also in contrast with the previous period, the civilian contacts during the "legalist" period tended to be defined within the framework of a subordinate relationship in which the armed forces, as an organization and according to the hierarchical lines of command, received "technical" information over a wide range of social problems offered by those contacts.

29. For an orthodox example of the "legalist" position (and its numerous ambiguities), see General B. Rattenbach, *El Sector Militar de la Sociedad,* (Biblioteca del Círculo Militar Argentino, 1966). P. Beltran and J. Ochoa de Eguilar (*Las Fuerzas Armadas Hablan,* Paidós, 1969) analyze the content of a number of military statements, among them those corresponding to the "legalist" period.

30. In this speech, General Onganía spoke in his capacity as commander-in-chief of the army with the specific purpose of outlining the armed forces' conception of its place and function in Argentine society. The complete text of this speech can be found in *La Prensa,* August 6, 1964.

31. *Ibid.*

32. See R. Girardet, ed., *La Crise Militaire Française, 1945–62: Aspects Sociologiques et Idéologiques* (Colin, 1964).

33. With respect to this particular motive, consult L. Veneroni, *op. cit.;* R. Barber and E. Ronning, *Internal Security and Military Power* (Ohio University Press, 1966); W. Just, "Soldiers", *Atlantic* (October–November, 1970); and R. P. Case, "El Entrenamiento de los Militares Latinoamericanos en los EEUU," *Aportes,* no. 6 (October 1967), pp. 44–56.

34. The phrases in quotations correspond to the definition of "internal warfare" according to the official doctrine of the Argentine army: "Conducción para las Fuerzas Terrestres," Anexo I, inciso F, número 37 (El Instituto Geográfico Militar, 1968).

35. The quotations are from an article by General J. Guglialmelli, "Función de las Fuerzas Armadas en la Actual Etapa del Proceso Histórico Argentino," *Estrategia,* no. 1 (May–June, 1969), pp. 8–19. For a similar vein of thought consult General O. Villegas, *Guerra Revolucionaria Comunista* (Pleamar, 1963), and *Políticas y Estrategias para el Desarrollo y la Seguridad Nacional* (Pleamar, 1969).

36. General J. Guglialmelli, *op. cit.;* the same conception is obvious in a number of speeches and statements by leaders of the armed forces from 1963–64 to the present.

37. The quote is from the definition of "national security" found in a document of the Superior War College, "La Seguridad Nacional. Un Concepto de Palpitante Actualidad," *Estrategia,* no. 4 (November–December, 1969), pp. 132–134. For a similar definition see the "Ley de Seguridad Nacional," no. 16.970. Also see General O. Villegas, *ops. cits.*

38. J. Guglialmelli, who points out that "development as an essential factor of national security constitutes a basic part of our military doctrine"; "Fuerzas Armadas y Subversión Interior," *Estrategia,* no. 2 (July–August, 1969), pp. 7–14. Also see General O. Villegas, *op. cit.,* 1969 and the Superior War College, *op. cit.*

39. Superior War College, *op. cit.*

40. J. Guglialmelli, *op. cit.,* July–August, 1969.

236 Guillermo A. O'Donnell

41. For a typical example of this feeling of superior capability see Colonel M. Orsolini, *Ejército Argentino y Crecimiento Nacional* (Arayú, 1965). Also, works by the military authors already cited.

42. Carlos Astiz ("The Argentine Armed Forces: Their Role and Political Involvement," *The Western Political Quarterly*, 22, no. 4, pp. 862–878, 1969) has compiled publications which openly discussed the coup d'état before its actual occurrence.

43. This interpretation of the choice of the date of coup d'état and of the reasons which led to that decision is taken from the primary information which came from interviews with "legalist" officials, in Robert Potash, *op. cit.*

44. *La Prensa,* May 30th, 1966.

45. For data on this and other matters alluded to in this section, consult my *Modernization and Bureaucratic Authoritarianism,* chapter 2; also see Carlos Astiz, *op. cit.*

46. Each of those processes are connected with a number of the propositions. The propositions group and organize them for easier comprehension.

47. For another South American example of high modernization, Brazil, consult Alfred Stepan, *The Military in Politics: Changing Patterns in Brazil* (Princeton University Press, 1971). This book and my conversations with its author have greatly influenced the present study.

48. The necessity for the qualification introduced in this paragraph is made evident by a third Latin American case of high modernization, Mexico. In spite of the fact that this country displays the structural characteristics of high modernization, (including an increasing concentration of resources in large organizations, in which private owners of foreign property predominate; see among others, M. Singer, *Growth, Equality and the Mexican Experience,* The University of Texas Press, 1969, and P. Gonzalez Casanova, *La Democracia en México,* México D. F., 1965), the legitimacy of the regime, of its institutions and of its governmental personnel—resulting from a still fresh revolutionary past—has impeded, until now at least, the emergence of mass praetorianism.

49. Propositions 1 and 2 are a synthesis of a theory of the emergence of bureaucratic authoritarian regimes in cases of high modernization. In my previously cited book, I have attempted a first statement of that theory in relation to contemporary South America and its two countries with the most highly modernized centers, Argentina and Brazil. The strong tendency toward mass praetorianism and authoritarianism in situations of high modernization suggests similarities to other, non-South American cases. Contemporary Greece, and various central European countries between the two world wars, merit detailed study in this direction. See especially K. Legg, *Politics in Modern Greece* (Stanford University Press, 1969), and A. Janos, "The One-Party State and Social Mobilization: East Europe Between the Wars," in S. Huntington and C. Moore, *Authoritarian Politics in Modern Societies, the Dynamics of Established One-Party Systems,* pp. 204–235 (Basic Books, 1970). Although the processes which preceded its inauguration registered a level of violence significantly greater than those already mentioned, contemporary Spain's authoritarian regime exhibits the characteristics associated with high modernization. See especially the study by J. Linz, "An Authoritarian Regime: Spain," recently reprinted in

S. Rokkan and E. Allardt, eds., *Mass Politics* (Free Press, 1970). I have proposed designating these regimes "bureaucratic" because of two of their more fundamental and distinctive characteristics: large public and private organizations on which they base their domination and the typical patterns of personal careers for most of their governmental personnel. These authoritarian regimes are certainly very different from the "traditional" authoritarian ones that correspond to societies predominantly agrarian, scarcely differentiated, and endowed with only a small nucleus of political activism. They are also very different from the "populist" authoritarian regimes. These latter regimes, of which the present Peruvian one seems to be a good example, include an attempt to expand popular political participation and activity, together with the adoption of measures to channel and limit this activity by means of rigid governmental controls. In these efforts the "populist" regimes should be contrasted with the bureaucratic-authoritarian regimes, which attempt the radical elimination of political participation by the popular sector, its political deactivation and its domination by a coalition of large organizations in which the role of foreign-owned firms which produce for the domestic market is increasingly important. On the bureaucratic regimes one can find more detailed accounts in F. Cardoso and E. Faleto, *Dependencia y Desarrollo en América Latina, Siglo XXI,* 1969 and in my work, *op. cit.*

50. This trend has been a healthy reaction against the "neo-realist" (or "militarist") focus which I will criticize later in this study. For a good examination of the various interpretations of the problem of military intervention see O. Cuellar, "Notas Sobre la Participación Política de los Militares en América Latina," *Aportes,* no. 19, pp. 7–41.

51. See J. Nun, "The Middle Class Military Coup," in C. Veliz, ed., *The Politics of Conformity in Latin America* (Oxford University Press, 1967), pp. 66–118. There is a slightly different Spanish version in *Desarrollo Económico,* "Crisis Hegemónica y Golpe Militar de Clase Media," no. 22–23. [An edited reprint of this article appears in this volume.—Ed.]

52. S. Huntington, *op. cit.,* 1968. This focus, which will be called "structuralist" for its emphasis on ordered factors situated at the global social structural level, is synthesized clearly in the following passage from the cited work: "[The military] become the guardians of the existing middle-class order. They are thus, in a sense, the door-keepers in the expansion of political participation in a praetorian society: their historical role is to open the door to the middle class and to close it to the lower class" (p. 222). Other authors have expressed similar points of view, either on Latin America (M. Needler, *Political Development in Latin America: Instability, Violence and Revolutionary Change,* Random House, 1968) or on "underdeveloped" countries (E. Nordlinger, "Soldiers in Mufti: the Impact of Military Rule upon Economics and Social Change in Non-Western States," *The American Political Science Review,* 64, no. 4, pp. 1112–1130, 1970). Nordlinger's article contains a good critique of the "neo-realist" or "militarist" conception, which I will analyze.

53. Again S. Huntington eloquently expresses this point of view: "The effort to answer the question, 'What characteristics of the military establishment of a new nation facilitate its involvement in domestic politics?' is misdirected because the most important causes of military intervention in

politics are not military but political and reflect not the social and organizational characteristics of the military establishment but the political and institutional structure of the society." *Op. cit.*, 1968, p. 194. The position is embellished further in the descriptive parts of the works by J. Nun and E. Nordlinger, but it is characteristic of the view which I have called "structuralist" that the explanatory arguments are centered on the level of the global social structure.

54. The "middle class" tends to be no more than an immense residual category consisting of those that are neither particularly rich nor particularly poor. Therefore, especially in the context of high modernization where social differentiation has increased enormously (especially in the large urban centers), this category includes such sectors as public functionaries, students, intellectuals, small businessmen, employees, and others, whose political behavior usually differs in many and very important respects. Which of these sectors is "represented" or "expressed" in the political behavior of the military? And although this question may have an answer, in what form does the link between the "middle class" and the political behavior of the military operate, especially with regard to the mediation of the organizational level of the military? For a similar critique, see A. Stepan, *op. cit.*, pp. 45–46. Of course, with these reflections I do not pretend to do justice to the works which represent a formidable advance with respect to those that I will analyze later on.

55. I am using the designation proposed by A. Stepan, *op. cit.* Possibly it would be more precise to give the name "militarist" to this conception, not only because of its kind evaluation of the "developmental" capabilities and potentialities of the military, but also because of its tacit prescription that the military should take over governmental power directly.

56. The quotation is from R. Price, "A Theoretical Approach to Military Rule in New States: Reference Group Theory and the Ghanaian Case," *World Politics*, 23, no. 3, pp. 399–430 (1971). This author adds some interesting alternatives to his critique of the "neo-realist" focus. See also A. Stepan, *op. cit.*, pp. 7, 253.

57. In the future when I refer to the attribution of "special abilities" to the military, it should be understood in the sense expressed here.

58. For additional works formulating this point of view, one can read G. Pauker, "Southeast Asia as a Problem Area in the Next Decade," *World Politics*, 11, pp. 325–345 (1959); L. Pye, *Aspects of Political Development*, pp. 172–187 (Little Brown, 1966); H. Daadler, *The Role of the Military in Developing Countries* (Mouton, 1962) and, with specific reference to the Latin American case, J. J. Johnson, *The Military and Society in Latin America* (Stanford Univ. Press, 1964). Other authors recognize a similar function by the military sector, but stop short of coming to the conclusion that those (presumed) characteristics allow the military to play a privileged role in "development." See, for example, S. Finer, *The Man on Horseback: the Role of the Military in Politics* (Praeger, 1962); M. Janowitz, *The Military in the Political Development of New Nations: An Essay in Comparative Analysis* (The University of Chicago Press, 1962); E. Shils, "The Military in the Political Development of New States," in J. Johnson, ed., *The Role of the Military in Underdeveloped Countries*, pp.

7–68 (Princeton University Press, 1962); and E. Lieuwen, *Arms and Politics in Latin America,* (Praeger, 1960).

59. On the basis of their case studies, A. Stepan and R. Price, *ops. cits.*, also argue that the position criticized here lacks all empirical substance. See, in the same sense, E. Nordlinger, *op. cit.*

60. Or, to put it more simply: disillusionment with the possibilities of "development" and the preoccupation (closely connected with the cold war) with the incorporation of "underdeveloped nations" into other international spheres of power.

61. This change of expectations and of tone, as well as their consequences on the analysis and recommendations that one derives, is particularly visible in the case of an author who has written influential works on Latin America. In his book published in 1958 (*Political Change in Latin America: The Emergence of the Middle Sectors*), J. J. Johnson attributes a privileged developmental role to the "middle sectors," and conceives of development politically in terms of the emergence and consolidation of democratic political regimes. In his later book (published in 1964), the optimism of the previous work has disappeared, his emphasis on order and stability is greater, and the military has displaced the "middle sectors" as the principal depository of the author's hopes. For a good analysis of the strong emphasis on political stability underlying a good part of the literature on "political development," see M. Blackman, "Latin American Political Development: the View from the U.S.," paper presented at the Seminario sobre Indicadoras de Desarrollo Nacional, Río de Janeiro, 1972.

62. G. Sartori, "Concept Misformation in Comparative Politics," *The American Political Science Review,* 64, no. 4 (1970). The quotes are from pages 1034 and 1054, and the emphasis is from the original.

63. This critique not only ignores the underlying differences between identical names, but also ignores the differences which, even between really similar sectors, would result from their insertion in different global social contexts (national units in this case).

64. For similar affirmations based on their own data see A. Stepan and R. Price, *ops. cits.* See also D. Rapoport, "The Political Dimensions of Military Usurpation," *Political Science Quarterly,* 83, pp. 551–573 (1968), and W. C. McWilliams, "Introduction," in W. C. McWilliams, ed., *Garrisons and Government* (Chandler Publishing Co., 1967).

65. Or, to be more exact: this level of vagueness.

66. The situation of various countries of the third world and the memoirs of military chiefs cited by R. Price suggest that not even these two characteristics of the military can yet be really taken for granted.

67. It could be argued that the armed forces can play its supposedly decisive or privileged role as vanguard or principal executor of "development" without the necessity of directly controlling the national government. But, to my knowledge, not even the most openly militaristic authors have attempted this argument. One apparent exception could be seen to derive from the arguments for implanting the doctrines of "civic action" among the Latin American armed forces. But no one seems to believe fully in the developmental consequences of activities oriented explicitly toward preventing "subversion" in particularly depressed areas and/or toward keep-

ing busy officers who, it is feared, would otherwise conspire against the national authorities. For this explicit motivation, consult L. Veneroni, R. Barber and E. Ronning, and W. Just, *ops. cits.*

68. This position is particularly visible in J. J. Johnson when he writes: "Social upheavals will keep societies [Latin American ones] in disequilibrium and will bring to the surface people who in their restlessness and insecurity will welcome ideologies requiring total commitment. . . . In any event, since the armed forces will probably remain for some time the only agency capable of countermanding rampant damagoguery, they will appear different to the states of Latin America than they do to states with great national cohesion. . . . Furthermore, for the next decade or more, they will on occasion be the most reliable institution to ensure political continuity in these countries. They will, in certain instances, stand as a bulwark of order and security in otherwise anarchical societies; at other times, if they were to follow a policy of non-intervention in the civilian area, it would remain the preservation of an unsatisfactory status quo" (*op. cit.,* 1964, pp. 260–61). Although from a different angle, the same proposition is expressed by L. Pye when he concludes that one positive characteristic of military governments is that it is more probable that they will be better allies of the "West" than civilian governments (L. Pye, *op. cit.,* pp. 185–186). In a very fundamental sense the premises of the "neo-realist" focus come to their logical conclusion with this: Some internally cohesive armed forces are capable of preserving "internal order" against "subversion" or "anarchy," but the "developmental" role that had been originally attributed to them disappears—except as the distant and less than likely result of the fulfillment of the role which remains really of interest, the preservation of the existing social structure.

69. The content of this proposition coincides closely with the model of the "moderating role" proposed by Stepan as typical of the Brazilian armed forces prior to the coup of 1964; see A. Stepan, *op. cit.,* especially p. 172.

70. Of course, neglecting to consider that the military has means for resolving internal conflicts (from purges to simple combat) usually not available to the civilian sectors.

71. Unless it is clear that the concept ends by being defined as "preservation of the existing order."

72. For analysis of the importance of this ideology in other South American countries see P. V. Beltran, ed., *Las Fuerzas Armadas Hablan* (Paidós, 1969); A. Stepan, *op. cit.,* especially p. 172; L. Einaudi, "The Peruvian Military: A Summary Political Analysis" (The Rand Corporation, 1969); and A. Quijano Obregón, *Nacionalismo, Neoimperialismo y Militarismo en el Perú* (Ediciones Periferia, 1971).

73. Unless, of course, one believes that the "doctrine of national security" is substantially correct.

74. An intuitive combination of attitudes to the military underlies the conclusions of authors such as S. Finer, M. Janowitz and E. Lieuwen (*ops. cits.*) who, although they avoid most of the failings criticized here, vacillate in their arguments, eventually concluding that military attitudes permit the armed forces to play a privileged "developmental" role.

75. That is to say, what is really important is not a list of presumed attitudes but the form in which these attitudes come together finally in each concrete case. To isolate them one from another is an intellectual exercise which permits arriving at conclusions previously anticipated by the value preferences of the author. For example, if one chooses to stress the dominant preoccupation with order and stability, one comes to conclusions of the type proposed by E. Nordlinger, which are clearly opposed to the ones postulated by the "neo-realist" authors: "The vision [of the military officers] of political stability hinders social and economic change insofar as such changes are a product of governmental responsiveness to articulated and forcefully promoted demands; repressing these demands largely rules out their fulfillment." Nordlinger, *op. cit.*, pp. 1137–38.

76. This argument should be understood in the sense of promoting a level of facts and of analysis which seems analytically more useful than the one implied by the attribution of attitudes just examined. Naturally, it does not imply that a choice must be made between the two levels of inquiry. Political ideologies and a presumed *ethos* are levels of analysis of different attitudinal "depths" and, as such, are both legitimate material for study. Moreover, one could imagine investigations at a level of even greater psychological "depth," such as trying to determine what type of personal characteristics (if any) can influence choice of the military profession and what effect educational experience in the military organization can have on these characteristics. All of these are interesting possibilities, but it would seem that the "deeper" the psychological factors analyzed, the greater the possible variation in the dependent variable of interest (political behavior), the more numerous the intervening variables and—perhaps above all, the more improbable it is that one could locate reliable, pertinent data. This last problem is far from being trivial, above all in a subdiscipline which, like that of the political sociology of the armed forces, is characterized by a paucity of available information and by a scarcity of reasonably confirmed theoretical propositions.

77. This tends to confirm the hypothesis that the influence of corporate interest (in other words, of the perception of such interest) will increase as the degree of professionalization increases. Although within different overall conceptions, various authors have emphasized the importance of the corporate interest of the armed forces; see S. Finer, A. Stepan, E. Lieuwen, *ops. cits.;* E. Lieuwen, *Generals vs. Presidents—Neo-Militarism in Latin America* (New York, 1964); M. Needler, "Anatomy of a Coup d'Etat: Ecuador 1963," (Institute for the Comparative Study of Political Systems, Washington, D.C., 1964).

78. As has been indicated in the previous sections, this is the real meaning of affirmations of the type made by General Onganía in the period 1963–1966, in the sense that the armed forces must refrain from intervening except in the case of "extreme circumstances." For a similar position taken by General Castello Branco prior to the Brazilian coup oᶠ 1964, see A. Stepan, *op. cit.* and T. Skidmore, *Politics in Brazil, 1930–1964* (Oxford University Press, 1967).

79. On the growing levels of political activity and of social protest in the period

242   Guillermo A. O'Donnell

which closely preceded the Greek coup, see K. Legg, *op. cit.;* for the Brazilian case, see A. Stepan, *op. cit.,* T. Skidmore, *op. cit.* and O. Ianni, *O Colapso de Populismo no Brasil* (Editorial Civilizacao Brasileira, 1968). For a more detailed analysis of the Argentine case and a more complete bibliography of the Brazilian example, consult my *Modernization and Bureaucratic Authoritarianism.*

80. The quote is from J. Thompson, *Organizations in Action* (McGraw Hill, 1967), pp. 159–160. See also J. Cyert and J. March, *A Behavioral Theory of the Firm* (Prentice Hall, 1963) and J. March and H. Simon, *Organizations* (Wiley, 1958).

81. An example of this is the concerted agreement on sale prices among "competitive" firms in a given market.

82. J. Thompson, *op. cit.,* p. 160. An example of this is the attempt to eliminate competition and establish a monopoly.

83. Any successful career in a large organization requires large "investment" in terms of specialization in matters considered highly "functional" to the activities of the organization. This, in turn, implies a high degree of "trained incapacity" to perceive, evaluate, and make decisions according to patterns different from those learned in the course of that career—although the problem to be faced may bear little relation to those typically confronted in the area of specialization. On the learning of these biases and "programs" of decision-making, see, above all, J. Cyert and J. March, *op. cit.*

84. As can be expected from what has already been said, this utopian view is particularly visible in the intervals immediately following the seizure of governmental power by professionalized militaries. The cases of presidents Onganía and Castello Branco are sufficiently illustrative.

85. I reiterate that the above-mentioned matter "contributes" to this implantation, because a complete explanation cannot exclude the critical independent effect of factors in the larger social context, alluded to in section 1 of this paper and studied in greater detail in my book *Modernization and Bureaucratic Authoritarianism.*

86. One theme treated only tangentially in this article, but which is the focal point for the different level of analysis used in my book, is the constellation of power in the larger social context. This constellation, also profoundly conditioned by the structural characteristics of a high level of modernization, leans toward the preservation of the existing social system and its international affiliations. It does this through the profound socioeconomic transformations involved in the attempt (more successful in Brazil than in Argentina, but in both cases considerably advanced) to concentrate even more socioeconomic resources and political power for the benefit of large public organizations (controlled, above all, by the military) and private ones (above all, foreign-owned). The great compatibility of interest among those sectors and organizations to which modernization has given progressively greater importance (at least at the moment of the coup d'état which implants a bureaucratic-authoritarian regime and closes those channels of political access still open to the popular sectors) helps to explain why the organizational goals of the military discussed here can express themselves within the larger social context.

87. In accordance with David Apter (*op. cit.*, 1971) this would be a case of "right-wing radicalization." The purpose (and to a large extent the effects) of the implantation of the new political regime is the introduction of a fundamental change in the allocation of social resources. There is a tendency to qualify these attempts as "reactionary" or "conservative," minimizing implicitly their effect in introducing important social changes. The content of these changes may be subjectively disagreeable (it is for me), but that is a question which differs from its detection and study. For a discussion of this matter in a vein similar to the one indicated here, see F. Cardoso's article, "El Modelo Politico Brasileno," *Desarrollo Económico*, 11, no. 42, pp. 218–247, (1972).

88. For a study of these matters I refer again to F. Cardoso and E. Faleto, *op. cit.*, and to my *Modernization and Bureaucratic Authoritarianism*.

89. On these concepts see David Apter, *op. cit.*, 1965.

90. More than a few functionaries at the highest level of the regime inaugurated in Argentina in 1966 have complained publicly of the slowness and the vetoes to which decision-making initiatives have been subjected. It seems safe to affirm that in this respect, a serious problem of the regime deposed in 1966 and one on which the first military proclamations placed great emphasis, has not been solved.

91. On the application of criteria of seniority in military command in deciding presidential designations in Brazil, and its close connection with the desire to avoid what would otherwise threaten division in the armed forces, see A. Stepan, *op. cit.*, pp. 253–266. In Argentina, the presidential designation of General Lanusse seems to have been dominated by similar factors.

92. In Argentina, the provinces, public enterprises and autarchic entities which have been assigned to particular branches are numerous. It should be evident that this phenomenon, as well as those already indicated, are hardly congruent with the probability of regularly "hitting the mark" in the designation of governmental personnel and in the coordination of their actions.

93. Although these characteristics of military rule are derived from the Argentine case, A. Stepan notes similar ones in the apparently more "successful" case of Brazil: A. Stepan, *op. cit.*

94. If I may be permitted a personal note, it may be, if a truly open electoral option finally prevails, and if the bureaucratic-authoritarian experience has taught a substantial proportion of the civil sector that it is in their interest to formulate their demands in a more regulated manner, a future government might be able to count on sufficient political time to institutionalize non-praetorian norms of competition and to resolve some of the more severe socioeconomic bottlenecks. These are big "ifs," but in the type of learning process involved in what we are discussing, a possibility might be found for the political democratization of highly modernized nations.

95. Insisting here upon something which emerges from all that has been said thus far, I hope it remains clear that in this article I do not attempt to explain coups-d'état (a task undertaken in my book, already cited numerous times), but rather, the military's contribution to those coups. It pays to insist on this point because serious errors of analysis tend to originate from the confusion of these two matters.

Alfred Stepan / # The New Professionalism of Internal Warfare and Military Role Expansion

Since 1964 the Brazilian military establishment has steadily assumed control over a widening area of the country's social and political life. Indeed, there exists the possibility that what we are witnessing in Brazil is the creation of a new political and economic model of authoritarian development. Others [have examined] the internal workings, policy outputs, and institutionalization possibilities of this model. My focus is on how changing military ideology contributed to the events leading up to the military coup of 1964 and the emergence of the military-bureaucratic and authoritarian-developmentalist components of the model.

In this [essay] I argue that what happened in Brazil was, to a significant extent, part of the wider military phenomenon of what I call the "new professionalism of internal security and national development." In analyzing how the ideology of new professionalism arose and how it contributed to the expansion of the military's role in politics, I also endeavor to identify some of the institutional and political variables that are peculiar to Brazil and that help account for some of the special characteristics of the military regime.

From Alfred Stepan, ed., *Authoritarian Brazil* (New Haven: Yale University Press, 1973), pp. 47–65. Reprinted by permission of the author and publisher.

**Conflicting Paradigms: New Professionalism
vs. Old Professionalism**

In the 1960s, the political roles of the Brazilian and Peruvian military establishments underwent a great expansion. Yet, as measured by a number of indicators, these military establishments are probably the two most professional in Latin America.[1] They have relatively universalistic procedures for the recruitment and promotion of officers, highly structured military schooling programs that prepare officers for passage to the next stage of their careers, highly articulated and well-disseminated military doctrines and well-programmed military-unit training cycles, all coordinated by extensive general staff systems. If there is one central concept of modern civil-military relations, it is the concept of "professionalism." According to this concept, as the professionalism of a military establishment increases along the lines indicated above, the military tends to become less political in its activities. In the case of Brazil, however, professional standards coexisted with increasinging politicization in the years leading up to 1964. Thus, either Brazil must be considered a deviant case, or one must suggest an alternative framework that is capable of incorporating Brazil, Peru (where a similar process of professionalization and politicization has been at work), and, I suspect, a number of other countries, such as Indonesia, as the predictable outcome of the new paradigm.

It is the argument of this essay that the highly bureaucratized, highly schooled, and yet highly politicized armies of Brazil and Peru are best viewed not as lapses from the paradigm of the "old" professionalism, but as one of the logical consequences of the "new" professionalism. To clarify the theoretical and empirical aspects of this assertion, I briefly consider first the components of the old professionalism. Though many aspects of the argument are widely reproduced by writers who have not studied his work, the classic formulation of the argument about military professionalism and its relation to the political activity of the military is Samuel Huntington's. As quoted or paraphrased from his own writings,[2] his argument is as follows:

1. *On the nature of modern warfare and the requisite skills.* Modern warfare demands a highly specialized military; the military cannot master the new skills needed to carry out their tasks while at the same time "remaining competent in many other fields" as well (*The Soldier,* p. 32).

2. *On the impact of pursuit of professionalism.* As a result of this specialization, "the vocation of officership absorbs all their energies and furnishes them with all their occupational satisfactions. Officership, in short, is an exclusive role, incompatible with any other significant social or political roles" ("Civilian Control," p. 381).

3. *On the relationship between political and military spheres.* The functional specialization needed for external defense means that "it became

impossible to be an expert in the management of violence for external defense and at the same time to be skilled in either politics and statecraft or the use of force for the maintenance of internal order. The functions of the officer became distinct from those of the politician and policeman" (*The Soldier,* p. 32).

4. *On the scope of military concern.* "At the broadest level of the relation of the military order to society, the military function is presumed to be a highly specialized one. . . . A clear distinction in role and function exists between military and civilian leaders" ("Civilian Control," pp. 380–81).

5. *On the impact of professionalism on military attitudes to politics.* "Civilian control is thus achieved not because the military groups share in the social values and political ideologies of society, but because they are indifferent to such values and ideologies" ("Civilian Control," p. 381).

6. *On the impact of professionalism on civil-military relations.* "The one prime essential for any system of civilian control is the minimizing of military power. Objective civilian control achieves this reduction by professionalizing the military" and by "confining it to a restricted sphere and rendering it politically sterile and neutral on all issues outside that sphere" (*The Soldier,* p. 84; "Civilian Control," p. 381).

This argument runs through a large part of American military writing and appears frequently in congressional discussions of the rationale for United States military assistance policies to developing countries. The argument that assistance policies should be given in order to professionalize the military has been rationalized on the grounds that in doing so the United States could help convert traditional, politicized armies into modern, apolitical ones. However, as the extensive quotations from Huntington illustrate, the professionalization thesis was rooted in the assumption that armies develop their professional skills for conventional warfare against foreign armies. In his later writing Huntington has stated that if the focus shifts from interstate conflict to domestic war it will encourage a different pattern of civil-military relations than that expounded in the passages quoted above.[3] Since many later writers have failed to note this qualification, the concept of military professionalism is still widely misunderstood, and it is useful to formulate explicitly the differences between the old professionalism of external warfare and the new professionalism of internal security and national development.

In reality, by the late 1950s and early 1960s, the success of revolutionary warfare techniques against conventional armies in China, Indochina, Algeria, and Cuba led the conventional armies in both the developed and underdeveloped world to turn more attention to devising military and political strategies to combat or prevent domestic revolutionary warfare. In fact, by 1961, the United States military assistance programs to Latin America were largely devoted to exporting doctrines concerned with the military's role in counterinsurgency, civic action and nation building [4] In Latin America the process by which the military came to define its mission primarily in terms of dealing with threats to internal security was accelerated by the defeat and destruction of the conventional army in Cuba by Castro's guerrilla force. In Brazil and Peru, where the military was highly institutionalized, the perception of the threat to the internal security of the nation and the security of the military itself led to a focusing of energies on the "professionalization" of their approach to internal security. The military institutions began to study such questions as the social and political conditions facilitating the growth of revolutionary protest and to develop doctrines and training techniques to prevent or crush insurgent movements. As a result, these highly professionalized armies became much more concerned with political problems.

Thus there was a dual process at work. Because of their preoccupation with subversion and internal security, many military establishments in Latin America attempted to undertake institutional professionalization and development and were given extensive United States military assistance in doing so. Yet, given the changed political climate, the formulators of United States military assistance programs and the chiefs of many Latin American military establishments now believed that professional military expertise was required in a broader range of fields. Instead of increasing functional specialization, the military began to train their officers to acquire expertise in internal security matters that were defined as embracing all aspects of social, economic, and political life. Instead of the gap between the military and political spheres widening, the new professionalism led to a belief that there was a fundamental interrelationship between the two spheres, with the military playing a key role in interpreting and dealing with domestic political problems owing to its greater technical and professional skills in handling internal security issues.[5] The scope of military concern for, and study of, politics became unrestricted, so that the "new professional" military man was highly politicized.

The new professionalism of internal security and national development almost inevitably led to some degree of military role expansion. However, variables stemming from the larger political system in addition to those associated with the military subsystem affect the degree of this role expansion. The weaker the civilian government's own legitimacy and ability to supervise a "peaceful" process of development, the greater the tendency will be for the new professionals to assume control of the government to impose their own view of development on the state.

The old professionalism of external security and the new professionalism of internal security and national development share many external characteristics, especially those of highly developed military schooling systems and elaborate military doctrines. However, the *content* and *consequences* of the two forms of professionalism are quite distinct, as is shown

Table 1. Contrasting Paradigms: The Old Professionalism of External Defense The New Professionalism of Internal Security and National Development

	Old Professionalism	*New Professionalism*
Function of military	External security	Internal security
Civilian attitudes toward government	Civilians accept legitimacy of government	Segments of society challenge government legitimacy
Military skills required	Highly specialized skills incompatible with political skills	Highly interrelated political and military skills
Scope of military professional action	Restricted	Unrestricted
Impact of professional socialization	Renders the military politically neutral	Politicizes the military
Impact on civil-military relations	Contributes to an apolitical military and civilian control	Contributes to military-political managerialism and role expansion

schematically in Table 1. It is useful to distinguish the two types of military professionalism for reasons of policy as well as theory. Since 1961, United States military policy toward Latin America has been to encourage the Latin American militaries to assume as their primary role counterinsurgency programs, civic-action and nation-building tasks. This policy has often been defended, in the name of helping to create a professional army, and by implication, an apolitical force in the nation. However, in terms of the schema presented in the table, technical and professional specialization of the military in conjunction with doctrines and ideologies of internal security will tend to lead toward military role expansion and "managerialism" in the political sphere.[6]

It also seems useful to point out for reasons of politics as well as theory that the new professionalism is not only a phenomenon of the developing countries. Some of the key ingredients of the new professionalism were observed in France in the 1950s and played a major role in the civil-military crises there in 1958 and 1961. Even in the United States, the military's development of the new professionalism in the fields of counterinsurgency and civic action has resulted in the development of skills that, though originally developed for export to the developing countries such as Brazil in the early 1960s, were by the late 1960s increasingly called upon within this country. Huntington's view of the old professionalism, where the military was functionally specific and unconcerned with domestic political events, is now less meaningful for this country. The United States Army has increasingly been used to quell riots and given the function of maintaining internal order. Once given this function, the internal logic of the new professionalism comes into play, and the military sets about in a "professional" way to train to perform this function. In the late 1960s, many units such as the crack 82nd Airborne Division spent an increasing amount of their time training how to occupy American cities in case of domestic riots. The next "new professional" question for the United States military was to inquire into the nature of the enemy. This involved the military in a surveillance and intelligence-gathering role within the United States.[7]

New Professionalism in the Brazilian Political Crisis

The processes leading toward the development of the new professionalism were evident in Brazil before 1964. In Brazil, many of the external standards of the old professionalism had greatly increased before this date. The military schooling system was highly evolved. To be eligible for promotion to the rank of general an army line officer was required to graduate from the Military Academy (Academia Militar das Agulhas Negras, AMAN), the Junior Officer's School (Escola de Aperfeiçoamento de Oficiais, EsAO), and the three-year General Staff School (Escola de Comando e Estado Maior do Exército, ECEME), whose written entrance examination is passed by less than a quarter of the applicants. In terms of rank structure, the rank distribution was roughly similar to that of the United States. According to Janowitz, 21.7 percent of officers in the United States Army were colonels or generals in 1950. In 1964, the figure for Brazil was only 14.9 percent.[8]

At the same time, new military institutions were developing in Brazil that were to become centers of the new professionalism. Of prime importance was the Superior War College (Escola Superior de Guerra, ESG) which was formally established by presidential decree under Dutra in 1949. At the time of its founding, the United States played a key role through a military advisory mission that stayed in Brazil from 1948 to 1960. By 1963, the ESG decreed its mission as that of preparing "civilians and the military to perform executive and advisory functions especially in those organs responsible for the formulation, development, planning, and execution of the policies of national security."[9] That the new professionalism of national security as developed at the ESG was very different in conception from that of the old professionalism, which in theory confines military activity to a more restricted sphere, is clear from an examination of the seven academic divisions of the college. These were (1) political affairs, (2) psychological-social affairs, (3) economic affairs, (4) military affairs, (5) logistical and mobilization affairs, (6) intelligence and counter-intelligence, and (7) doctrine and coordination.[10]

One interesting aspect of the new professionalism was its relation with civilians. In the 1950s in Brazil, the participation of civilians became a key aspect of the college's program. Precisely because the military viewed the situation in Brazil as going beyond questions handled by the old professionalism, and because the ESG was to be concerned with all phases of development and national security, it was felt the Brazilian military needed to socialize civilians from such fields as education, industry, communications, and banking into the correct national security perspective. By 1966, in fact, the ESG had graduated men from many of the key sectors of the political and economic power structure in Brazil: by this date, 599 graduates were military officers, 224 were from private industry and commerce, 200 from the major government ministries, 97 from decentralized government agencies, 39 from the federal Congress, 23 were federal or state judges, and 107 were various professionals, such as professors, economists, writers, medical doctors, and Catholic clergy.[11]

By the late 1950s and early 1960s, the ESG had developed its key ideological tenet: the close interrelationship between national security and national development. The doctrines taught at the college emphasized that modern warfare, either conventional or revolutionary, involved the unity, will, and productive capacity of the entire nation.

The low-mobilization, high-control policies of the military governments since 1964 had their intellectual roots in the ESG's doctrine that an effective policy of national security demands a strong government that can rationally maximize the outputs of the economy and effectively contain manifestations of disunity in the country. The new professionalism contributed to an all-embracing attitude of military managerialism in regard to Brazil's political system. The ideas and suggestions aired at the ESG at least five years before the coup of 1964 ranged from redrawing state boundaries (to eliminate old political forces and restructure the federation along "natural" economic boundaries) to the enforcement of a two-party system.[12] The language in the 1956 ESG lecture quoted below foreshadowed the tone, substance, and rationale of later military government attempts to impose a hierarchical, semicorporatist unity on the Brazilian political system.

> We live in a climate of world-wide war that will decide the destiny of Western civilization.
>
> A decentralized system is fundamentally weak in periods of war, which demand a centralized and hierarchic structure. As total war absorbs all people, institutions, wealth, and human and national resources for the attainment of the objectives, it seems certain that centralization and concentration will increase the efficiency and ability of the political and national power.[13]

Though the ESG always concerned itself to some extent with conventional warfare, it became the center of ideological thougnt concerning counterrevolutionary strategy in Brazil. In early 1959 the chief ideologue of the school, Colonel Golbery, argued that indirect attack from within was a much more real threat to Latin America than direct attack from without:

What is certain is that the greater probability today is limited warfare, localized conflict, and above all indirect Communist aggression, which capitalizes on local discontents, the frustrations of misery and hunger, and just nationalist anxieties. . . . Latin America now faces threats more real than at any other time, threats which could result in insurrection, outbursts attempting (though not openly) to implant . . . a government favorable to the Communist ideology and constituting a grave and urgent danger to the unity and security of the Americas and the Western world.[14]

It was this perception of threat, in conjunction with the ESG's underlying preference for "ordered politics," that led to their advocacy of the primacy of the politics of national security (implicitly directed by the military) over competitive politics. Golbery contended that in times of severe crises,

the area of politics is permeated . . . by adverse pressures, creating a form of universalization of the factors of security, enlarging the area of the politics of national security to a point where it almost absorbs all the national activities.[15]

It was from this perspective of the relation between internal security and national development that the ESG set about studying all problems viewed as relating to the security issue. Its civil-military, national security elites studied inflation, agrarian reform, banking reform, voting systems, transportation, and education, as well as guerrilla warfare and conventional warfare. In many of these studies, some of the fundamental aspects of Brazilian social and economic organization were depicted as needing change if Brazil were to maintain its internal security.

Initially, these critiques of Brazilian society by military intellectuals seemed academic, and the influence of the ESG's doctrine was not pervasive within the military in the mid-1950s. But by the early 1960s, as the military perceived a deepening crisis in Brazil, the ESG's emphasis on the need for a total development strategy to combat internal subversion found an increasingly receptive audience in the military. Through the military's highly structured and well-developed publication and education systems, the ideology of internal warfare was widely disseminated throughout the officer corps. The ECEME, one of the major institutions of the old professionalism, became a central vehicle for socializing an entire generation of military officers in the internal-warfare doctrines. The training program is three years long, and entrance is highly competitive. Unless an army line officer is graduated from the ECEME he is ineligible for promotion to general, for appointment to the teaching staff of any military school, or to the general staff of any senior command. Thus the ECEME is the central recruitment and socialization institution of the senior army officer corps of the Brazilian army.

An examination of the curriculum of the ECEME shows that, like the ESG, it increasingly became devoted to the doctrines of the new professionalism, with its emphasis on the expanded political, economic, and social roles of a modern army in times of internal-security threats. In the 1956 curriculum, for instance, there were no class hours scheduled on counterguerrilla warfare, internal security, or communism. By 1966, however, the curriculum contained 222 hours on internal security, 129 on irregular warfare, and only 24 hours on the "old" professional military topic of territorial warfare.[16] Through military publications, such as the newsletter *Boletim de Informações,* sent from the Estado Maior to key troop commanders, the content of the new professionalism was systematically disseminated to all army units.[17]

In their studies of the Brazilian political system the new professionals had, since the early 1960s, moved toward the position that (1) numerous aspects of the economic and political structures had to be altered if Brazil were to have internal security and rational economic growth and (2) the civilian politicians were either unable or unwilling to make these changes. By early 1964, through the prism of internal-warfare doctrines of the new professionalism, a substantial part of the Brazilian military establishment perceived the rising strike levels, the inflation rate of over 75 percent, the declining economy, the demands of the Left for a constituent assembly, and the growing indiscipline of the enlisted men as signs that Brazil was entering a stage of subversive warfare.

Moreover, the new professionals had come to believe that, in comparison to the civilian politicians, they now had constructed the correct doctrines of national security and development, possessed the trained cadres to implement these doctrines, and had the institutional force to impose their solution to the crisis in Brazil. Thus, after overthrowing the civilian president in 1964, the Brazilian military did not return power to new civilian groups, as they had in 1930, 1945, 1954, and 1955, but assumed political power themselves for the first time in the century.

Since 1964, the military has frequently been internally divided over specific policies and the problems of succession. Nevertheless, one must not lose sight of the important point that many of the doctrines of internal warfare, formulated originally at the ESG and later institutionalized in the ESG-influenced government of Castello Branco, permeated almost all major military groups in Brazil and were accepted as a basic new fact of political and military life. The central idea developed at the ESG was that development and security issues are inseparable. Even when differences over policies developed between the Castello Branco government and the Costa e Silva government, almost all military officers agreed that since labor, fiscal, educational, and other problems were intrinsic to the security of the nation, it was legitimate and necessary for military men to concern themselves with these areas. From this basic premise came the steady broadening of military jurisdiction over Brazilian life after the military assumed power in 1964, despite the fact that an important faction of the military had hoped to eventually allow the inauguration of liberal political forms.

Even within the military government itself, security matters have been given special prominence. A new agency, the National Information Service (Serviço Nacional de Informações, SNI), combining the functions of the FBI and CIA in the United States, has been created, and its director has been granted cabinet rank. In 1968 and 1969, national security laws were passed that have greatly increased the role of SNI and other intelligence units. Since 1969, every ministry has had an SNI representative, responsible for ensuring that all policy decisions of the ministry give full consideration to national security issues. Thus the new professionalism of internal warfare and national development contributed to the expansion of the military's role in Brazil that led ultimately to the military's assumption of power in 1964, and afterward to a widening of military control over those aspects of Brazilian life perceived in any way as threatening to the executors of the national security state—that is, the military.

New Professionalism in Peru

The argument that the internal logic of the new professionalism tends to contribute to an extension of the role of the military in politics receives support from a study of the only other country in Latin America to have developed fully an ideology relating internal security to national development and to have institutionalized that ideology within the military. This country is Peru.[18] The grouping of Peru with Brazil may at first seem incongruous because the policies of their military governments have been very different. However, the two countries are strikingly similar when analyzed from the perspective of the central part played by their respective war colleges in the process of military role expansion. In both countries the staffs and students at the war colleges attempted to systematically diagnose their nation's security-development situation. In the end both colleges had forged a docrine that implicitly "legitimated" long-term military supervision of the development process. Furthermore, in both military establishments there was the belief that the war colleges and general staff schools had trained the cadres capable of administering this military-directed process. Both, in short, are examples of the new professionalism.

In Peru, as in Brazil, reasonably developed standards for the professional officer's education, promotion, and training exist. In Peru, educational performance is central to any officer's advancement. Eighty percent of all division generals on active duty between 1940 and 1965, for instance, had graduated in the top quarter of their military academy class.[19] A comparable figure for generals in the United States Army in Morris Janowitz's 1950 sample was 36.4 percent.[20]

In 1950, the Peruvian military established its own superior war college, called the Center for Higher Military Studies (Centro de Altos Estudios Militares, CAEM). By the late 1950s, CAEM had largely turned its energies to analyzing the nexus between internal security and national development. As in Brazil, the military's assessment of the development process led the Peruvian military officers into political diagnosis, but in the case of Peru their orientation was markedly more nationalistic and antioligarchical in tone. Five years before the Peruvian military assumed power, a CAEM document stated·

> So long as Peru does not have programmatic and well organized political parties, the country will continue to be ungovernable. . . . The sad and desperate truth is that in Peru, the real powers are not the Executive, the Legislature, the Judiciary, or the Electorate, but the latifundists, the exporters, the bankers, and the American [United States] investors.[21]

CAEM studies in the late 1950s and early 1960s diagnosed a number of problems of Peruvian society. Against a background of growing social tensions and political paralysis, the organization of peasants by Hugo Blanco and later the guerrilla outbreak of 1965–66 served to broaden the consensus within the military that direct action was necessary. Though the military defeated the guerrillas in six months, they intensified their investigations of the causes of insurgency. They concluded that rural conditions in Peru were so archaic and unjust that, unless there was a profound change in the rural structure of the country, more guerrilla outbreaks could be expected. The military concluded from their studies that Peru was in a state of "latent insurgency," which could only be corrected, in their view, by a "general policy of economic and social development."[22] In Einaudi's words, "elimination of the latent state of subversion became the primary objective of military action."[23]

The military's analysis of the factors contributing to latent insurgency included elite intransigence, fiscal and technical inefficiencies, and a wide variety of administrative weaknesses traceable to the weakness of the government and the underlying contradictions of the social structure.[24] As in Brazil, the military educational system in Peru had produced a whole cadre of officers with a highly articulated ideology of internal security and national development, and with a new confidence as to the utility of their technocratic and managerial education. These officers feared that the country could evolve into a dangerous state of insecurity if fundamental changes in the polity and economy were not brought about. Like the Brazilian military officers schooled at the ESG, the Peruvian officers trained at CAEM came to the conclusion that civilian governments were incapable of bringing about these changes, and that their own CAEM training in the new professionalism gave them the trained cadres and correct ideology for the task of restructuring the country. This attitude strongly influenced the military's decision to assume and retain political control of the country.

Significantly, in Einaudi's interviews with key Peruvian generals, implicit reference was made to the impact the new professional training has had on military confidence to rule. A former minister of war commented that in the past the military felt culturally inferior and that "when a general met an ambassador, he turned red in the face and trembled." But a leading general in the current regime argued that whereas past military attempts to induce change, such as the regime of Colonel Sánchez Cerro, were doomed to failure because military men were not adequately trained in matters of national development, the present military officers possessed the correct training to be successful. He commented: "Sánchez Cerro was alone. I am but one of forty. And behind us comes a generation of still better trained officers ready to carry on should we falter."[25]

Brazil and Peru: Their Contrasting Policies

Peru is relevant for our analysis of Brazil not only because it is an example of the new professionalism, but also because it illustrates that the new professionalism contributes more to the military's general attitude to political action than to specific policies. In the two countries, the new professional military men have chosen quite different paths. Why has this occurred, and what are the chances that the military in Brazil might take a Peruvian turn?

This is not the place for an extensive comparative analysis of the two regimes, but some of the factors contributing to the different policies of the two military regimes should be stated. First was the impact of World War II. During the war, Brazil sent a combat division, the Fôrça Expedicionária Brasileira (FEB), to fight in Italy as allies of the United States. My extensive interviews with many of the key leaders of the 1964 military government in Brazil indicate that some of the distinctive characteristics of the Castello Branco government—its pro-Americanism, its favorable attitude toward foreign capital, its distaste for "excessive" nationalism—had their roots in this experience. The ally relationship also prepared the way for close personal and institutional ties between the United States and the Brazilian military establishment.[26] In this area, Peru has no comparable experience.

A second area of divergence between the two countries involves their superior war colleges. The Brazilian war college was established and largely dominated by veterans of World War II, who saw the college as the place to "institutionalize the learning experience of World War II." When officers training at the ESG were sent abroad, they were normally sent to United States military schools, and this experience reinforced the security emphasis, which had found a place in United States schools. Some of the officers associated with CAEM, however, had direct contacts with French-Catholic reformist priest Lebret or attended United Nations civilian-directed schools in Chile. These experiences reinforced CAEM's emphasis on development and helped cast the school's concern for development in a nationalistic light. At the Brazilian ESG many of those attending the courses were private businessmen, and undoubtedly this contributed to the ESG's bias in favor of capitalism and efficiency. The private civilian industrial sector has never been as heavily represented at CAEM.

A third factor influencing the direction and content of the military regimes in Brazil and Peru is the size of the private industrial sector. The
much larger and more powerful private industrial sector in Brazil conditioned military attitudes by inhibiting the adoption of the Peruvian approach, because the private sector is considered so large, dynamic, and
advanced that the military doubts its own ability to run the industrial
sector efficiently. Industrialists are therefore viewed as allies in the low-
mobilization, high-coercion development model in Brazil. In Peru, on the
other hand, the industrial sector is smaller and less dynamic. It appears
that in the less developed economy, the scope for military Nasserism is
greater and the working-class groups far more amenable to the military
nationalist-statist approach.

A final factor to be considered in this [essay] is the way in which the
nexus between security and development issues was viewed by military
officers at the time they seized power. In 1964, military officers in Brazil
were primarily concerned with what they viewed as the immediate security
threat. In Peru, on the other hand, the defeat of the guerrillas in 1966 gave
military officers time to focus almost exclusively on the long-term development aspects of security. The initial acts of the Brazilian military regime
after 1964 were consequently largely concerned with repression, which by
1968 had become institutionalized coercion. In Peru, the military government has been largely concerned with nationalism and development and
this has meant that significant internal opposition from the Left is absent.

Even this cursory analysis of some of the different historical, institutional, and economic legacies in the two countries helps clarify why the
"Peruvian wing" within the Brazilian military has not been able to assume
control in Brazil and why it is unlikely to do so in the future. What in fact
is the future of the new professionalism in Brazil?

One factor that must be taken into consideration is that in a number of
ways the Brazilian military in the 1950s and 1960s was for the first time
moving toward becoming a professional *caste*. In the period 1941–43, for
instance, sons of military families represented 21.3 percent of all cadets
admitted to the military academy. This figure had increased to 34.9 percent by 1962–66. More startling is the fact that, as the military professionalized its educational system, it expanded its military high schools in
order to ensure the entry into the military school system of a sufficient
number of attractive officer candidates. In 1939, 61.6 percent of all cadets
at the military academy had attended civilian high schools. By 1963–66,
only 7.6 percent of all cadets had attended civilian high schools. Thus,
probably about 90 percent of the present army officers in Brazil entered
the military educational system when they were about twelve years old.[27]

Once the military assumed power, the movement toward professional
homogeneity was accelerated. About 20 percent of the field grade officers
have now been purged from the military for ideological deviation. Possession of the "correct" revolutionary mentality is now indispensable for pro-

motion or assignment to a key command. The purging of a significant group of senior officers, together with the purging of politicians, has created an "Argentine" extrication dilemma. The military fears leaving office because of the threat posed by the return to power of previously purged officers and politicians. Institutional factors such as these must be borne in mind in any assessment of the possibility of military rule ending in Brazil.

On the other hand, despite the new professionals' agreement on the inseparability of internal security and national development, the contrast between Peru and Brazil has helped point out that the ideology itself leaves unspecified most concrete policy decisions. Nor can the particular ideological unity of the military help resolve succession crises. In fact, the nine years of Brazilian military rule have gravely injured military unity. The military experienced major internal crises in October 1965, November 1968, and September 1969. "Defense of the military institution" was one of the keys to the new professionals' entry into national politics. If, however, internal disunity increases over policy or succession problems, "defense of the institution" may well be one of the keys to extrication, via a caretaker junta. The military leaders are attempting to institutionalize the system so that levels of coercion and dissent diminish and support rises. The Mexican model of institutionalization is often mentioned by the military. However, the absence of a revolutionary myth in Brazil and the much more advanced state of both the economy and, more importantly, social groups would seem to rule out this possibility.

Notes

1. See Alfred Stepan, *The Military in Politics: Changing Patterns in Brazil* (Princeton: Princeton University Press, 1971), chap. 3; and Luigi Einaudi, *The Peruvian Military: A Summary Political Analysis* (Santa Monica: RAND Corporation, RM-6048-RC, May 1969).
2. Samuel P. Huntington, *The Soldier and the State: The Theory and Politics of Civil-Military Relations* (New York: Vintage Books, 1964); idem, "Civilian Control of the Military: A Theoretical Statement," in *Political Behavior: A Reader in Theory and Research,* ed. H. Eulau, S. Eldersveld, and M. Janowitz (New York: Free Press, 1956).
3. See in particular his "Patterns of Violence in World Politics," in *Changing Patterns of Military Politics,* ed. Samuel P. Huntington (New York: Free Press, 1962), pp. 19–22.
4. This shift has been well documented. For an overview and a guide to the United States government programs and publications see W. F. Barber and C. N. Ronning, eds., *Internal Security and Military Power: Counter-insurgency and Civic Action in Latin America* (Columbus: Ohio State University Press, 1966). See also M. Francis, "Military Aid to Latin America in the United States Congress," *Journal of Inter-American Studies* 6 (July

1964) : 389–401. A strong criticism of this policy from the Latin American perspective is John Saxe-Fernández, *Proyecciones hemisféricas de la pax Americana* (Lima: IEP ediciones y CAMPODÓNICOediciones, 1971).

5. A thorough and brilliant analysis of some psychological and political implications of this type of military ideology of total counterrevolutionary warfare (especially in the context of a weak political system) is Raoul Girardet's discussion of the French army. See his "Problèmes idéologiques et moraux," and "Essai d'interprétation," in *La Crise militaire française, 1945–1962: Aspects sociologiques et idéologiques,* ed. Raoul Girardet (Paris: Librairie Armand Colin, 1964), pp. 151–229.

    In the early 1960s the Indonesian army's Staff and Command School formulated a development and security doctrine that was later implemented in large part when the military assumed power in 1965. For the doctrine and an insightful analysis see Guy J. Pauker, *The Indonesian Doctrine of Territorial Warfare and Territorial Management* (Santa Monica: RAND Corporation, RM-3312-PR, November 1963).

6. I develop this argument at greater length in my congressional testimony; see U.S. Congress, House of Representatives, *Hearings before the Subcommittee on National Security Policy and Scientific Developments of the Committee on Foreign Affairs on Military Assistance Training,* 91st Cong., 2nd sess., October 6, 7, 8, December 8, 15, 1970, pp. 105–11, 117–29 passim.

7. For a more detailed discussion of these themes, see Bruce Russett and Alfred Stepan, eds., *Military Force and American Society* (New York: Harper & Row, Torchbook, 1973).

8. For documentation see Stepan, *The Military in Politics,* chap. 3.

9. Decreto No. 53,080, December 4, 1963.

10. Ibid.

11. For a short official history of the ESG, see the heavily documented essay by General Augusto Fragoso, written while he was commandant of the school, "A Escola Superior de Guerra (Origen—Finalidade—Evolução)," *Segurança & Desenvolvimento: Revista da Associação dos Diplomados da Escola Superior de Guerra,* año 18, no. 132 (1969), pp. 7–40. The figures on occupations of graduates were provided by the ESG and reprinted in Glauco Carneiro, "A guerra de 'Sorbonne,' " *O Cruzeiro,* June 24, 1967, p. 20.

12. See, for example, Christovão L. Barros Falção, Capitão-de-mar-e-guerra, *Mobilização no campo econômico,* Curso de Mobilização Nacional, Escola Superior de Guerra, C-03-59; and David Carneiro, *Organização politica do Brasil,* Escola Superior de Guerra, Departmento de Estudos, C-47-59. These and all subsequent ESG documents that I cite I found either in the archive of Castello Branco located in the library of ECEME or in the Biblioteca Nacional. Most ESG documents are still classified by the Brazilian government.

13. Ildefonso Mascarenhas da Silva, *O poder nacional e seus tipos de estructura,* Escola Superior de Guerra, C-20-56, pp. 32–34.

14. Golbery do Couto e Silva, *Geopolítica do Brasil* (Rio de Janeiro: José Olympio, 1967), pp. 198–99 (from a chapter originally written in 1959).

This book is based on ESG lectures. The developments in the Cuban revolution in late 1960 and 1961 intensified the ESG fear of the "communist threat."

15. Golbery do Couto e Silva, *Planejamento estratégico* (Rio de Janeiro: Biblioteca do Exército Editôra, 1955), pp. 38–39. Most of this book had its origin in lectures originally given at the ESG. The book is one of the major sources for the ideology of the ESG.

16. Based upon my examination of the curriculum of ECEME on file at their library.

17. Ministério da Guerra, Estado Maior do Exército, *Boletim de Informações*. Copies of this are on open file at the Biblioteca do Exército in Rio de Janeiro. Before October 1961 the format was that of a very straightforward review of professional topics and routine surveys of international news. From October 1961 on, the format changed to one much closer to the framework and terminology of the ESG and, most significantly, began to deal with the question of the threat to internal security presented by communism.

18. Argentina, which I would rank highest after Brazil and Peru among the countries of Latin America on a rough scale of new professionalism, experienced a military coup in 1966. Analysts specifically pointed to the evolution of a military ideology concerned with internal security and national development as an important factor in the inauguration of the authoritarian military regime. This would be in keeping with the thesis of the present essay. See Guillermo A. O'Donnell, "Modernización y golpes militares: Teoría, comparaciones e el caso Argentino," (Buenos Aires: Instituto Torcuato Di Tella, Documento de Trabajo, September 1972). [A translation appears in this volume.—Ed.]

19. Luigi Einaudi, *The Peruvian Military*, p. 7. The analysis of Peru owes much to my discussions with Einaudi. We coauthored the monograph *Latin American Institutional Development: Changing Military Perspectives in Peru and Brazil* (Santa Monica: RAND Corporation, R-586-DOS, April 1971), in which Einaudi is primarily responsible for Peru and I am primarily responsible for Brazil.

   In 1972, while on a SSRC-ACLS grant I carried out research in Peru and visited CAEM. Although the discussion in this essay reflects some of the results of this research, extensive analysis and documentation of the material must await a later publication. One particularly relevant finding is based on my study with Jorge Rodríguez of the University of York, England. Of the 404 articles to appear in the *Revista de la Escuela Superior de Guerra* (Peru) from 1954 to 1967, the percentage of articles whose content met our criteria of "new professionalism" increased from virtually zero in 1954–55 to well over 50 percent by 1964.

20. Morris Janowitz, *The Professional Soldier: A Social and Political Portrait* (New York: Free Press, 1960), pp. 134–35.

21. CAEM, *El estado y la política general* (1963), pp. 89, 92, cited in Einaudi and Stepan, *Latin American Institutional Development*. Víctor Villanueva, in his important book, *El CAEM y la revolución de la fuerza armada* (Lima: IEP ediciones y CAMPODÓNICOediciones, 1972), pp. 85–88,

notes that while this document was initially released with the approval of the director of CAEM, it was withdrawn due to pressure. Villanueva argues that this document is considerably more nationalistic and concerned with structural change than most CAEM studies in this period. Nonetheless for purposes of our comparison the document reveals a set of concerns very different from those found at the ESG in Brazil.

22. See Peru, Ministerio de Guerra, *Las guerrillas en el Perú y su represión* (Lima, 1966), p. 80. Articles in this vein had been appearing in Peruvian military journals even before the guerrilla movement of 1965–66. See in particular Lieutenant Colonel Enrique Gallegos Venero, "Problemas de la guerra contrarrevolucionaria," *Revista de la Escuela Superior de Guerra,* año 11, no. 2 (1964), pp. 97–106.

23. In Einaudi and Stepan, *Latin American Institutional Development.* A civilian social scientist who has been on the faculty at CAEM since 1959 told the author that from 1959 to 1962 CAEM experienced a phase of radicalization aimed at bureaucratic and organizational reform in Peru and that many of these policies were implemented by the 1962–63 military government. From 1964 to 1968 CAEM underwent a new phase of radicalization, but this time the studies explored and advocated much deeper social and structural changes because of the realization that organizational changes alone had been insufficient to resolve Peru's security and development crisis. Interview with Jorge Bravo Bresani, Lima, June 22, 1972.

24. See Brigadier General E. P. Edgardo Mercado Jarrín, "La política y estrategia militar en la guerra contrasubversiva en la América Latina," *Revista Militar del Perú* (Chorrillos), November–December 1967, pp. 4–33. In many ways this article is a classic example of new professionalism.

25. Einaudi and Stepan, *Latin American Institutional Development,* p. 59.

26. For a more detailed discussion and documentation, see Stepan, *The Military in Politics,* pp. 239–44.

27. The data on social origins and educational background of cadets at the Academia Militar das Agulhas Negras were obtained at the academy by the author.

Barry Ames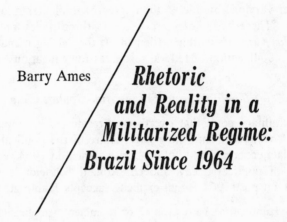

Rhetoric and Reality in a Militarized Regime: Brazil Since 1964

Introduction

Social scientists and historians have written elaborate explanations for the propensity of Latin American armed forces to overthrow established governments, but little attention has been paid to the consequences of military takeovers. The military leaders ruling Brazil after the coup of 1964 have not merely taken over the political system, they have thoroughly dominated it. More than ever before in Latin America, Brazil's leaders have articulated a set of goals which is both detailed and wide-ranging. Prominent among these goals has been the desire to institute a new kind of policy-making, replacing personalism, nepotism, and corruption with "planning," "rationality," and the "public interest."

This study focuses on changes made in the policy-making process following the coup.[1] It begins by discussing the background of the movement

Excerpted from Barry Ames, "Rhetoric and Reality in a Militarized Regime: Brazil Since 1964," *Sage Professional Papers in Comparative Politics,* H. Eckstein et al., eds., No. 01-402. Copyright © 1973 by Sage Publications, Inc. and reprinted by permission of the author and the publisher, Sage Publications, Inc.

Author's Note: The fieldwork for this study was made possible by grants from Stanford University, the National Science Foundation, and the University of New Mexico. I am indebted to many people for comments and advice, including David Abernethy, Frank Bonilla, Robert Daland, Richard Fagen, Paul Hain, Catherine MacKinnon, James McCormick, Martin Needler, Robert Packenham, Simon Schwartzman, Robert Slenes, Paula Sornoff, and Claude Welch.

against President João Goulart and the nature of the post-coup elite that emerged—who they were and what they wanted to do. Then problems in analyzing the implementation of the regime's rhetoric are confronted. Subsequently, the essay reviews various theories linking military regimes and policy outcomes and advances a few speculative hypotheses, predicting, under varying conditions, the degree of implementation of policy process goals. These hypotheses are tested in three policy areas: the removal of *favelas* (urban squatter settlements), the setting of national salary levels, and the allocation of federal resources for education.*

The Background of the Anti-Goulart Coup

The military coup that overthrew President João Goulart on March 30, 1964, resulted from a long-term failure of the political system and an immediate economic and political crisis. Brazil in 1964 seemed to be a classic case of political decay. Indeed, Ronald Schneider's (1971: 11) recent work on post-1964 Brazil explicitly accepts Huntington's analysis:

> Huntington's basic proposition is eminently applicable to Brazil, where the "lag in development of political institutions behind social and economic change" is a critical element in the "instability and disorder" that has characterized the past quarter century of national life. Urbanization and industrialization progressed apace during this period, while . . . political institutionalization made relatively little headway. . . . A notably complex and heterogeneous society, in Huntington's use of the term, the fragility of Brazil's political community resulted primarily from an inadequate level of institutionalization (see also Skidmore, 1967).

Though such analyses seem to fit Brazilian reality, they reify concepts like "political system" and "institutions" at the expense of understanding the people who make up the systems and institutions. Political systems are composed of people with values. While values are molded by cultural and institutional patterns, a person's values are often linked to the social class from which he comes. Brazil's political elite came from the upper-middle and upper classes. Elitist politicians generally strove to preserve existing patterns of social stratification while developing the economy along capitalist lines. Since mass participation in national politics had been extremely low since the beginnings of the Republic (at the end of the nineteenth century), Brazil's elites could maintain their status with little coercion and with a political style based on mutual accommodation among the elites and recognition of the sanctity of the vital interests of each elite sector (for a similar analysis, see Love, 1971).

Economic development in Brazil increased the size of the working class and concomitantly increased demands for basic reforms. Such demands

---

* The original article examines these three policy areas. The material on setting national salary levels, plus the general conclusion and all references, have been included in this edited version.—Ed.

could not be met, because the political system still overrepresented the traditional upper classes and the middle class, all unwilling to accept fundamental changes in the society. The pressure on the system was alleviated when the economic pie was expanding (as in the late fifties), but capitalist systems are notoriously prone to cyclical depressions, and inevitably a downturn would spell the end of the unlikely combination of unresponsive but low-coercion politics (see Skidmore, 1967).

The immediate causes of the coup were both political and economic. Goulart had never inspired great loyalty or respect from senior military commanders. A protégé of twice-overthrown President Getúlio Vargas, Goulart had moved from a Rio Grande do Sul ranch to Labor Minister under Vargas, to Vice President in a regime in which the President, Jânio Quadros, had triumphed over Goulart's party, and to the presidency upon the resignation of Quadros. Opposition by military and civilian leaders to Goulart's ascendancy to the presidency led to a brief parliamentary regime, but Goulart was able to return Brazil to a presidential system with himself as President in 1963.

Goulart's style and political background were unsuited to the task of dealing with senior military officers. Accustomed to a patronage-based system, Goulart relied on promotions of friendly officers to assure himself military support. Since the officer corps was oriented to seniority and merit as criteria for promotion, Goulart gained little from his attempts to recruit military officers to his side, while he gradually alienated the vast body of centrist officers who had been committed to legality.

Brazil's economic momentum in the early 1960s ran out of steam. Nothing Goulart tried worked. Increases in the gross national product declined steadily, and in 1963 growth was negative. Goulart first relied upon a group known as the "positive" left. Its members, including well-known economist Celso Furtado, wanted development and stabilization at the same time. Though emphasizing the need for basic reforms, they were not seriously nationalistic or socialistic. To the left of this group was the "negative" left, a more radical and anti-American faction. As the economy worsened, Goulart turned from the former group to the latter, but the economic crisis could not be alleviated by slight modifications of old policies.

Goulart's political manipulations achieved no more than his economic efforts. Basically a nonideological centrist within his own party, the Brazilian Labor Party, Goulart tried to prevent the radical left from outflanking him. Such a strategy had little payoff, since the left would never really trust Goulart and since each move left further strengthened and polarized his opposition. Goulart vastly overestimated the strength of the left and vastly underestimated the willingness of the military to intervene. As a result the coup was remarkably quick and bloodless.

In the analysis of Latin American coups linkages between social sectors and military officers are often overemphasized to the detriment of institutional factors affecting the military directly. The latter are clearly relevant in the 1964 coup. Enlisted men and noncommissioned officers responded to Goulart's moves to the left by demanding their own political rights. To their senior officers such demands represented a breakdown in the chain of command for which Goulart, who refused to support the officers in crucial confrontations, was responsible. Unfortunately for Goulart, the rebellious soldiers were conspicuous by their failure to take up arms in his defense as the coup unfolded at the end of March.

The Composition of the Post-Coup Policy Elite and Its Goals

At the time of the coup, three groups comprised the anti-Goulart forces: Castello Branco and officers and civilian technicians associated with the Higher War School, the Escola Superior de Guerra or ESG,[2] civilian politicians, and non-ESG officers. The Castello Branco regime was soon dominated by the ESG group. Civilian politicians like Adhemar de Barros and Carlos Lacerda lost their political influence. Generals sympathetic to the coup but not to the ESG were purged, including Olympio Mourão Filho and Amaury Kruel.

The dominance of post-coup policy-making by officers and civilians with essentially ESG goals was facilitated by heavy civilian participation in the Escola. Though assisted by a United States Military Mission during its formative years, the ESG differed from the U.S. National War College in its emphasis on joint military-civilian participation in courses and activities. In fact, 646 of the 1276 ESG graduates between 1950 and 1967 were civilians (Stepan, 1971: 176). Drawn from education, industry, communication, and banking, these civilians remained active in the ESG after graduation through its alumni activities, which included a traveling informational lecture series, journals, and luncheons.

The ESG taught a systematic set of beliefs. Similar to the military in other developing countries, ESG ideology stressed nationalism, a puritanical outlook, acceptance of collective public enterprise, and a planning mentality based on an anti-politics position (see Janowitz, 1964: 63–65). ESG beliefs also demonstrated a strong anti-communism (helped along by the Cuban experience) and a definite alignment with the U.S. in the Cold War. Some ESG publications argued that Brazil's political parties were too many and too localistic (Carneiro, n.d.: 18–20). Others stressed the need for a strong central government, economic planning, and mobilization of resources (Stepan, 1971: 178–182).

The ESG itself did not rule Brazil,[3] but the ruling coalition of officers and civilians grounded their policy orientations in ESG doctrine. Their positions included short-term responses to the economic crisis, such as halting inflation and restoring economic growth, and long-term economic goals, such as maintaining private enterprise, a strong state role in the economy, and friendliness to foreign investment. Ideologically, they were strongly anti-communist and sided with the United States in the Cold War. Their institutional commitments included reducing party strife and eliminating demagoguery by populist politicians and union leaders. In policy-making, they were committed to authority and decision-making by planning and rationality.

These orientations produced changes in policy input and in policy-making structures. The political activity of thousands of people was repressed, and elections were devalued by reducing their number and restricting potential candidates' eligibility. Leaders of over 400 labor unions were replaced, liberal newspapers were attacked, and the right to strike was nearly eliminated. The regime attempted to repress the National Student Union (UNE) and prohibited marches and demonstrations. Changes in the policy-making structure included centralizing authority by decreasing the power of the legislature and the states and increasing the power of the executive, creating new ministries (e.g., the Ministry of Planning and General Co-ordination, to control budget design), removing authority to initiate new programs from certain ministries (e.g., Education and Culture), and attempting to improve bureaucratic performance by encouraging full-time work in government agencies.

These changes themselves are less important than their actual effects. Before evaluating the implementation of goals which affected the policy-making process itself, the elite's conception of a rationalized policy process must be analyzed. Then the question of whether policy outcomes actually measure true goals can be confronted. Subsequently, the literature linking military regimes and policy outcomes can be consulted so that some hypotheses guiding the analysis of our three cases can be developed.

Elite informants were asked what they meant by a rationalized policy process and how they planned to improve it. Their vision of improved policy-making called for an increase in the number and authority of technically trained administrators (*técnicos*)[4] employed in decision-making posts. Elite informants expected técnicos to make decisions on technical criteria, but they did not expect perfectly rational and omniscient policy makers (see Braybrooke and Lindblom, 1963). To assess the success of attempts to improve policy-making, information was sought both on increases in the number of técnicos and on differences between their behavior and that of nontécnicos.

Since all regimes face constraints, using policy outcomes as tests of true goals really asks whether the regime was powerful enough to realize its goals.[5] Brazil may be an ideal test case, since the regime was rarely forced to compromise its strongly held preferences. It crippled the unions, repressed student organizations, devalued elections, persecuted intellectuals, and emasculated the Congress. And although the regime faced financial limitations, its expectations did not overestimate Brazil's economic potential.

Outcomes under Militarized Regimes

Policy outcomes from military-dominated regimes have traditionally been viewed in two ways (see Schmitter, 1970)‌ In the first, which can be called the "conservative-incompetent" model, officers are thought to be defenders of status quo interests, expected to identify with the upper class, and labeled as poor planners and technicians. The foremost exponent of this position, Edwin Lieuwen, has argued that in general the military in power has no concern for civil rights or representative government, that professional careers isolate officers from the main currents of society, that officers' understanding of national problems may be defective, and that officers do not make capable technicians (Lieuwen, 1961: 134–154). Edward Shils (1962: 55–56), whose position is quite close to Lieuwen's, believes that once the military has succeeded in

> suppressing attempted *putsches*, cleaning up streets, removing beggars from the center of the main town, prosecuting the beneficiaries of the preceding regime . . . there is not much more they can do to support their own self-confidence and to impress themselves on the public mind. Since they have very little of a program except what they take over from the planning boards and civil servants of the old regime, for whom they have no respect, they are left directionless . . . so there is a danger that they will come to feel suspended in a void of clean government and clean streets.

In recent decades the officer corps has increased its level of technical skill, and officers have come from middle- as well as upper-class backgrounds. These tendencies have encouraged scholars to develop a second model, a developmental-proficient position. Its advocates point to the advantages of the military as an "engine of development" by virtue of its cohesiveness, ability to use force of arms, propensity toward state intervention in the economy, and basically middle-class orientation. The best-known exponent of this position, John Johnson (1962: 127), sees the changes in officers' class origins and professional backgrounds as vital keys to their new emphases on nationalism and industrialization:

> When military governments do exist they will tend to be oriented toward the urban propertied elements rather than otherwise. . . . Pressures for redistribution of land are building up . . . it is becoming politically injudicious to defend the interests of the great landholders. Politically, then, the militarists who seek power . . . may be expected to bid for popular support from the same socio-economic groups—ranging from the urban workers through the bureaucracy and professions to the owners and managers of commercial enterprises—as the middle sectors have done for half a century. The social and economic slogans of the militarists need not differ substantively, and probably will not in most cases, from those offered by the civilian elements.

The developmental-proficient model is really the core of Nasserist theories. Manfred Halpern (1962: 300) suggests:

> As a ruling power, an army has several extraordinary advantages. Because of historical circumstances Middle Eastern armies tend to produce

butes from the two ideal types, may represent actual empirical outcomes. In effect, the third model suggests that the explanation of policy outcomes under military regimes requires much more explicit attention to variables which have heretofore been ignored.

Given both the absence of developed and tested theories of policy outcomes in either military or civilian regimes and the unreliability of incomplete data from a police state, it would be foolish to attempt to develop a general theory of policy outcomes. Instead, the explanation of outcomes can be advanced if we focus on hypotheses predicting the regime's implementation of goals affecting the policy-making process itself.

Hypotheses

It is now well established that policy-making structures may vary according to the nature of the policy problem (see Lowi, 1966). Variations can include the composition and goals of the policy-making elite, its need for supportive coalitions, the social groups making demands on policy makers, the nature of policy-making structures during previous regimes, the amenability of the problem to technical solutions, and the experience of technically trained administrators in forming earlier policy.

While the Brazilian regime's desire to improve the policy-making process was to affect all policy areas, many of its goals which related to specific groups pertained mainly to a single policy area. The priority the elite placed on "process" goals as opposed to "group" goals may differ among policy areas. This ranking will be affected by the aspects of the policy process mentioned above. Economic policy, for example, has traditionally been an area in which technically trained administrators wielded influence. In addition, a general perception also exists that economic issues are more amenable to technical inputs than, say, housing policy. Thus economic policy outcomes under a new military regime are more likely than other policy outcomes to reflect the impact of increased technical inputs.

All regimes develop clientele groups, and policy problems arise which affect them. Unless there is a complete harmony of interest between clienteles and the elite, the ability of clientele groups to influence policy ought to be inversely proportional to the unity and intensity of elite preferences on the issue. Technically trained administrators (*técnicos*) frequently must compete against clienteles of the regime. Técnicos are likely to be strongest when their competitors oppose the regime and weakest when their competitors support it. In addition, technical inputs should influence policy less when the policy elite is not united.

Other things being equal, it is likely that the more technical expertise a decision maker has, the more his behavior will be guided by it. Frequently, however, expertise may make little difference. Often the data available to a decision maker are spotty, inaccurate, and biased, encouraging him to make decisions on other grounds. Frequently data are supplied by groups interested and involved in the policy process, so their biases tend to be reflected in decisions. Sometimes the context of policy-making does not encourage technically trained decision makers to use their skills. In milieus dominated by administrators lacking technical training, técnicos are less likely to behave differently from nontécnicos, because technically grounded decision-making may not be encouraged. Técnicos are most likely to utilize their technical expertise in policy milieus which reward such behavior and have utilized it in the past.

Some factors influence outcomes more uniformly. Samuel Huntington (1962: 36) points out that "prolonged military participation in politics inevitably means that the military reflects the divisions, stresses, and weakness of politics." The longer the military is in power, the less characteristically military is its behavior, and the less independence it has from the clientele groups.

Finally, a regime's success is limited by scarce technical and financial resources. If a regime concentrates technical personnel in one policy area, others will be shortchanged. In areas of less importance to a regime, policy-making patterns from earlier regimes are likely to persist.

Methods for a Study of Policy-Making

In testing these hypotheses, two methodological problems present themselves: the question of the choice of cases and their representativeness, and the question of the techniques used in analyzing each case and the validity of the resulting data.

When the analysis of a series of cases is intended to yield general hypotheses, the choice of cases becomes crucial. The general policy areas and the specific decisions analyzed in this study were chosen because they involved at least the potential for conflict among social classes. This does not mean that all social classes were necessarily represented in the policy process or that final outcomes necessarily penalized one class for the benefit of another, but on the basic issues involved in the arena the interests of different social classes were opposed.

This criterion of "potential for conflict among social classes" excludes such issues as administrative reforms, which do not a priori discriminate between classes, at least in the short run. The policy problems it includes are those we normally consider important; they are part of the "who gets what" process which is the heart of politics. The areas chosen, involving housing for urban migrants, national salary levels, and resources for education, clearly meet the criterion of potential class conflict, and they also are among the most widely recognized problems facing policy makers throughout Latin America. However, in no sense do they constitute a random sample of Brazilian policy-making.

In each policy area the analysis is developed chronologically. Within the narratives, data gathered in 1969 and 1970 from about 67 interviews with knowledgeable informants plus high- and low-level policy makers are presented. These data, revealing the behaviors, attitudes, and perceptions of policy makers, were gathered in interviews which were about half open-ended, concentrating upon the details of the case, and about half structured, utilizing memorized translations of questions regarding the decision-making process. Few interviewees were active military officers, but this does not mean that the interviews underrepresented the influence of the military in policy-making, because the military controlled policy by dominating the very highest levels of government (like the presidency) while most administrators have remained civilian (see Daland, 1972a: 192–199; Schmitter, 1971a).

Brazil is a police state. Data gathered in such conditions from high-level informants are inherently unreliable. This was especially true in the arena of education policy, many of whose participants were under attack by the regime. It was least true in salary policy, since in this arena the regime had great pride and confidence. Nevertheless, none of the interview data can be rigorously quantified. They can only support essentially subjective conclusions. . . .

Salary Policy after 1964

In salary policy the benefits of técnico decision-making should be most evident. The elite was united in its general ideological preferences, economic problems were salient at the time of the coup, and technically trained administrators had considerable influence even before 1964.

On the surface, salary policy does appear to conform to a rational model. Salary increases were regularly held below the rise in the cost of living, and the inflation rate dropped dramatically. However, it is questionable whether salary policy caused the reduction in the inflation rate. Albert Fishlow, a member of the U.S. AID Economic Mission to Brazil, argues that the dominant diagnosis of pre-1964 problems made by post-coup policy architects (especially Roberto Campos) led to excessive salary repression and an over-tightening of credit. This produced a decrease in investment and continuing high levels of inflation without corresponding growth. Increased growth between 1967 and 1970 resulted partly from the development of exports, but mainly from a business-cycle upswing. Government policies, according to Fishlow, were not primarily responsible for the economic reversal.[7]

The 1964 coup unquestionably increased the técnico presence in salary policy-making. To determine whether the presence of more técnicos improved the quality of decisions (given the goals of the elite) we will examine the background of Brazilian economic policy, the views of high-level economic policy makers, the general outlines of government wage policy, and a specific group faced with implementing an emergency wage increase in 1968.

The federal government in Brazil has long occupied a dominant role in its economy, owning all or most of many industries, including maritime, river, and rail transport; petroleum, steel, and alkali production; and controlling the exportation of coffee, sugar, rubber, and other crops. It produces most iron ore, regulates mining rights, and controls communications and transport concessions, exchange and interest rates, and insurance. It attempts to fix prices of basic goods, rents, and most short-term and almost all long-term credit. It finances port facilities, housing projects, and warehouses, and it exerts strong controls over monetary, fiscal, investment, education, and health policies (see Leff, 1968; Schmitter, 1971b).

Government economic dominance extends to the setting of salaries. Besides controlling wages of civil servants, the government has set wages for workers in government-related industries since the *Estado Nôvo* of 1937–1945. The government-established minimum salary, first decreed in 1940 during the Vargas regime, theoretically applies to all adult workers, and is designed to provide sufficient income to satisfy "normal necessities of food, housing, clothing, hygiene, and transportation."[8] It has usually paid between $30 and $42 per month. The minimum is important in Brazil precisely because it is a real social minimum, at least in urban areas. About half the work force receives the minimum salary, and most of the remainder receive some fixed multiple of the minimum (Gregory, 1968). Though the actual level of the minimum salary varies from region to region, the levels are set after collection and analysis of living cost data by the National Salary Department of the Labor Ministry.

Coupled with the dominance of the central government in economic policy-making is a long tradition of attempts to regulate and manipulate employers' and workers' associations in order to control dissent and coopt opposition. This corporatist policy began during the Vargas period (in the 1930s) as a device to undermine the power of state governors (see Skidmore, 1967: 34). Both workers' and employers' organizations are regulated by the national government, receive funds from it, and hold legally established places on consultative councils in their policy areas.

In the case of the employers' organizations it is difficult to determine whether business or government benefits more from this corporatist relationship. Leaders in the National Confederation of Commerce believed that they profited, because they could inform the government of their problems and provide technical assistance. But it would be impossible to tell what would happen in the absence of such participation, since neither government decision makers nor CNC officials perceived their interests as basically in conflict.[9]

The weakness of workers' organizations is quite apparent. During the Estado Nôvo the state initiated a policy of preemptive cooptation, sponsoring and supporting representative associations before they were able to emerge spontaneously and manipulating the unions through control of their finances. The Labor Code, consolidated and revised after 1943, provided registration of every aspect of unionism and working conditions, including a syndical tax, labor courts, and the minimum salary, but these gains were not won through struggle. The "thirteenth-month salary," child allowances, and unemployment compensation were not labor-management issues, but grants from the government. When the government wanted to diminish labor's bargaining ability after 1964, a full range of time-tested controls, such as the practice of installing pro-government agents in union leadership positions (*peleguismo*), stood ready (see Skidmore, 1967: 40).

Given the economic situation in 1964, it is not surprising that the new government would be concerned with labor's power. The litany of ills besetting Brazil at the end of March 1964 has been recited often enough. We need only note that inflation had risen to a level such that the annual rate for 1964 would have been 140 percent. During 1963, the GNP had actually declined. Labor troubles were an important aspect of the turbulent political environment. In the month before the coup there had been two major strikes, among bus drivers and cigarette makers. The steel workers, one of Brazil's most powerful unions, had settled their wage dispute for a 90 percent increase. And in the week before the coup, 5,380 rebellious and unemployed workers in Brasilia were given jobs by the President (*Jornal do Brasil,* 1964b, 1964c, 1964e).

The Coup and Economic Ideology

Interviews and documentary evidence revealed that economic policy makers generally shared goals.[10] Respondents (primarily connected with the Ministries of Labor, Treasury, and Planning) stressed the need to control the cost of living. Inflation was either first or second as the most important problem for every government policy maker interviewed. Economic conditions in 1964 were so bad that it was unnecessary to consider the possibility that deflationary policy might be counterproductive for growth. A much simpler solution was to control inflation.

A kind of capitalism and free enterprise value underlay respondents' answers to "What do you believe is the basic role of the State in economic development?" and "Do you believe that the major sectors of the economy now in private hands should remain there?" Representative answers included aiding free enterprise, helping foreign investment, and providing capital to national industry. Few respondents were interested in nationalizing industry.

These economic policy makers unanimously believed that the labor movement in 1964 had become Communist-dominated and demagogic. They felt that its leaders were calling for raises far in excess of cost of living increases and were thus fueling the inflation. Some unions, such as the steel workers, were perceived to be getting extraordinary raises simply because of their credible strike threat.[11]

Alternative weapons to salary restriction for fighting the inflation were rejected on a number of grounds. Asked why profits could not be restricted by profit-ceiling legislation, progressive taxation, or price control, some respondents argued that there were insufficient data to analyze profits, and/or that profits were not high anyway. Others thought that profit restriction was antithetical to free enterprise. Many believed that such moves would be self-defeating, because they would cut investment and restrict growth.

Policy makers seem to have reasoned that forced saving by the lower class was necessary, and that only when nonmarket forces such as unions interfered with this classical pattern of capitalist development would the real wage of the salaried class rise and become inflationary. Roberto Campos explained his unwillingness to control inflation through freezing prices by arguing that

> it would be counterproductive: it would impede the readjustment of agricultural prices, essential for the modernization of agriculture; it would congeal the prices of basic services, diminishing the capacity of investment in energy and transportation, and finally, it would lend itself to fraud and abuse, because of the inefficiency of the administrative machinery and the inadequate moral discipline of our controls (*Correio da Manhã*, 1966c).

The policy elite also wanted a definite policy. When asked "What have been the major achievements of the salary policy?" about one-third of those interviewed mentioned the need for one policy. Others concurred spontaneously; the remainder agreed when asked if they thought just having one policy was a virtue in itself. (For an illustration of this terminology, see Pinheiro, 1968: 491.)

The Development of Government Wage Policy

Although the conspirators took office without fully developed economic plans, the unions received quick attention. Forty labor leaders were replaced within the first month after the coup, including the heads of the National Confederation of Industrial Workers (CNTI), the General Labor Command (CGT), the National Confederation of Workers in Agriculture (CONTAG), and the National Confederation of Workers in Establishments of Credit (CONTEC). By the end of May the government admitted intervening in 300 unions, including almost all the important national unions. Overt opposition to these interventions was extremely rare.

A comprehensive wage policy emerged slowly. The National Council of Salary Policy was reorganized, and the government declared its intent to maintain the working-class share of the national wealth. The current share to be maintained would be the average salary for the previous 24 months. In 1964 this formula was applied almost literally, causing a sharp decline in real wages, because, with continuing inflation, only immediately after the adjustment did a worker's salary actually equal even the 24-month mean.

At this stage the federal government lacked the legal power to fix salaries for most nongovernmental workers. Thus the bank workers were not bound by the nonstrike decree or by the wage guidelines. Typically, however, their government-imposed leader announced in September 1964 that his union would neither strike nor appeal the bankers' offer to the arbitrational labor courts.

Official strictness on salary hikes in 1964 brought support and encouragement from industry. *Desenvolvimento e Conjuntura* (1964: 3), the journal of the National Confederation of Industry, argued that salaries ought to be raised less than the increase in the cost of living:

> The adoption of a policy of elevation of salaries below the growth in the cost of living in the molds proposed by the "Action Program" (the first full-scale plan of the new regime) constitutes the only way to continue a policy of control of inflation without interrupting development.

By 1965, however, the unanimity of support from business and media began to break down, and splits appeared within the government as well. The business community divided over wage policy because commercial interests began to suffer from the decline in middle- and lower-class buying power which resulted from wage repression. The split was reflected in certain quasi-governmental consultative councils. For example, a faction of the National Economic Council (CNE)[12] led by Fernando Gasparian began attacking government wage policy as monetarist and orthodox.[13] By July 1965 *Correio da Manhã* was talking about serious unemployment in textiles and arguing that government credit tightening was discouraging modernization. Gasparian was soon joined by another highly placed critic, Antônio Dias Leite, an economics professor from São Paulo. Their anti-monetarist criticisms began appearing in trade journals such as *Digesto Econômico*, the journal of the Commercial Associations of São Paulo. The opponents of the policies of Campos and Treasury Minister Bulhões began to form a political alliance. Dias Leite and Gasparian allied themselves with members of the "undespicable" (*Não begorrilha*) wing of the old Brazilian Labor Party, to members of the "Compacts" of the Social Democratic Party, and to Carlos Lacerda and the *bossa nova* wing of the National Democratic Union. These factions, composed of the right wing of the more leftist party and the left wings of the rightest parties, pursued a strategy based on the electoral strength of the working class and the presidential desires of Carlos Lacerda. But since Lacerda was not allowed to seek public office, this essentially in-house protest of a faction of the CNE and their allies yielded nothing.

In May of 1965 the first formal plan was published by the Ministry of Planning and General Coordination. Known as the Program of Economic Action of the Government 1964–66, it established guidelines for wage policy:

> The salary readjustment will be determined so as to equal the real average salary for the last 24 months, multiplied by a coefficient which measures the increase in productivity estimated for the previous year, plus a provision to compensate for the chance inflationary residual allowed in the financial programming of the Government.[14]

In July 1965 this formula was extended to all collective agreements and labor court decisions, and in 1966 the government began formally applying the inflationary residual to salary increases.

The inflationary residual was designed to compensate workers for the continuous decline in their buying power each month after their annual wage increase by including a prediction of the inflation in the year to come. In 1966, for example, the predicted inflation was 10 percent, which meant that salaries were increased by 5 percent extra (one-half the prediction). The increase in the cost of living between July 1965 and July 1966 was 40.5 percent. The next prediction, August 1966 to August 1967, was again 10 percent. The real cost-of-living increase was 30.1 percent (Gregory, 1968). In both years the real value of salaries dropped due to the over-optimism of the government prediction.

Did high-level decision makers actually believe that inflation could be kept to 10 percent? Or were they simply striving to achieve the maximum deflationary effect with the minimum political difficulty? Journalistic discussions presumed that the economic policy makers were simply over-optimistic, that they were making honest errors. But the técnicos in the Ministries of Planning and Treasury admitted that no one really believed inflation could be kept to 10 percent either in 1966 or 1967. Ten percent was picked as an optimum goal. If salaries were adjusted on that basis, they could not contribute to inflation. If salaries were adjusted at some likely level, then a rise in the cost of living in that range might be accelerated by salary increases. It was safe to underestimate the prediction—it might help and it could not hurt. High-level policy makers pursued this line of reasoning because their true objective was to restrain inflation at any cost. Maintaining the workers' share of the national product was official policy, but it was a goal of lower priority.[15] In this case deficient technical expertise, i.e., the inability to predict accurately the inflation rate for the next year, led to a salary repression even beyond the intentions of government policy makers, although it was acceptable to them.

By May 1966 anti-governmental forces had picked up another ally, if a very inconsistent and uncertain one. The *Jornal do Brasil* (1966b) editorially supported Dias Leite's criticism and pointed out that between 1964 and 1965, those receiving the minimum salary had lost 8 percent of their real buying power, bank workers had lost 15 percent, textile workers had lost 7 percent, steel workers had lost 5 percent, and civil servants had lost 13 percent. These figures were not debated by government leaders— Minister of the Treasury Bulhões said that workers have to suffer "temporary losses to benefit from sound wisdom in the near future" (*Correio da Manhã*, 1966b).

Businessmen were beginning to attack government policy not from love of workers, but because aggregate demand was slipping. Pro-government economist Mário H. Simonsen (1968a) had argued that salaries were neither the exclusive nor predominant component of aggregate demand.

Because it discounted any negative effects on growth, such reasoning led to maximal salary repression. The commercially oriented sector of business, first to feel losses in demand, understandably refused to accept Simonsen's argument.

In 1967 the Costa e Silva government assumed power. Bulhões and Campos were replaced, and Delfim Neto, a former economist at the University of São Paulo, became Treasury Minister and the real architect of economic policy. The attack on government policy by the commercial sector continued, and almost immediately there was a period of confessions inside the government. Everyone admitted that the salary policy of Campos and Bulhões had injured the workers. In May, Jarbas Passarinho, the new Minister of Labor, charged the National Council of Salary Policy with the task of bringing in suggestions for changes in the policy, adding that if the problem were not resolved by September 1, he would resign (*Correio da Manhã*, 1967b). Unfortunately for the Labor Minister, the post-coup policy-making pattern had relegated his ministry to a secondary role. When Passarinho announced on August 31 that the current salary policy would remain in effect until inflation dropped to 10 percent (a figure it has not even approached), it was clear that the monetarism of Delfim Neto had prevailed with Costa e Silva (*Correio da Manhã*, 1967c).

In September of 1967 the inflationary residual was increased to 15 percent, meaning that salaries would be 7.5 percent higher to account for the next period's inflation. In the next year the cost of living rose 21.5 percent. So although real salaries continued to drop, they dropped at a lesser rate. Salary increases in both the civil servant and minimum salary categories for 1968 were pegged at about 20 percent, much closer to the expected inflation.

A Second Slice into the Policy Process: The Emergency Bonus of 1968

In spite of Passarinho's efforts, opposition continued to grow in Congress. In the Chamber of Deputies forty members formed the Frente Parlamentar Anti-Arrôcho (Anti-Strangulation Parliamentary Front), composed of 28 MDB deputies and 12 from the official government party, the National Renovating Alliance (ARENA). Senator Carvalho Pinto, a *paulista ARENA* member and a pre-coup Finance Minister, introduced a bill granting a 10 percent advance to all workers who had not received one within the last six months. The advance would be financed mostly from excess welfare funds, but partially (one-fourth) by the employers. This bill was conceded a good chance to pass the Congress, and even if vetoed, it would embarrass the government.

In April 1968 Passarinho proposed his own version of the *abono de emergência* (emergency bonus), which was similar to that of Carvalho Pinto. Unfortunately the Labor Minister had not cleared the plan with the other ministers, especially those of Treasury and Planning. Apparently he had received general approval from Costa e Silva, but given Costa's penchant for decentralizing authority to lower officials, this did not ensure unwavering support. Minister Delfim Neto criticized the abono as inflationary, and Housing Bank officials complained about a potential cutback in their fund supply. It was also discovered that Treasury officials had been using the unemployment fund, from which the abono would largely be financed, to cover short-term federal budget deficits.

Manufacturers strongly opposed the plan. Heads of various industrial confederations immediately denounced the abono as demagogic and inflationary.[16] Their discovery that the plan had not been cleared with other ministries was used as evidence that it was ill-planned. The manufacturers' pressure was directed at the Ministers of Treasury and Planning. They in turn protested to Costa e Silva, who decided that Passarinho was being too hasty. A five-man committee consisting of two representatives from the Ministries of Labor and Treasury and one from the Planning Ministry was formed to study the abono and make recommendations.

The official mandate of the group was to design a noninflationary solution to the abono dilemma acceptable to both Delfim and Passarinho. After an intensive week-long session such a plan, differing considerably from the Passarinho proposal, was developed. Recipients of the minimum salary (about one-half the labor force) were excluded from its benefits, and no one could receive a payment of more than about one-third the minimum ($12). Rather than the unemployment fund financing most of the abono, it would be paid for by the welfare institutes. The government also agreed to cut back a part of a projected increase in the Merchandise Consumption Tax (ICM).[17] This rollback enabled some businesses to profit from the abono, since the difference in the ICM was greater than the payout the abono required.

After the decision group had reached an agreement and the ministers had concurred, the plan was proposed to representatives of business. In a ceremony in the Treasury Ministry in Rio, the heads of the CNI and the Federations of Industry of Rio and São Paulo signed an agreement not to raise prices as a result of the abono. The force of the agreement, however, was purely moral.

The bureaucratic group which designed the abono was selected for intensive analysis in this study, because it seemed typical of the kind of decision-making the regime wanted to institute. Intensive interviews were conducted with all members of the group. All of them were technically trained, had worked together before, and professed mutual respect (in contrast to CEPE-3* members). Within the broad constraints imposed by

---

* Executive Commission for Specific Projects, mandated in 1968 to design a definitive solution for the problem of favelas in the state of Guanabara.—Ed.

the ministers, the group had considerable power, because the potential costs to the ministers of deciding the issue themselves were high, and a plan devised by a respected group of técnicos would have the legitimacy to ensure acceptance.

The techniques used for evaluating proposals differed sharply from those of CEPE-3. Proposals were not distorted; these técnicos understood each other's ideas and language. Alternatives were not dismissed as impossible without analysis. Group members did not apply cost-benefit analysis to every proposal, but they did avoid intense involvements in their own proposals and concomitant distortion of alternatives.

Since the técnicos on CEPE-3 did not display a noticeably technical decision style, the behavior of the abono group cannot be explained by its técnico composition. The most striking differences between the two groups lie in their internal dynamics. In contrast to CEPE-3, the abono group had to come up with a plan. (The ministers insisted on this.) In addition, the members of the abono group agreed on goals, and they liked each other personally. When an issue remained in dispute even after long discussion, the group compromised. All the members supported the final solution, even though aspects of it contravened the wishes of the superiors of individual members. Such actions would have been impossible on CEPE-3.

Members of the CEPE-3 group seemed to use the language of comprehensive planning as a rationale for inaction. In the abono group talk of total planning was much less heard. Members seemed much more concerned with particular bottlenecks, and they used terms like "flexible" and "pragmatic" instead of "integrated" or "comprehensive" (see Hirschman, 1965). Perhaps part of the difference can be explained by the problems faced by the two groups. Certainly a one-month salary increase is simpler than a solution for the problem of Rio's favelas. However, when the abono group members were quizzed about their subsequent participation in a commission to design a new salary policy, they continued to avoid terms such as "comprehensive planning." Perhaps their incentives for action discouraged the use of terms which appear to hinder task fulfillment.

The increased effectiveness of decision-making does not mean that decisions were made on narrowly technical grounds. In fact, key choices were made to satisfy particular influential people or groups whose approval was needed. The abono was financed by the welfare institutes rather than by the unemployment compensation fund not because it was economically better, but because this choice reduced opposition from inside the government. The ICM was reduced 1 percent to provide a carrot to business. Even if the members had wanted to perform more technical analysis, it would have been difficult, because time and data were limited. This technical weakness led to a bizarre outcome: a supposed emergency raise for workers actually added to business profits, because the tax break was bigger than the payout. Since the task of this group was to avoid an inflationary solution, both weak and strong firms had to be protected. Since the weak firms could not be identified and exempted, all firms had to be protected, giving the stronger firms a break. . . .

Conclusion

The Policy-Making Process

Formal governmental positions were more likely to be filled by técnicos after the coup. Both in education and housing, increased centralization and shifts in authority to certain ministries increased the percentage of técnicos in formal authority positions. In salary policy, pre-1964 decisions were also made by técnicos, but the ideological unity and loyalty of decision makers increased in the post-coup period.

Evidence for differences in decision-making behavior among different kinds of personnel was inconclusive. Differences emerged between the behavior of the groups making salary and favela policy. Members of the favela group had a much less evidence-based decision style, and their emphasis on the necessity for global planning seemed to rationalize inaction.[18] But while the favela decision group included both técnicos and nontécnicos, no consistent differences in behavior were found between the two. This suggests that the nature of the groups and the kind of problems they must solve are important determinants of decisional behavior.

The salary group members had high positive affect, faced a specific task, and would be negatively evaluated by their ministers if they failed to solve it. The favela group participants had a mandate to solve the whole favela problem of the state of Guanabara, but they had strong incentives to do nothing, because action invited penalties and would bring few rewards. Decision-making behavior might be quite different for each group in a different setting.

A related aspect of technically oriented behavior involves the criteria used to choose among alternatives. Even though participants in the salary group were much more likely to evaluate alternatives according to evidence, their criteria were political rather than technical. Their goals included getting the solution accepted by the ministers, enforcing it, and so on. These criteria were unrelated to the effects of the wage increase on living standards, aggregate demand, or inflation. Moreover, the outcome in the salary group was clearly affected by shortages of time and deficiencies in data.

In spite of similiarities in decision making behavior between técnicos and nontécnicos, technically trained personnel might gain influence because they are listened to by the elite. This seems to have occurred in salary policy, where técnicos were, if not supreme, certainly dominant. The other cases, however, show the limitations of técnico influence. While técnicos filled formal governmental positions, real influence was retained by people who did not hold official posts. Certain people in favela policy, for instance, influenced outcomes even though they represented the kind of particularistic interest supposedly alien to the regime. Advocates of experimental solutions, regardless of technical knowledge, fared poorly because of the paternalistic and anti-lower-class values of high officials. In allocating education resources, técnicos were also mostly ineffectual. They did not generally advocate increased spending on universities; the policy elite, however, responded to the demands of students and university administrators and increased expenditures in this area. The elite talked about planning, but such talk was really a screen used to justify decisions made on other criteria.

The Incompleteness of Goals

The coup elevated to power men with goals affecting some policy areas but not others. If a policy problem fell into an area affected by regime goals, outcomes would be fairly predictable. But what if no intensely held common goal applied?

Apparently the regime was determined to preserve political and social calm. Both the storm of criticism which arose following the rains of 1966 and 1967 in the state of Guanabara and the pressure from rectors, parents, and university students in 1967 and 1968 came from sources either friendly or neutral to the regime. Neither could be repressed by military action or political persecution. In both cases the regime responded with vigorous measures designed to alleviate the immediate crisis rather than solve the long-range problem. The favela problem was federalized, thus meeting the criticism that the state was incompetent. But the regime was unwilling to commit enough resources to deal seriously with squatter settlements. Similarly, the initial response to the pressure for higher university enrollment was to create more places without increased expenditures, producing overcrowding. Later expenditures did go up sharply, but at the cost of decreases for other educational levels and without consideration for the effects on the labor market.

Since the desire to improve decision-making supposedly applied to all policy areas, it might be expected that once a new policy problem arose, decision-making in that area would be modified and técnicos would gain influence. This did not occur. In favela policy Carlos Costa's ability to force favela removals ended only upon the death of Costa e Silva. In educational policy, the rectors were far stronger than the técnicos. Técnicos in education competed with people better connected to the President and ministers. As long as technical inputs themselves were not valued highly, the ability of técnicos to achieve their objectives through bargaining was limited, because técnicos could operate only inside the government and depended upon an organizational hierarchy. So técnicos did little to promote their own policy goals, but it is doubtful that more activity would have yielded greater success.

Toward a Ranking of Elite Goals

The findings of this essay help differentiate between regime rhetoric and real priorities. While economic goals seem to have been foremost both in rhetoric and actual behavior, it proved impossible to develop a consistent ranking of goals beyond them. For example, the elite implemented its desire to end excessive fractionalization of parties, demagogic labor leadership, and the *jogo de política* (the game of politics). But this implementation was much more thorough in some policy arenas than others. It was effective in economic policy: the repression of labor and centralization of policy-making power in the Ministries of Planning and Treasury facilitated a rigorous wage policy. But in favela and education policy particularistic forces retained power, and técnico decision makers were overruled by regime clienteles. Similarly, the regime's desire to institute rational policy-making was partially realized in economic policy, given limitations of time and data. But técnicos were scarcer in favela and education policy and received little support even when they participated in the policy-making process.

In sum, in those policy arenas in which the regime had intense goals and in which technical expertise was traditionally utilized, the regime's desire to rationalize policy-making was at least partly implemented. But in arenas in which the regime had no intensely held goals and in which the *jogo de política* had traditionally held sway, the regime seemed unable or unwilling to modify policy-making. In these latter arenas policy-making was considered rationalized once the regime had attained power. Any outcomes were considered better than pre-coup outcomes simply because the regime had produced them.

These findings also illuminate problems in the three models linking military regimes to policy outcomes. Ideological attributes such as developmental and conservative have generally been regarded as opposites, apparently in the belief that a developmental approach would necessarily favor different social groups than a conservative approach. Such a belief represents confusion about the kind of modernization occurring in Latin American military regimes and about the different components of any regime's ideology or goals.

The military in both Brazil and Peru are attempting to accelerate economic development and modernize administrative structures. Barrington Moore, Jr. (1966), would call this kind of development "revolution from above," because both regimes are simultaneously developmental and authoritarian; i.e., they actively intervene in the processes of change while trying to restrict mass involvement and initiative. In this sense developmental really implies an active rather than a passive stance toward change. It does not imply any particular direction of change nor does it identify the social groups which the regime will perceive as obstacles.

The goals of any military elite identify reactionary and progressive social groups. Whether the groups labeled obstacles include urban labor or bourgeoisie, rural proletariat or landowners, depends upon the political experiences of the military elites. While the Brazilian military cannot be said to favor only traditional upper-class interests, it has clearly not favored the short-run interests of the poor. Brazil's emulation of the repressive modernization of Germany and Japan may or may not prove successful, but its claim to the developmental label should be based on its active stance vis-à-vis intervention in political and economic structures rather than on its particular friends and enemies.

This study also demonstrates that military regimes cannot be easily categorized as either proficient or incompetent. Brazil's military has a rising level of professional skill, but these military skills are not necessarily transferable to nonmilitary problems. The training school of the armed forces has long been associated with civilians, and this helped the military elite improve policy-making somewhat, because it could call on a corps of trained and ideologically sympathetic técnicos led by Roberto Campos. However, economic policy was dominated by técnicos long before the new regime assumed power, and in other policy areas the outcomes of military rule were not systematically distinguishable from those of civilian regimes.

In fact, military regimes may commonly be labeled proficient because their domination of the political process is accompanied by policy formation with fewer of the visible signs of bargaining, compromise, and shifting coalitions characteristic of civilian regimes. This surface smoothness of the military-dominated policy process is not proof of technically superior decisions. Técnicos in Brazil were powerless when the regime wanted to ignore them, and decisions legitimated on planning criteria were actually made to satisfy clienteles of the regime.

Should the proficient-incompetent dimension be totally rejected? Perhaps not, because in policy areas in which the military is intensely interested, there may be a concentration of técnicos holding real authority. Técnicos made economic decisions in Brazil, and in Peru government técnicos implemented the regime's land reform. Students of military regimes should search for a flow of técnicos toward policy areas of high priority to the elite, but whole regimes should not be characterized as proficient or incompetent.

What can be said about the attempted synthesis of the third model? Is the military really just another interest group, embedded in a mesh of alliances? The argument that outcomes lose their uniquely military cast when the military elite is less cohesive and when the regime has been in power longer seems to explain differences between the regimes of Castello

284   Barry Ames

Branco and Costa e Silva. Nevertheless, the argument that this discontinuity has been exaggerated finds substantial support in the policy cases. Salary policy was not really modified until economic conditions compelled it, well after Costa e Silva assumed power. The political forces which led to an increase in university-level spending were latent until the problem of the excedentes could command attention. And the regime never really had any policy toward favelas until the political battles in Guanabara proved embarrassing. True, the elite had lost cohesiveness and had been in power longer, but these policy outcomes seem better explained by the incompleteness of the regime's goal structure.

This incompleteness seems generally characteristic of third world militaries. Policy problems arise which are unrelated to any regime goal, thus enabling the participation of clientele groups. Lacking a common goal, elite cohesiveness drops, and the elite loses the special characteristics distinguishing military from civilian regimes.

In sum, the findings of this study suggest a reassessment of the traditional models linking military regimes to policy outcomes. The concepts that different policy-making structures characterize different arenas and that the goals of the governmental elite have varying degrees of applicability to policy problems suggest that outcomes cannot be adequately predicted with single models totally characterizing each regime. A more flexible multimodel approach may be needed, especially one which incorporates the hypotheses that the rank order of the regime's goals and the conflicts between these goals in different policy arenas powerfully affect outcomes.

Notes

1. In this study, policy-making and decision-making will be distinguished by positing that decisions are choices between alternative solutions to single problems, while policies are collections of related decisions. No precise boundary can be drawn between policies and decisions, but in most cases (and in all the cases of this study) the language used by the actors themselves is indicative. A policy provides constraints guiding subsequent decisions. Each discrete decision may gradually or sharply change the broad policy. A policy maker is an actor who is involved in a series of related high-level decisions. A decision maker is a participant in a specific decision group. All policy makers are decision makers, but the reverse is not true.
2. Stepan (1971: 240–241) found that graduates of the *Escola* had participated in the coup much more than non-ESG graduates. Of those generals who had attended the ESG, 60 percent were defined as active plotters by Stepan, compared to only 15 percent of those who had not attended the ESG.
3. Some recent writings have questioned the similarity of the goals of the various groups who have dominated post-1964 politics. The strengthening of the non-ESG hard-line wing of the military in the debacle following the

elections of October 1965 has been called a coup within a coup by Ronald Schneider, and both Alfred Stepan and Cândido Mendes see a sharp contrast between the governments of Castello Branco and Costa e Silva. In some areas of policy these analysts are clearly correct—both key policy makers and their goals changed. The internal coup of 1965 did affect the composition and goals of the policy elite, but mainly in such areas as elections, parties, and purges. With the selection of Costa e Silva as the second President a gradual modification of economic and social policies began, including a humanization of development which supposedly meant a less repressive wage stabilization program and a more nationalistic attitude toward foreign investment. Moreover, the independence of the military elite from demands by nonmilitary groups which had supported the coup decreased during the Costa e Silva regime. Generally, I would argue that the discontinuity between the two regimes has been exaggerated and that many basic policies either were not modified under Costa e Silva or would have changed even if Castello Branco and the ESG group had continued in power. Schneider suggests that Castello agreed in 1966 to support Costa e Silva's bid for the presidency in return for a commitment to continue his program, and that after Castello's death the regime followed a more Castellist line, especially in economic policy. In any event, this problem will be clearer after a discussion of the policy cases (see Schneider, 1971: 173, 223; Mendes, 1967: 107–111; Stepan, 1971: 230–239).

4. Técnicos in this analysis refers to administrators who have some expertise in their area of authority. They may be civilian or military. For a general discussion of Brazilian public administration, see Graham (1968).

5. Throughout this analysis the term "ideology" will be avoided. Discussion of authoritarian regimes often revolves around their ideologies or lack of ideologies, while tending to ignore the wide variations possible in regimes without comprehensive Nazi or Communist-type belief systems. All elites have goals; the real questions concern the nature of these goals, the intensity with which they are held, and the unity of beliefs among the elite.

6. The one exception, a measure of "leaders' commitment to economic growth and development" is of questionable validity, since it relies on expert ranking of such items as the existence of national plans. In Latin America, rhetoric about planning may be negatively related to actual plan implementation.

7. Speech by Albert Fishlow at the Stanford-Berkeley Latin American Colloquium, April 7, 1971.

8. This is from the first minimum salary law, "lei no. 2.162, May 1, 1940."

9. The importance of the way problems are viewed by petitioner and legislator was demonstrated in the case of the trade expansion in the United States by Bonilla (1956: 39–48).

10. Roughly 25 people were interviewed in the area of economic policy. Most were or had been high-level government officials in ministries concerned with economic policy or members of the technical staffs of interest associations in this area. About one-third the number interviewed were then working for the government.

11. An economist's perspective on the wage situation would differ somewhat. According to Peter Gregory's study of industrial wage policy between 1959

and 1967, real wages rose by 4.1 percent per year between 1959 and 1962, and by 7 percent per year in 1963 and 1964. The 1959–1962 period was one of expansion in which market forces produced a rise in real wages, because many categories of skilled labor were in short supply. The 1962–1964 period was characterized by high inflation, lessened growth, and a very loose labor supply, so the rise in the real wage must have been a function of such nonmarket forces as unions or government. The real losers in this period were not the industrialists, who were able to defend their profit position, but property owners and agriculturalists. In urban areas rents were largely fixed, and the government kept basic food prices low as a subsidy to urban workers (see Gregory, 1968). The government's salary policy did not really take hold until 1966.

However, the argument that salaries were the main cause of inflation seems erroneous. Albert Fishlow (1971), a member of the Agency for International Development Economic Mission to Brazil from 1964 to 1968, argued that the real causes of the inflation and the decline in growth were an inability to continue import substitution coupled with a normal business-cycle depression. Fishlow believes that the Campos-monetarist interpretation of Brazil's economic troubles was simply wrong.

12. The CNE is a kind of free-advice commission which united representatives of major economic sectors: labor, manufacturing, commerce, and so on, with técnicos from various ministries.

13. Some of the policy makers interviewed discounted the criticism leveled by Gasparian on the grounds that his textile family background biased his views, because textiles in Brazil were largely obsolete technologically and were among the first to feel declines in buying power.

14. See Brasil. EPEA (1965: 85). The first formula for wage increases can be expressed as follows:

$$W_0 = \frac{1}{24} \sum_{i=1}^{24} \frac{W_i}{C_i} \frac{R}{1+2+P}$$

where W_0 = newly adjusted wage level; W_i = the money wage in force during the preceding 24 months; C_i = a price index with a base equal to 1.00 in month 1, the last month prior to the effective month of the new adjustment; R = expected rate of inflation over the forthcoming twelve months; P = national average of increases in productivity. (This did not reflect increases in utility prices or rents, since these had been subsidized by the government before 1964, and were returning to natural levels.)

15. As Peter Gregory rightly notes, Campos and Bulhões believed that staple foods and utilities were unnaturally subsidized before 1964, and therefore these price increases should not count in figuring the new cost of living. See, for example, the *Boletim* of the Ministry of Labor, January and December, 1966, for an article by Francisco de Paula de Castro Lima, Head of the National Salary Department and an appointee of Campos, for an exposition of this viewpoint.

16. *Jornal do Brasil* (1968b). The newspaper attacked the abono editorially on April 26, branding it opportunistic and suggesting that the Ministry of

Planning was doubtful on it and that the Treasury Ministry was in the dark. (See also *Correio da Manhã*, 1968b.)

17. The ICM is a state tax, but its level is set by the federal government following negotiations with the states. It was regarded by businessmen as one of the most oppressive taxes.

18. Richard Fagen (1972: 34) points out that the Cuban revolutionary leadership has an anti-planning mentality precisely because of its belief that "too much thought given in advance to the possible consequences of a program tends to erode revolutionary will and courage."

References

Albano, J. (1961) "O fator humano nos programas de recuperação das favelas." (unpublished)

Banas Informa (1964) December.

Bonilla, F. (1956) "When is petition pressure." Public Opinion Q. 20 (Spring).

Brasil. CHISAM (1969) CHISAM Origem-Objectivos.

————. EPEA (1965) Programa de Ação Econômica do Governo 1964–66.

————. Instituto de Geografia e Estatística (1970) Anuário Estatístico do Brasil.

————. (1969).

————. (1968).

————. (1965).

Brasil. Instituto de Pesquisas Econômicas Aplicadas (1968) "Recursos públicos aplicados em educação—1960–1967."

————. Ministério do Planejamento e Coordenação Geral (1969) Programa estratégico de desenvolvimento 1968–1970 (February).

————. (1965) Programa de Ação Econômica do Governo (1964–66) Documenta EPEA (May).

Braybrooke, D. and C. Lindblom (1963) A Strategy of Decision. New York: Free Press.

Campos, R. (1968) Estado de São Paulo. June 2, in Lima L. (1969) O Impasse na Educação Rio: Editôra Vozes.

Carneiro, D. (n.d.) Organização Politica do Brasil. Rio: Escola Superior de Guerra, Depto. de Estudos, c-47-59.

Carta Economica Brasileira (1966) May.

Cole, H. J. (1966) Revista de Administração Municipal. 79 (March and April).

Correio da Manhã (1968a) April 14.

————. (1968b) April 24, 25, 26.

————. (1968c) April 27.

————. (1967a) April 28.

————. (1967b) May 9.

———. (1967c) August 31.

———. (1966a) June 7.

———. (1966b) June 22.

———. (1966c) August 5.

———. (1965a) February 3.

———. (1965b) July 11.

———. (1965c) September 5.

———. (1964a) May 30.

———. (1964b) June 21.

———. (1964c) October 21.

———. (1964d) December 23.

Cotler, J. (1970–1971) "Political crisis and military populism in Peru." Studies in Comparative International Development 21.

Daland, R. T. (1972a) "Attitudes toward change among Brazilian bureaucrats.' J. of Comparative Administration 4.

———. (1972b) "The paradox of planning," in H. J. Rosenbaum and W. Tyler, Contemporary Brazil: Issues in Economic and Political Development. New York: Praeger.

———. (1967) Brazilian Planning. Chapel Hill: Univ. of North Carolina Press.

Desenvolvimento e Conjuntura (1964) October.

Downs, A. (1967) Inside Bureaucracy. Boston: Little, Brown.

Doxiadis (1965) Guanabara: A Plan for Urban Development. Athens: Commissão Executiva para o Desenvolvimento Urbano.

Fagen, R. (1972) "Continuities in Cuban revolutionary politics." Monthly Rev. (April).

Ferraz, E. (1966) CAPES (special edition).

Graham, L. (1968) Civil Service Reform in Brazil. Austin: Univ. of Texas Press.

Gregory, P. (1968) "Evolution of industrial wage policy in Brazil, 1959–1967." Rio: USAID Brazil Summer Research Program (September).

Guanabara (1969) Rio: Operação Favela.

———. COHAB-GB (1970) "Historia da COHAB." (mimeo)

Halpern, M. (1962) "Middle Eastern armies and the new middle class," in J. J. Johnson, The Role of the Military in Underdeveloped Countries. Princeton: Princeton Univ. Press.

Hirschman, A. (1965) Journeys Toward Progress. New York: Anchor.

Huntington, S. (1962) Changing Patterns of Military Politics. New York: Free Press.

Janowitz, M. (1964) The Military in the Political Development of New Nations. Chicago: Univ. of Chicago Press.

Johnson, J. J. (1962) "The Latin American military," in J. J. Johnson, The Role of the Military in Underdeveloped Countries. Princeton: Princeton Univ. Press.

Jornal do Brasil (1968a) April 24.

————. (1968b) July 11.

————. (1966a) January 7.

————. (1966b) May 29.

————. (1964a) February 9.

————. (1964b) March 3.

————. (1964c) March 4.

————. (1964d) March 15.

————. (1964e) March 21.

————. (1964f) May 8.

————. (1964g) September 11, 12.

————. (1964h) September 19.

————. (1964i) December 11, 12.

Leeds, A. (1969) "The significant variables determining the character of squatter settlements." America Latina 12 (July–September).

Leff, N. (1968) Economic Policy-Making and Development in Brazil, 1947–1964. New York: John Wiley.

Lieuwen, E. (1961) Arms and Politics in Latin America. New York: Praeger.

Lima, F. (1966) Boletim. Ministry of Labor (January and December).

Love, J. (1971) Rio Grande do Sul and Brazilian Regionalism, 1882–1930. Stanford: Stanford Univ. Press.

Lowi, T. (1966) "Distribution, regulation, redistribution: the functions of government," in R. R. Ripley (ed.) Public Policies and Their Politics. New York: Norton.

Mangin, W. (1967) "Latin American squatter settlements: a problem and a solution." Latin Amer. Research Rev. 2 (Summer).

Mendes, C. (1967) "O Governo Castello Branco: paradigma e prognose." Dados 2/3.

Moore, B. (1966) Social Origins of Dictatorship and Democracy. Boston: Beacon Hill.

Myhr, R. (1972) "Student activism in development," in H. J. Rosenbaum and W. Tyler (eds.) Contemporary Brazil: Issues in Economic and Political Development. New York: Praeger.

Nordlinger, E. (1970) "Soldiers in Mufti: the Impact of Military Rule upon Economics and Social Change in Non-Western States." The American Political Science Review 64, 4.

Parisse, L. (1969a) Favelas do Rio de Janeiro: Evolução-Sentido. Caderno do CENPHA, 5.

————. (1969b) "Las favelas en la expansion urbana de Rio de Janeiro: Estudio Geografica." America Latina 12 (July–September).

Pasquale, C. (1966) O desenvolvimento do ensino primário e o plano nacional de educação. São Paulo: Instituto Nacional de Estudos Pedagógicos.

Petras, J. and N. Rimensnyder (1970) "What is happening in Peru?" Monthly Rev. 21 (February).

Pinheiro, I. (1968) Visão (October).

Pye, L. (1962) "The army in Burmese politics," in J. J. Johnson, The Role of the Military in Underdeveloped Countries. Princeton: Princeton Univ. Press.

Quijano, A. (1971) "Nationalism and capitalism in Peru: a study in neo-imperialism." Monthly Rev. 23 (July–August).

Revista Brasileira de Estudos Politicos (1966) 21 (July).

Revista dos Mercados (1968) 14 (May).

Salmen, L. (1972) "Urbanization and development," in H. J. Rosenbaum and W. Tyler, Contemporary Brazil: Issues in Economic and Political Development. New York: Praeger.

Schmitter, P. (1971a) Interest Conflict and Political Change in Brazil. Stanford: Stanford Univ. Press.

———. (1971b) "The Portugalization of Brazil." University of Chicago (unpublished).

———. (1970) "Military intervention, political competitiveness and public policy in Latin America: 1950–1967." Harvard Center for International Studies. [This paper was later published in Morris Janowitz and Jacques van Doorn, eds., *On Military Intervention* (Rotterdam: Rotterdam Univ. Press, 1971). An edited version appears in this volume.—Ed.]

Schneider, R. (1971) The Political System of Brazil. New York: Columbia Univ. Press.

Shils, E. (1962) "The military in the political development of new states," in J. J. Johnson, The Role of the Military in Underdeveloped Countries. Princeton: Princeton Univ. Press.

Simonsen, M. H. (1968a) "O problema educacional." Industria e Produtividade (April).

———. (1968b) "Salários e inflação." Mundo Econômico (April).

Skidmore, T. (1967) Politics in Brazil. New York: Oxford Univ. Press.

Steinbrunner, J. (1968) "The mind and milieu of policy makers: a case-study of the MLF." Ph.D. dissertation. MIT.

Stepan, A. E. (1971) The Military in Politics. Princeton: Princeton Univ. Press.

Teixeira, A. (1960) Educação e um Direito. São Paulo: Cia. Editora Nacional.

Wirth, J. (1970) The Politics of Brazilian Development 1930–1954. Stanford: Stanford Univ. Press.

Zolberg, A. (1964) "Military rule and political development in tropical Africa," in J. van Doorn (ed.) Military Profession and Military Regimes. The Hague: Mouton.

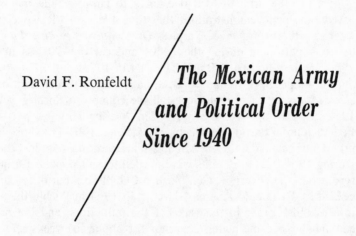

David F. Ronfeldt

The Mexican Army and Political Order Since 1940

I. Introduction by Illustration

The Mexican army, many feel, has become since the 1940s an increasingly professional force, one that obeys civilian authorities and defends the constitution in apolitical fashion. Others argue that the army has become an increasingly conservative force, still wielding political influence and repressing popular elements. These prevalent, opposing viewpoints reflect a quiet debate about the contemporary institutional history of the Mexican army and its impact on the course of the Mexican Revolution since 1940. The purpose of this paper is to offer a variety of partial observations and speculative impressions on this topic.

From *The Mexican Army and Political Order Since 1940*, Rand Corporation Paper P-5089.

Author's Note: This paper incorporates some research materials provided by Lt. Col. Franklin D. Margiotta into the revised version of a paper I originally presented at the Fourth International Congress of Mexican Studies in October 1973. My original version will appear in *Contemporary Mexico: Papers of the IV International Congress of Mexican History* (UCLA Latin American Center, forthcoming). Margiotta has written "Patterns of Civilian Control in Mexico," delivered at the 1974 Conference of the Inter-University Seminar on Armed Forces and Society, State University of New York at Buffalo, October 18–19, 1974.

Though I alone am responsible for the contents of this paper, I wish to express my appreciation for the helpful comments received on the original version from Luigi Einaudi, Edward Gonzalez, Elizabeth Hyman, Brian Jenkins, Edwin Lieuwen, Jorge Lozoya, and G. Harvey Summ.

What, in fact, does the Mexican army do? What is its record in national life since the 1940s? Systematic information is lacking, but its roles may be illustrated by a variety of cases culled mainly from the recent national press.

In 1968 the army helped decisively to suppress the massive student-based riots and demonstrations that took place in Mexico City and elsewhere on the eve of the Olympics. Other *university disturbances* also led to troop patrolling during the 1960s and early 1970s, as in Morelia in 1966, Hermosillo in 1967, and Tlaxcala in 1973.

Army units have frequently been called upon to maintain order during *electoral disturbances* or to forestall the collapse of local governments. In 1952 army troops put down riots in Mexico City by partisans of the Federación del Partido del Pueblo Mexicano (FPPM), whose founder and presidential candidate, Gen. Miguel Henríquez Guzmán, lost the campaign. During 1960–62, army units were needed to halt popular turmoil in Guerrero, when the governor, Gen. Arturo Caballero Aburto, fell and was succeeded by Raimundo Abarca Alarcón. In 1964 in Puebla the army helped to reestablish order in the wake of the milk riots, and the military zone commander became acting governor for about six weeks after the fall of Governor Gen. Antonio Nava Castillo. Major violence that accompanied a gubernatorial campaign in Sonora in 1967 also led to relatively heavy troop patrolling throughout the state.

At the municipal level, the presence of army patrols helped to subdue electoral disturbances during major campaigns in Mérida in 1967 and Tijuana in 1968, campaigns that were hotly contested by the official Partido Revolucionario Institucional (PRI) and rival Partido de Acción Nacional (PAN). Other incidents that involved violent or potentially violent conflicts among rivals affiliated with these and different parties occurred in Huehuetlán, Puebla in 1969, and in Tacámbaro, Michoacán in 1972. Sometimes the municipal conflicts involved rival factions of the PRI, as in Ciudad Valles, San Luis Potosi in 1971, and in Santa Cruz, Tlaxcala in 1972. Other incidents that led to small unit patrolling might better be described as an uprising of townspeople against town officials and police, as in Atencingo, Puebla in 1968.

The army has been deeply involved in the control and pacification of numerous *rural political disturbances*. These have included: elections of *ejidal,* credit society, and cooperative officers from among polarized peasant factions; large peasant demonstrations and hunger marches, such as those conducted during the early 1960s by candelilla and ixtle gatherers from Coahuila; threatened peasant uprisings in the early 1960s in the sierras of Guerrero, Oaxaca, Puebla, and Veracruz by FPPM affiliates; and numerous land invasions throughout Mexico, especially those led by the Central Campesina Independiente (CCI) and Unión General de Obreros y Campesinos de México (UGOCM). Furthermore, the army has helped to hunt down, and enforce some official control over the domains of such regionally powerful social bandits and agrarian radicals as Rubén Jaramillo (killed by an army unit in 1962), Genaro Vásquez Rojas, and Lucio Cabañas, whose insurgencies have had some revolutionary qualities. In early 1973, army units enabled government officials to regain physical control of the important San Cristóbal sugar mill in Veracruz and halt a potentially violent rebellion by some cañeros and outside supporters.

Though the army appears to be more active in rural than in urban areas, *industrial and labor disturbances* have also led to the use of troops. A major contemporary example is the railroad workers' strike during 1958–59. More recently, at the end of 1972 soldiers helped to dislodge members of a rebellious railroad workers' movement from union buildings they had seized in Durango, Oaxaca, and Torreón, so that the offices could be returned to the control of the dominant, officially-favored railroad workers' union. Also in 1972, military vigilance was required during elections for the leadership of the petroleum workers' union section in Poza Rica.

The army has fought the occasional outbreak of *guerrilla insurgency and urban terrorism* led by aspirant revolutionaries. In the mid and late 1960s, army units destroyed at least a half dozen very minor attempts by leftist intellectuals and students to establish guerrilla *focos* in various places, notably at Madera, Chihuahua in 1965 (and again in 1967 and 1969). In Guerrero the recent campaigns against Vásquez, Cabañas, and their allies have had counterinsurgency aspects, with the army engaging in civic action as well as strictly military activities. The army has also worked closely with the police to detect and eliminate urban terrorists and urban elements who have endeavored to organize national revolutionary movements, as in the recent case of the Revolutionary Action Movement (MAR-Action) and the 23 September Communist League. Along the southern border the army also pursued Guatemalan guerrillas operating from, or retreating to, Mexican territory during 1972.

Many of the army's activities are *socioeconomic and humanitarian in nature*. Their impact is strongest in isolated rural areas, where the civilian bureaucracies have little presence. Soldiers help to hunt down cattle rustlers and bandit bands in the countryside, and to prevent smuggling and narcotics cultivation. Through a long history of rural civic action, the army has engaged in health education, provided applied medicine from dentistry to minor surgery, undertaken school and road construction and repairs, dispensed food supplies and clothing as well as tools and utensils, and has also carried out reforestation programs. In recent years major civic action campaigns have developed in Chihuahua, Guerrero, and Yucatán. Taking over duties from civilian officials of the Finance Ministry, military officers are also now in charge of arms registration throughout the country, and head customs posts in order to halt contraband. In the wake of natural calamities such as floods and earthquakes, the army frequently provides disaster relief and protects property. Soldiers are also used to guard certain valuable economic enterprises, including private ones.

In sum, these varied examples indicate that the Mexican army has been extensively—even if perhaps only instrumentally—involved in the promotion of public order in constitutional ways that have apparently had considerable impact on local security and on local political and socioeconomic conditions. Moreover, far from being intermittent or unusual, army involvement in national development since 1940 has been quite constant and enduring, even though at a relatively low level compared to that of most Latin American militaries.

II. The Residual Political Roles of the Mexican Army

The Mexican army is reputed to be one of the best "tamed" and least political in Latin America. During the period from 1920 through the 1940s the army of the Mexican Revolution was carefully reorganized and subordinated to the civilian authorities of the party-government; military coups have become virtually impracticable; and political participation by individual officers has declined over the decades.[1] One prominent analyst, Edwin Lieuwen, concludes that the "political role of the army has all but disappeared."[2]

The comparatively high degree of civilian authority cannot be denied, and the military's loss of political power remains an important research topic. As the examples cited above suggest, however, the army may not be so inactive, nor the political system as highly demilitarized, as it often appears. For the post-1940 period, the historical emphasis on depoliticization should not mislead the researcher into neglecting the extent and significance of the army's residual political roles, just because they are exercised in subordination to civilian ruling groups and strong political institutions.

What are the residual political roles of the military, if any? How are they exercised? What is the extent of military influence? On what kinds of issues? Under what conditions? At what levels of government? Are they policy-making or instrumental roles? Are they institutional roles, like those of a lobby or pressure group? Or are they the individual roles of special officers? Do such roles make much difference for the functioning of the political system? How have they changed in recent decades? Students of Mexican history offer a few paragraphs or pages of stimulating judgments about such questions. Yet none has offered convincing documentation for the post-1940 period.[3]

The recent date of many of the introductory examples emphasizes a great problem for the researcher in answering even simple questions about what the army does. There is no readily accessible, running record of its activities—and this fact makes it an extremely difficult subject for historical analysis. Contemporary Mexican institutions are among the most studied in Latin America. Yet civil-military relations since 1940 remain quite a mystery. For a country of Mexico's importance, its army is one of the least studied in Latin America. Indeed, the contemporary Mexican military may be the most difficult such institution to research in Latin America. Certainly it is the most difficult national institution to research in Mexico. The few studies that have been completed, the statistical data that can be compiled, and the press and biographical materials that are available enable the historical analyst to gain only a cursory knowledge of post-1940 processes and seminal events. Without new field work the roles and contributions of one of Mexico's most important national institutions will likely remain the target more of rumor than of serious analysis.[4]

Some Specific Roles in Conflict Management

The army's continuing political roles relate mainly to conflict management.[5] This is a major activity of party-government elites, especially since the resort to violence, or threat of it, is a relatively common and even institutionalized tactic used by discontented groups.[6] Though civilian party and government leaders dominate the management of conflicts, army officers may be involved at almost every step. Their roles relate mainly to political communication (by conveying information upward to higher levels) and enforcement (by maintaining order on behalf of partisan elites).

In the area of political communication, army officers may affect political intelligence and interest articulation, especially in rural areas. Zone commanders, who are appointed by the president, are significant sources of political intelligence on state government activities for the Presidency and the Secretariat of the Interior. In addition, the paramilitary, peasant-based "rural guards" are under army command. A reason for their current existence is "mostly political: to provide to the government an unusual mechanism of information that leads to immediate knowledge of all subversive action in any corner of the country."[7] Furthermore, army officers have evidently served since the 1940s as potential alternative channels for interest articulation. If discontented peasants feel that the state governor or other civilian officials have blocked their petitions from reaching presidential attention, peasant leaders have sometimes protested to the zone commander and sought his help in getting the president's attention.

The introductory examples also show that the army has served as a major constitutional instrument for political enforcement during conflicts. Zone commanders remain an important presidential agent for replacing state governors during crises. The army is frequently used to separate and prevent violence between rival political factions in provincial areas, while civilian officials seek to resolve the conflict. Electoral defense for the PRI and suppression of political rebels and radicals are other uses that the army has served. Indeed, citizen groups sometimes address their public petitions, printed in newspapers, to the local zone commander or even the secretary of national defense, urging him, as well as the political authorities, to correct some serious abuse or restore order in some conflict situation.[8] The army has also helped the government to secure control over isolated, unruly rural areas. The expansion of the government's politico-administrative control has often followed the extension of economic and social services to needy peasant populations in isolated areas. Such developments may disturb the traditional forms of local politics; and thus in high conflict areas such as Guerrero, the army may become an indispensable participant in the process.

Participation in policy decisions by officers of the regular army or Presidential Guard, however, is extremely unclear, even on questions of mobilizing troop units. It has surely diminished at the federal level since 1940; and aside from normal bureaucratic and budgetary politics, there is no satisfactory evidence that it has not disappeared. It is more likely that some policy influence persists at state (i.e., zone commander) levels—and in some states more than others. But research is also lacking on this point.

Something can perhaps be inferred from enduring patterns of officer recruitment to formal political and bureaucratic roles (e.g., governor, congressman, subordinate to the secretary of the presidency, as well as many lesser posts). Such participation has declined but far from disappeared. Since 1964, politicians have stopped naming a general as president of the PRI. There has been a steady decline in the number of generals that become state governors (see Table 1). And the only cabinet members recruited from the officer corps are the secretary of national defense and the secretary of the navy.

However, there is still a moderate recruitment of officers to fill senior and subordinate bureaucratic positions in other federal ministries (see Table 2). Officers on leave in 1970 occupying nonmilitary positions included the regent (mayor) of Mexico City; the chief of police, director

Table 1. Military Officers as Governors

Year	President in Office	Number of Officers as Governors (out of 31)
1948	Alemán (1946–1952)	15
1953	Ruiz Cortines (1952–1958)	8
1959	López Mateos (1958–1964)	6
1965	Díaz Ordaz (1964–1970)	3
1972	Echeverría Alvarez (1970–)	1

Source: Margiotta, 1974, p. 27.

Table 2. Military Officers in Executive Branch

Non-Military Position	1948	1961	1970	1971
Senior Level Bureaucrat	13	8	10	8
Subordinate Level Bureaucrat	7	16	7	16

Source: Margiotta, 1974, p. 25.

general of roads, and the director general of sports in Mexico City; the federal director of security in the Secretariat of the Interior; and the head of the Department of Press and Information in the Attorney General's Office. In addition, the constant recruitment of officers as personal aides or staff assistants by high-level government and party officials is a frequently overlooked form of participation.

Military officers, retired or on leave, have also held from 20 to 30 congressional seats during the 1950s and 1960s, and of course larger numbers have appeared as candidates, mainly for the PRI and the Partido Auténtico de la Revolución Mexicana (PARM), which was formed in 1958 by three veteran generals of the Revolution. In this regard Margiotta makes an interesting observation: "While the electoral picture was dominated by Generals and Colonels over the early years, since 1964 about half the candidates were of the rank of Lieutenant Colonel or below. In fact, with the decline of the Revolutionary Generals, there seems to be an increasing awareness and interest in electoral politics among the younger officers."[9]

Surely most officers in such political and bureaucratic posts act merely as private individuals. The opportunities for such participation provide a nonmilitary outlet for personal ambitions, and may help give them a stake in the established system. As an indirect minimum policy influence, it is conceivable that officers serving in military or nonmilitary posts can personally affect the formation of political cliques or *camarillas*, and therefore the future of aspirant civilian politicians within the PRI and the Revolutionary Family.[10]

In sum, it appears that the army and its officers have remained significantly involved in political activities. Instrumental roles in political communication and enforcement predominate, but some policy-making influence cannot necessarily be discounted. The Mexican army is, of course, much less active politically than its counterparts in other Latin American countries. But if one focuses on the lesser political conflicts rather than on attempted coups and other major public disturbances elsewhere in Latin America, then it would appear that the Mexican army is not much less active than its counterparts, especially in relation to the control of agrarian struggles.

It seems likely, moreover, that the army's performance of its residual political roles has made a significant difference for the Mexican political system. Had the army behaved as a strictly professional and apolitical military that was mobilized only in case of major domestic disturbances, the president would have lost considerable capacity to control state governors. Both the president and governor would have lost considerable control over isolated rural areas. And, in general, government and political elites would most likely have had to increase their dependence upon police and paramilitary forces, whose conduct would be much less professional and politically more manipulable than that of the contemporary Mexican army.[11] Although the comparison is difficult to draw, I would even suggest that the army has had greater political impact than any opposition party, including PAN.

Impact on the Political System: Four Current Views

How important are the army's continuing political roles? Four views of the army's relationship to the broader political system have been advanced. According to one, the army serves in political as well as military capacities *as a major institutional pillar of the government*.[12] In this view, the missions of the army center on the protection of the president and the Revolutionary party-government institutions, and the defense of the Constitution; the military (including the Presidential Guard) and the PRI form the acknowledged pillars of government stability and elite integration.

The PRI has, in fact, sometimes needed army support to help maintain control of certain localities, although party strength has allowed general reliance on the military to subside over the decades. And even so, there is continued, if only incidental, dependence upon the army and its officers for electoral defense, internal security, enforced subordination of local to presidential interest, political intelligence, and even for the channeling of interests articulated by discontented peasants. All these indicate a continuing, politically significant, partisan role for the army as a legitimate defender of the established institutions in those circumstances where party or bureaucratic mechanisms may prove inadequate, especially in isolated rural areas.

According to a second view, individual army officers have served *as important participants in the broad ruling coalition,* the Revolutionary Family.[13] Through the president, in particular, civilian elites certainly predominate. But some officer participation in, and support for, the Revolutionary Family has helped and perhaps been essential to maintaining the presidential supremacy and the elite integration upon which civilian dominance and political stability have depended. Of course, the influence of individual officers varies greatly from time to time and place to place; but in certain respects civil-military coalitions remain as much a factor in Mexican politics as in many other Latin American countries. This is particularly true in the case of certain state administrations.[14]

Whereas the first two views of the army focus on potential bases of partisan roles, the third and fourth describe the consequences of actually assuming such roles. Basic to the third point of view are the beliefs that

Mexican political structures have attained some valuable attributes of democratic responsiveness, and that PRI supremacy has been essential for their development. Just as the substantial imposition of government control over the military may have helped in establishing certain democratic practices in civilian institutions, so in recent decades the army's performance of its residual political roles may have enabled the civilian institutional framework to remain very stable despite considerable socioeconomic problems and periodic political opposition struggles. Moreover, through civic action, the army has helped to establish government services in isolated rural areas. Therefore, the army deserves credit *as a partner in political responsiveness and democratization.*[15]

A fourth tentative view, however, is virtually the reverse. Its proponents focus on the authoritarian and inequitable processes that persist in the Mexican political system. During recent decades certain government and party factions (reportedly including military as well as civilian elites) have afforded powerful resistance to legitimate pressures for increased democratization of party politics and for increased responsiveness to lower class socioeconomic demands. The army has played a major conservative role in this process, helping to defend the institutional status quo against political struggles and public disorder. Therefore, it is concluded, the army has behaved in part *as a significant force for authoritarian control and occasional political repression.*[16]

It should be noted that these are not, of course, alternative or mutually exclusive views. They can all be partially valid.[17] Indeed, with regard to the last two, it is fairly common for governments to respond to demands from some sector while simultaneously seeking to repress certain activities or groups associated with it.

My impression is that three of the four views have considerable merit: namely, that the army has political significance as an institutional pillar of the government, as an agency for limited democratization under the PRI, and as a force for authoritarian control. Lack of evidence makes the view that army officers are essential participants in the broad ruling coalition seem less convincing. But for that matter, except for presidents, cabinet members, and governors, the importance of other civilian government and party elites in the Revolutionary Family is also difficult to clarify in Mexico's centralized system. In any case, these views do indicate that the army's roles have had partisan consequences in Mexico's contemporary political development.

III. Factors Affecting the Army's Residual Political Roles

As noted, the post-1940 history of the army is relatively obscure. The available historical sketches generally treat it as a gentle evolution of trends established around 1940, and highlight only such major events as the removal of the military sector from the PRI. Yet it is not even clear whether that development took the military further out of politics, or conversely concentrated its lessening influence in the executive bureaucracy closer to the president.

In what general ways have army roles changed since 1940? What factors may account for such changes? And what may be the future implications? These questions may be approached by considering, first, conditions internal to the military institution, and second, developments in the external context.

Internal Military Constraints: Limited Professionalism

The original measures to bring the army under central control during the 1920s and 1930s imposed strong internal obstacles to military participation in politics on either an individual or institutional basis. These measures, as treated in various writings, may be considered to include: the rotation of zone commands, so that officers do not acquire large personal followings; the splitting of infantry commands around Mexico City among the Presidential Guard, the secretary of national defense, and the I zone commander; retention of political generals in top commands; presidential control of the promotion and assignment system for the ranks of colonel and above; limitation of the size, budget, and equipment of the armed forces;[18] establishment of professional education and training programs; the encouragement of private economic, rather than political, profiteering by individual officers; and also—since 1940—government restrictions placed on military relations with the United States and with hemispheric security activities. Though the links are often uncertain, these and other measures have reportedly helped civilian officials to centralize governmental control, discourage military rebellions, focus loyalty on the established party-government institutions, and foster limited military professionalism.[19]

The trend toward institutional professionalism is often singled out as having inhibited political participation. Yet the relationship is quite uncertain and a different interpretation may be added.[20] Professionalism within the Mexican army has increased considerably since the 1940s, but it has reportedly not yet attained a high level compared to other Latin American militaries. One reason is the constant circulation of officers between military and other government, party and business posts, combined with the essentially part-time status of many officers. With the possible exception of the instruction offered by the small and select Escuela Superior de Guerra (Advanced War College), the professional education and training programs for the officer corps are apparently less advanced than those of the South American systems, where officers study the entire development of their societies at length, as well as strictly operational matters. Mexican officers who want to study nonmilitary subjects seriously are generally advised to attend the national university.[21] A further sign of limited professionalism has been the erratic promotion and retirement practices, which until recently resulted in a very top-heavy and aged officer corps in the upper ranks.[22]

The original reorganization and professionalization of the Revolutionary army certainly constrained the potential for military participation in politics. However, the subsequent slow growth of military professionalism has inhibited the development of military autonomy in various ways, and has helped to enable the government to use the army for some limited partisan purposes under fairly strong civilian control. A more professional army would likely be a politically less tractable institution.[23]

Constraints placed upon political concerns within the military appear to be very effective. Generational differences between older and younger officers and bureaucratic disputes involving the army occasionally surface. Yet the picture that emerges is one of a unified and well-disciplined corps. Indeed, while factional divisiveness has sometimes appeared publicly within three major institutions responsible for Mexico's historical political stability (namely, the PRI, the executive administration, and the Catholic Church), the one national institution in which elite integration has consistently appeared to persist is the military.[24]

Still, internal arrangements within the military institutions do not fully account for the changing roles of the army. Many of the changes that originally helped constrain its impact on Mexican politics (e.g., rotation of zone commanders) have been undertaken in other Latin American countries with only marginal effect, confirming that internal military developments are only part of the answer.

The External Political Context: Four Perspectives

The course of the army's political roles since 1940 probably has depended more upon developments in the external political environment than upon internal institutional changes. Most importantly, while Mexico's Revolutionary elites incorporated the army into politics in order to later exclude it from overt roles, they also fashioned strong party and government institutions on which to base their rule and manage conflicts.

In Mexico today, problems of political conflict have been subjected to four alternative—though not mutually exclusive—interpretations. These identify unrest and violence as being (1) permanent and developmental in nature; (2) periodic or cyclical in character; (3) subversive in origin; and/or (4) the manifestation of institutional crisis. Each view of conflict has had different implications for military roles. The army exists to deal constitutionally with violent and potentially violent conflict; and conflict, of course, cannot be interpreted apart from the context in which it occurs.

Permanent Developmental Unrest. One interpretation treats the varied unrest as being essentially permanent and developmental in nature. Mexican politics has always been somewhat violent, coercive, and anarchistic; and rural and urban unrest, student rebellions, intraelite frictions, etc., have never been particularly uncommon since 1940. There were workers' strikes during the presidency of Miguel Alemán, intraelite difficulties under Ruiz

Cortines, wide-ranging unrest during López Mateos' first years in office, and student, agrarian, and intraparty conflicts under Gustavo Díaz Ordaz. Yet, despite changing conditions, and despite variations in presidential policies, the basic structure of the post-Revolutionary institutions has remained relatively stable, intact, resilient, and progressive, capable of simultaneously increasing both responsiveness and repression.[25]

Indeed, all political systems, including Mexico's, are naturally characterized by a certain amount of unrest and violence. Moreover, it appears that different stages or conditions of development seem to be characterized by different types or patterns of unrest. Thus, major peasant revolts have typically occurred in postfeudal economies and societies that are undergoing a new centralization and bureaucratization of political power and authority. This may be currently the case in isolated areas of the state of Guerrero, though no longer in Mexico as a whole. Under later conditions of modernization, urban unrest in the form of electoral shifts, student rebellions, and worker discontent may become a natural, even temporarily routine, pattern. This has recently been the case in some of Mexico's cities.

If this interpretation is correct, we can expect that Mexico's current government and its successors will continue to manage the occasional conflicts and challenges pragmatically, as have their predecessors. Fundamental institutional change need not result—though government policies may take somewhat new directions following the historical alternation of "reformist" and "consolidationist" presidents. Military political roles will continue to be residual in nature, probably declining as the resilient post-Revolutionary governments strengthen their administration in rural areas.

Periodic or Cyclical Unrest. A second interpretation—in a sense a variant of the first—is that some unrest is periodic or cyclical in character. It is the natural accompaniment of a presidential (or gubernatorial) succession and the consolidation of a new presidential regime in power in the Mexican system.

A pattern appears to have developed whereby the initial and final years of a presidential regime are the most opportune times for pressure groups to demand attention for their particular grievances, and for ambitious leaders to seek gain through conflict. During his final years, an outgoing president (or governor) can make concessions at lowered personal political cost, or decisions that might relieve his successor from the onus of a difficult or unpopular move in his early years. On the other hand, during the initial years in office, while a new president is forming his regime and impressing himself upon his role, he may be most vulnerable to the bargaining power of interest groups. Consequently, groups or leaders with old and new grievances may mobilize and compete fiercely for federal attention, especially if the new PRI candidate conducts a long, intense campaign.[26]

Though to some extent this cyclical unrest resurfaces during every presidential succession, an outstanding case appears to have occurred during the changeover to López Mateos. He was confronted with an extremely diverse set of political and economic pressures, in part inflamed by the local impact of the Cuban Revolution. Important—and often interrelated —problems and developments reportedly included:[27]

- An intraelite struggle between Cardenista and Alemanista elements, combined with public appeals for more leftist policies by ex-president Lázaro Cárdenas himself.

- Slowdowns in foreign investment, private business fears of a deteriorating business climate, and some threatened flight of domestic wealth.

- A resurgence of communist agitation and subversion.

- The formation of radical movements among intellectuals (the Movimiento de Liberación Nacional, MLN), and peasants (the Central Campesina Independiente, CCI).

- Widespread peasant unrest and demonstrations, including hunger marches in northern states.

- Student agitation and rebellions among normal school and university students.

- A severe railroad workers' strike, and an attempt by leader Demetrio Vallejo to secede with his following from the CTM (Confederación de Trabajadores Mexicanos).

- Rightist Church reactions.

- Constant criticism of the PRI as an unrepresentative and undemocratic organ.

- Pressures from young army officers for better pay and benefits.

- Electoral difficulties for the government in several states, including open-armed revolt against the state governor in Guerrero.

- Foreign policy problems with Cuba and the United States.

This reads much like the agenda of political troubles that have confronted President Echeverría: the similarities are striking, though Echeverría's difficulties have been perhaps less severe. I would not be surprised if some military resurgence in politics were regarded as having occurred during the 1958–62 period.

The regime of López Mateos responded with pragmatic, maneuverable policies that he declared exemplified the extreme left of Mexican nationalism within the Constitution. These reportedly included:

- The jailing of certain communist and radical leaders and the suppression of allegedly communist-influenced demonstrations and rebellious activities.

- Symbolic and verbal soothing of the Revolutionary Family's left wing, ultimately combined with a reaffirmation of Family unity through the appointment of all ex-presidents to government posts.

- Pay increases for the army.

- An expansion of the public sector of the economy into areas long ago targeted because of majority control by foreigners.

- Laws which allowed worker sharing in profits.

- Increased attention to land reform, *ejidal* agricultural systems, and rural credit.

- Extension of social security benefits to the army, government bureaucrats, and sugar cane workers.

- Reimbursement for nationalized business interests and economic measures concerning inflation and the foreign debt which encouraged private enterprise.

- A neutralist policy toward Cuba, declared independence from the United States, and expanded relations with the rest of Latin America.

Thus, despite a few dire predictions of internal upheaval, despite intraelite conflicts, and despite an economic slowdown, political stability was restored. Once again, there are certain similarities between these policy directions and those which have taken effect under President Echeverría— although by now it is clear that the unrest and his difficulties have continued well beyond the opening years of his administration.

Thus a period of skillful maneuvering and bargaining by the then incumbent president will enable the cyclical unrest to subside and the political system to restabilize itself along durable traditional lines. There may be temporary new directions in policy (especially in the foreign affairs and public economic sector areas), but major institutional changes will be avoided or forestalled. Accordingly, the military may seem sporadically quite active, but its roles continue to be essentially residual.

Subversion. Subversion is sometimes identified as a major cause of unrest, radical organization, and occasional violence. Local and international communist and noncommunist revolutionaries are generally viewed as having occasionally targeted Mexico. The 1958–59 labor unrest, the 1965 guerrilla front in Chihuahua, the alleged Maoist revolutionaries arrested in 1967, the 1968 student riots, the conversion of Guerrero state's leading social bandit into a revolutionary figure, the formation of the Revolutionary Action Movement (MAR-Action) by members trained in North Korea, and the recent terrorism attributed to the 23 September Communist League are sometimes said to confirm the practice of international and domestic subversion in Mexico.[28] Most of the so-called subversive violence in Mexico, however, has been treated by the government and the military as criminal activity that requires little more than policing action. Subversive activities are also attributed to right-wing imperialist or neofascist elements operating in the country.

While identifying conflict as subversive in origin is less satisfying as a general view than the other interpretations advanced, it now seems clear that the incidence of violence in Mexico has equalled or surpassed that characterizing Brazil, Peru, Venezuela, and possibly Uruguay (though not Argentina and Colombia) when, at an earlier period, their conditions did give rise to guerrilla and terrorist organizations. The implications of similar subversion depend mainly upon domestic conditions within Mexico, and on the analysis made by military elites. If the current manifestations of unrest are seen as generally developmental or cyclical in nature, then the major policy consequences of subversion might be simply somewhat greater government attention to the limited problems of discontent, and/or temporarily more active security roles for military and police agencies, and/or slight shifts in foreign policy directions—though the linkages are uncertain.

If an institutional crisis were to arise, however, then the opportunities might increase for subversion to affect institutional stability, policy directions, and military roles. A military analysis that treats subversive activities as essentially criminal ones that require little more than a policing response is not likely to lead to an expansion of the army's political roles, in contrast to an analysis that the subversion or insurgency results from dangerous systemic conditions that require political and socioeconomic as well as security responses.[29]

Institutional Crisis. A fourth interpretation of conflict is gaining in credibility, though it is not entirely convincing. It holds that Mexico may be entering, or has now entered, a period of institutional crisis, and that current political unrest and violence are manifestations of this condition. Accordingly, the very success of political and economic development has brought Mexico to a point where force will be increasingly required to maintain the political system if reforms are not enacted.

In essence the potential crisis is said to consist in excessive concentration of power in the Presidency, unresponsiveness of government bureaucracies to popular needs, and unrepresentative and undemocratic features of the government party. Though to some extent these have been long-term features of Mexico's political development, they have never before been tested in a context that newly combines: generation gaps in most major institutions and pressures from the newer elites; economically inequitable rural-urban conditions; population, employment, public service, and patronage pressures; little land left for agrarian distribution; electoral abstentions and voting shifts in some modernizing urban centers; structural needs to reduce dependence on the U.S. economy; open reliance on military, police, and paramilitary forces for maintaining public order; and a multiplication of organized interest groups and elite sectors with often contradictory factional demands.[30]

Under such circumstances, skillful maneuvering by the president and other members of the Revolutionary Family may periodically restore a semblance of stability and temporarily forestall any major changes. Yet, in the long run, forces inside and outside the established institutions will persist and may ultimately bring about major institutional changes, whether resulting in a more democratic, populist, or authoritarian government. In Mexico the alternatives are commonly said to be a conservative dictatorship, radical democratic reform, or chronic disorganization.

The development of an institutional crisis could have—but would not necessarily have—profound effects on the military's residual political roles. As Mexican officials have repeatedly observed, the two institutional pillars of stable government are, and will continue to be, the official party and the army. Developments that led to an increasing ineffectiveness of civil-military conflict management techniques, and that also involved a marked weakening of party control through its sectoral organizations, would tend to make government elites more dependent upon army support in order to maintain internal political order and defend federal over state and local interests. Severe challenges to PRI supremacy from without, and deterioration from within, would probably induce some expansion of the political and administrative roles of the army.

Concluding Comment

Whichever interpretation one prefers, the endurance of the established Mexican political system has probably depended significantly—and will continue to depend—upon the army's performance of its residual political roles. Because of the army's impact on conflict management, through political communication and enforcement, it remains important for party-government stability and for elite integration within the Revolutionary Family.

Mexico has a highly civilianized political system by Latin American standards. Yet acting constitutionally, the Mexican military has continued since 1940 to be engaged in a number of inherently partisan political activities, especially at the middle levels of the regime. Attempts to eliminate (or conversely, to expand) the few remaining political roles would probably lead to political instability. This suggests that Mexico, while having a resilient political system of distinctive genius since 1940, is not so unlike other Latin American countries, and that there are limits to the demilitarization that can benefit or be achieved in a developing Latin American country.

Notes

1. According to Francisco A. Gómez Jara, *El Movimiento Campesino en México,* Editorial Campesino, México, 1970, p. 174, however, politician General Henríquez Guzmán considered a military coup against Adolfo Ruiz Cortines, and even approached U.S. officials in a search for support.
2. See Edwin Lieuwen, *Mexican Militarism: The Political Rise and Fall of the Revolutionary Army, 1910–1940,* The University of New Mexico Press, Albuquerque, 1968, p. 148. Jorge Alberto Lozoya, *El Ejército Mexicano (1911–1965),* Jornadas 65, El Colegio de México, México, 1970, goes a step further, arguing that militarism never was established in Mexico. Also see Frederick C. Turner, "México: las causas de limitación militar," *Aportes,* 6, October 1967, pp. 57–65.
3. Recent scholarly claims that the military has continued to have political roles are found in: Frank Brandenburg, *The Making of Modern Mexico,* Prentice-Hall, Englewood Cliffs, 1964, passim. Alberto Ciria, "Cuatro ejemplos de relaciones entre fuerzas armadas y poder político," *Aportes,* 6, October 1967, pp. 30–43. Pablo González Casanova, *Democracy in Mexico,* Oxford University Press, New York, 1970, passim. Francisco González Pineda and Antonio Delhumeau, *Los Mexicanos Frente al Poder: Participación y Cultura Política de los Mexicanos,* Instituto Mexicano de Estudios Políticos, México, 1973, pp. 303–6. Pedro Guillen, "Militarismo y golpes de estado en América Latina," *Cuadernos Americanos,* 24, No. 3, May–June 1965, esp. pp. 9–10. Franklin D. Margiotta, "Patterns of Civilian Control in Mexico," paper delivered at the 1974 conference of the Inter-University Seminar on Armed Forces and Society, State University of New York at Buffalo, October 18–19, 1974. Lyle N. McAlister, "Mexico," in McAlister and others, *The Military in Latin American Sociopolitical Evolution: Four Case Studies,* American University Center for Research in Social Systems, Washington, 1970, pp. 197–258. Martin C. Needler, *Politics and Society in Mexico,* University of New Mexico Press, Albuquerque, 1971, chap. 6 entitled, "The Political Role of the Military," pp. 65–72. Peter Nehemkis, *Latin America: Myth and Reality,* Alfred A. Knopf, New York, 1964, p. 54. L. Vincent Padgett, *The Mexican Political System,* Houghton Mifflin, Boston, 1966. Karl M. Schmitt, "The Role of the Military in Contemporary Mexico," in Curtis A. Wilgus, ed., *The Caribbean: Mexico Today,* University of Florida Press, Gainesville, 1964, pp. 52–62. Robert E. Scott, "Mexico: The Established Revolution," in Lucian W. Pye and Sidney Verba, eds., *Political Culture and Political Development,* Princeton University Press, Princeton, 1965, pp. 380–83; and *Mexican Government in Transition,* University of Illinois Press, Urbana, 1964, 2nd ed. rev., p. 134. Norman M. Smith, *The Role of the Armed Forces in Contemporary Mexican Politics,* M.A. thesis, University of Florida, 1966. Philip B. Taylor, "The Mexican Elections of 1958: Affirmation of Authoritarianism," *The Western Political Quarterly,* 13, 3, September 1960, pp. 722–44. Hans-Werner Tobler, "Las paradojas del ejército revolucionario: su papel social en la reforma agraria mexicana, 1920–1935," *Historia Mexicana,* 81, July–September 1971, pp. 38–79.

4. The possibilities for research are quite limited—but some do exist, mainly in archives and through oral interviews. Direct research through military libraries, archives, and interviews seems extremely difficult, but is not impossible. González Pineda and Delhumeau, 1973, Lozoya, 1970, Margiotta, 1974, and McAlister, 1970, are all based in part on informal interviews with a few officers. The main library at the Secretariat of National Defense is open to the public, but access to the general staff library requires special arrangements. The military archives are essentially closed, except to historians interested in precontemporary affairs.

Much might be learned from indirect research through nonmilitary archives and interviews, that is, from case studies of developments that partly involved the military and that generated a considerable number of documents which were subsequently filed in various public government archives. For example, Agrarian Department archives surely contain voluminous material on political, economic, and even some military developments pertaining to the struggles of Rubén Jaramillo in Morelos since the 1940s, and of Genaro Vásquez Rojas in Guerrero since the 1950s. Other subjects might be the 1952 presidential election, the history of the FPPM and other examples of military populism, and the removal of the military sector from the party. This indirect approach would probably not produce much data on the army; but the researcher interested in such topics as agrarian struggles, electoral processes, leadership formation, or party development might nevertheless be able to test some specific propositions and highlight some activities concerning the army's roles in broader political processes.

5. The best treatments to date of points in this section are in McAlister, 1970, and González Pineda/Delhumeau, 1973.

6. Conflict management among discontented cañeros is analyzed in David Ronfeldt, *Atencingo: The Politics of Agrarian Struggle in a Mexican Ejido,* Stanford University Press, Stanford, 1973. Conflict management among rebellious railroad workers, medical doctors, and university students is analyzed by Evelyn P. Stevens, *Protest and Response in Mexico,* The MIT Press, Cambridge, 1974.

7. Lozoya, 1970, p. 81.

8. For example, during a wave of local and national terrorism in 1974, business groups in Guadalapara called on the regional zone commander to help restore political order, while they also blamed the policies of the federal government for creating a climate that stimulated terrorism.

9. Margiotta, 1974, p. 31.

10. Perhaps the close working ties between officials in the Secretariats of the Interior and National Defense is one factor that has facilitated the frequent presidential candidacy of the secretary of the interior.

11. Paramilitary and parapolice forces are not widespread in the cities or the countryside, but it is not unusual to read about one or another occasionally in newspapers. For an analysis of the potential incentives to use extralegal or extraconstitutional methods in dealing with some conflict situations, see Evelyn P. Stevens, "Legality and Extra-legality in Mexico," *Journal of Inter-American and World Affairs,* January 1970, pp. 62–75.

12. An apolitical, nonpartisan version of this view is found in Mexican government documents and military publications such as *Revista del Ejército* and *Armas*.
13. Standard U.S. academic analyses cited in note 3 above have provided major sources for this interpretation.
14. There have been numerous, unsubstantiated rumors of military coup plots during the current presidential administration—rumors that have been matched by the president's praise of the institutional loyalty of the armed forces, and by their professions of loyalty to his administration. While the rumors have attained an unusual level in the last few years, my sense is that publicly unsubstantiated coup rumors have appeared during every presidential administration since 1940, and that at moments every president has had to verify military loyalty to his regime. There were rumors that General Andréu Almazán might lead a coup attempt after his unsuccessful presidential bid in 1940 against the victor, General Manuel Avila Camacho. I am unfamiliar with any coup rumors during the presidency of Miguel Alemán—but I would not be surprised if some were evoked by the removal of the military sector from the PRI. There were rumors of a pending coup against Adolfo Ruiz Cortines soon after he assumed the presidency—and this may help explain the numerous changes he made in zone commander appointments. I can only guess that coup rumors arose during the presidency of Adolfo López Mateos, because there was so much internal unrest during 1958–62. And of course there was at least one coup rumor when President Gustavo Díaz Ordaz was having difficulty with the 1968 student rebellion.
15. This interpretation is common in official Mexican publications, though stated in an apolitical sense.
16. In various versions this interpretation has been most strongly argued by certain Mexican intellectuals, by the radical opposition, and by PAN leaders. A representative PANista expression is Gerardo Medina Valdés, *Operación 10 de Junio*, Mexico, 1972, second edition.
17. To say that Mexican political practices are both democratic and authoritarian seems to be a meaningful but rather unsatisfactory approach. Corporatism may be a better concept for capturing and combining these ideas.
18. Two types of budget figures must be taken into account: the expenditures proposed at the beginning of the budget cycle, and the actual expenditures by the end of the budget cycle. The proposed expenditures as a percentage of the government budget have declined from about 25% in 1940, to 13% in 1950, to 11% in 1960, to 10% in 1970. The actual expenditures as a percentage of the government budget ranged downward from 17% in 1940, to 10% in 1950, to 6% in 1960, and 5% in 1970. The actual expenditures have begun to climb above 6% since 1972, as President Echeverría has granted improvements in the living conditions and professional infrastructure of the armed forces.

    The armed forces have small procurement budgets. The principal equipment items are transport aircraft, light tanks, armored personnel carriers, armored cars, and trucks that are useful for internal security operations.

The army air force also has some subsonic jet-trainer fighter bombers. The navy is mainly equipped with coastal patrol vessels.

The armed forces total about 80 thousand members, which is small for such a large, populous country. The army accounts for 65 thousand, up from 55 thousand five years ago.

19. A close examination of the impact of these contemporary measures on the institutional development of the military is beyond the scope of this paper. In some cases (e.g., restriction of foreign military relations) the impact may be quite debatable.

20. Earlier studies on general civil-military relations argued that professionalism would lead to depoliticization. Recent studies, reflecting on the roles of the South American militaries, show that professionalism leads to changes in the modes of military participation in politics without necessarily reducing the level of participation. See Luigi Einaudi and Alfred Stepan, *Latin American Institutional Development: Changing Military Perspectives in Peru and Brazil,* The Rand Corporation, Santa Monica, R-586-DOS, April 1971; Richard Maullin, *Soldiers, Guerrillas and Politics in Columbia,* A Rand Corporation Study, Lexington Books, Massachusetts, 1973; and Elizabeth H. Hyman, "Soldiers in Politics: New Insights on Latin American Armed Forces," *Political Science Quarterly,* September 1972, pp. 401–18.

21. Preliminary data indicate that political, economic and social aspects of Mexico's security and development are treated in the education received at the prestigious Escuela Superior de Guerra, which may be Mexico's counterpart to Brazil's Escola Superior de Guerra (ESG) and Peru's Centro de Altos Estudios Militares (CAEM).

    Mexico's military medical schools are also excellent and might serve as models for the improvement of civilian medical schools, according to Charles N. Meyers, "Demand and need for doctors in Mexico: a reply," appearing in Spanish in *Demografía y Economía,* 6, No. 1, 1972, pp. 99–106.

22. President Echeverría has accomplished a major circulation of military as well as civilian elites. Indeed, he has promoted and retired far more military officers than any of his predecessors since 1940. The long duration of aging veterans and other established officers at high level ranks and posts led to open discontent among colonels and junior officers during his term. Graduates of the prestigious Escuela Superior de Guerra in particular have gained important positions. They now account for all (or almost all) zone commander posts; and for the first time the next minister of defense will surely be a graduate of that school. For additional information, Margiotta, 1974, provides broad data on contemporary institutional developments and the living conditions of officers.

23. Under the growing leadership of graduates from the Escuela Superior de Guerra, military professionalization is currently accelerating. But a discussion of recent institutional developments is beyond the scope of this paper.

24. Reports vary, however. According to Daniel Cosío Villegas, "Un país en dura preuba," *Visión,* 8 April 1972, p. 8, "Two great unknowns confuse the present condition of Mexico. . . . The second is the army. No one knows for certain what it is like today, since it is commanded by entirely unknown

leaders and officers. There is no lack of persons who fear that in a crisis it would incline toward a politics of order at any cost."

Manuel Moreno Sánchez, *Crisis Política de México,* Ed. Extemporáneos, México, 1970, pp. 77–78, distinguished between older and newer officer generations: "That minority [group that forms the privileged oligarchy] is supported by high-ranking military officers under the pretext of defending the institutions, in spite of distrust and discontent among the younger officers. They [i.e., the high-ranking officers] consider every instance of nonconformity with the established institutions to be threatening or prejudicial."

A U.S. analyst, McAlister, 1970, p. 245, says that the army's air force officer ranks contain a group of technocratic reformists, graduates of the Escuela Superior de Guerra, who would like to expand military contributions to national development, especially in the civic action and education fields. According to González Pineda/Delhumeau, 1973, p. 305, the officer corps contains political outlooks as diverse as those found in the broader civilian middle classes. As a contrast, one official report in 1975 stated that a former army officer, and deserter, was the leader of a guerrilla splinter group of the 23 September Communist League.

25. This seems to be the standard, most widely accepted interpretation, elements of which I have only sketched here. The best full representation is found in Roger D. Hansen, *The Politics of Mexican Development,* The Johns Hopkins Press, Baltimore, 1971. One potential weakness in this persuasive analysis, and others like it, is the strong emphasis on political culture as a stabilizing factor: specifically, that the large size of the so-called "parochial" and "subject" subcultures effectively limits burdensome demands on the political system. However, although those subcultures comprised even larger portions of the population at the turn of the century, this did not prevent the Revolution in which "parochials" and "subjects" participated extensively. For predictive purposes, then, such analyses may need to pay greater attention to changes within the small elitist "civic culture," and to institutional along with cultural tendencies.

26. My statement of this interpretation expands upon comments in: Taylor, 1960, especially, p. 19n; González Casanova, 1970, pp. 14–17; and Scott, 1964, p. 201.

27. An addition to other sources cited, Olga Pellicer de Brody, *México y la Revolución Cubana,* El Colegio de México, México, 1972, contains illuminating research.

28. On the Chihuahua guerrilla episode, see Prudencio Godines, Jr., *Que Poca Mad . . . Era! de José Santos Valdés,* publisher unknown, 1968, and compare with José Santos Valdés, *Madera, Razón de un Martiriologio,* Imprenta "Laura," México, 1968. On the 1967 Maoists, see Cecil Johnson, *Communist China and Latin America, 1959–1967,* Columbia University Press, New York, 1970, pp. 274–80. On the MAR, see John Barron, "The Soviet Plot to Destroy Mexico," *Readers Digest,* November 1971, pp. 227–68.

29. See Maullin, 1973, and Einaudi/Stepan, 1971, for extensive discussions and examples of this point.

I think a further point may also be worth some thought. In those countries where the established political institutions have remained relatively strong, the process of dealing with mainly rural insurgencies seems to have led to the strengthening of liberal or reformist elites—as in Colombia, Peru, and Venezuela. In contrast, urban terrorism seems associated with the strengthening of anti-liberal, conservative, or reactionary elites—as in Argentina, Brazil, and Uruguay. The reasons for this association are unclear, but may depend upon which elites are "in" and "out." Rural insurgency aims mainly at traditional landed elites who are generally on the way "out" as powerful figures, thus providing an issue whereby liberal and reformist elites from the middle and urban sectors can improve their position. Urban terrorism, however, poses a direct threat to business, financial, and government elites who are very much "in," and may thus effectively use their positions to pressure for authoritarian, conservative, even repressive solutions.

. In the case of Mexico, liberal tendencies in the Echeverría administration were strongest during the early years when it mainly faced a minor rural insurgency problem. In the wake of the recent urban terrorism, however, conservative pressures have mounted, leading to heavy public criticism of the president's foreign and domestic policies.

30. While not necessarily reflecting all these briefly stated points, some significant Mexican writings on the subject are: Daniel Cosío Villegas, *El Sistema Político Mexicano, Las Posibilidades del Cambio,* Ed. Joaquín Mortiz, México, 1972; Manuel Moreno Sánchez, *Crisis Política de México,* Ed. Extemporáneos, Mexico, 1970; Carlos Fuentes, "La Disyuntiva Mexicana," pp. 147–93 in his *Tiempo Mexicano,* Ed. Joaquín Mortiz, México, 1971; Octavio Paz, *The Other Mexico: Critique of the Pyramid,* Grove Press, New York, 1972, a translation from his Spanish original; Pablo González Casanova, *Democracy in Mexico,* Oxford University Press, New York, 1970, a translation from his Spanish original; L. Dario Vasconcelos, *Madrazo, Voz Postrera de la Revolución, Discursos y Comentarios,* Costa-Amic, México, 1971; and Fernando Carmona and others, *El Milagro Mexicano,* Ed. Nuestro Tiempo, México, 1970.

As a word of caution, it should be pointed out that ever since the 1940s one set of Mexican intellectuals or another has argued that the country was suffering from some serious institutional crisis.

Abraham F. Lowenthal / *The Political*
Role of the
Dominican Armed Forces:

A Note on the 1963 Overthrow
of Juan Bosch
and on the 1965
Dominican "Revolution"

Several years ago, in a general essay on Dominican politics, I wrote a few
pages about the political role of the Dominican Armed Forces. I argued
that "the history of the past few years in the Dominican Republic may best
be viewed as a constant struggle among changing alliances, not in terms of
confrontation between civilian authority and the military establishment"
(Lowenthal, 1969: 40). I suggested that "far from being a professional
institution dedicated to certain principles that impel its occasional entry
into politics, the Dominican Armed Forces have never had any significant
function beyond politics, except for plunder" (Lowenthal, 1969: 40).
Painting a picture of constant struggle within the Dominican Armed Forces,
for power and a chance at the spoils, I played down the importance, for
understanding the political role of Dominican military officers, of institutional and ideological considerations. Perhaps my most controversial proposition was that both the 1963 overthrow of Juan Bosch (the elected social
democratic president) and the 1965 "constitutionalist" attempt to restore
Bosch to the presidency owed less to ideology than to intramilitary struggles among competing cliques and to rival civilian efforts to enlist the

From Abraham F. Lowenthal, "The Political Role of the Dominican Armed
Forces: A Note on the 1963 Overthrow of Juan Bosch and on the 1965 Dominican
'Revolution,'" *Journal of Interamerican Studies and World Affairs*, 15, no. 3 (August
1973): 355–61. Copyright © 1973 by Sage Publications, Inc. and reprinted by permission of the publisher, Sage Publications, Inc. [A table has been omitted from this
edition.—Ed.]

Author's Note: I express here my appreciation to Christopher Mitchell, Peter
Smith, and Peter Winn for their comments on a draft of this note.

support of various military factions. I asserted that "there does not seem
to have been any appreciable difference . . . between the top military
leadership of the two sides" in 1965 "with respect to previous ideology or
degree of honesty. . . . The major distinction between the military leaders
on either side . . . was that of age and rank: the established leaders were
of higher rank precisely because they had prevailed in previous struggles to
reach the top" (Lowenthal, 1969: 41–42).

My view has been considered exaggerated by several other observers
(see Slater, 1970). The 1963 coup against Bosch is still often treated in
the general literature on Latin American politics as a classic example of
institutional military opposition to reform (Lieuwen, 1964; Needler,
1966). A specific case study of the 1963 coup interprets it as the coherent
institutional response of the Dominican Army to perceived threats to its
status and prerogatives (Chung, 1966). And a major study of the 1965
"revolution" distinguishes the "rebels" from the "loyalists" on two grounds,
one of which is that "the rebels had an ideology which advocated greater
participation of all classes of people in the cultural life of the nation, together with some specific ideas on means to achieve this goal" (Moreno,
1971).

Conclusive demonstration of my view is perhaps impossible to achieve;
it is certainly beyond my present capacity given available time and materials. I do wish, however, to support my interpretation, and to provide
further material for others, by providing previously unpublished data that
I submit as an extensive "footnote" to the work I have previously presented on Dominican politics.[1]

When the Bosch government was toppled on September 25, 1963, its
demise was marked by an official *comunicado* signed by 25 high-ranking
Dominican military officers, all of them united at that moment in their
agreement that Bosch should be replaced. The *comunicado,* later repub-
lished in an official Dominican military "white paper" on the overthrow of
Bosch, is often cited as an indication of the supposed institutional view of
the Dominican military establishment (Centro de Enseñanza, 1964:
90–95).

Still skeptical about the attribution to the Dominican Armed Forces of
the qualities of institutional coherence and ideological unity others have
posited (extrapolating from their interpretations of the Dominican officers'
role in ousting Bosch), I decided recently to compare the political role
played by these same 25 officers just seventeen months later, when the
next Dominican government (headed by Donald Reid Cabral) was being
ousted by a coup aimed at returning Bosch to the presidency.

. . . No information is available to me on one of the officers. Four of
the remaining 24 were out of the country in April 1965, sent abroad because they were out of favor with the Reid Cabral regime; in at least two
cases, and perhaps in all, this disfavor resulted from the officers having
plotted to overthrow Reid. Of the remaining 20, 8 supported the pro-
Bosch movement on April 25, despite the stance they had adopted in 1963;

in at least half the cases the officers had been fired, usually for plotting, during the Reid government. Six of the remaining 12 were busy on April 25 trying to set up their own juntas, supporting neither the Reid government nor the pro-Bosch coup. The remaining 6 officers, whose actions on April 25 may be interpreted as having supported the Reid government, comprised the core of the faction the United States government represented in 1965 as the loyalists, as if they were the established governmental authority. Even among these 6, however, most were really members of General Elias Wessin's clique; they actually failed to support Reid Cabral during the crucial first hours of the coup, thus assuring his regime's fall, and did not become loyalists until late in the day!

What these data suggest is simply that the political behavior of Dominican military officers during the 1965 crisis cannot easily be reconciled with a view of the Dominican Armed Forces as an autonomous and coherent professional institution, or with a view of Dominican officers as primarily or even importantly motivated by ideological considerations. The fact that virtually all Dominican officers were anti-Reid by April 1965 might suggest an institutional and conceivably even ideological rejection of that regime, were it not for the chaotic pattern of individual actions. . . . Individual conversions to the pro-Bosch cause, for instance, might be attributed to belated ideological commitment, but the overall pattern—clusters of officers seeking to prevail through a variety of quickly changing alignments—may be more easily explained in cruder terms.

Showing that the Dominican Armed Forces was composed of struggling cliques in 1965 does not prove, of course, that the same was the case when Juan Bosch was overthrown, though whoever posits the institutional integrity and ideological concern of the Dominican military in 1963 might be asked to explain its apparently complete transformation by 1965. (I would attribute the apparent unanimity of the Dominican officers' cliques at the moment of Bosch's overthrow primarily to the fact that his power bases, including United States support, had so obviously crumbled that nothing was to be gained by staying off the bandwagon. There were other reasons, too, including the way Bosch handled his relations with key officers and perhaps even some "institutional" fear of Bosch, his colleagues, and their [probably falsely] reported intent to establish a civilian militia. But however genuine the Dominican officers' statement on September 25, their *comunicado* only temporarily obscured the existence of competing cliques that had been struggling for predominance ever since Trujillo's death and were still at it in 1965.)

I do not mean to indicate that there were no differences between the followers of the two sides in the 1965 crisis. "The crisis certainly divided Dominican society, bringing together a coalition of the aggrieved in support of the constitutionalist cause and organizing on the anticonstitutionalist side some of the country's most retrograde elements" (Lowenthal, 1969: 41). Nor do I mean to suggest that none of the constitutional leaders was motivated by the ideologically based desire to reinstate the elected government (nor, for that matter, that none of those who opposed the coup in 1965 was acting out of loyalty to the incumbent regime). Motivations are far too complicated to exclude any from possibly important influence, or to treat them without full reference to the changing context in which they come into play.

What I do mean to argue, emphatically, is that a view of the Dominican Armed Forces in the 1960s as basically comprised of competing factions of officers concerned more about spoils than about ideology is more helpful than one that treats the Dominican Armed Forces as fundamentally a professional military institution comparable to those in many other countries in Latin America. Assuming that similar labels necessarily identify comparable phenomena is a dangerous practice—for political scientists as much as for policy officials.

What I believe but cannot show on the basis of material in hand is that a specific focus on the various intramilitary rivalries in Santo Domingo would immeasurably enhance our understanding of Dominican politics since Trujillo's death. A good dissertation, or book, is waiting to be written.

Note

1. I collected the material here summarized in the course of my research on the 1965 Dominican crisis, drawing on an extensive number of interviews, access to restricted documents, and review of the public record. My sources are detailed in the preface and appendices of *The Dominican Intervention* (1972).

References

Centro de Enseñanza de la Fuerza Armada (1964) Libro Blanco de las Fuerzas Armadas y de la Policía Nacional de la República Dominicana. Santo Domingo: Editora del Caribe.

Chung, H. M. (1966) "The case of the muffed mission: the 1963 coup d'état in the Dominican Republic." Caribbean Project, Foreign Policy Research Institute, University of Pennsylvania.

Lieuwen, E. (1964) Generals versus Presidents. New York: Praeger.

Lowenthal, A. F. (1972) The Dominican Intervention. Cambridge: Harvard Univ. Press.

———. (1969) "The Dominican Republic: the politics of chaos," pp. 34–58 in A. Van Lazar and R. R. Kaufman (eds.) Reform and Revolution: Readings in Latin American Politics. Boston: Allyn & Bacon.

Moreno, J. A. (1971) Barrios in Arms: Revolution in Santo Domingo. Pittsburgh: Pittsburgh University.

Needler, M. (1966) "Political development and military intervention in Latin America." Amer. Pol. Sci. Rev. 60 (September): 616–626.

Slater, J. (1970) Intervention and Negotiation: The United States and the Dominican Revolution. New York: Harper & Row.

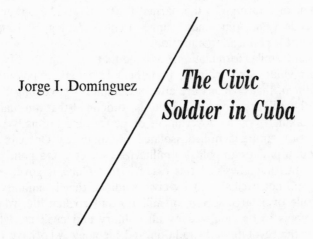

Jorge I. Domínguez / *The Civic Soldier in Cuba*

Two major patterns of civilian control over the military have been identified.[1] One, subjective civilian control, maximizes civilian power over the military by increasing the power of a governmental institution (such as parliament) or of a social class (such as the bourgeoisie) or of a political party (such as the Communist Party) over the military institutions. The other, objective civilian control, maximizes military professionalization, that is, the increase of military expertise, responsibility and corporate autonomy.

Civilian control over the military is not a worldwide norm. Among economically underdeveloped states and new states with relatively weak political institutions in particular, military control over civilian institutions often prevails. Two basic types of military intervene in politics.[2] The arbitrator military tend to have no independent political organization, little interest in constructing an independent political ideology, and are often content merely to supervise leading civilians in government. When arbitrator armies take over power directly, they set a time limit on their trusteeship

From Jorge I. Domínguez, "The Civic Soldier in Cuba," in *Political-Military Systems: Comparative Perspectives*: 209–36, ed. C. M. Kelleher, Vol. 4 *Sage Research Progress Series on War, Revolution, and Peacekeeping.* Copyright © 1974 by Sage Publications, Inc. and reprinted with the permission of the author and publisher. [A table and accompanying text have been omitted from this edition.—Ed.]

Author's Note: The original version of this essay was presented at the Inter-University Seminar on Armed Forces and Society, held in Chicago, October, 1973. I am grateful to Abraham Lowenthal, Alfred Stepan, other seminar participants and Timothy Colton for comments on that version.

and hand the government back to "acceptable" civilians. The arbitrator accepts the existing social order, and places relatively high value on civilian government. The ruler military tend to have, in contrast, little confidence in civilian rule, reject the legitimacy of the existing social order, have little expectation of returning to the barracks after they take power, construct an independent and sometimes change-oriented ideology and may develop an independent political organization.

These and similar formulations[3] assume that one can identify with some precision civilians and military, that there is actual or potential conflict between them, that civilians are always capable of governing the country, and that the military scope of activity is so defined that unusual behaviors (such as taking over the government or performing normally civilian unskilled labor) can be identified, isolated and analyzed. One can, therefore, think about a praetorian polity, a militarized society, or a politicized army.

The central hypothesis of this essay is that Cuba is governed in large part (though not exclusively) by civic soldiers, that is, military men who actually rule over large sectors of military and civilian life, who are held up as symbols to be emulated by all military and civilians, who are the bearers of the revolutionary tradition and ideology, who have civilianized and politicized themselves by internalizing the norms and organization of the Communist Party and who have educated themselves to become professionals in military, political, managerial, engineering, economic and educational affairs. Their civic and military lives are fused. It is, therefore, inaccurate to speak of civilian control over the military, military control over civilians, the politicization of the military or the militarization of society as if the civic and military spheres were clearly distinct.

The civic soldier is the key political role in Cuba.[4] Civic soldierly behavioral patterns are expected of about two-thirds of the occupants of top elite positions. Most civic soldiers were socialized into their role during the insurgency against Batista in the 1950s and during the counter-insurgency against anti-communists in the early 1960s. This type of warfare, more than any other, tends to fuse military and political roles in the battlefields. Civic soldiers head both military and civilian agencies in Cuba and, just as military agencies have civilian tasks, civilian agencies have military tasks and use military symbols and organization. Therefore, the sent roles of a military commander or the Minister of Education or a sugar harvest administrator include both civilian and military elements. While the sent role of a military commander may have more military elements, there are still strong civilian elements.

This has important implications for the nature of political conflict and adaptive behavior. First, there is relatively little evidence (though there is some) of conflict between persons in distinct civilian and military roles. Conflicts in various issue areas tend to occur between civic soldiers; the more "pure" civilian minority of the leadership tends to split, too, but there are rarely clear civilian and military sides to a dispute. Second, there is *no* issue area in which civic soldiers are totally disinterested. Civic soldiers are engaged in disputes in military, political, economic, artistic, educational, and social deviance issue areas. When conflict occurs, for example, over the defense budget, civic soldiers are found on both sides of the dispute. Thus the presence of conflict in the military issue area can co-exist with the civic soldier role, though it may increase role pressures.

Third, the civic soldier role, theoretically, seems fraught with objective role conflict. How many resources will be diverted from the defense to the industrial investment budget, when both goals are prescribed by the Party leadership to which one belongs (intra-sender conflict)? If one is in charge of a motorized brigade, does one emphasize training for combat or for a mechanized harvest, that is, does one respond more to the strict military or strict economic organizations (inter-sender conflict)? The leadership has addressed itself primarily to the second type of role conflict by seeking to prevent extreme organizational specialization, and by relying on long-standing interpersonal bonds from the shared guerrilla experience. Thus the Ministry of the Armed Forces will demand both economic and military performance: but what is the field officer supposed to do when he must apportion his own time?

One may continue theoretically to expect inter-sender role conflict. The civic-military fusion creates a host of potential role conflicts. But, empirically in Cuba, the meager evidence suggests thus far little conflict between different organizational senders. The organizational pull of the Armed Forces and Education Ministries clash little by preventing extreme organizational specialization. The civic soldier concept has permeated many organizations, too. And too little is known about intra-sender conflict.

Fourth, because the civic and the soldierly elements of the role are equally legitimate, organizational adaptation is facilitated. For example, if the defense budget is threatened because threats to the state decline, it is feasible to stress more the non-defense elements of the civic soldier role. The objectives of the military institutions include both elements; as H. A. Simon argued, loyalty to the organization will support opportunistic changes of emphasis to promote organizational survival and growth; the legitimacy of civic soldiership facilitates the shift. Blau has argued that the attainment of organizational objectives (e.g., military security) generates a strain toward finding new objectives (e.g., politics, or economics). It can be hypothesized that organizational growth is a specific goal of the military institutions or, at the very least, that the prevention of organizational decline is certainly such a goal. The civic soldier concept helps to legitimize a shift in objectives or missions of the military organization as perceived by the entire elite. In turn, the ability to shift objectives, as Huntington has argued, adds to the organizational age of the military organization so it becomes more institutionalized.[5]

In this essay, we will pay attention only to the military as an institution of government, emphasizing the strictly military, the socio-economic and the political objectives or missions of the armed forces from the view of the party-military relationship. We will pay little attention to the military as a re-socializing institution or as a symbol or norm for civilians (especially for children) or to matters purely internal to the armed forces such as training, schools.[6] Thus we consider the civic soldier hypothesis in order to explain the fusion of civilian and military aspects of governing Cuba.

Background

Cuba has experienced three distinct periods of civil-military relations. The first, from qualified independence in 1902 until the 1933 revolution which overthrew President Machado, emphasized subjective civilian control. The military served in large part as a Presidential political machine, insuring the victory of the President's party at the polls in return for participation in a system of widespread and institutionalized graft. The military also defeated insurrections by the opposition after the elections. These insurrections were usually minor, designed to provoke U.S. interference to annul the elections. There were no military coups during this period.[7]

The second period, from 1933 until the 1958 revolution which overthrew President Batista, emphasized arbitrator military behavior. There were two successful military coups, in September 1933 and in March 1952, but no military rule. The military placed their chosen civilians in power, including a thoroughly civilianized Senator Batista in 1952. In 1936, the military forced Congress to impeach the President and replace him with the Vice President. From 1933 to 1940, effective political power was held by the Commander-in-Chief of the Army, Colonel Fulgencio Batista, who often removed civilian Presidents. But a military officer on active duty never served as President of the Republic. All military coups attempted between 1940 and 1952 failed.

Batista relied on existing political parties, whose ideas he borrowed, in both periods of effective rule, 1933–1944 and 1952–1958. Though he eventually developed a political organization, it was not the military's, but his own. As Army Chief in the 1930s, he toyed with corporatist political ideology but abandoned it swiftly. He expanded the role of the military extensively into civilian areas, especially education and public health, yet he kept the military out of economic tasks. He emphasized the more effective distribution of resources, such as education and public health, which did not require taking from some social groups to give to others. In literacy and public health, the military supplanted civilians and brought no skills which could not have been provided by civilians if resources had been channeled through civilian rather than military agencies. A technically or managerially competent military, stressing development, was *not* the role performed; rather, the military were the distributors of basic values by using "cheap labor" through enlisted men.[8]

During the course of the 1940s, the scope of army "non-military" activities was sharply restricted, as many educational and health functions were transferred from military to civilian agencies. The Batista government in the 1950s turned to repression of the opposition but without militarizing the social system. The President chose to risk defeat in combatting the insurgency rather than disrupt the economy. He allocated troops to protect enterprises, and to guarantee production, rather than to facilitate military offensive operations.[9] At the end of the Batista regime, therefore, the scope of military activities was restricted, the weight of the military on the national economy and life was limited (as shown below) and attitudes toward the armed forces were negative.

The third period, from 1959 until the present, is the rule by the revolutionary government headed by Fidel Castro. It fits none of the theoretical categories. While one can identify a ruling elite and "pure" civilians, it is not always easy to identify the "pure" military. A large majority of Cuba's contemporary ruling elite have military rank. There is no identifiable alternative "pure" civilian elite capable of ruling the country without the military politicians. There is only limited evidence of civil-military conflict, not only because the "pure" civilian share of the elite is small, but also because the military's decisive political role is perceived to be legitimate. Finally, the scope of activity of the military is not well defined, and it is becoming more ill defined with the passing of time.

The Military Mission of the Military

The "military" mission of the Cuban military has been to provide for external defense and to suppress internal challenges to the authority of the government. Since the early summer of 1960, the Soviet nuclear shield has protected Cuba against U.S. attack. The Cuban armed forces are responsible for sub-nuclear defense. The major external attack was the Bay of Pigs invasion in 1961. Since then, though with declining frequency, various exile groups have launched hit-and-run attacks on the island or have landed small parties, which have typically been captured quickly.

Cuba's external defense, in practice, rests with the navy, equipped to intercept landings and prevent hit-and-run raids, with the air and the anti-aircraft defense forces, equipped to intercept exile bombings of the island, and with the Frontier Corps, which serves as the first line of territorial defense against a successful landing, prior to calling the regular army units. Cuba's other military capabilities are not necessary to the daily practice of external defense. In 1970 total navy size was between 6,000 and 7,500; the size of the air force and the anti-aircraft defense units was between 12,000 and 20,000. The army had about 90,000. In short, the bulk of Cuba's military force is not externally but internally oriented.[10]

Cuba faced internal war, with some interruptions, from December 1956 through 1965. Since then, the pockets of internal resistance have been few and have been eliminated quickly. From December 1956 to January 1959, Batista's forces fought against the insurgency led by Castro and allied organizations. During the second half of 1960 insurgents rose against

Table I.[12] The Military Burden, 1940–1970

	Military Expenditures				Military Personnel (in thousands)	
	Millions current pesos[a]	Millions current dollars[b]	% of national income[a]	% of GNP[b]	Regular forces[c]	Regular and para-military forces[b]
1940	19		4.5			
1949-50	40		2.6			
1951-52	42		2.2		25	
1958	50		2.3		29	
1961		175		7.6		270
1962		200		8.0		280
1963	213	200	6.5	7.4	300	285
1964	223	200	5.6	6.7		175
1965	214	220	5.5	6.9		175
1966		230		6.6		175
1967		250		6.3		175
1968		300		6.0		200
1969		250		5.0	116	200
1970		290		5.6	110	200
1971						
1972	365					

[a] From Cuban government data.
[b] From ACDA data.
[c] From various sources cited in note 12.

Castro's government, primarily in the Escambray mountains at the center of the island, in Las Villas province. This was followed by the Bay of Pigs invasion in April 1961. The defeat of the invasion and the containment of the Escambray insurrection slowed down the internal war, which resumed in 1962. In July 1962, the government created the Anti-Bandit Struggle Corps throughout the island (Lucha Contra Bandidos, or LCBs). Although the LCBs undoubtedly fought against some bandits, their clear target was political insurrection against the revolutionary government.[11]

Table I shows the military burden. National income estimates between the 1950s and the 1960s are not strictly comparable. Budget statistics, however, are even less comparable. The budget is vastly larger after 1959 than before because it encompasses operations for a socialized economy. Therefore, the national income estimates are preferred.

Table I shows that the highest level of military expense weight on national income in pre-revolutionary Cuba came in the period through 1940, when the Batista-led armed forces were engaged in fairly extensive activities beyond the strict military mission. But the weight of military expenses declined to a low point just as Batista staged his coup of March 1952. Among the first measures after the coup were pay raises for all military forces. Although the military budget grew during the Batista regime, its weight on national income remained virtually unchanged because the economy also grew. In 1958, as his government was threatened with widespread insurrection, the Batista government still registered a very low commitment of national resources to military ends. In contrast, the Castro government has committed a share of national income which is two to three times the size of Batista's.

Table I shows a reasonable (though not exact) correspondence between the ACDA estimates and the computations based on direct Cuban government data. In particular, both sets of data point to a decline in the weight of military expenditures on the economy after 1963, as the intensity of internal war declined and the economy recovered from its near-collapse of 1962–1963. The decline in the economic weight of the military was steady throughout the second half of the 1960s, to be interrupted only by the rise in activities by the military in connection with the 1970 sugar harvest.

Cuba's regular armed forces grew from 24,797 when Batista took over on March 10, 1952, to 29,270 on the day he fell (in addition, Batista created army and navy reserves amounting to 18,542 by December 1958). The revolutionary government had 300,000 regular forces, with a reserve of approximately the same size, at the peak of the insurrections against its rule. Table I shows the shrinking of the size from 1963 to 1970, to correspond with the reduced threat to the government's survival. . . .

Castro's forces had numbered no more than 300 in mid-1958; no more than 2,000 in early December, 1958, and no more than 3,000 by the end of the month. . . . Approximately 2,000–2,500 persons (or two to three times the 898 reported in the only detailed count ever published) were killed on both sides during the insurrection against Batista. . . . In the first half of the 1960s there were insurrections against the Castro government in each of the six provinces. There were at one time as many as 179 insurrectionary bands. The revolutionary government estimated the size of this armed opposition at 3591 (dead plus captured), and has reported about 500 military deaths from the Anti-Bandit struggle, independent of other military deaths from other actions or terrorism. Anti-government forces numbered 1000 at their peak.[13] Because the government won and the insurrectionists lost, more insurrectionist than government deaths may be expected. Indeed, one gets into the same range (2000–2500 deaths) for the 1960s as for the 1950s.

In sum, the number of regular troops committed by the Cuban government against insurrection was ten times greater under Castro than under Batista; the reserve forces under Castro were ten to fifteen times greater than under Batista; the level of fighting was probably the same. Batista's government lost; Castro's government won. Revolutionary government in Cuba could not have survived without the military's effective performance in their strictly military role.

Once survival of the revolution was assured, broad shifts in the posture of the military occurred. In the early 1960s, the Cuban military had a large standing force but with limited professional competence. The military could defeat an internal insurrection or exile landing, but would have had to rely on Soviet protection against a major external attack. By the late 1960s, the desire for greater strategic autonomy joined the wish to reduce the burden of the military on the Cuban economy. The size of the standing force shrunk; the military share of national income declined. But the actual military budget remained high and rose moderately. The new funds were used for the modernization of inventories and the professionalization of the officer corps. The new Cuban strategic doctrine emphasized more self-reliance on a modernized and professionalized "small" standing force *plus* a capability for full and swift mobilization of the reserves.[14]

The shift in strategic doctrine, therefore, provided more autonomy at less economic cost. The real cost to the civilians—and gain to the military—was the expansion of military training and military control over the lives of young and middle-aged adults. Civilians were militarized. But another trend began simultaneously. The armed forces became much more involved in activities which were not strictly military. Their socio-economic and political missions became paramount. The military were civilianized. More appropriately, it is arguable that these joint trends have led to civilian and military role fusion in many areas, and to the diffusion of the civic soldier concept within both military and civilian sectors.

The Socio-Economic Mission of the Military

Upon the suppression of the insurgency by 1965, the military searched for new or expanded roles. One was the supervision of social deviants and their presumed rehabilitation, the other was the promotion of economic growth. It had been foreseen for some time that the military would perform such roles. In 1963 the compulsory military service law was discussed and implemented. Although external and internal defense were its foremost military justifications, there were additional public justifications. Armed Forces Minister Raúl Castro argued that a three-year military tour of duty for draftees was justified in order for the military to perform in missions other than external defense and internal order:

> If we emphasize military training alone, if we want but an army, we can have them [the draftees] for two years . . . [but] because we believe that the armed forces should help in national production . . . [we intend to make] a bit lighter the burden of military expenditures on our people, that is, we must work during a part of the service, first of all in the sugar harvest. . . .[15]

Secondly, the lazy, the corrupt, the homosexual, the religious proselytizer (especially Jehovah's Witnesses) would be drafted into special military units. They would be given no weapons; they would be socially "rehabilitated." Although it was emphasized that the compulsory military service was not designed primarily for this purpose, this would be a subsidiary benefit.[16]

When the internal armed challenge to the revolutionary government was defeated and the objective of state security achieved, the military sought to find new organizational objectives to promote organizational growth by emphasizing the non-defense elements of the civic soldier role. In November 1965, the Army High Command proposed the formation of Military Units to Aid Production (Unidades Militares de Ayuda a la Producción—UMAP) and Prime Minister Castro agreed. UMAP would be nourished by the often arbitrary draft of social deviants. Deviancy included "bad" work habits, intense religious beliefs, homosexuality, and all those traits not in strict accord with a public perception of the "good citizen." As the first UMAP draftees arrived, they were treated so brutally that some of their officers were court-martialled and convicted.[17] The initial brutality by military officers was brought under control by one of the leaders of the revolution against Batista, Ernesto Casillas, who headed the UMAP in its formative months. . . .

UMAP remained through two sugar harvests (1965–1966, 1966–1967). It was not universally applauded. The Cuban Union of Writers and Artists protested to Prime Minister Castro, because many intellectuals and members of the universities were sent to UMAP as alleged homosexuals. Although the Prime Minister had approved UMAP and spoke well of it as late as March 1966, the scandalous treatment of UMAP draftees was unacceptable, and UMAP was eliminated after the end of the 1967 harvest. This decision was resisted by the Army High Command, whose journal ran articles in four different issues in the spring of 1967 defending UMAP's record.[18] The defeat of the military establishment on this issue highlights both the decisive role of Prime Minister Castro—a civic soldier —and the limits on military expansion. The military would still recruit and train "good revolutionaries." Their positive socializing mission would continue. Their repressive, "rehabilitative" mission was sharply curtailed.

The military expanded their role in economic production more successfully. Even in the early 1960s, when the strict military mission was paramount, military units contributed to production. LCB units in the Escambray mountains in the fall of 1963 helped the peasants. This work was also part of the counter-insurgency strategy in this threatened area. Similar LCB work with the peasants occurred elsewhere in 1962, 1963 and 1964.[19] As in the case of UMAP, the major expansion in the economic role of the military came only after the external and internal military threats declined. Economic objectives flowed also from emphasizing the non-defense aspects of the civic soldier role, were thereby legitimized, and contributed to military organizational growth.

Table II.[20] Military Participation in the Sugar Harvest

	Number of soldiers	% (range)
1968	51,000	44-47
1969	38,000	32-35
1970	70,000	60-64
1971	43,000	37-40

Table II shows military participation in sugar harvests. Cutting sugar cane requires limited skills. This use of the military, therefore, does not stress military technical or managerial skills, though these would be used in other ways in the harvest. The chief military contribution in cutting cane was to guarantee a cheap labor supply in conditions of labor scarcity. Though the specific tasks were different, this use of the military was similar to Army Chief Batista's in his role expansion programs of the 1930s, except that the role expansion of the 1960s emphasized growth, that of the 1930s, distribution. Normal military participation (1968, 1969, 1971) was just over 40,000 men, somewhat over one-third of the armed forces. The 1970 harvest was extraordinary. Cuba sought to produce ten million tons of sugar; it actually produced 8.5 million tons, the largest harvest in its history. Almost two-thirds of the armed forces cut cane in 1970.

Unlike Batista's military in the 1930s, whose technical and managerial contribution to economic growth was minimal, the revolutionary armed forces also took on important technical and managerial economic roles in the late 1960s to promote growth.[21] This began in 1967, when the air force took charge of 60 airplanes devoted to aerial fumigation and fertilization of agricultural areas. In the fall of that year the army formed a motorized brigade to take over mechanized or motorized equipment, first to open up new fields for cultivation and subsequently for the sugar harvest. By the spring of 1969 all farm machinery was under military authority. Officers and enlisted men who had worked in tank or motorized military units were shifted to the new brigade. Since the fall of 1968, the Che Guevara Brigade had been organized into 36 sub-units, throughout the six provinces. Its Commander-in-Chief, Raúl Guerra Bermejo, was also a member of the Party's Central Committee. The Brigade retained a strict military organization and hierarchical chain of command, but it operated entirely in the economic field. It took over all the machinery formerly administered by the State Farms and civilian personnel.

In the giant 1970 sugar harvest, the military cut 20 percent of the sugar cane harvested. They organized and operated the Henderson combines, which sought to mechanize the cane cutting. The military coordinated the cane loading at strategic locations and supervised the transportation of cane for the sugar mills in the more important eastern provinces. They operated all tractors and cane lifters. They built roads, railroad tracks and temporary housing. The military brigade Luis Turcios Lima, of the Eastern Army, won the coveted title of National Heroes of Labor. The harvests since the late 1960s—and especially in 1970—have been directed from a national command post, linked to the field through provincial, regional and municipal posts. The symbolism is strongly military: the harvest is a battle, a struggle, portrayed as no less essential to the survival of the revolution than the real military battles of the earlier 1960s.

Contrary to some expectations that the military economic role expansion fever of 1967–1968 would subside, it continued and became institutionalized with each subsequent harvest. There is now nothing unusual about military participation in Cuba's annual battle of the sugar harvest. The military have yet to prove that they are more successful than civilians in rescuing the Cuban economy, but their commitment to large scale economic participation and the general acceptance of such participation are now unquestionable.

The growing economic role of the Cuban military gave it a new mission. It has also blunted a criticism that the armed forces were an excessive burden on the Cuban economy. The previously cited 1963 speech by Armed Forces Minister Raúl Castro suggests that this concern was prevalent even when it was clear that the government needed the military for survival. This criticism was stronger in the mid-1960s, as the insurrection against the government was defeated and the military's economic role had not yet expanded. The old objectives had been achieved. Until new ones were found, the organizational health of the military organization was at stake because of the pressures of civic soldiers heading civilian agencies. In 1966 the military agreed to cancel purchases of helicopters and military transport aircraft in order to divert such resources to the purchase of the airplanes for aerial fumigation; and the transfer of no less than 250 pilots on active military service to aerial agricultural service was justified on similar budgetary grounds.[22]

In mid-1967, however, the reductions in the economic weight of the military budget and in military manpower had not yet satisfied some critics. The military responded in two ways. One was the sharp increase in economic activities that has been described. The other was the renewed assertion of the priority of the military budget. Raúl Castro noted on July 22, 1967, that the country may have to "sacrifice even some aspects of its social development in construction work in order to earmark more of our resources to prepare the country for a war whose outbreak we cannot foresee." By January 1968, after the military's economic role had expanded, Fidel Castro acknowledged the priority of the military in the allocation of scarce strategic resources such as petroleum.[23]

Table I shows how the conflict was resolved. The defense budget rose 20 percent and military manpower rose 14.3 percent from 1967 to 1968. The armed forces, therefore, registered the largest annual increase on either indicator for the entire decade. However, military expenditures as a percentage of Gross National Product continued to decline. The military budget grew, but at a rate slower than the economy in a good year (1968). And almost one-half of all military personnel in the regular army had to cut sugar cane in 1968. Though the defense budget retrenched in 1969 to the 1967 level, it almost reached the 1968 level again in 1970, and reached a new height in 1972.

Other communist and non-communist armed forces have also engaged in what is variously called the peaceful uses of military forces, civic action programs, non-military uses of the military or productive work. The scope and domain of the Cuban military's involvement in social and economic tasks is, however, vast compared to many other reported instances of this kind of military behavior.[24] Among communist armed forces, the Soviet military have strongly and repeatedly emphasized professional, strictly military concerns; they have argued that modern military technology requires their full attention to military tasks. But even in the early years of the Soviet revolution, there was little of the kind of role expansion into non-military employment that the Cuban armed forces have embraced.[25] This may have resulted from a regime decision or from military resistance. The point is that role expansion did not occur.

The closest parallel to the Cuban performance is the Chinese military. The Chinese military's reported involvement in the Great Leap Forward was probably comparable to the Cuban military's reported involvement in the Giant Harvest of 1970. A remaining difference with the Chinese is that a significant number of military officers in the Chinese army resisted such role expansion into social and economic tasks, and argued, as did their Soviet colleagues, that the profession of arms was a full-time profession.[26]

There is very little evidence of comparable resistance within the Cuban military. On the contrary, the evidence strongly suggests that the military have embarked on their economic tasks with eagerness and enthusiasm. The only instance when the Cuban military may have resisted involvement was in the 1970 harvest. As Table II showed, however, their participation in that harvest was clearly extraordinary; in 1971, they reverted quickly to their "normal" rate of participation. There are indications that Fidel Castro wanted, but did not get, additional military participation in the 1970 harvest.[27] Noting that limited exception, the generalization is that the Cuban military have and want a very large involvement in social and economic tasks. One reason for this important difference is the Cuban military's efforts to redesign their mission to remain useful to society, to protect their budget, and to promote their organizational growth in size and function. This explanation, while necessary, is not yet sufficient to distinguish between Cuban and other comparable armed forces. What sets them apart is a set of political variables.

The Political Mission of the Military

The political mission of the Cuban military has four components. First, the internalization of the structure of the Communist Party, so that the corporate autonomy of the military institutions is preserved and party-military conflict contained. Second, the elimination of historical cleavages which plagued the armed forces prior to the revolution: conflicts between commissioned and non-commissioned officers, and between professional and non-professional commissioned officers. Third, the political indoctrination of recruits, and the weeding out of military men with undesirable traits. And fourth, the organization of modes of party organization and control, and the development of leadership cadres that can be exported to the civilian sectors and, in particular, to the top elite. It is at this high level that the fusion between the civic and military tasks of the soldier is climaxed by placing the civic soldier in charge of the highest commands in both the party and the military. The military commander is not a mere technician of arms, but also a political officer; the party national leader is not only a politician but also an officer with technical and managerial competence for civilian and military work.

The civic soldier hypothesis does *not* apply for the early years (1961–1962) of party-military relations. This period ended wth a large scale expulsion of party members in 1962 (most of the expellees were members of the pre-revolutionary Communist Party, faithful to Moscow and not especially close then to Castro's movement) and the large scale recruitment of new members.[28] The party's crisis was caused primarily by a confrontation between Fidel Castro and pre-revolutionary Communists, not by civil-military friction. But the latter was a contributing factor and steps were taken to correct the problem. The bitter memories of civil-military relations in 1961–1962 spurred the civic soldier concept.

During 1961–1962, the party sought control over the armed forces. Political instructors were trained in the Osvaldo Sánchez School for Revolutionary Instruction of the Revolutionary Armed Forces, and then assigned to military units. These political instructors lacked any military training or operational field experience. There was a separation of political and military tasks in the military units. Military commanders strongly opposed both the division of command and the imposition of political instructors outside the military chain of command. These early political instructors explicitly copied the experience of political commissars in the military from other communist countries. One result of the great purge of the party in 1962 was the abandonment of this system. Beginning early in 1963, prospective students for the Osvaldo Sánchez School were drawn directly from the military ranks, particularly officers. The curriculum in the school was revamped so that 40 percent of the time would be spent on military topics.[29]

By the end of 1963, party recruitment and organization in the military had begun.[30] There was a trial run in the Mountain Corps (Compañías Serranas) of the easternmost province, to be followed in December 1963 by the beginnings of party organization in the regular units of the Eastern Army. The formation of the party in the military has observed this procedure. All members of a military unit are classified into eight ranks, from soldiers to commanding officers. Each rank has an assembly—directed by a Commission of political instructors appointed by the party's political bureau in the armed forces—to elect "exemplary combatants" (except that all commissioned officers are automatically assumed to be "exemplary combatants"). The exemplary combatants are then interviewed individually by the Commission. Exemplary combatants meet also as groups with the Commission, separately for each of the eight categories of military rank, for criticism and self-criticism. The Commission members select new party members after discussing the candidates among themselves and with ranking officers. The new members are presented to the rest of the unit, and to the party cell (núcleo) which is established in the military unit, and includes all party members regardless of military rank. Party officers are elected at the cell level in the unit and progressively upward in battalions, armies, etc.

At the outset, neither the military orders of the officers nor the officers' own personal and political behavior could be criticized in the party cell. By the mid-1960s, this rule held only during the course of the first year of party formation in the military units. By the second year of party formation in a military unit, though military orders and regulations issued by the officers could still not be questioned in the cell, the personal and political behavior of the officers could be criticized, regardless of the military ranks of the officer and his critic. However, the officers and their orders could at all times be criticized by higher ranking military officers and by political instructors assigned to higher ranking military units.

Political work in the armed forces was directed by the National Commission of the Party in the Armed Forces, whose chief was Raúl Castro—Armed Forces Minister, Deputy Prime Minister, and Second Secretary of the national party. The political instructors are not elected, but appointed by the National Commission upon the completion of their training. There are two political channels within the armed forces. One is the party, organized from the bottom up; the other, from the top down, is the set of Political Sections in the military units, at all levels of aggregation, composed of the political instructors. The two channels, however, are merged in two ways. First, the political instructors and all party members belong on equal footing to the party's political organs at each level of military organization. Second is the principle of the unified command.

In contrast to the early 1960s and possibly to other communist countries, "command and party go forward together; they are not parallel. The content of the party's work is determined according to the Work Plan of the military unit, according to the specific tasks which it is expected to perform. There is no separation of activity between military and party obligations."[31] Party organization within the military is hierarchical. The upward flow of criticism is difficult, but possible. Innovation remains at the top. Though the party penetrates the military, the military has also penetrated the party. The party in the military is led by the military high command, not by party cells or agencies outside the military. The party in the military is self-contained. Non-military party members have no authority over the party in the military. Party criticism in the military is, at once, criticism within the party, criticism of the military by the party, and criticism of the party by the military, because party and military are fused.

The formation of the party in the military was complete by the end of 1966. The party's formation moved geographically from the eastern to the western provinces, and hierarchically from the bottom up. The last military sector to organize party cells was the National Headquarters of the Army Chief of Staff. By the fall of 1970, 69.6 percent of all officers in the armed forces belonged to either the party or the Communist Youth Union. By the summer of 1973, the proportion rose to 85 percent. The 15-member Advisory Commission of party members to the Political Bureau of the Armed Forces in 1970 was composed entirely of commissioned officers, of whom 7 were *Comandantes* (the highest rank in the Cuban military). In the fall of 1970, 69 percent of the members of the party in the military were commissioned officers. Enlisted soldiers and draftees were a larger, though unspecified, proportion of the membership of the Communist Youth Union.[32] The high overlap between the officer corps and party-youth union membership further facilitates the fusion of party and military.

Though such membership overlap is a necessary condition for fusion, it is not sufficient. In the Soviet military, the proportion of military officers who have belonged to the party has varied over time: 32 percent in 1924, 65 percent in 1928, 86 percent in 1952, 90 percent in the early 1960s, 93 percent in 1966, when 80 percent of the total personnel of the Soviet armed forces were in the party or in the Communist Youth Union (mostly the latter).[33] And yet, there has been repeated conflict between the party and the military throughout Soviet history.[34] What is crucial, beyond the overlap, is the militarization of the political instructors within the armed forces, the internalization of politics by the military officers, the principle of unified command which preserves, in practice, the military chain of command, the self-containment of the party within the military so that the corporate integrity and autonomy of the military are not threatened, and the presence of civic soldiers at the core of the top elite and in charge of both military and civilian organizations. Thus, in the Soviet Union, even when political commissars and military commanders coalesce on a specific issue,[35] the central organs of the party have limited representation from either of them. In the absence of fusion in the top elite, conflict between central civilian party organs and military leaders and units can continue.

The chief problem in the party-military relationship in Cuba has not been partisan interference with military matters, but the lack of fulfillment of political programs in military units. Military commanders tend to leave political matters to the political instructors. In the spring of 1968, according to the Army Chief of Staff, the net result was not the agglutination of power in the hands of the political instructors, but rather the downgrading of political work within the armed forces. Military commanders were urged to become responsible for the political education of all their subordinates, even if the daily political tasks were implemented directly by the political instructors.[36] At the military unit level, therefore, there did not seem to be a politico-military conflict.

The proportion of soldiers and non-commissioned officers in the party in the military—almost one-third—is comparatively high. In the Soviet military, the proportion of soldiers and non-commissioned officers fell as low as 3 percent of all military party members in the 1940s.[37] The relatively high proportion in Cuba can be explained as a part of the democratic commitment of the revolution within the armed forces. The revolutionary leadership has also been aware of the historical cleavage between commissioned and non-commissioned officers in the Cuban military prior to the revolution. Though such cleavages are latent in most military institutions, Cuba experienced a comparatively rare event: On September 4, 1933, army sergeants and corporals headed by then Sergeant Fulgencio Batista overthrew the government and the officer corps. Sergeant Batista promoted himself to Colonel, and other Sergeants and Corporals were equally promoted. Many former officers gathered at the National Hotel to fight back; Batista's forces attacked and killed 14 officers, wounded 17, and took the rest prisoner.[38] Subsequent Cuban military leaders have been concerned lest anything resembling those events should recur.

The second major cleavage within the military prior to the revolution existed between professional officers, who had received formal military training in Cuba or abroad, and non-professional officers, who owed their position to their participation in military coups and shrewd politicking. In the 1950s about one-sixth of the officers were non-professionals, including Generals Juan Rojas González, Luis Robainas, Martín Díaz Tomayo, Pilar García, and Roberto Fernández Miranda.[39] The revolutionary government sought to prevent the recurrence of such a cleavage through its promotion policy.

Table III shows that no less than three-quarters, and typically nine-tenths, of all professional officers promoted and graduating cadets are members of either the Communist Party or the Communist Youth Union. Among the officers promoted, party membership is widespread; among the

Table III.[40] Professional Military Promotions and Party-Communist Youth Membership

Ranks and dates	N	% in rebel army	% in party	% in Youth Union	% party + % Youth Union
April 1968					
First Captains	35	100.0	94.3	0.0	94.3
Captains	56	100.0	100.0	0.0	100.0
All lieutenants	1757	33.7	69.3	8.8	78.1
March 1969					
Graduate Cadets	414	1.2	48.5	48.5	97.0
August 1969					
Graduate Cadets	731	N.A.	N.A.	N.A.	89.0
August 1970					
Graduate Cadets	1304	N.A.	N.A.	N.A.	87.0
August 1973					
Graduate Cadets	N.A.	N.A.	N.A.	N.A.	95.0

N.A. = not available

cadets, Youth Union membership is even more pervasive. The share of officers or cadets promoted with any rebel army experience is declining to zero. Party membership has become a prerequisite for promotion to the upper ranks of the military, and Youth Union membership for promotion from the cadet level. The sharp conflict between party and military of the early 1960s in part occurred because so few military men were in the party. By the 1970s, however, the policy for officer promotion was guaranteeing near-perfect overlap between military officership and party membership. Politically connected officers would also be military professionals and vice versa.

A second aspect of the promotion policy was to send military officers with very low levels of formal training to military school to acquire professional skills. According to Fidel Castro, it would become policy to promote only those who had had professional training in military schools; but, in the late 1960s, those officers with operational experience but no school training were still being promoted. However, the problem of professionalizing the military was quite severe. For example, the Ignacio Agramonte School for Officers in the city of Matanzas required officers to have completed the fifth grade of elementary school prior to admission. Throughout most of the 1960s, this rule was frequently broken. It was not until the spring of 1967 that all new students admitted to the school had prior schooling equal to a sixth grade education. The military were not very different from—and actually a bit ahead of—the rest of the political leadership. In 1969, 79 percent of all national party members lacked a sixth grade education.[41]

In sum, the revolutionary government sought to politicize the entire officer corps, but especially the younger officers who had good professional training but little or no operational experience. It also sought to professionalize, and partly politicize, those non-professional officers with a great deal of operational experience. These joint promotion policies sought to reduce the historical cleavages which had weakened the Cuban military in the past.

The main tasks of the party are to support the authority and enhance the prestige of the military chain of command. The party is expected to strengthen troop morale and combat preparedness through propaganda, political education, and surveillance, not only during uneventful periods of military life, but also in the midst of tactical maneuvers. Political instructors accompanied the LCB units in their struggle against internal insurrection in the early 1960s.

There are additional pay-offs from party work in the military. The process of party formation in the military yielded a lot of information about the troops and the officer corps, which could subsequently ease decisions concerning promotion or forced retirement. The system of criticism and self-criticism institutionalized this pay-off and led to greater discipline in the military. The process of party formation activated latent support for the government, and exposed opposition. The introduction of the party established political criteria for promotion beyond normal military criteria.[42]

Moreover, the party in the military organized a program of *captación*. Party and Youth Union members are assigned a number of military men for their supervision. They were expected to "find out about his anxieties, find out about his personal or family problems," engage in political education, and take the tutee to political meetings and activities. The program was supposed to uplift morale, discipline and education. Its by-products, according to Raúl Castro, included repression of homosexuals and of deeply religious soldiers. The program also stimulates competition within military ranks for promotions, through separate political activity amidst soldiers, NCO's, and commissioned officers. When serious problems appear, a court-martial may be in order. Service on all military tribunals is limited to party and Youth Union members. In the fall of 1970, when the second all-military party national meeting gathered, among the chief criticisms of the weaknesses of party work in the military were the insufficiency of criticism and self-criticism and greater need to survey the personal needs of members of the armed forces—suggesting that both programs had yielded rich results in the past and that more was wanted.[43]

This concern for the individual and for small group ties within the military in Cuba is similar to findings about the Chinese army in the early

1950s. Both leaderships took an active interest in the development and control of small group ties. Political judgments were made to control interpersonal relationships and to erode their autonomy. Autonomous, small group social cohesion would not be allowed to threaten the political and military capabilities of the armed forces. Here the interests of party and military clearly went hand in hand.[44]

The political missions of the military discussed above are largely operative within the military organizations. Another mission, in contrast, aims to export political models and personnel from the military to the rest of the political system. The military experience in forming the party preceded the formation of the party in most of the civilian central administrative agencies. While the party in the military finished its process of construction by the end of 1966, the construction of the party in most of the civilian ministries only began in the spring of 1967. The party drew on the experience of party building in the military and, in particular, on the principle of unified command. As the party began its organization in the civilian ministries, its national Secretary of Organization, Armando Hart, noted:

> There cannot be dual leadership in a central State organization. The maximum authority of the party, in each branch of the State apparatus, will be that of the minister or president of the organization, who works under the direction of the Party Central Committee and Political Bureau. If in any case this should turn out to be impossible, we will have to consider the demotion of the executive. . . .[45]

The party in the military also developed a regular practice of holding assemblies to evaluate its work in the military units. These assemblies were held at all levels of command virtually every year. National meetings to evaluate party work in the military were held in 1966 and in 1970.[46] This regularity in the party's organization within the military would serve as a model for non-military branches of the party. Though there had been provincial (civilian) party assemblies since the early days of the party,[47] the especially impressive feature of the party in the military—and a contribution for export to the civilian sectors—was the seriousness and relative regularity of party work in the military.

Finally, the military have developed cadres that can be and have been exported to the civilian sectors. Table IV shows the military shares of the Central Committees of the Communist parties in China, Cuba and the Soviet Union. The data for Cuba have been divided into "total" and "strict' The "total" statistic includes all those members of the Central Committee with military title and rank. The "strict" statistic includes only those members of the Central Committee who were primarily engaged in military affairs most of the time, including political work within the military. Military for these purposes also includes the Ministry of the Interior (internal security). The difference between the "total" and "strict" percentages is a measure of the export of cadres from the military to the civilian sectors

Table IV.[48] Military Shares of the Central Committees of the Communist Parties of China, Cuba and the Soviet Union: Selected Years

	% military	N
China,[a] 1949-1950	38.1	168
China,[a] 1962	24.6	171
China,[b] 1969	51.2	170
China,[b] 1973	31.8	195
China,[a] 1973	31.3	319
Cuba,[b] 1962, total	56.0	25
Cuba,[b] 1962, strict	28.0	25
Cuba,[b] 1965, total	69.0	100
Cuba,[b] 1965, strict	51.0	100
Soviet Union,[b] 1956	7.5	122
Soviet Union,[b] 1966	8.2	195
Soviet Union,[b] 1971	10.2	235

a = all members; b = full members only

that is, of the diffusion of civic soldiers in Cuban public life. Under either measure, the military share of the Cuban Central Committee is very high, and it was greater in 1965 than 1962. In 1962, the Central Committee in fact had not yet been established: it was then called the National Directorate of the United Party of the Socialist Revolution; it was obviously quite small.

Since 1965, men who were classified as "strict" military at the time have taken on new tasks in the civilian economy. For example, . . . former Army Chief of Staff Belarmino Castilla became Minister of Education; his successor as Chief, Diocles Torralba, joined Castilla in late 1972 in the super-Cabinet which was organized to direct all Cuban government policies. Lesser military lights have followed the same path. The process of export of cadres from the military to the civilian sectors, which had begun in the early 1960s, has continued to accelerate through the early 1970s. Leaders are trained in the military ranks; as they have matured, and as the strict military mission of the military has become less important, civic soldiers have shifted their attention to the civilian sectors. In the central ministries as well as at various levels of the "civilian" party ranks one finds civic soldiers again and again. Of the eleven men in the Political Bureau and the Secretariat of the Central Committee, the highest organs of the revolution, there are seven Comandantes who fought in the insurrection against Batista, but who increasingly devote their attention to the widest range of matters.

In the 1950s, the military share in a modern, complex, mature communist political system such as the Soviet Union was small. The Soviet pattern—about 10 percent of the Central Committee coming from the military, with a range between 7 percent and 13 percent, was set by the late 1930s. Prior to that time, the military share of the top elite had been much less.[49] The Table shows that the Chinese case is more complex. We noted in the discussion of social and economic role expansion that the Chinese case came closer to the Cuban, and it is useful to spell out similarities and differences.[50]

First, as Table IV shows, the normal participation of the military in the top elite is much higher in Cuba than in China. The "normal" rate of military participation in the Chinese Central Committee is about one-third, well above the Soviet, well below the Cuban cases. The 1969 Central Committee, at the end of the Cultural Revolution, is exceptional. The participation of the Cuban military in central decision making is apparently more stable and institutionalized than in China. There has been no purge of the Cuban military comparable to the effects of the Lin Piao affair. Second, as the discussion of social and economic role expansion indicated, there has been resistance by professional Chinese officers to engaging in non-military tasks. Cuban military officers have welcomed such role expansion. In China, professional resistance to role expansion existed also just prior to, during, and after the Cultural Revolution. The entry of the armed forces into the Cultural Revolution was no military coup; it was the result of a decision by the political leadership. The People's Liberation Army (PLA) did not set out to expand its role, as the Cuban armed forces did between 1965 and 1968; power gravitated to the PLA and its role expanded. The impetus came from outside the military. During the Cultural Revolution, the professional vs. political dispute was less salient, but it simmered beneath the surface. The professional officers still opposed the large-scale involvement of the PLA in politics. An important element in the anti–Lin Piao coalition were the professional commanders who had opposed political involvement and favored its reduction so that the armed forces could concentrate again on professional military tasks. Thus, though both the Cuban and the Chinese military have engaged in role expansion, Chinese professional officers have resisted while Cuban professional officers have favored it. The impetus in China was primarily external to the military organization; it was both internal and external in Cuba.

Third, the Cuban armed forces have institutionalized the export of political models and cadres to the rest of the political system. In 1964, the Chinese were publicly called upon to "learn from the experience of the PLA in political education and ideological work." The PLA did, indeed, become a model for the rest of the political system. But the "learn from the PLA campaign" lasted only four or five months. During the course of the Cultural Revolution, though the PLA played a decisive role, the export of political models to the rest of the political system was not emphasized. The PLA intervened generally to restore order. It exported middle and low level cadres who became regional or local political leaders through the

Revolutionary Committees. But in the years since the Cultural Revolution there seems to have been a gradual restoration of civilian rule and a retrenchment of the export of cadres from the military to the political system (some of it reflected in Table IV). Thus the Chinese case shows some elements of the civic soldier concept, but not all elements simultaneously. And, whereas the Cuban civic soldier pattern is quite stable, the Chinese clearly is not. Though some Maoists may have had a civic soldier model in mind, though they may have intended its implementation, it was not, in fact, achieved to the degree that it was in Cuba.

A Paradox

Cuba is governed, in large part though not exclusively, by civic soldiers. The leaders of the insurrection against Batista were socialized into a fusion of civilian and military roles. They have remained the top government elite and have turned the civic soldier concept into a dominant norm in civilian organizations. The Cuban military organization has undertaken, both simultaneously and sequentially, important tasks in the Cuban revolution. As the strictly military mission or objective faded, social, economic and political missions became more important. The result has been the gradual spread of civic soldier roles within the military organization. Therefore, a government led by civic soldiers has sought to induce convergence of goals and structures in civilian and military organizations.

Since the beginning of the 1960s, Cuba has not had an alternative civilian elite within the system capable of governing it. And there is relatively little evidence of conflict between persons in distinct civilian and military roles. Conflict occurs not only among civic soldiers; civilians, too, divide. For example, some leading old-Communists and cultural bureaucrats are evidently in agreement with new-Communists in the armed forces concerning the decadence of many Cuban intellectuals.[51] There are, of course, conflicts in the "military issue area." However, these conflicts, as in other issue areas (budget, harvest participation, UMAP), are settled by civic soldiers. Conflicts in this issue area may have been less severe than in other issue areas, such as economic policy and incentives policy.[52]

Organizational survival and growth were achieved by reemphasizing the continuing legitimacy of old objectives and by finding and implementing new, non-defense objectives within the civic soldier role. The civic soldier concept legitimated role expansion. The military organization has not faded away, but organizational boundaries have become blurred. Organizational survival and growth led leaders of the military institution to seek to expand organizational objectives in the mid-1960s as strategic security seemed assured. Strategic doctrine shifted to emphasize civilian mobilization rather than a standing army. Social, economic and political roles were sought and obtained. The UMAP affair was but a minor setback in a story of organizational success. The broadened scope of organizational activity assured organizational survival, and promoted growth in size, functions and resources.

At the same time, inter-sender role conflict was reduced by reversing the organizational specialization of the military. The sent roles of subordinates would be less incompatible because the military organization became more compatible with civilian organizations. The role pressures on civic soldiers serving in civilian agencies were reduced too. They no longer had to argue to reduce the budget of their former comrades-in-arms, because the military organization now performed civilian tasks. Party structures learned from the military experience; party hierarchies were populated by civic soldiers. These changes were, therefore, generally welcomed by the elite because they reduced intra-elite disputes, role pressures on civic soldiers in civilian agencies, and inter-sender role conflict for subordinates. They may, however, have increased intra-sender role conflict, about which, unfortunately, little is known.

It has become fashionable to write about the militarization of the Cuban revolution. That approach has suggested that the events of the late 1960s were drastically different from earlier ones; in fact, a continuum of behavior, with an admitted acceleration in recent years, is closer to the facts. But the concept of militarization is inappropriate in itself, because it fails to identify the special political quality of the soldiers who are clearly so important. These are soldiers who went to military school *after* they had become military commanders and ministers of state,[53] and who have had extra-military concerns from the day they learned that the insurrection against Batista required not only military but also political skills. The Cuban civic soldier, therefore, is different from military men in both communist and non-communist countries because of his eagerness and conviction that military and political tasks require a fusion of personnel and methods.

Yet the civic soldier is a soldier still, and Cuba's reliance on him bespeaks important failures of the revolutionary government. The need to employ the armed forces in the sugar harvest highlights the failure of economic production, and the inability to handle labor supply problems. The use of military methods in the political field has stifled criticism from the bottom of the system, has shut off the upward flow of political communication, and has curtailed the adaptability of the political system. The thorough use of military techniques in the 1970 harvest ended with a quasi-strike by labor in the summer of 1970 and emergency measures to correct a serious problem by the Labor Confederation.[54]

The successful development of the civic soldier concept in Cuba has occurred in the context of political and economic failure. Nor has the civic soldier's performance in economic production been any more successful than that of civilians. The problems are too profound for the Cuban leadership to rely as exclusively as it has on the fusion of military and political methods into a single, unified tool. The various tasks of the revolution require various tools, but the Cuban leadership has yet to implement an approach that makes separate and distinct use of political, economic and military tools according to the ends pursued.

Notes

1. Samuel P. Huntington, *The Soldier and the State* (Cambridge: Harvard University Press, 1957), pp. 80–85.
2. Amos Perlmutter, "The Praetorian State and the Praetorian Army: Toward a Taxonomy of Civil-Military Relations in Developing Polities," in J. L. Finkle and R. W. Gable, eds., *Political Development and Social Change* (New York: John Wiley and Sons, Inc., 1971), pp. 314–324.
3. Gino Germani and Kalman Silvert, "Politics, Social Structure and Military Intervention in Latin America," *European Journal of Sociology*, vol. 2, 1961 [reprinted in this volume]; Morris Janowitz, *The Military in the Political Development of New Nations* (Chicago: University of Chicago Press, 1964); and Samuel P. Huntington, *Political Order in Changing Societies* (New Haven: Yale University Press, 1968), chapter 4.
4. The usage of role theory in this and the following paragraphs follows R. L. Kahn *et. al.*, *Organizational Stress: Studies in Role Conflict and Ambiguity* (New York: John Wiley and Sons, Inc., 1964), pp. 11–35.
5. H. A. Simon, *Administrative Behavior* (New York: Macmillan Co., 1961), p. 118; P. M. Blau, *The Dynamics of Bureaucracy* (Chicago: University of Chicago Press, 1955), p. 195; Huntington, *Political Order, op. cit.*, pp. 13–17; and W. H. Starbuck, "Organizational Growth and Development," in J. G. March, ed., *Handbook of Organizations* (Chicago: Rand McNally and Co., 1965).
6. For the guerrilla experience and the early 1960s, see Louis A. Perez, *The Rise and Fall of Army Pre-Eminence in Cuba, 1898–1958* (Albuquerque: The University of New Mexico, unpublished Ph. D. dissertation, 1971), chapters 10 and 11; Louis A. Perez, "Perspectives on the Rebel Army," unpublished manuscript (I am grateful to Nelson P. Valdés for showing this manuscript to me); and Ramón Bonachea and Marta San Martín, *The Cuban Insurrection, 1952–1959* (New Brunswick: Transaction Books, 1974), pp. 85–105, 187–197, 226–301; and on military symbolism and socialization functions, see Marta San Martín and Ramón Bonachea, "The Military Dimension of the Cuban Revolution," in I. L. Horowitz, ed., *The Cuban Revolution* (Second edition; New Brunswick: Transaction Books, 1972).
7. R. Adam y Silva, *La gran mentira* (La Habana: Editorial Lex, 1947).
8. Fulgencio Batista, *Revolución social o política reformista* (La Habana: Prensa Indoamericana, 1944), pp. 58–59, 62, 82–85, 123–124, 127; *Cuba's Three Year Plan* (La Habana: Cultural S.A., 1937); Consejo Corporativo de Educación, Sanidad y Beneficencia, *Militarismo, anti-militarismo, pseudomilitarismo* (Ceiba del Agua: Talleres del Instituto Cívico-Militar, 1939), pp. 5–6, 8, 82, 106; Edmund Chester, *A Sergeant Named Batista* (New York: Henry Holt and Co., 1954); and Perez, *The Rise, op. cit.*

9. J. Suárez Núñez, *El Gran Culpable* (Caracas: 1963), pp. 89–90, 94–98, 170.
10. Institute for Strategic Studies, *The Military Balance, 1970–1971* (London: ISS, 1970), p. 76; Subcommittee on Inter-American Affairs of the Committee on Foreign Affairs, House of Representatives, "Hearings on Cuba and the Caribbean," Ninety-first Congress, Second Session (Washington: U.S. Government Printing Office, 1970), pp. 37, 125–126; Subcommittee on Inter-American Affairs of the Committee on Foreign Affairs, House of Representatives, "Hearings on Soviet Activities in Cuba," Ninety-second Congress, Second Session, Part 3 (Washington: U.S. Government Printing Office, 1972), pp. 6, 18–19, 22; and H. I. Blutstein *et al.*, *Area Handbook for Cuba* (Washington: U.S. Government Printing Office, 1971), p. 439.
11. J. Suárez Amador, "Octavo aniversario de L.C.B.," *Verde olivo*, vol. 11, no. 28 (July 12, 1970), pp. 4–5; *Verde olivo*, vol. 4, no. 47 (November 24, 1963); *Granma*, March 5, 1966, p. 8; March 13, 1966, p. 8.
12. Entries under *b* are taken from U.S. Arms Control and Disarmament Agency, *World Military Expenditures, 1971* (Washington: U.S. Government Printing Office, 1972). Entries on military expenditures under *a* have been computed from the Cuban Economic Research Project, *A Study on Cuba* (Coral Gables: University of Miami Press, 1965), pp. 455, 461, 621, for the pre-revolutionary period; and for the revolutionary period from Junta Central de Planificación, *Compendio Estadístico de Cuba, 1966* (La Habana: JUCEPLAN, 1966), p. 13; Carmelo Mesa-Lago, "Economic Policies and Growth," in Carmelo Mesa-Lago, ed., *Revolutionary Change in Cuba* (Pittsburgh: University of Pittsburgh Press, 1971), pp. 319, 331; and *Granma*, August 6, 1972, p. 4. Entries on military personnel under *c* are taken from A. Reyes, "Ejército de la tiranía," *Verde olivo*, vol. 7, no. 45 (November 12, 1966), pp. 23, 27–28 for the 1950s; and from *Granma*, December 12, 1971, p. 3, for 1963; Blutstein *et al.*, *op. cit.*, p. 439, for 1969; and Institute for Strategic Studies, *op. cit.*, p. 76, for 1970.
13. Raúl Castro, "Graduación del III curso de la escuela básica superior 'General Maximo Gómez,' 22 de Julio de 1967," *Ediciones al orientador revolucionario*, no. 17 (1967), p. 11; *Granma*, June 13, 1971, pp. 2–3 and December 12, 1971, p. 6.
14. Raúl Castro, "Las FAR rinden profundo y sentido homenaje al vigésimo aniversario," *Bohemia*, vol. 65, no. 31 (August 3, 1973), p. 28; Raúl Castro, "Graduación," *op. cit.*
15. *Verde olivo*, vol. 4, no. 47 (November 24, 1963), p. 19.
16. *Ibid.*, pp. 19–20, 52; and "El proyecto de ley del servicio militar obligatorio," *Cuba socialista*, no. 28 (December, 1963) pp. 85–87.
17. *Granma*, April 14, 1966, p. 8.
18. *Ibid.*, p. 8; and March 16, 1966, p. 4; *Verde olivo*, vol. 7, no. 43 (October 30, 1966), pp. 14–15, supplement; vol. 8, no. 11 (March 19, 1967), pp. 34–38; vol. 8, no. 12 (March 26, 1967), pp. 27–30; vol. 8, no. 18 (May 7, 1967), pp. 19–21; vol. 8, no. 19 (May 14, 1967), pp. 36–39; see also José Yglesias, *In the Fist of the Revolution: Life in a Cuban Country Town* (New York: Vintage Books, 1968), pp. 274–302; and Lourdes Casal, "Literature and Society," in Mesa-Lago, ed., *Revolutionary Change in Cuba, op. cit.*, p. 459.
19. *Verde olivo*, vol. 4, no. 47 (November 24, 1963), pp. 10–11; vol. 4, no. 4

(January 27, 1963), pp. 52–53; vol. 11, no. 28 (July 12, 1970), p. 5; *Granma*, March 5, 1966, p. 8.

20. Computed from *Granma*, July 18, 1971, p. 9, and from data in Table I.
21. Fidel Castro, "Brigada invasora Che Guevara," *Verde olivo*, vol. 8, no. 44 (November 5, 1967), pp. 6–7; F. Vascos, "Brigada invasora Che Guevara: Año 1," *Verde olivo*, vol. 9, no. 45 (November 10, 1968), pp. 6–7; *Verde olivo*, vol. 10, no. 45 (November 9, 1969), pp. 7–9, 62, vol. 11, no. 4 (January 25, 1970), p. 32; "Algunas tareas cumplidas por las FAR en 1970," *Verde olivo*, vol. 11, no. 52 (December 27, 1970); René Dumont, "The Militarization of Fidelismo," *Dissent* (September–October, 1970), pp. 417–420; K. S. Karol, *Guerrillas in Power* (New York: Hill and Wang, 1970), pp. 444–450, 534–544.
22. *Política internacional*, vol. 4, no. 16 (Fourth quarter, 1966), pp. 214–215.
23. Raúl Castro, "Graduación," *op. cit.*, p. 22; *Granma*, January 7, 1968, p. 3.
24. H. Hanning, *The Peaceful Uses of Military Forces* (New York: Frederick A. Praeger, Inc., 1967).
25. Roman Kolkowicz, *The Soviet Military and the Communist Party* (Princeton: Princeton University Press, 1967), pp. 36–79, 309–321.
26. J. Gittings, *The Role of the Chinese Army* (New York: Oxford University Press, 1967), pp. 29–32, 176–201; E. Joffe, *Party and Army: Professionalism and Political Control in the Chinese Officer Corps, 1949–1964* (Cambridge: Harvard University, East Asian Research Center, 1965), pp. 80–87.
27. Karol, *op. cit.*; Dumont, *op. cit.*; and Andrés Suárez, "How the Cuban Regime Works," (University of Florida at Gainesville, unpublished manuscript, 1972).
28. Jorge I. Domínguez and Christopher Mitchell, "The Roads Not Taken: Institutionalization and Political Parties in Cuba and Bolivia," *Comparative Politics* (1976, forthcoming).
29. *Verde olivo*, vol. 4, no. 7 (February 17, 1963), pp. 6–7.
30. José Causse Pérez, "La construcción del partido en las Fuerzas Armadas Revolucionarias de Cuba," *Cuba socialista*, no. 47 (July, 1965); Raúl Castro, "Problemas del funcionamiento del partido en las FAR," *Cuba socialista*, no. 55 (March, 1966); *Verde olivo*, vol. 4, no. 44 (November 2, 1963), pp. 35–41; vol. 4, no. 50 (December 15, 1963), pp. 3, 12; vol. 4, no. 51 (December 22, 1963), pp. 3–10, 58–59, 66.
31. E. Yasells, "Reseña de una asamblea," *Verde olivo*, vol. 8, no. 51 (December 24, 1967), p. 11.
32. *Verde olivo*, vol. 7, no. 52 (December 13, 1966), p. 4; vol. 8, no. 51 (December 24, 1967), p. 12; vol. 11, no. 40 (October 4, 1970), pp. 8, 10; *Granma*, March 1, 1966, p. 4; *Bohemia*, vol. 65, no. 31 (August 3, 1973), p. 28.
33. R. Garthoff, "The Military in Russia, 1861–1965," in J. van Doorn, ed., *The Armed Forces and Society* (The Hague: Mouton and Co., 1968), pp. 247, 253.
34. Kolkowicz, *op. cit.*
35. For a fascinating discussion of this behavior, see Timothy Colton, *Army, Party and Development in Soviet Politics* (Cambridge: Harvard University, unpublished dissertation, 1974).

36. Quoted in R. Gutiérrez, "Segunda asamblea de balance," *Verde olivo*, vol. 9, no. 9 (March 3, 1968), p. 11.
37. Kolkowicz, *op. cit.*, p. 74.
38. Luis Aguilar, *Cuba: 1933* (Ithaca: Cornell University Press, 1972), pp. 187–188.
39. Suárez Núñez, *op. cit.*, pp. 64, 91–92.
40. Computed from *Política internacional*, vol. 6, nos. 22–24 (second half, 1968), p. 93; *Granma*, March 16, 1969, p. 7, and August 31, 1969, p. 1; *Verde olivo*, vol 11, no. 34 (August 23, 1970), p. 8; *Bohemia*, vol. 65, no. 31 (August 3, 1973), p. 27.
41. *Verde olivo*, vol. 9, no. 17 (April 28, 1968), pp. 5–6; vol. 8, no. 19 (May 14, 1967), p. 7; vol. 8, no. 20 (May 21, 1967), p. 18; *Granma*, July 20, 1969, p. 10.
42. Causse Pérez, *op. cit.*, pp. 54–55; *Granma*, January 10, 1971, pp. 10–11; January 24, 1971, pp. 10–11; March 5, 1966, p. 8.
43. Raúl Castro, "Problemas," *op. cit.*, pp. 56–57; *Verde olivo*, vol. 10, no. 2 (January 12, 1969), p. 29; vol. 11, no. 40 (October 4, 1970), pp. 8–9.
44. A. George, *The Chinese Communist Army in Action* (New York: Columbia University Press, 1967), pp. 26–55; Morris Janowitz, "Social Cohesion under Prolonged Stress," and R. W. Little, "Buddy Relations and Combat Performance," in Morris Janowitz, ed., *The New Military* (New York: Russell Sage Foundation, 1964).
45. *Granma*, May 14, 1967, p. 11.
46. *Granma*, May 20, 1966, p. 5; Yasells, *op. cit.;* "Primera asamblea de balance del partido," *Verde olivo*, vol. 8, no. 51 (December 24, 1967); "Sección política de la marina de guerra revolucionaria," *Verde olivo*, vol. 9, no. 2 (January 14, 1968); "Primera asamblea de balance del partido comunista de Cuba en el cuerpo blindado," *Verde olivo*, vol. 9, no. 7 (February 18, 1968); Gutiérrez, *op. cit.;* "Asamblea de balance del partido en el ejército de Oriente," *Verde olivo*, vol. 10, no. 5 (February 2, 1969); "Balance del partido en el cuerpo ejército de Camagüey," *Verde olivo*, vol. 10, no. 42 (October 19, 1969); "Segunda asamblea de balance del partido comunista de Cuba en una unidad en Matanzas," *Verde olivo*, vol. 10, no. 42 (November 2, 1969); "Segunda asamblea de balance del partido en el ejército del centro," *Verde olivo*, vol. 10, no. 44 (November 2, 1969); "Segunda asamblea de balance del partido comunista de Cuba en el estado mayor general," *Verde olivo*, vol. 10, no. 49 (December 14, 1969); "Segunda reunión del partido en las Fuerzas Armadas Revolucionarias," *Verde olivo*, vol. 11, no. 40 (October 4, 1970).
47. L. Méndez, "La asamblea provincial del PURS en Matanzas," *Cuba socialista*, no. 31 (March, 1964).
48. D. W. Klein, "The 'Next Generation' of Chinese Communist Leaders," *The China Quarterly*, no. 12 (October–December, 1962), p. 66; E. Joffe, "The Chinese Army after the Cultural Revolution: The Effects of Intervention," *The China Quarterly*, no. 55 (July–September, 1973), p. 457. Computations based on *China News Summary*, no. 483 (September 6, 1973); R. H. Donaldson, "The 1971 Soviet Central Committee: An Assessment of the New Elite," *World Politics*, vol. 24, no. 3 (April, 1972); and a biographical data file kept by the author.

49. Colton, *op. cit.*
50. The following comments on China are based mainly on Joffe, *Party and Army, op. cit.*, pp. 57–72; Gittings, *op. cit.*, chapters 5, 8, 11, 12; J. Domes, "The Cultural Revolution and the Army," *Asian Survey*, vol. 8, no. 5 (May, 1968); H. Nelson, "Military Forces in the Cultural Revolution," *The China Quarterly*, no. 51 (July–September, 1972); P. Bridgham, "The Fall of Lin Piao," *The China Quarterly*, no. 55 (July–September, 1973).
51. Karol, *op. cit.*, pp. 394–395; Casal, *op. cit.*, pp. 458–464; and Mario Benedetti, "Present Status of Cuban Culture," in Rolando Bonachea and Nelson P. Valdés, eds., *Cuba in Revolution* (Garden City: Anchor Books, 1972), pp. 520–524.
52. Jorge I. Domínguez, "Sectoral Clashes in Cuban Politics and Development," *Latin American Research Review*, vol. 6, no. 3 (Fall, 1971); and Bertram Silverman, ed., *Man and Socialism in Cuba: The Great Debate* (New York: Atheneum, 1971).
53. *Granma*, July 24, 1968, p. 1, makes references to courses taken by Political Bureau members, Comandantes R. Castro, del Valle and Valdés.
54. Domínguez and Mitchell, *op. cit.*

Contributors

Gino Germani is professor of social relations at Harvard University. He is the author of numerous works on politics and society in Latin America, including *Estructura social de la Argentina* (1955) and *Política y Sociedad en una época de transición* (1962).

Kalman Silvert was professor of political science at New York University, and program advisor for the Ford Foundation's Office for Latin America and the Caribbean. Among his many works are *Man's Power* (Viking, 1970) and, with Leonard Reissman, *Education, Class, and Nation* (Elsevier, 1976).

José Nun is professor of political science at the University of Toronto. His research has focused on the politics of Argentina, and the politics of the military throughout Latin America.

Robert D. Putnam is professor of political science at the University of Michigan. He is the author of *The Beliefs of Politicians: Ideology, Conflict, and Democracy in Britain and Italy* (New Haven, 1973).

Philippe C. Schmitter is professor of political science at the University of Chicago. His main works include *Interest Conflict and Political Change in Brazil* (Stanford, 1971) and "Still the Century of Corporatism?" in Frederick Pike, editor, *The New Corporatism* (Notre Dame, 1974).

Liisa North is assistant professor of political science at York University in Toronto. She is the author of *Civil-Military Relations in Argentina, Chile, and Peru* (Berkeley, 1966).

Guillermo O'Donnell is director of the Center for Studies of State and Society in Buenos Aires, Argentina. His publications include *Modernization and Bureaucratic Authoritarianism: Studies in South American Politics* (Berkeley, 1973).

Alfred Stepan is associate professor of political science at Yale University. His publications include *The Military in Politics: Changing Patterns in Brazil* (Princeton, 1971), and (ed.) *Authoritarian Brazil: Origins, Policies and Future* (New Haven, 1973).

David Ronfeldt is a member of the staff of The Rand Corporation, Santa Monica, California. He is the author of *Atencingo: The Politics of Struggle in a Mexican Ejido* (Stanford, 1973).

Barry Ames is assistant professor of political science at Washington University in St. Louis. Professor Ames is currently working on a study of patterns of public spending in Latin America.

Jorge Domínguez is professor of politics at Harvard University. He is the author of *Governing Cuba: Political Order, Change, and Revolution in the Twentieth Century* (forthcoming, Belknap Press of Harvard University Press). He has also written numerous articles on Cuba, Latin America, and international politics.

Abraham F. Lowenthal is acting director of studies, Council on Foreign Relations, and lecturer in public and international affairs, Woodrow Wilson School, Princeton University. His publications include *The Dominican Intervention* (Cambridge, 1972) and *The Peruvian Experiment: Continuity and Change under Military Rule* (Princeton, 1975)

Index